Disability in Medieval Christian Philosophy and Theology

This book uses the tools of analytic philosophy of disability (and disability studies more generally) and close readings of medieval Christian philosophical and theological texts in order to survey what these thinkers said about what today we call "disability." The chapters compare what these medieval authors say with modern and contemporary philosophers and theologians of disability. This dual approach enriches our understanding of the history of disability in medieval Christian philosophy and theology and opens up new avenues of research for contemporary scholars working on disability.

The volume is divided into three parts. Part I addresses theoretical frameworks regarding disability, particularly on questions about the definition(s) of "disability" and how disability relates to well-being. The chapters are then divided into two further parts in order to reflect ways that medieval philosophers and theologians theorized about disability. Part II is on disability in this life, and Part III is on disability in the afterlife. Taken as a whole, these chapters support two general observations. First, these philosophical theologians sometimes resist Greco-Roman ableist views by means of theological and philosophical anti-ableist arguments and counterexamples. Here we find some surprising disability-positive perspectives that are built into different accounts of a happy human life. We also find equal dignity of all human beings no matter ability or disability. Second, some of the seeds for modern and contemporary ableist views were developed in medieval Christian philosophy and theology, especially with regard to personhood and rationality, an intellectualist interpretation of the *imago Dei*, and the identification of human dignity with the use of reason.

This volume surveys disability across a wide range of medieval Christian writers from the time of Augustine (4th century) up to Francisco Suárez (17th century). It will be of interest to scholars and graduate students working in medieval philosophy and theology or disability studies.

Scott M. Williams is Assistant Professor of philosophy at the University of North Carolina Asheville. He publishes in the areas of medieval theology and philosophy, philosophy of religion, and philosophy of disability. He has published several articles in philosophical theology on the Trinity and recently published a response article, in *Faith and Philosophy*, called "In Defense of a Latin Social Trinity: A Response to William Hasker." He is currently writing a book, *Henry of Ghent on the Trinity*, and is co-editing a special issue of the journal *TheoLogica* on conciliar trinitarianism.

Disability in Medieval Christian Philosophy and Theology

Edited by
Scott M. Williams

NEW YORK AND LONDON

First published 2020
by Routledge
52 Vanderbilt Avenue, New York, NY 10017

and by Routledge
2 Park Square, Milton Park, Abingdon, Oxon OX14 4RN

Routledge is an imprint of the Taylor & Francis Group, an informa business

© 2020 Taylor & Francis

The right of Scott M. Williams to be identified as the author of the editorial material, and of the authors for their individual chapters, has been asserted in accordance with sections 77 and 78 of the Copyright, Designs and Patents Act 1988.

All rights reserved. No part of this book may be reprinted or reproduced or utilised in any form or by any electronic, mechanical, or other means, now known or hereafter invented, including photocopying and recording, or in any information storage or retrieval system, without permission in writing from the publishers.

Trademark notice: Product or corporate names may be trademarks or registered trademarks, and are used only for identification and explanation without intent to infringe.

Library of Congress Cataloging-in-Publication Data
Names: Williams, Scott M. (Scott Matthew), 1977– editor.
Title: Disability in medieval Christian philosophy and theology / edited by Scott M. Williams.
Description: New York : Routledge, 2020. |
Includes bibliographical references and index.
Identifiers: LCCN 2019051514 (print) |
LCCN 2019051515 (ebook) | ISBN 9780367195229 (hbk) |
ISBN 9780429202919 (ebk)
Subjects: LCSH: Disabilities—Religious aspects—
Christianity—History—To 1500. | Disabilities. |
Philosophy, Medieval.
Classification: LCC BT732 .D57 2020 (print) |
LCC BT732 (ebook) | DDC 261.8/3240902—dc23
LC record available at https://lccn.loc.gov/2019051514
LC ebook record available at https://lccn.loc.gov/2019051515

ISBN: 978-0-367-19522-9 (hbk)
ISBN: 978-0-429-20291-9 (ebk)

Typeset in Sabon
by codeMantra

For Lisa and Olivia

"Better to sit at the waters' birth,
Than a sea of waves to win;
To live in the love that floweth forth,
Than the love that cometh in.

Be thy heart a well of love, my child,
Flowing, and free, and sure;
For a cistern of love, though undefiled,
Keeps not the spirit pure."

– George MacDonald, *Phantastes*

"For love is long and longs to love,
Ever blessed by God's Holy dove."

– Anonymous

Contents

Acknowledgments ix

Introduction 1
SCOTT M. WILLIAMS

PART I
Theoretical Frameworks 23

1 Plurality in Medieval Concepts of Disability 25
KEVIN TIMPE

PART II
Disability in This Life 49

2 Medieval Aristotelians on Congenital Disabilities and Their Early Modern Critics 51
GLORIA FROST

3 Personhood, Ethics, and Disability: A Comparison of Byzantine, Boethian, and Modern Concepts of Personhood 80
SCOTT M. WILLIAMS

4 The *Imago Dei/Trinitatis* and Disabled Persons: The Limitations of Intellectualism in Late Medieval Theology 109
JOHN T. SLOTEMAKER

5 Remembering "Mindless" Persons: Intellectual
  Disability, Spanish Colonialism, and the Disappearance
  of a Medieval Account of Persons Who Lack
  the Use of Reason   134
  MIGUEL J. ROMERO

6 Deafness and Pastoral Care in the Middle Ages   179
  JENNI KUULIALA AND REIMA VÄLIMÄKI

7 Taking the "Dis" Out of Disability: Martyrs, Mothers,
  and Mystics in the Middle Ages   203
  CHRISTINA VAN DYKE

PART III
Disability in the Afterlife   233

8 Separated Souls: Disability in the Intermediate State   235
  MARK K. SPENCER

9 Disability and Resurrection   258
  RICHARD CROSS

10 Relative Disability and Transhuman Happiness:
   St. Thomas Aquinas on the Beatific Vision   277
   THOMAS M. WARD

List of Contributors   287
Index   291

Acknowledgments

When I was 19 years old, I was diagnosed with Type 1 diabetes, and it changed my life in several significant ways. I had to learn about my condition from the doctors, and how to treat it (so as not to die any time soon). I had to teach my friends about it, and even more, we had to learn together what it meant for our social lives. I didn't understand myself to have a disability because I didn't really have a concept of disability nor understood that it could apply to me. In any case, I have learned to live with diabetes (which involved learning about, and in some cases, surviving, various medical systems). I am thankful for my friends who were willing to learn with me what this meant (and in some cases, getting me to the hospital when I desperately needed it), especially Micah Hayes and Jeff Malas. Thanks also to my parents, Will and Jackie, for their support over the years as I adjusted to living with diabetes. And, I want to acknowledge my mother's work as a high school special education teacher; her care for her disabled students' well-being has been a source of inspiration to me. These experiences have played an important role (intellectually and affectively) in how I come to the philosophy and theology of disability.

While I was in graduate school, I met Professor Essaka Joshua. She taught me, and her husband, Professor Richard Cross, about disability studies. She pointed me toward nuanced ways of understanding "disability" and how these understandings can be personally and socially empowering. There is an important sense in which *Disability in Medieval Christian Philosophy and Theology* would not have been made if it were not for her witness to me (and to Richard Cross) about the importance of disability studies. Subsequent to our schooling in disability studies, Richard published several articles on disability in medieval theology. I found these to be inspiring and creative engagements with the medieval authors whom we study. So, thanks go to Essaka Joshua and Richard Cross for helping me, and inspiring me, to want to put this volume together.

The idea for this volume came to me about six years ago (not too long after Richard had published his first few articles on the intersection between disability and medieval philosophy and theology). I wanted to teach my students about disability in medieval philosophy and theology; given that there were no such books, I decided I should try to do something about it. Initially, it was challenging to find a sufficient number of scholars of medieval philosophy or theology who were able and willing to do the kind of work that you now hold in your hands, or see with your eyes, or hear with your ears.

Fortunately, after lots of social networking over the years, we have the line-up of authors who have contributed to *Disability in Medieval Philosophy and Theology*. To get this new kind of work in medieval philosophy and theology going, we needed to meet together at a workshop to share our chapters and offer feedback to each other. So, in April 2018, most of the contributors presented their chapters at a workshop held at the University of Notre Dame. I wish to thank all of the contributors to this volume. For some, this was their first step into the philosophy and theology of disability. For others, this is an extension from their previous work in the philosophy or theology of disability. I am especially grateful for the mutually supportive and inspiring ways in which everyone worked together, particularly at our workshop at the University of Notre Dame.

Special thanks are owed to different departments and institutes at the University of Notre Dame for supporting our workshop: Department of Philosophy, Department of Theology, Disability Forum, the Medieval Institute, the Nanovic Institute, and the Institute for Scholarship in the Liberal Arts. Thanks also to Therese Scarpelli Cory for comments on early drafts of several of the chapters. I also wish to thank my colleagues at the University of North Carolina Asheville, who have been so supportive of my work and teaching in the philosophy and theology of disability. This has been particularly evident in the campus-wide support for hosting a biennial conference on the philosophy of disability at UNCA.

Further, thanks go to Andrew Weckenmann, our Routledge editor, who enthusiastically embraced this new kind of project in medieval philosophy and theology. Thanks also go to Allie Simons, who guided this project along to its completion.

Finally, I wish to thank my wife, Lisa Toland Williams, for all her love and support over the years as I worked on this volume. She shows me again and again that disability is not merely something one lives with that makes differences to one's life, but that it can enrich our lives together. This became even more evident to me as Lisa found, and then we adopted, two congenitally disabled dogs who are brothers, namely, our double-dapple dachshunds, Origen Clement and Didymus Severus (who is blind). While the sighted one sees for the blind one, the blind one's augmented sense of smell helps them discover otherwise unnoticed things in the garden. Disability gain isn't just individual, it's social!

Scott M. Williams
Feast of All Saints, 2019
Asheville, North Carolina

Introduction
Scott M. Williams

The Intersection: Disability in Medieval Christian Philosophy and Theology

Over the last few decades literary scholars,[1] social historians,[2] and religious historians[3] have focused on ways in which what we call "disability" intersects with medieval texts (e.g., canon law, canonization documents, and literary texts) and medieval social and religious practices. However, there has not been any book-length treatment of the intersection between disability and medieval Christian philosophy and theology. This is a significant gap in the literature that *Disability in Medieval Christian Philosophy and Theology* aims to fill. Given that this book is a first attempt at such a project, it is far from being fully representative of the issues and it makes no claim of being exhaustive. However, it is representative of different issues and methodologies so as to be a fruitful first attempt to engage this intersection. *Disability in Medieval Christian Philosophy and Theology* is intended to introduce the intersection – what topics might be discussed and which texts and which methodologies are fruitful for this kind of project – and in so doing to suggest pathways for future exploration in medieval Christian philosophy and theology, and medieval philosophy and theology more generally. The chapters (taken altogether) include not only the usual suspects in medieval philosophy and theology (e.g., Albert the Great, Aquinas, Augustine, Boethius, Bonaventure, Duns Scotus, and William Ockham) but also others such as Bartolomé de Las Casas, Bernard of Trilia, Catherine of Siena, Dante Alighieri, Durand of St. Pourçain, Francisco Suárez, Francisco de Vitoria, John Mair, John Maxentius, Julian of Norwich, Matthew of Aquasparta, Mechthild of Magdeburg, Raymond of Penyafort, and Thomas Chobham.

Academic interest in disability is (partly) reflective of cultural shifts that began around the 1960s. With the advent of the disability-rights political movement, there has been intense public, governmental, and scholarly debate on the relationship between disability and human well-being and on how to define disability. (In the 20th century, there have been two general models of disability, namely the medical model and the social model. Each of these have been subject to wide-ranging criticisms.)[4] These two issues, disability and human well-being, and the definition of disability, permeate much of contemporary philosophy of disability and theology of disability, and this is no less true of *Disability in Medieval Christian Philosophy and Theology*. The term "disability" is (at least) a 19th century term meant to group together disparate subclasses of conditions: deafness, blindness, mild to profound cognitive impairment, paraplegia, and so on.[5] One might wonder, then, how there can be a book on disability in medieval Christian philosophy and theology if the term is relatively recent. The short answer is that even though the term "disability" is only relatively recent, the various referents of this term are not. Nonetheless, those working in medieval history are attentive to ways in which contemporary definitions of disability or associations with disability are useful for historical investigations, even if at times not wholly reliable. As Jenni Kuuliala puts it,

> The modern theories of disability do not work for the student of medieval history as such, but the conceptions are helpful in the attempts of detecting not only the paradigms of medieval society, but also the attitudes of the historians trying to reach them.[6]

In a similar vein, Richard Cross says that

> The history of notions of disability is complex and contested. One reason is that our contemporary notions of disability are themselves complex and contested: there are popular, pre-theoretical notions and highly theorized notions, and, between the two, varieties of practical and political notions – I mean notions identified with governmental administration, and with activism of identity politics. Another reason is that the very notion of disability is itself modern. So the history of disability involves the isolation and examination of concepts ancestral to our own ones, along with frank acknowledgement that our own ones are far from clear.[7]

This description of the intersection between disability and medieval Christian philosophy and theology is apt and ought to guide those working in this intersection. This sensitivity to different notions of a disability is a guiding assumption throughout *Disability in Medieval Christian Philosophy and Theology*. This assumption is crucial for understanding medieval texts on their own terms; otherwise, one might project onto the medieval texts what is not there. In addition to understanding the medieval texts for their own sake, we can investigate these texts in order to discover what their significance(s) may be for contemporary theorizing in, for example, ethical theory, political philosophy, philosophy of mind, and metaphysics.

As a history, *Disability in Medieval Philosophy and Theology* gives close textual readings in order to establish an understanding of the texts on their own terms. This is a historical methodology. But this book is more than a history. It brings understandings of medieval Christian philosophical and theological texts regarding what we call disability together with evaluative judgments that are informed by concerns raised in contemporary philosophy and theology of disability.[8] This is a comparative and evaluative methodology. All chapters employ a historical methodology, and most add a comparative or evaluative methodology too. For example, in Chapter 9, Richard Cross uses a "disability-theoretic perspective" to describe and evaluate specific claims. By employing these different methodologies, this book is better able to raise awareness of some of the important and complex issues that arise in the intersection of disability and medieval Christian philosophy and theology. It makes no claims of being exhaustive; instead, it is a collective attempt by scholars of medieval Christian philosophy and theology to engage the topic of disability while being sensitive to contemporary philosophy and theology of disability. *Disability in Medieval Philosophy and Theology* draws attention to specific medieval topics and how they compare to contemporary (and in some cases, modern) philosophy and theology.

Disability has been largely ignored by scholars of medieval Christian philosophy and theology. For example, disability (or any terms akin to it) is not discussed or mentioned in the two-volume *The Cambridge History of Medieval Philosophy* (2012), nor in John Marenbon's *Medieval Philosophy: An Historical and Philosophical Introduction* (2006), nor is disability found in a word search in Peter Adamson's otherwise extensive *History of Philosophy without Any Gaps* (as of October 2019). Although Adamson has several episodes on health, which has some overlap with disability, and has edited a book, *Health: A History* (2018), health and disability are not the same thing. (This overlap between health and disability is discussed in the working group called ReMeDHe-L, which stands for Religion, Medicine, Disability and Health in Late Antiquity.)[9] Further, the most popular medieval survey textbook assigned in undergraduate medieval philosophy classrooms (according to an informal survey by Robert Pasnau),[10] namely *Philosophy in the Middle Ages: The Christian, Islamic, and Jewish Traditions*, does not include any text in which what we call disability is prominently represented. This lack of representation, in the secondary literature mentioned above and in the most popular survey textbook, gives the false impression that medieval philosophers and theologians (including Christian ones) have nothing to say about what we call disability.

Fortunately, there are signs of change. Some scholars of medieval Christian theology have engaged with the philosophy of disability and have made new connections. They have drawn attention to neglected texts. For example, Brian Brock and John Swinton have edited the book

Disability in the Christian Tradition: A Reader, in which they include primary texts regarding disability from, for example, Cappadocian theologians like Basil the Great, from Augustine, from Thomas Aquinas, and from Julian of Norwich. Further, Richard Cross has published several articles on the intersection between medieval Christian philosophy and theology, and contemporary philosophy and theology of disability. Specifically, he has written on disability as it intersects with medieval discussions of the sacrament of baptism, the metaphysics of the Incarnation and personhood (as requiring dependency), and the moral status of disability in relation to original justice and original sin.[11] These discussions not only point toward specific textual and topical *loci* for future research but also provide insightful and fruitful ways to engage the intersection between what we call disability and medieval philosophy and theology. Miguel Romero is another who has published several articles on disability and medieval Christian philosophy and theology, with a focus on Thomas Aquinas.[12] Romero has shown that Aquinas discusses what we call disability – particularly intellectual disability – in different contexts, and he has drawn attention to the significance of Aquinas's thoughts on disability for contemporary normative ethical questions regarding human well-being. This work on disability in medieval Christian philosophy and theology over the last ten years has jump-started recent interest in this particular intersection and, to some extent, has laid the groundwork for *Disability in Medieval Christian Philosophy and Theology*.

The quotation from Richard Cross (above) reports some of the conceptual challenges that scholars face when engaging with disability in medieval (Christian) philosophy and theology. Elsewhere I have argued that facing this challenge becomes more manageable if one is familiar with contemporary philosophy and theology of disability.

> Why *contemporary* philosophy and theology of disability? First, it draws attention to the relevant diverse phenomena and explananda that are referred to by the term "disability." Second, it provides concept frameworks for understanding the diverse phenomena and explananda that are called "disability." Third, it provides arguments for competing (moral) evaluations of "disability" and for competing definitions of "disability."[13]

Just as medieval scholars are trained to some extent in contemporary philosophy (e.g., logic, epistemology, metaphysics) in order that they can better understand and evaluate medieval philosophical and theological texts (albeit, this is not sufficient for a proper *historical* understanding), so too should they be familiar with contemporary philosophy of disability if they are going to be better situated for understanding and evaluating medieval philosophical and theological texts on what we call disability. If scholars are not sufficiently familiar with contemporary debates on disability, whether on the relation between disability and well-being or debates on defining disability, then they would be at a disadvantage in understanding and interpreting what medieval texts claim or do not claim, imply or do not imply. Of course, familiarity with contemporary philosophy and theology of disability is only one resource for addressing the conceptual challenges. For, medieval philosophers or theologians may (or may not) share certain conceptual frameworks for thinking about disability. (For example, are 'disabilities' intrinsically bad, neutral, or good? We get different answers from medieval philosophers and theologians in different contexts.) Still, it is useful to be acquainted with contemporary philosophy of disability while engaging with medieval philosophers and theologians because there might be nuances in the contemporary literature that assist (to some degree) in interpreting and understanding medieval texts. As will become clear, contributors to *Disability in Medieval Christian Philosophy and Theology* have benefited in one way or another from the work of, for example, Elizabeth Barnes, Nancy Eiesland, Eva Feder Kittay, Jeff McMahan, Irina Metzler, Tom Shakespeare, or Anita Silvers in the philosophy of disability, and this is reflected in how they engage particular issues.

The time is ripe for scholars of medieval Christian philosophy and theology to investigate the ways in which disability was understood and evaluated by medieval Christian philosophers and theologians. (Some work has already been done on disability in Judaism and in Islam, but we hope for more in-depth research on medieval Jewish and Muslim philosophers and theologians in the future.)[14] Moreover, those working in disability studies, whether in academia or in government or the public sector, will benefit (in many and perhaps unpredictable ways) from learning what medieval Christian philosophers and theologians had to say about what we call disability. It is useful to be able to compare contemporary understandings with, for example, medieval understandings because it helps us to become aware of things that we might have overlooked (and perhaps should not have) or help us to re-interrogate and reassess our own assumptions about what we call disability.

Disability in Medieval Christian Philosophy and Theology is useful not only for comparing medieval with contemporary positions but also for comparing medieval philosophers and theologians with other medieval texts and social practices. Social historians tell us that a common medieval view was that there is a very close connection between one's disability and one's own sin or one's parent's sin. This is labeled the "religio-moral" view of disability. In short, if one sins, then one may be punished by means of acquiring a disability; or, if parents sin, then their child may acquire a disability.[15] Nancy L. Eiesland describes this sort of view as follows:

> The persistent thread within the Christian tradition has been that disability denotes an unusual relationship with God and that the person with disabilities is either divinely blessed or damned. ... In

the Hebrew Scriptures, in particular, the conflation of moral impurity and physical disability is a common theme. ... The New Testament also supports this theme of a link between sin and disability.[16]

However, when we turn to Christian theologians like Thomas Aquinas and Duns Scotus, we find different positions that sound superficially the same as this, but the difference is significant. As Richard Cross argues in an article on Aquinas on physical impairment, for Aquinas, disabilities *in this life* are a punishment for Adam and Eve's original sin. A disability is not a punishment for one's own personal sin(s), nor are one's parents necessarily personally morally blameworthy for producing a congenitally disabled human being.

> Aquinas sees physical impairments – things that constitute a subclass of what he labels "bodily defects" – fundamentally as punishments for original sin. He is (generally) very careful to distance his accounts of defects from notions of individual punishment. (When he is not, it is because of pressure from Scriptural sources .... [H]e believes that by and large the Bible, too, explicitly rejects the view that disability could be a punishment for individual sin.) So whatever we think of punishment models more generally, Aquinas's certainly removes one of the least appealing aspects of such models as typically understood. And Aquinas is careful, too, to associate many features of the human condition – not just those identified as a certain subclass of defects – with corporate punishment for original sin. To this extent, his account of physical impairments tends to normalize such impairments, and to de-emphasize their distance from other features of post-lapsarian human existence. While I doubt that what Aquinas says about bodily defects would satisfy many contemporary disability theorists, it seems to me that parts of his account – and not least this normalization strategy – may appeal to more theologically-inflected accounts of the human condition.[17]

In another article, Cross argues that for Duns Scotus, disabilities (e.g., blindness) are *de facto* a punishment for original sin but are not intrinsically punitive. If there had been no original sin, there could have been disabilities (that were not punishments).[18] Aquinas and Duns Scotus's positions make different connections between disability and sin than the one posited by the religio-moral position. This helps us to understand that there were different accounts of the relation between disability and sin in the medieval period.

Survey of the Chapters

Disability in Medieval Christian Philosophy and Theology is divided into three parts. Part I, "Theoretical Frameworks," addresses the definitional question, "what is a disability?" and some implications for human well-being. Part II, "Disability in This Life," investigates what medieval Christian philosophers and theologians have to say about disability occurring after Adam and Eve's original sin but before death and the afterlife. This context is significant because what these authors say about disability depends on the specific context, or as they would put it, on the specific "state of human nature." Disability before the fall is different from disability after the fall, and likewise disability is different for disembodied human souls and different again for those resurrected to damnation in hell and those resurrected to eternal life in heaven and the beatific vision of God. Consequently, Part III is on "Disability in the Afterlife."

Christian theological beliefs about different states of human nature make a difference in medieval philosophers' and theologians' theorizing about what we call disability. This is in contrast to contemporary philosophy of disability that is (typically) limited to disability as it currently exists or has existed in the past as reported by commonly accepted historical records. There is also another contrast. Suppose you are going to theorize about "ideal" human nature: What would it be like? What constraints would be assumed? For medieval theologians (and philosophers), ideal human nature would be ambiguous between human nature in the state of innocence with original justice (i.e., Adam and Eve before their original sin), Christ's sinless human nature, and the resurrected saints in heaven. Each of these examples call for different detailed answers. In short, medieval discussions of what we call disability is complicated. By attending to these complications, we may be surprised by what we find. In some cases, we find resources that have a significance for contemporary theorizing; in other cases, we find interesting counterexamples to what we find in medieval social history; and yet in other cases, we find significant connections with other historical phenomena – including political history, social history, and the history of ideas.

In Chapter 1, "Plurality in Medieval Concepts of Disability," Kevin Timpe examines two medieval understandings of disability (*defectus*) with a view toward ways that they might be brought into contemporary discussions, particularly as found in Elizabeth Barnes's work in the philosophy of disability. A central concern is that medieval discussions of many issues, including disability, use different concepts than contemporary discussions even though similar names are used for that concept. As a result, we can think we're talking about the same thing as medieval authors when we're not. Timpe's discussion seeks to show that Thomas Aquinas does not have a single, unified concept of disability, compared to Duns Scotus, who, arguably, has a univocal concept of disability (*defectus*). Timpe concludes with a reflection on Aquinas's multiplicity of concepts of disability and its implications for whether disability makes (what Barnes calls) a bad-difference or mere-difference to human well-being or flourishing. The issue is raised whether a univocal concept of disability or a multiplicity of concepts of disability are compatible with one or more answers to the question, how does a disability affect one's well-being?

Part II, "Disability in This Life," surveys disability in the context of a *fallen* human race. Medieval Christian theologians believed that Adam and Eve were created in a state of innocence, free from sin. While they disagreed on details regarding things like original justice and grace in relation to Adam and Eve's unfallen human nature, they held that in the state of innocence, for example, Adam's body was ordered toward Adam's soul, and Adam's soul was ordered toward knowing and loving God. The same was true for Eve. But when they originally sinned, Adam and Eve lost this ordering of body to soul, and soul to God. As mentioned above, Aquinas and Duns Scotus take disabilities in this life among human beings to be punishments for Adam and Eve's original sin. This involves a disorder between body and soul, and soul and God. This general story is an assumption that medieval Christian philosophers and theologians typically have when theorizing about disabilities in this life.

In Chapter 2, "Medieval Aristotelians on Congenital Disabilities and Their Early Modern Critics," Gloria Frost discusses what Augustine, Albert the Great, and Thomas Aquinas say about the causes of congenital disabilities (which they call monstrosities (*monstra*)). For these theologians, original sin plays a causal role in the generation of the congenitally disabled. Frost shows, however, that for Albert the Great and Thomas Aquinas, original sin is not the only cause of congenital disability. She examines Albert the Great's full taxonomy of the causes of congenital disabilities in particular because his discussion is (perhaps) the most detailed and extensive discussion on this topic among medieval Christian philosophers and theologians. Given that Albert's analysis of the causes is broadly Aristotelian, Frost also surveys Aristotle's account of the generation of living organisms. She reflects on whether Albert's taxonomy of the causes of congenital disabilities is misogynistic. Contra Irina Metzler, Frost contends that this close examination of Albert's taxonomy shows that his analysis is not misogynistic. It is not misogynistic because Albert posits that the father's sperm (a form) and mother's menstrual blood (matter) can each be causally responsible for the generation of a congenitally disabled human fetus. This contrasts with Aristotle, for whom the only causal explanation for congenital disability has to do with the mother's contribution to the generation of a human fetus.

Moreover, Frost compares what Albert the Great and John Locke say about the congenitally disabled, namely those called "monsters," and evaluates their accounts on the basis of a disability-positive perspective. For example, for Locke, a subclass of the congenitally disabled fails to be (full) human beings. But for Albert the Great, their humanity is not in question given his Aristotelian hylomorphism. Frost reasons that if one's humanity is a basis on which one has moral status and equality in the moral community, then Albert's account of monsters is more supportive of a disability-positive perspective than, for example, a Lockean one.

The question about disability in relation to moral status is taken up again, in different ways, in Chapters 3–5. Chapter 3 examines different accounts of personhood in relation to moral status and equality. Chapter 4 examines different accounts of the image of God (or image of the Trinity) in relation to moral status and equality. And, Chapter 5 discusses different accounts of rationality in relation to human nature, moral status, and equality.

In Chapter 3, "Personhood, Ethics, and Disability: A Comparison of Byzantine, Boethian, and Modern Concepts of Personhood," Scott M. Williams compares two early medieval accounts of personhood (Byzantine and Boethian) with some modern accounts of personhood in order to evaluate which of these is supportive (or more supportive) of a disability-positive perspective. (The Byzantine authors surveyed are Gregory of Nyssa and John Maxentius and, to a lesser extent, Maximus the Confessor and John of Damascus.) Williams argues for the conditional claim that if personhood is the sole basis on which one has intrinsic and equal moral status and the disability-positive perspective is correct, then the Byzantine and Boethian accounts of personhood are preferable to the modern accounts of personhood that are surveyed. Williams concludes by comparing the Byzantine and Boethian accounts of personhood using a disability-positive perspective and argues that the Byzantine account is even more friendly to a disability-positive perspective than the Boethian account. While both accounts agree that personhood (*hypostasis, prosopon, persona*) requires being an individual of some nature, Boethius adds that personhood also requires rationality. Given the significance and influence of Boethius's additional criterion for personhood in the Latin west, Williams offers an explanation for why Boethius supposed he needed to stipulate that rationality is required for personhood.

While this chapter offers a close reading of the medieval texts, the understandings of the medieval texts are for the sake of comparative evaluation. This dual methodology is what Richard Cross once described to me as "medieval with a twist."[19] What makes this approach different from more standard approaches is that the evaluative criteria are not limited to the stock philosophical criteria of, for example, internal consistency, contradiction to known principles, or explanatory adequacy, but also includes the disability-positive perspective. This evaluative criterion may not be shared by others who engage the intersection of disability and medieval Christian philosophy and theology. But debate about this additional evaluative criterion would be another topic for another time.

In Chapter 4, "The *Imago Dei/Trinitatis* and Disabled Persons: The Limitations of Intellectualism in Late Medieval Theology," John T. Slotemaker surveys early medieval and medieval discussions of the image of God, and in some cases the image of the Trinity, in human beings.

The scriptural basis for philosophical and theological reflection on the image of God is Genesis 1:26. Slotemaker focuses on the tradition of interpretation of this passage from Augustine up to Thomas Aquinas and William Ockham. Having described what he calls the intellectualist tradition, he asks whether the intellectual gloss on the image of God is a useful resource for thinking about individuals who have significant intellectual impairment. While some contemporary theologians wish to ground human moral status and dignity in human beings being made in the image of God, Slotemaker judges that the intellectualist tradition is not an adequate resource for establishing the moral status and equality of human beings with significant intellectual impairment. Nevertheless, he identifies a minority report on the image of God, found in Irenaeus of Lyon and again in Gregory of Rimini, that may be more useful for grounding human moral status and equality.

In Chapter 5, "Remembering 'Mindless' Persons: Intellectual Disability, Spanish Colonialism, and the Disappearance of a Medieval Account of Persons Who Lack the Use of Reason," Miguel J. Romero retraces the origin and development of an interpretive shift in the way the 16th century Spanish Dominican interpreters of Thomas Aquinas spoke about the significance of our rational faculties. These include Ginés Sepúlveda and Bartolemé de Las Casas. He shows how Aquinas's ways of thinking about the intellectual dignity and inalienable contemplative aptitude of persons who "lack the use of reason" came to be displaced from the main currents of Thomistic theological discourse. This shift in outlook was an unintended by-product of the Salamancan Thomist defense (by, e.g., Bartolemé de Las Casas) of the rational status and moral aptitude of the Amerindian peoples. Conscious of the worthiness of the Dominican cause, Romero makes a distinction between the specific topic of the Spanish colonial debates (concerning the anthropological status and moral aptitude of the Amerindian people) and the theoretical subject of the debates (the anthropological status and moral aptitude of persons who seem to lack the use of reason). Romero's focus is on persons who actually (and not allegedly) lack the use of reason. Romero's entry point into this complex historical period is John Mair's novel interpretation (in 1510) of Aristotle's account of the "slave by nature" in the *Politics* and Mair's unprecedented claim that the Amerindian peoples are slaves by nature. Mair's interpretation became the cornerstone of the various Spanish colonial arguments, by, for example, Ginés Sepúlveda, against the Amerindian peoples. From there, Romero offers a focused genealogy of the reception history of Aristotle's *Politics*, book 1. Romero highlights key Aristotelian distinctions that were conflated in the 16th century and shows ways in which book 1 of the *Politics* could be interpreted as a deeply problematic account of persons who we today identify as intellectually disabled. Romero then shows how Aquinas recognized that Aristotle's subject was persons who "lack the use of reason" and outlines

Aquinas's subversive revision of Aristotle's figure of the "natural slave." He also points out that not all 16th century theologians agreed with Mair's conflation. By drawing attention to Francisco de Vitoria, Romero shows us someone who rejected Mair's conflation altogether and returned to a closer reading of Aquinas to find an account according to which all human beings are rational given that they have a bare intellectual aptitude for intellectual acts. The use of reason (e.g., producing complex thoughts for means-to-ends reasoning) is consequent to this intellectual aptitude. Human dignity and equality, for Romero, are based on this bare intellectual aptitude, which all humans have, and are not based on the use of reason. Consequently, when theorizing about cognitive disability and moral status, Romero contends that, for example, Aquinas and de Vitoria are on the right track in distinguishing a bare intellectual aptitude and the use of reason and identifying human dignity and equality with the former and not with the latter. This position is much more supportive of a disability-positive perspective than is the position that requires the use of reason for human dignity and equality.

Whereas Chapter 5 examines a reception history of Aristotle's category of the natural slave that had implications for those who lack the use of reason, in Chapter 6, "Deafness and Pastoral Care in the Middle Ages," Jenni Kuuliala and Reima Välimäki investigate the ways in which Christian theological reflections on deafness (as found in Augustine and the Fourth Lateran Council) were transmitted through influential confessors' manuals to parish priests and in turn to the laity. Overall, this chapter is concerned with medieval pastoral care for deaf individuals, theological views of deafness, and deaf people's ability to participate in religious life. Moreover, they challenge some current interpretations of Augustine that claim that Augustine endorses a disability-positive perspective – understood as a denial of a bad-difference interpretation of disability in relation to well-being.

Having discussed different medieval theories about the relation between deafness and perceived intelligence, they survey ways in which deaf individuals were included in the sacraments or rites of marriage, confession, and religious devotion. While some medieval authors made a hasty generalization from one's being deaf to one's lacking intelligence, not all did. They point to the scholastic Jean de Jandun, who

> was able to determine that a congenitally deaf person's inability to speak was caused by the lack of exposure to speech, not by the lack of neural connection between the ear and vocal organs. This distinction, in theory, allowed him to perceive deafness simply as an inability to hear, not as a more comprehensive neural or mental defect.[20]

Nonetheless, they observe that the lack of a sophisticated sign language for teaching the meaning of religious sacraments and rites posed a significant challenge to pastoral care.

12 Scott M. Williams

In Chapter 7, "Taking the 'Dis' out of Disability: Martyrs, Mothers, and Mystics in the Middle Ages," Christina Van Dyke draws attention to some ancient and medieval conceptions of physical disability and the ways in which certain medieval theologians resisted some ableist theories in the Platonic and Aristotelian traditions. Van Dyke begins by laying out a general picture of the universe that was commonly held in the Middle Ages. On this picture, the universe has a natural, hierarchical order – with God being the source of all things, followed by lesser beings (angels, then humans, then animals, then plants, then elements). Each natural-kind has distinctive capacities (cognitive, or physical, or both), and when members of each natural-kind actualize their capacities, then they are instances of flourishing or well-being, relative to that natural-kind. In contrast to the contemporary social model of disability, according to which departures from the statistical average are construed as bad or undesirable only because of discriminatory social practices, institutions, and the like, the hierarchical medieval view would contend that departures from one's (fixed) nature count as a defect and as undesirable (especially so in the case of congenital disabilities). However, Van Dyke argues that there was a medieval resistance to this way of understanding defects because of the intense devotional practices in the 13th–15th centuries regarding the incarnate Son of God. That is to say, by taking the humanity of God the Son as the paradigm case of human nature (and not Aristotle's ideal of a fully actualized male), it became understood that mothers, mystics, and martyrs were not defective nor undesirable. Instead, these groups were understood as having perfected human nature. Van Dyke is careful to point out that these were not the only ways human nature was to be understood as perfected, but they are (*contra* Aristotle) some ways in which human nature is perfected. This chapter includes several medieval images of Christ to support Van Dyke's contention that these depictions of Christ's human nature reflected the view that mothers, mystics, and martyrs were non-defective human beings because of the ways in which they imitate "mother Jesus." The chapter concludes with a reflection on the medieval claim that

> the ultimate end of human nature is knowing and loving God, and that human beings can fulfill their potentialities in any way that does this. … Martyrs imitating Christ by retaining their wounds in the afterlife (without pain) and mothers' bodies mirroring Christ's body in their bleeding (and feeding) also present examples in which God is understood as able to glorify any sort of embodiment, whether standardly-able-bodied or not.[21]

Van Dyke's chapter concludes Part II and turns our attention to disability in the afterlife. In medieval Christian theology, it was believed that when humans die, their rational immortal souls continue to exist albeit separated from their human organic bodies. Human souls are in an intermediate state between "this life" and the general resurrection in which humans are resurrected to damnation in hell or resurrected to eternal life in heaven that includes the beatific vision. Part III consists of three chapters to represent this additional context for theorizing about disability in medieval Christian philosophy and theology. In Chapter 8, Mark K. Spencer writes about disability in the intermediate state; in Chapter 9, Richard Cross writes about disability and resurrection (for those in hell and those in heaven); and in Chapter 10, Thomas M. Ward writes about disability and the beatific vision. What may be surprising to those who have not yet read what medieval theologians wrote about the afterlife is that they had a lot to say and there were significant debates. What may be surprising to those already familiar with these discussions is that once we re-examine these texts from a disability studies perspective, what we find are fine-grained discussions that can speak to contemporary concerns. In this way, Spencer's, Cross's, and Ward's discussions each bring a welcome zest and intrigue to texts that haven't received as much attention as they deserve. (That's "medieval with a twist!")

In Chapter 8, "Separated Souls: Disability in the Intermediate State," Mark K. Spencer draws parallels between different medieval theories of separated souls and their cognitive activities (or inactivity), on the one hand, with three contemporary theories of disability (i.e., the medical model, the social model, and the cultural model), on the other hand. These parallels are instructive in helping us to understand the medieval theories better and to be made aware of the relevant normative issues (regarding disability and well-being) from a disability-positive perspective. Spencer follows Richard Cross's suggestions that certain Franciscan theologians' views of impairment and disability parallel some aspects of the contemporary social model of disability, and Aquinas has views that parallel the contemporary medical model of disability. But whereas Cross's observations arose from texts dealing with disability in this life, Spencer draws attention to these parallels in the intermediate state. Spencer makes several surprising connections with contemporary philosophy of disability. For example, he identifies a case of what philosophers of disability call "disability advantage" or one's gaining an advantage in some way on the basis of one's disability. Spencer says

> Some contemporary disability theorists argue that the impairment of certain abilities leads to the heightening of others or to alternative abilities. Aquinas affirms this for the separated soul, but goes further: while the separated soul is in a worse condition than the embodied soul with regard to being a mere part, it is in a better and freer condition with regard to its intellectual nature. We see this further in Bernard of Trilia's argument that the separated soul cannot engage in discursive reasoning, since that requires returning to

> phantasms, but this is an improvement in the soul's understanding: it directly and intuitively understands things, without needing to move from premises to conclusions.[22]

The cognitive disability of not being able to use reason to go from premises to conclusions, which arises for the soul from being separated from its organic human body, is an intriguing claim. Moreover, it would be an interesting topic for future research, especially in relation to the subclass of human beings that Romero identified, that is, those who lack the use of reason (*amentia*).

In Chapter 9, "Disability and Resurrection," Richard Cross surveys several topics that pertain to those who are resurrected (according to the medieval Christian theologians that are considered here): impassibility, sensation, agility, and mobility. Disability intersects with each of these in at least two ways. First, disability is understood as lacking something (*defectus*) that is apt or natural for human beings. So, we can observe medieval theologians discussing various defects. Second, Cross uses a disability-positive or disability-theoretic perspective as a basis on which to evaluate different theories. Cross shows that certain normative views of the body made on the basis of ableist pre-suppositions are alien to at least some traditional theological reasoning about the resurrected body. In particular, mobility was not taken to require limbs, and certain kinds of sensation were held to be alien to the resurrected body – either superfluous, or actively harmful of it. Nevertheless, Cross points out instances in which we find "scholastic ableism" on display in their discussions of what the resurrected bodies of the damned will be like. Aquinas claims, for example, that the damned will suffer "defects which naturally follow the natural principles of a human body – such as weight, passibility, and such like ..., which defects the glory of the resurrection will exclude from the bodies of [the blessed in heaven]."[23] Cross concludes by comparing these medieval accounts of resurrected bodies with the contemporary transhumanist movement. He shows that while there are some similarities (e.g., positing radically new powers for the resurrected body and mechanisms by which those powers might be instantiated), Cross points out crucial differences between them. The transhumanist movement is concerned with *posthuman* survival in this life, but these medieval theologians are concerned with resurrected *human beings* in heaven (and hell) and give due weight to the importance of specifically human embodiment.

In the final chapter, "Relative Disability and Transhuman Happiness: St. Thomas Aquinas on the Beatific Vision," Thomas M. Ward discusses Aquinas's account of the beatific vision and shows that for Aquinas, human beings are naturally disabled with regard to it. He reports Dante's gloss on this as the need for humans to be "trans-humanized." What, then, is the beatific vision? According to Ward, medieval Christians took it that the highest human good is a certain kind of relationship to God, a relationship of enjoyment, often referred to as beatific vision, in which the intellect has immediate access to the divine essence such that the desires of the will are fully satisfied. But, according to Aquinas, no human being is naturally equipped to have such access to the divine essence. We need both an extrinsic power added to our nature and divine actualization of that power. In the language of contemporary philosophy of disability, human happiness requires a prosthesis (i.e., an extrinsic, added cognitive power) and an external source to activate the prosthesis; on Aquinas's view, only God can give this prosthesis and only God can actualize it. This tells us something about the relationship between human nature (conceived along Aristotelian lines) and human well-being. For Aquinas, success in the category of human nature radically underdetermines human well-being. Our human nature just doesn't give us the capacities we need in order to achieve the highest human good. Ward concludes that relative to the saints who enjoy the beatific vision, every merely human being is disabled.

Lessons from *Disability in Medieval Christian Philosophy and Theology*

As the above summary indicates, there are many different *loci* in which one can engage the intersection between disability and medieval Christian philosophy and theology. What uniquely characterize this intersection are the dual methodologies of historical exegesis and disability-theoretic concerns and evaluations. Both methodologies are essential to this task. Without awareness of a disability-theoretic framework, historical exegesis of medieval texts runs the risk of ableist interpretations. (This is the case because ableism is very common in contemporary society; scholars today are not immune to it simply by virtue of being medieval scholars.) That is not to say that a disability-theoretic framework makes it impermissible to ascribe ableism to a medieval text; rather, what is meant is that this framework attunes one to the relevant issues and concerns, and in turn enables one to locate a medieval text's anti-ableist claim(s), or ableist claim(s), or ambiguity regarding a text's normative evaluation of the condition in question. In short, familiarity with contemporary philosophy of disability, and theology of disability, gives one many conceptual tools that can help one to locate where a text or claim is in relation to positions that have been (or need to be) identified in disability studies. The chapters in this book have attempted this task, and I believe they have done so in an exemplary fashion.

Still, there are different ways to go about this task. In some cases, we find that historical exegesis of the texts themselves gives us various understandings of disability, for example, etiological, social, definitional, or normative evaluations. In other cases, historical exegesis of texts is put in service of comparing theories in light of disability-positive criteria. This might be construed as reading *against* the texts, to the extent that the exegete makes the text answer a question that the text itself is not directly answering. However, there is nothing hermeneutically problematic about discussing the significance of a text's claims for the readers' (and contemporary scholarships') own questions. What would be problematic is if the exegete presented the medieval text as if the reader's questions are in fact the medieval text's own questions. This is eisegesis. What is required is that the exegete clearly distinguish the *meaning* of the text on its own terms (understanding) from the *significance* of the text for the reader's own questions (overstanding).

There are several lessons that *Disability in Medieval Christian Philosophy and Theology* has uncovered. These lessons can be divided between comparisons between ancient and medieval claims, between different medieval claims (e.g., medieval theologians compared to commonly held views by medieval non-academics), and between medieval claims and modern or contemporary claims.

Some of the lessons to be found in comparing ancient and medieval claims and theories are as follows. It is well known that Aristotle's biology is false and is an expression of sexism.[24] One false claim is that in procreation, the mother does not provide any active contribution, but only provides passive menstrual blood. Moreover, only the father provides the active contribution, but only the mother's contribution explains congenital disabilities. Regarding sexism, Aristotle presents the female sex as defective human beings – defective in the sense of being non-paradigmatic and lesser in well-being by virtue of being female. Furthermore, Aristotle presents paradigm humanity as the adult male who actualizes all of his potentialities in accordance with (moral and intellectual) virtue. What do medieval theologians and philosophers make of all of this? The medieval authors surveyed here contest all of these claims and revise them. (One of Marilyn McCord Adams's research agendas was to map out medieval responses and revisions to Aristotle, given Christian theism. To this extent, *Disability in Medieval Christian Philosophy and Theology* is an extension and development of this research agenda.)[25] We find a revision of the causes of congenital disabilities by claiming that in various cases, it is not the mother's but the father's contribution that explains kinds of congenital disability (Chapter 2). We find a rejection of Aristotle's claim that only fully actualized adult males are paradigm cases of human nature, because mothers, mystics, and martyrs – individuals who are vulnerable, dependent, and nurturing in various ways – are also fully flourishing human beings (Chapter 7). We also find a rejection of the claim that the actualization of all sensitive and intellectual powers is required for a fully flourishing human life (Chapters 8, 9, and 10).

There are a few lessons in the second group, namely comparisons between different medieval claims. First, by comparing philosophers' accounts of the causes of congenital disabilities with more commonly held views in the wider medieval public, we learn that not all medieval authors supposed that the causes are explained by one's parents' personal sins (see Chapters 2 and 6), but rather there are natural causes of congenital disabilities in addition to original sin. Second, we learn that there were different perceptions of deaf individuals – while some (wrongly) inferred from deafness to intellectual impairment, others did not (Chapter 6). Third, while some medieval theologians proposed and accepted that there is a subclass of human beings called "natural slaves" who were thought to be "bestial" and that all of the Amerindian peoples are included in this subclass of human beings, there were others who firmly rejected this empirical claim, and still others who denied the empirical claim and denied the equation of human dignity and the use of reason (Chapter 5).

There are a few lessons from the third group too, namely comparisons between different medieval claims and modern, or contemporary, claims. First, we learn that it is a rather complicated affair in trying to identify the definition of disability (e.g., *defectus*) in relation to contemporary definitions. It remains an open challenge to identify overlaps and non-overlaps between medieval terms for what we call disability and for what contemporary philosophers of disability call disability (Chapter 1). Second, we learn that a *medieval* Aristotelian approach to procreation clearly establishes the humanity of each and every human fetus, in contrast to modern philosophers like John Locke, who doubt or deny the humanity of an "oddly shaped fetus" (Chapter 2). Third, if we accept, for the sake of argument, the modern contention that personhood is the basis on which one has moral status and equality, then we may do well to consider pre-modern accounts of personhood. In doing so, we find that if personhood is the basis on which an individual has moral status and equality and a disability-positive perspective is correct, then Byzantine and Boethian accounts of personhood are preferable to various modern accounts of personhood (Chapter 3). Fourth, some contemporary Christians claim that being made in the image of God secures each human being's moral status and equality with others, including severely cognitively impaired human beings. However, by looking at the medieval history of theorizing about the *imago Dei/Trinitatis*, we find that this claim does not necessarily provide the succor one may wish to find in the *imago Dei/Trinitatis*. The intellectualist interpretation of the *imago Dei* might be rejected in order to try to make it do the ethical work that one wishes it to do in ethical theorizing. One might explore a minority report on the *imago Dei* for this purpose; or, one might have independent reason to give up this sort of ethical project altogether because the *imago Dei* is not technically fit for such a modern ethical project (Chapter 4). Fifth, there are some observations to be made about what might be called bad seeds (from a disability-positive perspective) planted in the medieval period that were developed in the early modern period and following. By connecting the Boethian account of personhood, the intellectualist interpretation of the *imago Dei*, and the equation of human dignity with the use of reason, we can better understand how "modern personhood" came to be so pervasive. The invention of modern personhood has played a significant role in the oppression of cognitively disabled human beings (during the modern period and following). But, sixth, despite the development of modern personhood as a basis for discriminating against cognitively disabled human beings, there are some medieval resources to weed out, so to speak, the growth of modern personhood.

Now that "medieval with a twist" has been opened, I hope that many more will join this fellowship of scholars, disabled and temporarily non-disabled alike.

Notes

1 On disability and medieval literature, see Tory Vandeventer Pearman, *Women and Disability in Medieval Literature*; Joshua R. Eyler, *Disability in the Middle Ages: Reconsiderations and Reverberations*; Connie L. Scarborough, *Viewing Disability in Medieval Spanish Texts: Disgraced or Graced (Premodern Health, Disease, and Disability)*.
2 On disability and medieval social and religious history, see Irina Metzler, *Disability in Medieval Europe: Thinking about Physical Impairment in the High Middle Ages, c.1100–c.1400 (Routledge Studies in Medieval Religion and Culture)*; Irina Metzler, *A Social History of Disability in the Middle Ages: Cultural Considerations of Physical Impairment (Routledge Studies in Cultural History)*; Irina Metzler, *Fools and Idiots?: Intellectual disability in the Middle Ages (Disability History MUP)*; Jenni Kuuliala, *Childhood Disability and Social Integration in the Middle Ages: Constructions of Impairments in Thirteenth- and Fourteenth-Century Canonization Processes*.
3 On disability and medieval history of religion, see Caroline Walker Bynum, *Jesus as Mother: Studies in the Spirituality of the High Middle Ages*; Caroline Walker Bynum, *Fragmentation and Redemption: Essays on Gender and the Human Body in Medieval Religion*; Caroline Walker Bynum, *The Resurrection of the Body in Western Christianity, 200–1336*. For a more general discussion of disability and religion, see Schumm, Darla and Michael J. Stultzfus, *Disability in Judaism, Christianity, and Islam: Sacred Texts, Historical Traditions, and Social Analysis*.
4 See Tom Shakespeare, *Disability: The Basics*, 1–23. Also, Tom Shakespeare and Nicholas Watson. "The Social Model of Disability: An Outdated Ideology?" 9–28.
5 See Adrienne Asch, Jeffrey Blustein, Daniel Putnam, and David Wasserman, "Disability: Definitions, Models, and Experience."
6 Jenni Kuuliala, "In Search of Medieval Disability," 3.
7 Richard Cross, "Duns Scotus on Disability: Teleology, Divine Willing, and Pure Nature," 72–73.
8 For a classic example of theology of disability and evaluations of disability, see Nancy Eiesland, *The Disabled God: Toward a Liberatory Theology of Disability*.
9 See <https://remedhe.com>

10 See <https://inmediasphil.wordpress.com/2018/08/25/the-medieval-survey-class-pt-ii-textbooks/>
11 See Richard Cross, "Disability, Impairment, and Some Medieval Accounts of the Incarnation: Suggestions for a Theology of Personhood," 639–658; Richard Cross, "Baptism, Faith, and Severe Cognitive Impairment in Some Medieval Theologies," 420–438; Richard Cross, "Aquinas on Physical Impairment: Human Nature and Original Sin," 317–338; Richard Cross, "Duns Scotus on Disability, Teleology, Divine Willing, and Pure Nature," 72–95. Cross has also published a constructive piece on disability; see "Impairment, Normalcy, and a Social Theory of Disability," 693–714.
12 See Miguel Romero, "Aquinas on the *corporis infirmitas*: Broken Flesh and the Grammar of Grace," 101–151; Miguel Romero, "Happiness and Those Who Lack the Use of Reason," 49–96; Miguel Romero, "The Goodness and Beauty of Our Fragile Flesh," 206–253. For a discussion of mental disorder according to Peter John Olivi, John Duns Scotus, and William Ockham, see Vesa Hirvonen, "Mental Disorders in Late Medieval Philosophy and Theology," 171–188.
13 Scott M. Williams, "Disability, Ableism, and Anti-Ableism in Medieval Latin Philosophy and Theology," 37.
14 For a discussion of Judaism and Disability, see Tzvi C. Marx, *Disability in Jewish Law*. For a discussion of Islam and Disability, see Mohammed Ghaly, *Islam and Disability: Perspectives in Theory and Jurisprudence*. Also, for a more wide-ranging discussion and representation, see Darla Schumm and Michael Stoltzfus, *Disability in Judaism, Christianity, and Islam: Sacred Texts, Historical Traditions, and Social Analysis*.
15 For a discussion, see Edward Wheatley, *Stumbling Blocks before the Blind: Medieval Constructions of Disability*, 10ff. For rejection of this normative view, see Dan Goodley, *Disability Studies: An Interdisciplinary Introduction*, 5–10.
16 Nancy L. Eiesland, *The Disabled God*, 70–71; quoted in Richard Cross, "Duns Scotus on Disability, Teleology, Divine Willing, and Pure Nature," 73.
17 Richard Cross, "Aquinas on Physical Impairment: Human Nature and Original Sin," 317–318.
18 Richard Cross, "Duns Scotus on Disability, Teleology, Divine Willing, and Pure Nature," 75–95.
19 In personal correspondence Richard Cross elaborates on this, saying, "Now I suppose we need to know whether the cocktail use of 'with a twist' is an instance of the general sense (i.e. 'with something unexpected'), or a distinct and independent development proper to the world of alcohol." The analogy being made is as follows: just as standard approaches to medieval philosophy and theology are akin to standard cocktail recipes, so too are medieval philosophy and theology with a twist akin to cocktails with a twist. In this quotation, Cross distinguishes two senses of "with a twist."
20 Jenni Kuuliala and Reima Välimäki, "Deafness and Pastoral Care in the Middle Ages," 193.
21 Christina Van Dyke, "Taking the 'Dis' Out of Disability," 224–225.
22 Mark K. Spencer, "Separated Souls: Disability in the Intermediate State," 240.
23 Richard Cross, "Disability and Resurrection," 271.
24 Prudence Allen, RSM, *The Concept of Woman: The Aristotelian Revolution, 750BC – AD 1250*, 83–126.
25 See Marilyn McCord Adams, "The Resurrection of the Body According to Three Medieval Aristotelians: Thomas Aquinas, John Duns Scotus, and William, Ockham," 1–33; Marilyn McCord Adams, "What's Metaphysically

Special about Supposits? Some Medieval Variations on Aristotelian Substance," 15–52; Marilyn McCord Adams, "The Metaphysics of the Trinity in Some Fourteenth Century Franciscans," 101–168; Marilyn McCord Adams, *Some Later Medieval Theories of the Eucharist.*

References

Adams, Marilyn McCord. "The Resurrection of the Body According to Three Medieval Aristotelians: Thomas Aquinas, John Duns Scotus, and William Ockham," *Philosophical Topics* 20.2 (1992) 1–33.

——— "What's Metaphysically Special about Supposits? Some Medieval Variations on Aristotelian Substance," *Proceedings of the Aristotelian Society, Supplementary Volumes* 79 (2005) 15–52.

——— "The Metaphysics of the Trinity in Some Fourteenth Century Franciscans," *Franciscan Studies* 66 (2008) 101–168.

——— *Some Later Medieval Theories of the Eucharist: Thomas Aquinas, Giles of Rome, Duns Scotus, and William Ockham.* Oxford: Oxford University Press, 2010.

Asch, Adrienne, Jeffrey Blustein, Daniel Putnam, and David Wasserman. "Disability: Definitions, Models, and Experience." In *Stanford Encyclopedia of Philosophy* (Summer 2016), <https://plato.stanford.edu/entries/disability/>.

Allen, Prudence, RSM. *The Concept of Woman: The Aristotelian Revolution, 750BC – AD 1250.* Grand Rapids, MI: Eerdmans, 1997.

Brock, Brian and John Swinton (eds.). *Disability in the Christian Tradition: A Reader.* Grand Rapids, MI: Eerdmans, 2012.

Bynum, Caroline Walker. *Jesus as Mother: Studies in the Spirituality of the High Middle Ages.* Berkeley: University of California Press, 1982.

——— *Fragmentation and Redemption: Essays on Gender and the Human Body in Medieval Religion.* New York: Zone Books, 1992.

——— *The Resurrection of the Body in Western Christianity, 200–1336.* New York: Columbia University Press, 1995.

Cross, Richard. "Disability, Impairment, and Some Medieval Accounts of the Incarnation: Suggestions for a Theology of Personhood," *Modern Theology* 27.4 (2011) 639–658.

——— "Baptism, Faith, and Severe Cognitive Impairment in Some Medieval Theologies," *International Journal of Systematic Theology* 14.4 (2012) 420–438.

——— "Impairment, Normalcy, and a Social Theory of Disability," *Res Philosophica* 93.4 (2016) 693–714.

——— "Aquinas on Physical Impairment: Human Nature and Original Sin," *Harvard Theological Review* 110.3 (2017) 317–338.

——— "Duns Scotus on Disability, Teleology, Divine Willing, and Pure Nature," *Theological Studies* 78.1 (2017) 72–95.

Eiesland, Nancy. *The Disabled God: Toward a Liberatory Theology of Disability.* Nashville, TN: Abingdon Press, 1994.

Eyler, Joshua R (ed.). *Disability in the Middle Ages: Reconsiderations and Reverberations.* Burlington, VT: Ashgate, 2010.

Ghaly, Mohammed. *Islam and Disability: Perspectives in Theory and Jurisprudence (Routledge Islamic Studies Series).* Oxford: Routledge, 2010.

Goodley, Dan. *Disability Studies: An Interdisciplinary Introduction*. London: Sage Publications, 2011.

Hirvonen, Vesa. "Mental Disorders in Late Medieval Philosophy and Theology." In *Mind and Modality: Studies in the History of Philosophy in Honour of Simo Knuuttila*. Edited by Vesa Hirvonen, Toivo Holopainen, and Miira Tuominen. Leiden: Brill, 2006: 171–188.

Kuuliala, Jenni. *Childhood Disability and Social Integration in the Middle Ages: Constructions of Impairments in Thirteenth- and Fourteenth-Century Canonization Processes*. Turnholt: Brepols, 2016.

——— "In Search of Medieval Disability," *J@rgonia* 21 (2013) 1–6.

Marx, Tzvi C. *Disability in Jewish Law*. London: Routledge, 2002.

Metzler, Irina. *Disability in Medieval Europe: Thinking about Physical Impairment in the High Middle Ages, c.1100–c.1400 (Routledge Studies in Medieval Religion and Culture)*. Oxford: Routledge, 2006.

——— *A Social History of Disability in the Middle Ages: Cultural Considerations of Physical Impairment (Routledge Studies in Cultural History)*. Oxford: Routledge, 2013.

——— *Fools and Idiots?: Intellectual disability in the Middle Ages (Disability History MUP)*. Manchester, UK: Manchester University Press, 2016.

Pearman, Tory Vandeventer. *Women and Disability in Medieval Literature*. New York: Palgrave MacMillan, 2010.

Romero, Miguel. "Aquinas on the *corporis infirmitas*: Broken Flesh and the Grammar of Grace." In *Disability in the Christian Tradition: A Reader*. Edited by Brian Brock and John Swinton. Grand Rapids, MI: Eerdmans, 2012, 101–151.

——— "Happiness and Those Who Lack the Use of Reason," *The Thomist* 80 (2016) 49–96.

——— "The Goodness and Beauty of Our Fragile Flesh: Moral Theologians and Our Engagement with 'Disability,'" *Journal of Moral Theology*, Vol. 6, Special Issue 2 (2017) 206–253.

Scarborough, Connie L. *Viewing Disability in Medieval Spanish Texts: Disgraced or Graced (Premodern Health, Disease, and Disability)*. Amsterdam: Amsterdam University Press, 2018.

Schumm, Darla and Michael Stoltzfus (eds.). *Disability in Judaism, Christianity, and Islam: Sacred Texts, Historical Traditions, and Social Analysis*. New York: Palgrave MacMillan, 2011.

Shakespeare, Tom. *Disability: The Basics*. Oxford: Routledge, 2018.

Shakespeare, Tom and Nicholas Watson. "The Social Model of Disability: An Outdated Ideology?" *Research in Social Science and Disability* 2 (2002) 9–28.

Wheatley, Edward. *Stumbling Blocks before the Blind: Medieval Constructions of Disability*. Ann Arbor: University of Michigan Press, 2010.

Williams, Scott M. "Disability, Ableism, and Anti-Ableism in Medieval Latin Philosophy and Theology." In *The Edinburgh Critical History of Middle Ages and Renaissance Philosophy*. Edited by Richard A. Lee and Andrew LaZella. Edinburgh: Edinburgh University Press, 2020, 37–57.

Part I
Theoretical Frameworks

1 Plurality in Medieval Concepts of Disability

Kevin Timpe

Introduction

In recent years, contemporary history of philosophy has broadened its scope in at least two ways. First, previously ignored or under-valued figures are receiving increased attention. This increased in breadth of figures is good, as the Western canon has often been limited in ways that is hard to justify. Second, there is an increase in topics being explored historically. (And sometimes, these two ways of broadening contemporary philosophy's focus go together, as is the case, I think, with the volume you are holding as a whole.) While this second increase in scope is also good, there are methodological challenges of bringing historical figures from different contexts and with different assumptions into discussion with contemporary treatments. As the present volume indicates, one of the topics of renewed historical treatment is disability. Part of this renewal is an attempt to bring medieval and contemporary figures into discussion. As Richard Cross writes, such attempts are "complex and contested":

> One reason is that our contemporary notions of disability are themselves complex and contested: there are popular, pre-theoretical notions and highly theorized notions, and, between the two, varieties of practical and political notions .... Another reason is that the very notion of disability is itself modern. So the history of disability involves the isolation and examination of concepts ancestral to our own ones, along with a frank acknowledgement that our own ones are far from clear.[1]

This chapter acknowledges these difficulties and seeks to further develop a particular sort of challenge: that we can't always simply assume, in the way that some scholars seem to, that medieval concepts map onto the contemporary debates they're often taken to connect with. If the concepts don't closely map onto each other, then attempts to foster a cross-historical dialogue can be instances of talking past each other, even if we don't realize it. More specifically, I explore the thought of two medieval theologians and philosophers, Thomas Aquinas and John Duns Scotus, with a focus on how they understand the concept of disability.[2] I begin with Aquinas, where I'm interested in whether he would think we have a single univocal concept of disability that applies to all disabilities[3] – that is, to all things that contemporary disability studies and philosophical reflection on disability would typically recognize as a disability. In her recent book on physical disabilities, *The Minority Body*, Elizabeth Barnes argues that we should work from paradigmatic instances of disability toward an account of what disability generally is, rather than privileging an account of what disability is that may not accurately reflect the experiences of those that have the range of disabilities that the account is supposed to include:

> A successful account of disability needs to say that paradigm cases of disability are in fact disabilities (and that paradigm cases of non-disability are not) …. We want to know what *these kinds of things* – deafness, blindness, paralysis, achondroplasia, MS, etc. – are, such that they have something in common with each other.[4]

Her treatment in *The Minority Body* is limited to only physical disabilities. She is supportive of others who work up from different ground, who want to focus on other disabilities. But she points out that such projects may be aiming at something different than what she is aiming at (namely physical disabilities):

> I don't think we should infer that there is a unified category – or a unified connection to wellbeing – covering psychological, physical, and cognitive forms of disability simply because our word "disability" can refer to physical, cognitive, or psychological disability. Modifiers like "physically", "mentally", "psychologically", etc. can do a lot of work.[5]

Barnes isn't committed to the claim that there *isn't* a unified category of disability. Rather, on her view the mere fact that we use the word "disability" with this range of modifiers doesn't entail that there is. For Barnes,

> the best way to approach the question of whether and to what extent different types of disability form a common kind … is by first engaging in detailed analysis of the different varieties of disability and then exploring the potential commonalities.[6]

Furthermore, she encourages us to keep in mind that there is great variation within each kind of disability. Not all physical disability has a particular feature in common, and some physical disabilities may be more similar to, say, a psychological disability than it is to other physical disabilities.[7]

Another debate in contemporary philosophy of disability is about the normative status of disability – that is, whether disability involves, in Barnes's terminology, "mere-difference" or "bad-difference."[8] While Aquinas's corpus doesn't offer an extended or systematic treatment of the nature of disability, his writings on philosophy of human nature offer important insights regarding his understanding of disability. Through an exploration of Aquinas's understanding of the nature of concepts, I argue that Aquinas would agree with Barnes's suggestion above that we should reject the assumption that all disability is of the same kind. That is, Aquinas would reject that there is a species which tracks the range of what we currently call disabilities and that there thus isn't a single univocal concept of disability that captures all and only disabilities. Relatedly, Aquinas thinks that one can't have *scientia* of things that are only known by the senses or what comes about merely by fortune, as opposed to what is necessary given things' natures.[9] Aquinas thinks that "to know scientifically we must know them all at once in the universal."[10] Thus, if there isn't a single univocal concept that captures the nature or essence of what disability is, we won't be able to have scientific knowledge of disability.

It follows from the discussion of Aquinas's view that we can't always assume that a particular historical figure has the same concept as contemporary discussions, since it may not be the case that they have a single concept in the first place. But bringing historical figures into dialogue with contemporary discussions is also difficult given that not all figures in a particular discussion have the same concept as others in that same period. So if we want to bring, for example, contemporary philosophical discussions into dialogue with historical figures such as Aquinas and Scotus or if we want to mine the thought of those historical figures to offset lacunae in contemporary discussions, we must pay attention to the differences between how the relevant historical figures understand the concepts in question and how those concepts may not have the same parameters as those that we're seeking to deploy.

I begin, in the first main section, *The Concept of a Concept*, by briefly examining how Aquinas understood the nature of concepts and cognition. For Aquinas, the ultimate object of human cognition is grasping the essences (or *quiddities*) of things. Complete understanding of an object requires the formation of a concept or mental word (*verbum*). Furthermore, an individual cognizes the more universal prior to the less universal; this means that an individual comes to know the genus first and then the differentia that marks off a particular species within that genus (the characteristic of a thing constituting it in its species).[11] In the second section, *Thomas Aquinas on Disability*, I then turn toward disability. While Aquinas's corpus doesn't offer an extended or systematic treatment of the nature of disability, his writings on philosophy of human nature do offer important insights regarding his understanding of disability. In the third section, *The Differentia of Disability*, I argue that Aquinas would deny that there is a single concept of disability that captures all and only disabilities.[12] In the fourth section, *Further Complexities from Duns Scotus*, I look at another medieval figure, Duns Scotus, who has an importantly different account of disability than Aquinas. Given the difference between figures such as Aquinas and Scotus, we can't even assume that two medieval figures have the same concept when contemporary discussion seeks to mine those historical texts for insight into contemporary debates. In the fifth and final section, *Plurality in Context*, I briefly consider how the multiplicity of concepts of disability gives figures like Aquinas a flexibility that isn't always present in contemporary discussions – a flexibility that can be seen in some of the subsequent chapters to this volume. However, this same flexibility makes bringing medieval figures into discussion with contemporary treatments a trickier issue than is sometimes expected. The chapter thus seeks to show the need for extended and careful treatments of the very sort that this volume as a whole seeks to provide.

The Concept of a Concept

I begin with some Thomistic philosophy of language. This treatment is in no way intended to be exhaustive; rather, I limit the discussion to just enough of Aquinas's thought as I think is needed for later purposes in the next two sections.

Aquinas thinks that human language, despite the finitude that makes univocal talk about God impossible,[13] can capture the essence of that which we speak about when we are speaking about creation:

> The universality of our words, on account of which they are related not just to *one particular sort of thing*, a universal, but rather to a multitude, indeed, a potential *infinity* of ordinary things, is the result of our ability to conceive of these things in a *peculiar manner*, namely, universally, and to use the word to express this universal conception, or as Aquinas often refers to it, the universal *ratio* of these ordinary things. Aquinas's notion of ratio is what we can justifiably identify as Aquinas's idea of *mental content*, the information encoded by our mental concepts about the things we conceive.[14]

So, for example, I can speak both of the feline nature but also a potentially infinite number of cats by employing the English word "cat" and, more importantly, the concept picked out by that particular phonetic signifier.[15]

The cognitive act by which we conceive of what a particular word signifies is, for Aquinas, a concept. Human thought and concept appropriation is linguistic for Aquinas, for he also refers to concepts as "mental words."[16] As Anthony Kenny puts it, "the grasp of a concept ... is expressed by the mastery of the use of a word."[17] On Aquinas's view, "to think about something is to *produce* a concept," that is a mental word, "of a thing."[18] Following "the Philosopher," Aquinas thinks that not every description of a thing is equally apt regarding that thing in terms of what it is *per se*, in its very being.[19] While Socrates is "a snub-nosed thing" (i.e., "snub-nosed" is *said in* Socrates), he is better signified under the concept of "rational substance" (i.e., "human" is *said of* Socrates). Some true predications are of a substance, and other true predications are of a substance's accidents. So not all concepts that we use to conceive of kinds of objects will be equally good or equally apt in characterizing those objects.

As the previous example indicates, a concept of a rational substance can relate to not just the genus as a whole but also all the particulars that belong to that genus. This is because, as Aquinas puts it, "the individual shares the nature, or falls under the concept."[20] So, continuing to use the example of rational substance, the concept can relate to every primary substance that falls under that genus. Rational substance as a concept relates to every human (and to every angel). But the concept can also relate to those species or substances that the genus is "said of."[21] At this point we can see the relationship between concepts and the standard medieval use of Porphyrian Trees to sub-divide genera. According to Eleonore Stump:

> [A] Porphyrian Tree begins with an Aristotelian category (*substance* is the standard medieval example) and moves via a series of dichotomous differentiae [i.e., a characteristic constituting only one species within that genus] from that most general genus through its species. (In theory, all its possible species can be uncovered by this means.) The dichotomies produce progressively more specific species by the application of a pair of complementary differentia to a less specific species or subordinate genus already in that tree.[22]

For Aquinas, the ultimate object of human cognition is the substance in which we grasp the essences of things. The concept of a species is "made up of its two constituent concepts,"[23] namely the concept of the genus and the concept of the differentia. So, cognition of a species within a genus will require grasping not only the genus but also the differentia that distinguishes that species from others in the same genus. Likewise, cognition of a particular within a species will require grasping not only the right genus and specific difference but also what individuates that particular from other members of the same species. In the next section, I argue that there is not a single differentia that marks off disability as a species within a genus. Thus, there is not a single concept of disability that captures all and only what we refer to as disabilities.

Thomas Aquinas on Disability

Like other medieval philosophers and theologians,[24] Aquinas doesn't give us an explicit or extended treatment of the nature of disability, or what he might call a "defect."[25] Instead, his discussion of disability is almost always in passing when discussing human nature. John Berkman lists a number of such instances and concluded that "examples of persons with physical or mental disabilities are employed to illustrate general points about human nature, its end and its perfections, whether the perfection be physical, intellectual, moral or spiritual."[26] Aquinas does not have a treatise or question in which he sets out to give a scientific definition of what he calls a defect. In fact, if defects come about *per accidens* rather than *per se*, as suggested above, then he couldn't give a scientific account. Instead, Aquinas discusses defect in many different questions, often when discussing human nature. Given his endorsement of a privation view of evil, his account of defects needs to be understood within this larger framework of privations – not merely lacks – within a thing's nature.[27] So it will be useful to look, even if just briefly, at what Aquinas says about human nature as it relates to disabilities before we examine directly the concept of disability.

Aquinas's account of human nature, like his account of creation as a whole, is inherently teleological. It is in virtue of its formal cause – that is, the rational soul – that human nature has the final cause that it does. And that final cause is the beatific vision.[28] While the specifically rational faculties that are given by the rational soul are necessary (and must also be used in a particular way pertaining to their proper function) to achieve their final end,[29] humans cannot reach the beatific vision simply by proper use of their natural powers. That requires grace.[30]

As Richard Cross makes clear in his treatment of disability in Aquinas, Aquinas thinks all post-Fall humans have defects of some sort. Perhaps surprisingly, even the human nature united to the Second Person of the Trinity in the Incarnation has defects.[31] The fact that Aquinas thinks that even the Incarnate Christ has defects (with respect to his human nature) should reinforce the claim that there's not necessarily blame or sin involved in every defect. This leads Berkman to claim that for Aquinas "all humans, as wayfarers on the road to God, are to a greater or lesser degree impaired."[32] Human nature, post-Fall, lacks an internal ordering that it had in the pre-lapsarian state.[33] And this disordering is what opens the possibility for disability. Furthermore, for Aquinas, particular disabilities are defects that themselves serve no ultimate purpose, either for the individual who has that defect or for human nature as a whole, even if the possibility of defect is a punishment for original sin.[34]

For Aquinas, then, disabilities are integrally related to how he understands human nature. According to Richard Cross, Aquinas differentiates defects into two general classes: "those that do, and those that do not, impact on the teleological orientation of an organism."[35] But this cannot be the differentia for disability, as it would be too broad. Both vice and sin more broadly also impact the teleological orientation of the organism. And while, as seen above, Aquinas thinks that disability is caused by sin (in particular, original sin), he does not think that all disability is sin (or vice more specifically): "Aquinas sees physical impairments – things that constitute a subclass of what he labels 'bodily defects' – fundamentally as punishments for original sin. He is (generally) very careful to distance his account of defects from notions of individual punishment."[36] This severing of disability and personal sin and punishment is what allows Aquinas to hold that individuals with severe cognitive impairment are more capable of achieving happiness than we might initially expect.[37] Even though they're not to be attributed to individual sins, Aquinas does think that disabilities are defects that undermine or completely destroy a natural principle of activity, without thereby ending the life of the individual. However, note that some illnesses also impact an agent's teleological functioning with regard to their natural principles of activity without thereby ending the life of the individual. But surely not all illnesses that have these characteristics involve disability. Having a cold, for instance, doesn't entail having a disability, even temporarily. So "impact on the agent's teleological functioning" also cannot be the differentia for a disability, since that concept is too broad and thus too inclusive. For that we have to look elsewhere.

As mentioned, Aquinas understands disabilities to be a certain species (or, if my argument in the next section is correct, certain *species* [plural]) of defects in human nature.[38] As a result, a fuller discussion of human nature than can be done here would be necessary for a complete discussion of human disability.[39] In one such larger context, Berkman talks about five ways that humans can have defects (or, in his language, impairments):

i The first kind of impairment is at the organic or vegetative level and involves impairment of the basic biological functioning of the individual. Berkman writes of this category:

> Aquinas calls all of these ills physical evils, or evils of nature, since they are a privation of human physical perfection. Of course, if the impairment is great enough, it leads to death, which is the greatest of physical evils.[40]

ii The second kind of impairment is a privation in the proper functioning of one of the senses, either the five physical senses (e.g., blindness) or one of the four internal senses (e.g., amnesia or dementia).[41]

iii The third kind of impairment is one involving the intellect's use of theoretical reason. (Like other kinds of impairments, these impairments come in degrees, and it may not always be clear where natural variation ends and a genuine disability begins.)

iv The fourth is also an impairment in the intellect, but this time with respect to practical or moral reason.

> This is the inability (or failure) to choose and act well, which is encapsulated in the moral virtues and vices. Aquinas is fully aware that some who are intellectually virtuous may be morally impaired, and vice versa. But in many places Aquinas does place clear boundaries between mental and moral disabilities.[42]

v The fifth and final kind of impairment involves spiritual deficiency.[43]

Berkman is also correct to see that "these levels are clearly related, as impairment at one level can cause or contribute to impairment at another level,"[44] a claim that even a quick examination of the contemporary psychological and biological literature on disabilities will attest.

While much – and perhaps the majority – of contemporary disability studies as a discipline focuses on physical or cognitive impairment, for Aquinas these two types of disability are not as important as other kinds, for two reasons. First, as already mentioned above, Aquinas thinks that all humans have defects. Physical and cognitive impairments are just part of a Fallen creation and thus aren't as problematic as are other sorts. Second, and relatedly, given the fundamental theological orientation of all of his thought, an orientation that is not standard in contemporary reflection on disabilities, moral and spiritual impairment (i.e., the fourth and fifth kinds mentioned by Berkman) are for Aquinas the most significant sorts.[45] However, in the present context I want to engage with contemporary disability studies rather than ethics or theology and thus will not focus on those impairments that Aquinas thinks are most important.

The Differentia of Disability

In the previous section, we've seen that disabilities, for Aquinas, are a kind of defect. But, from the first section, we've seen that for there to be a single concept of a species within a genus, there must be a constituent differentia that, when joined with the genus in question, demarcates the species. Is there such a concept of disability that can do this work? I think the answer is no, though it's an admittedly tentative answer. There may be details in aspects of Aquinas's corpus that I'm not aware of that would count against the argument to follow. But if we consider various elements gleaned from Aquinas's discussions about the nature of disability, I think that we'll see that none of these elements will suffice to serve as the needed differentia.

Consider first defect itself. If the differentia that marks off humans with disabilities from those without is defect, then the concept of disability would be too broad, as mentioned above, including things under the concept of disability that ought not be included under that concept.

For some defects are brought about by, or indeed identical with, sins. My gluttonous act of consuming too much espresso this morning, for instance, is a defect in my moral character and thus an act of sin. But it's not a disability. Furthermore, as seen above, all post-Fall humans have defects to some degree or other. If the concept of disability was to stretch this far, then it's simply not clear that the concept connects with what current disability studies aims at.[46] Even a specifically *physical* defect won't be sufficient for disability. Having the flu or a bout of gastrointestinal bleeding (caused either by peptic ulcers or by diverticulitis) doesn't entail a disability.[47]

It's worth noting here, even if just in passing, that Richard Cross has developed an account, drawing on Duns Scotus and Hervaeus Natalis, according to which "the model or archetype of human personhood is something that is *dependent* in various ways on some kind of prosthesis."[48] Cross suggests that the instrumentality relation can sometimes provide for a union between a person and an instrument, such as a prosthetic limb:

> I shall assume that this kind of unity–satisfied *merely* by relations of efficient causation–obtains between a person and an external tool or (in effect) a prosthetic limb. But I shall assume too that this unity is just as strong as obtains between a substance and an intrinsic part (e.g. a limb united to its whole by some kind of relation of formal causality). The only significant difference is that external tools and prostheses are in principle easier to detach and attach than intrinsic parts are (compare a knife with an arm-blade).[49]

If this kind of unity is possible, then Cross suggests that in the Incarnation the assumed human nature becomes a "total prosthesis"[50] of the Incarnate Second Person of the Trinity, where a total prosthesis performs "*all* human vital functions for a person, and [is] the instrument of that person in all human causal activity in the world."[51]

> On this view, the model or archetype of human personhood is something that is *dependent* in various ways on some kind of prosthesis. ... Given that the incarnate divine person is the normative case of what it is to be a human person, the incarnation shows that persons, normatively, are substances that include and depend on prostheses. Putting it another way, we might say that, *normatively*, human persons are intrinsically disabled or impaired.[52]

In a footnote later in the paper, Cross clarifies:

> I distinguish impairment and disability below .... As I make clear there, in line with suggestions made in my introduction, above, impairment is dependence; disability is the failure of the environment – be

> it the physical environment or the activities of other human agents – to provide the conditions for provide [*sic*] for opportunities for dependence necessary for flourishing. So, strictly speaking, human persons are intrinsically impaired, but not disabled.[53]

Thus, on this view by Cross, it's an intrinsic part of human nature to be dependent and impaired: "We are all, in different ways, givers and recipients and these kinds of relations clearly fall under the general scope of dependence."[54]

Whatever else one thinks of Cross's suggestion, it won't serve as an account of disability for Aquinas, for three reasons. First, the view depends on metaphysical and theological claims drawn from Scotus that Aquinas would reject.[55] (I come back to Scotus in the next section.) Second, on this view the kind of dependency at issue is built into human nature. Disability, or impairment in Cross's terminology, is a good part of human nature and thus not a defect, as it is for Aquinas. Third, while I agree it's not always clear exactly where to draw the bounds between individuals with disabilities and those without, expanding the boundaries of disability, or again to use Cross's terminology impairment, to include all instances of human nature – including the human nature assumed by the Second Person of the Trinity – violates Barnes's advice with which this chapter began that we should begin by ostension. Disability would no longer be recognized as that which disability discussion aims to be about.[56]

Disability can't be broader than defect, for Aquinas. But we've also seen that the genus of defect is too broad to be equivalent with disability. Not all defects are disabilities. If all disabilities are defects, then disability would be a species of defect – and so a further concept would be needed to differentiate those defects that are disabilities from those that aren't. But what could serve such a role? It's not clear that any consideration we've seen from Aquinas will be able to play this role.

Consider the various kinds of impairments that Berkman categorizes. Let's begin with biological impairment at the organic or vegetative level of functioning. While such might be sufficient for certain disabilities,[57] biological impairment at the organic or vegetative level isn't necessary either for disability. Mild or moderate cognitive impairments, for example, needn't involve an impairment of basic organic functioning[58] – they involve an impairment of the rational capacities. Similarly, impairment in one of the physical or internal senses also won't be necessary, since the need for a mobility aid doesn't involve any of the nine senses. Something similar is true of the next two categories from Berkman: impairment of right reason, that is, theoretical reasoning and moral reasoning. Perhaps such impairments are sufficient for disability, but they won't be necessary – as should be expected if we can't give a scientific definition of disability.[59] Finally, I think it's obvious that spiritual deficiency cannot be the relevant sort of defect that demarcates disability; such a suggestion reinforces the worst of ableist equating of disability and sin that has marked too much of Christian theology.[60]

Now, perhaps there are other concepts in Aquinas that might serve the relevant role of differentiating those defects that are disabilities from those defects that aren't. My inability to find one might simply be a function of failure in my philosophical imagination or my unfamiliarity with all of the relevant primary texts. But suppose that I'm right. Suppose there isn't a single concept of disability in Aquinas; in such a case, we might have reason to doubt that there is a single particular sort of thing in Aquinas's thought that is the universal disability, which all and only those qualities that are disabilities instantiate. It's possible, of course, that there is a universal that simply fails to track our concepts, such that the multiplicity of the former doesn't entail the multiplicity of the latter.[61] But Aquinas's understanding of *ratio* and its connection with concepts gives us reason to think this isn't the case:

> The *ratio* of every single thing is what its name signifies, as the *ratio* of a stone is what its name signifies. But names are the signs of intellectual conceptions, whence the *ratio* of any single thing signified by a name is the conception of the intellect that the name signifies. And this conception of the intellect is in the intellect as in its subject, but it is in the thing thought of as in that which is represented: for the conceptions of the intellect are certain similitudes of the things thought of. But if the conception of the intellect were not assimilated to the thing, then the conception would be false of that thing.[62]

For Aquinas, predications can only be true if the qualities predicated of things actually inhere in them. So if there isn't a single concept of disability, then the various predications (e.g., "2p15–16.1 microdeletion syndrome is a disability," "alexithimia is a disability," "paralysis is a disability," etc.) would involve not a single universal of disability but instead a plurality of qualities that are disabilities. Disability might involve ontological multiplicity and not just conceptual multiplicity.

Finally, if there is no such singular univocal concept of disability, that would mean that Aquinas's use of "defect" was either equivocal or analogical. Though I can't rule out here that his use of "defect" is equivocal and signifies a plurality of different objects with different meanings that are, at least at times, unrelated to each other, I'm inclined to think that he would understand it analogically, given that I think there is a general similarity between the various concepts that the use of the term seems to pick out.[63] A challenge for thinking that it's used analogically is specifying what meaning plays the role of the central unifying concept that the analogy is constructed around.[64]

Further Complexities from Duns Scotus

The previous sections sought to show some of the difficulties in seeking to bring a medieval figure's thoughts on disabilities into contemporary discussion. If, as I've argued, Aquinas doesn't have a single univocal concept of disability, then attempts to bring his views into discussion with contemporary treatments, as is increasingly happening with disability (among other topics), require a great deal of methodological and interpretive care. In the present section, I want to further illustrate these difficulties by pointing out how this project will be even more difficult once we broaden beyond just a single medieval figure. Even two figures who in broad strokes are as similar as Aquinas and Duns Scotus are have significant differences on the nature of disability.

There are important similarities between Aquinas and Duns Scotus related to how they'd understand the nature of disability. Like Aquinas, Scotus's account of individuation of a species includes a specific difference that distinguishes two different species within a genus. In fact, for Scotus a specific difference is "primarily diverse" from any other, meaning that the specific difference involves a concept that is absolutely simple and cannot overlap with the concept involved in another specific difference.[65] For Scotus, haecceities differentiate membership of the same species from each other in a way parallel to how specific differences differentiate two species within the same genus. However, unlike specific differences, haecceities lack shared conceptual contents.[66] Like Aquinas, Scotus also considers disabilities a kind of defect (*defuctum*) of one's teleologically normative powers. This, however, can't be the specific difference for disability in Scotus for the same reasons discussed in the previous section. In his discussions of specific disabilities, he understands them as the absence of one or more properties that are necessary for an individual but not included in that individual's essence. "The substance is appropriate for the properties, and the properties for the substance. In some sense it satisfies the *purpose* of each of these things that they go together."[67] This understanding of the kinds of properties that are lacking in a disability might provide a way of developing a specific difference that might unify disability into a species; but so far as I am aware, Scotus does not develop this possibility. In his investigation of Scotus on disability, Cross argues that it can be:

> this gets us Scotus's general account of what we would call disabilities: cases in which human nature fails to cause one or more teleologically normative *propria* [i.e., necessary but non-defining properties] – in a human individual – in particular, teleological normative *powers* whatever the explanation for this failure.[68]

If Cross's interpretation is correct, then unlike Aquinas, one may be able to give a univocal concept of disability.

Beyond this, however, there are also further differences between the two figures. A central difference between Aquinas and Scotus on the nature of disability is that Scotus rejects the connection between sin and disability as punitive that we saw in Aquinas's thought.[69] As Richard Cross puts it in a recent article on disability in Scotus,

> Scotus rejects the strong punishment found in Aquinas. He agrees that there is de facto a punitive element to disability in the context of original sin, but he disagrees with the view that it is a necessary feature of disability.[70]

In fact, Scotus thinks that it's possible that there be disability even had there been no sin. And the reason for this difference is that Scotus thinks that it isn't necessary for God to secure the non-necessary *propria* of creatures in the way that Aquinas does.[71] Scotus's thought not only eliminates the punitive nature of disability that figures into Aquinas' treatment but naturalizes disability as a result.[72]

The central thrust of this section ought to be obvious. Philosophical discussions of, for example, realism or hylomorphism or accounts of the nature of *liberum arbitrium* from the medieval period pay careful attention to the relevant differences between different individuals' views. But as these same figures are increasingly explored for what they thought about less well-known topics, greater care needs to be taken to keep the nuances and differences in their views in mind, elsewise we'll flatten a very nuanced and textured landscape. As Joshua Eyler notes, this flattening can be found in scholarly work that needs to be more careful:

> Beyond this issue of sources, though, lies a more damaging stereotype concerning medieval disabilities. As Irina Metzler has recently explained, the "belief of modern authors that ancient or medieval societies *invariably* saw a link between sin and illness appears to be the dominant historiographical notion on the subject of disability." While it is certainly accurate to say that *some* people in the Middle Ages believed disability to be God's punishment for sin, this way of understanding medieval disability has only a limited viability. In truth, there were many lenses through which medieval societies viewed disability, as the current research is beginning to demonstrate.[73]

Plurality in Context

The previous sections have explored how two medieval figures thought about what we now refer to as disability. I've argued that, in Aquinas, there is not one univocal concept which tracks our contemporary use of disability; rather, disability is a cluster concept that picks out a plurality of conditions that can't be unified under a single differentia. I then showed how Scotus's understanding of disability is importantly different from Aquinas's, thus illustrating some of the diversity that needs to be recognized in the medieval period. In this final section, I want to bring these discussions into dialogue with a number of recent debates in philosophy of disability and show two consequences of this conceptual plurality.

First, this conceptual plurality means that we need to be very careful when bringing medieval figures into discussion with the contemporary debates. As mentioned in the introduction, disability is one of the topics where historical treatments are presently being mined to see if they can shed light on contemporary discussions. But as with others of these topics, there's a methodological challenge in that we can't always assume that medieval concepts map onto the contemporary debates they're often taken to connect with.

With respect to philosophical discussions of disability, Elizabeth Barnes's work, mentioned earlier, has had a large influence on contemporary debates. Barnes's objective, very broadly but somewhat crudely put, in *The Minority Body* is to address a gap – a gap between how disability is thought of in the disability rights movement and how it's often understood in analytic philosophy. More specifically, she aims to give an exposition and defense of the former approach (or at least, a version of the former approach) in terms of the language and methodology of the latter. While much of the philosophical work on disability focuses on issues in bioethics or the justice of resource allocation, these issues presuppose a view about what disability is. And that is what Barnes aims to give us, though she restricts her project to physical disability. She's well aware of other sorts and the need for philosophical reflection on them; they just aren't her focus. Why this restriction? Barnes gives two main reasons. The first is simplicity. "The task of saying what (if anything) disability is, or what its connection to wellbeing is, gets complicated enough given the heterogeneity of things we classify as physical disability."[74] The second reason she focuses on physical disability has to do with her reliance on the epistemology of testimony. As she writes, "psychological and cognitive disabilities raise complicated issues for the reliability of testimony that simply aren't present in the case of physical disability."[75]

The core of Barnes's book focuses on the relationship between disability and well-being and the contrast between what Barnes calls "mere-difference" and "bad-difference" views.[76] The "rough and ready" distinction between the two is as follows: those views that hold that "disability is by itself something that makes you worse off [are] 'bad-difference' views of disability."[77] In contrast, mere-difference views are those according to which having a disability doesn't by itself or automatically make you worse off. And while she sometimes refers to *the* bad-difference view and *the* mere-difference view, each should be understood as a family of views. The "connection" between the disability and the difference in well-being is important here. It is consistent with a rejection of a bad-difference view that disabled people are in fact worse off than non-disabled people, insofar as that difference may be caused by social structures or ableism. Furthermore, there can be bad effects of disabilities that would still exist in the absence of ableism. But those same disabilities might allow for other goods that are perhaps unique to or even just more common for those with the disability. So the question is if the effects caused by disability are net-negative and these effects are "counterfactually stable – disability would have such effect even in the absence of ableism."[78] Now, I described this way of putting the contrast (following Barnes) as rough and ready, but that will be sufficient for the present point. Making it more precise is complicated given that she – understandably – wants to be neutral with respect to the particulars of the required theory of well-being.[79]

If we assume that there is just one univocal concept of disability at work, we can ask if disability makes a bad-difference or a mere-difference to one's life. And if there is just one thing that the concept of disability picks out, we might think that we need to give a single answer to this question. But not having a single normative concept of disability, medieval authors such as Aquinas have the conceptual flexibility to see some disabilities as involving bad-differences and others to involve mere-differences. Aquinas's position takes the lack of conceptual unity for disability to be an insufficient basis to support a mere-difference view or a bad-difference view for all cases. In fact, if disability really is a plurality of concepts rather than a single concept, there is conceptual space for Aquinas to think that some disabilities are good things. Given Aquinas's account of disability, disability *as such* has no such difference-making, precisely because there isn't a single thing that *is* disability *as such*. Rather, some conditions called disability might be good-differences, while others might be bad-differences.[80]

So one consequence of Aquinas's conceptual plurality is that we can't assume from the beginning that all disabilities will share some feature (such as involving mere-difference or bad-difference, being neutral with respect to well-being or counting against well-being) simply because some disabilities have that feature.[81] It is because of the diversity of the concept that one can even find disability positive aspects in the Latin medieval tradition,[82] even if the medieval tradition as a whole tends to think in ableist ways.[83]

Relatedly, especially given the conceptual plurality of disability from medieval Christian philosophers and theologians like Aquinas, we can't always assume that the extension of disability (*defectum*) for these figures has the same boundary as does our modern concept of disability.[84]

We should expect to find that there are some conditions that amount to having a disability, according to one or more of Aquinas's concepts, that doesn't fall within the extension of the concept of disability that current disability studies and philosophy of disability works with, and vice versa. As with other medieval treatments and figures, the project of mining historical figures and texts for input on contemporary debates needs to be done very carefully lest we fail to recognize the conceptual difference. As Romero remarks, "ambiguity on the nature and meaning of 'disability' ... limits both the analytic stability and theological utility of the concept,"[85] particularly when speaking across nearly a millennium of theology and philosophy. This doesn't mean the two can't be brought into discussion; rather, it just shows that the care that needs to be taken in the process. This care is something that the present volume aims to illustrate.[86]

Notes

1 Richard Cross, "Duns Scotus on Disability: Teleology, Divine Willing, and Pure Nature," 72f. See also Jan Branson and Don Miller, *Damned for Their Difference*, for a discussion of the historical complexities surrounding disability as a concept.
2 I'm restricting my attention in this chapter to specifically *human* disability. Similar considerations to those I explore here would likely apply to, for instance, feline or formicid disability, though the details of that would depend on the ontology of cat or ant natures, respectively.
3 If, as I argue, there isn't, then the question comes up of whether the concept is equivocal or analogical (akin to a cluster concept). I return to this issue in brief in the section "Thomas Aquinas on Disability" of this chapter.
4 Elizabeth Barnes, *The Minority Body*, 10.
5 Ibid., 3.
6 Ibid., 4.
7 I think these points are extremely important to keep in mind when evaluating both contemporary discussions of disability and their medieval precursors. I worry, for example, that Barnes's argument for why physical disability involves mere-difference rather than bad-difference doesn't generalize to all other kinds of disabilities, although that's not a line of criticism I can explore at present.
8 See especially Elizabeth Barnes, *The Minority Body*; more on this issue in section "Further Complexities from Duns Scotus."
9 See Aquinas's *Commentary on the Posterior Analytics of Aristotle*, lecture 42.
10 Ibid.
11 Aquinas, *ST* Ia 85.3.
12 Though I won't have time to consider why in the present chapter, I think that (if this chapter's arguments are right) Aquinas would have been correct to reject a single concept of disability. I develop such an argument in Timpe unpublished.
13 See Aquinas, *ST* Ia 13; Eleonore Stump, *Aquinas*, 146f; Rudi Te Velde, *Aquinas on God*, Chapter 4; and Klima, "Theory of Language," 379ff.
14 Gyula Klima, "Theory of Language," 373f. See Aquinas, *Resp. ad lect. Vercell. de art.* 108.1 and Aquinas, *ST* Ia 13.4.

15 Jeffrey Brower and Susan Brower-Toland, "Aquinas on Mental Representation: Concepts and Intentionality," is an excellent discussion of the various options for how concepts can be likenesses of the various particulars that fall under them. Reductive interpretations hold that the likeness should be analyzed, at least partially, in terms of sameness of form. Brower and Brower-Toland, on the other hand, favor a non-reductive interpretation as involving a primitive and unanalyzable feature of the objects in question. Their account

> takes Aquinas's notion of intentional likeness as primitive or basic .... It accounts for intentionality, not by *reducing* it to, or *explaining* it in terms of, something more basic [like sameness of form], but rather by postulating it as an *unanalyzable* feature of its possessors.
> ("Aquinas on Mental Representation: Concepts and Intentionality," 225)

So far as I can tell, nothing in the present chapter hangs on a resolution to this particular interpretive debate.
16 According to Jeffrey Brower and Susan Brower-Toland, Aquinas sometimes refers to concepts as "intelligible species"; see ibid., 194.
17 Anthony Kenny, *Aquinas on Being*, 56.
18 Giorgio Pini, "The Development of Aquinas's Thought," 498.
19 See Aquinas's *Commentary on the Posterior Analytics of Aristotle*, lecture 10.
20 Anthony Kenny, *Aquinas on Being*, 198.
21 See Aristotle, *Categories*, 1a.
22 Eleonore Stump, *Aquinas*, 75; see also ibid., 225:

> The Porphyrian tree of substance begins with *substance*, which is divided into *corporal substance* and *incorporeal*. Each of these subaltern genera of substance is divided in its turn until the single highest genus *substance* has been divided into all its subaltern genera and species. Medieval philosophers were fond of this device and extended its use as a means of showing structured relationships in many other areas besides the Aristotelian categories.

23 Anthony Kenny, *Aquinas on Being*, 18.
24 For discussions of disability in the medieval period, see Joshua R. Eyler, "Introduction: Breaking Boundaries, Building Bridges;" Irina Metzler, *Disability in Medieval Europe*; and Vesa Hirvonen, "Mental Disorders in Late Medieval Philosophy and Theology."
25 Miguel Romero describes Aquinas's treatment of a particular kind of disability, namely *amentia*, to be "integrated into his thought as a whole" ("The Happiness of 'Those Who Lack the Use of Reason'," 51). But Romero also notes the challenge of approaching Aquinas's thoughts on disability apart from his theological anthropology as a whole, including his doctrine of creation and Christology. See Miguel Romero, "The Goodness and Beauty of Our Fragile Flesh;" see also Deborah Creamer, *Disability and Christian Theology*, 3–33.
26 John Berkman, "Are Persons with Profound Intellectual Disabilities Sacramental Icons of Heavenly Life? Aquinas on Impairment," 84.
27 It's also important, for those not used to the privation view of evil, to remember that not all evils are moral evils or involve blame in any way. See Richard Cross, "Aquinas on Physical Impairment: Human Nature and Original Sin," 317f.
28 See Aquinas, *ST* IaIIae 1.8 and 2.8. See also Miguel Romero, "The Goodness and Beauty of Our Fragile Flesh." Berkman calls the view that roots

human nature primarily in terms of the human telos the "*telos* view" (Berkman, "Are Persons with Profound Intellectual Disabilities Sacramental Icons of Heavenly Life? Aquinas on Impairment," 92). He contrasts this with "the *genesis* view according to which "human dignity and significance arise from the fact the person is born of human parents" (ibid). Furthermore, there's a worry that Aquinas's account of the beatific vision is too cognitive. For a version of this worry that I'm sympathetic with, see Christina van Dyke "Aquinas's Shiny Happy People: Perfect Happiness and the Limits of Human Nature," 269–291.
29 See Aquinas, *ST* IaIIae prologue.
30 Aquinas, *ST* IaIIae 5.6 and 109.5.
31 See Aquinas, *ST* III 14.1, which states that in the Incarnation, Christ assumed defects and infirmities of the body, as was fitting.
32 John Berkman, "Are Persons with Profound Intellectual Disabilities Sacramental Icons of Heavenly Life? Aquinas on Impairment," 84.
33 Given that in assuming a human nature in the Incarnation Christ didn't also assume original sin, the human nature assumed by Christ in the Incarnation is a counterexample to the general claim; see Aquinas *ST* III 15.1.
34 Richard Cross, "Aquinas on Physical Impairment: Human Nature and Original Sin," 323. For an account of how disabilities that might be defeated even if they are not permitted because they serve a greater good or help prevent a worse evil, see Kevin Timpe and Aaron Cobb, "Disability and the Theodicy of Defeat," 100–120.
35 Richard Cross, "Aquinas on Physical Impairment: Human Nature and Original Sin," 320.
36 Ibid., 317; see also 324. Some evils – what we might call moral evils – are the results of particular human sins. And these sins can cause defects and disabilities. But the point here is that disabilities and defects *per se* are not the result of particular sinful actions.
37 See Miguel Romero, "The Happiness of 'Those Who Lack the Use of Reason'," 55f.
38 Given his endorsement of the privation view of evil, Aquinas also sees disabilities as evils; see, for instance, Aquinas's *Compendium of Theology*, § 114. However, it is important here to keep in mind that evil for Aquinas is not an essentially moral category. See also Terrence Ehrman, "Disability and Resurrection Identity," 732: "Disability is a privation of what naturally 'should' be present, but it does not exclude the person from being imago Dei or impair one's human dignity .... Those who have physical and/or mental impairments and disabilities are no less human persons, rather the impairments and disabilities are frustrated capacities and not an indication of a qualitatively different nature."
39 While such a discussion would be necessary, it would not be sufficient because of Aquinas's account of grace. See John Berkman, "Are Persons with Profound Intellectual Disabilities Sacramental Icons of Heavenly Life? Aquinas on Impairment," 89ff; Miguel Romero, "The Goodness and Beauty of Our Fragile Flesh," 206–253; Aquinas, *ST* IaIIae 5.6 and 109.
40 John Berkman, "Are Persons with Profound Intellectual Disabilities Sacramental Icons of Heavenly Life? Aquinas on Impairment," 89. Miguel Romero argues, conclusively in my view, that Berkman's larger discussion of the "final end" of individuals with cognitive disability wrongly suggests that they're an outlier to Aquinas's anthropology. Romero argues instead that corporeal vulnerability – including our vulnerability to bodily impairment, infirmity, illness, or injury – is built into Aquinas's understanding

of human nature; see Miguel Romero, "The Goodness and Beauty of Our Fragile Flesh," 231–243. This vulnerability is, as Aquinas puts it, suitable to our natural human end (*ST* I 76.5 ad 1). And that is why, as Miguel Romero ("Aquinas on the *corporis infirmitas*: Broken Flesh and the Grammar of Grace," 101–125) argues, one must begin a thorough treatment of what Aquinas thinks about disability with a careful investigation of what it means to be a human being. Nevertheless, I don't think Romero's corpus, for all its other virtues, succeeds in giving us a differentia of disability. Corporeal limitations (*defectum*), weaknesses (*infirmum*), and instrumental infirmities are too broad, given that such limitations are part of human nature and capture things that aren't disabilities (Miguel Romero, "The Goodness and Beauty of Our Fragile Flesh," 246; idem, "Aquinas on the *corporis infirmitas*: Broken Flesh and the Grammar of Grace," 106, 110). The experience of affliction is also too broad, since even the Incarnate Christ does this (see Miguel Romero, "Aquinas on the *corporis infirmitas*: Broken Flesh and the Grammar of Grace," 108).

41 See also Miguel Romero, "Aquinas on the *corporis infirmitas*: Broken Flesh and the Grammar of Grace," 110f for a discussion of infirmity in the external or internal senses.

42 John Berkman, "Are Persons with Profound Intellectual Disabilities Sacramental Icons of Heavenly Life? Aquinas on Impairment," 90.

43 Ibid., 91: "It is extremely important to note that for Aquinas, while moral choice is the typical seed of spiritual growth, it is ultimately not necessary and certainly not sufficient for the spiritual perfection of human beings."

44 Ibid., 89.

45 This isn't to say that the other categories are not important. They are, for instance, capable of leading to moral and spiritual harms. Berkman himself recognizes this (ibid., 85):

> Aquinas is certainly not immune from the difficulties of our life as wayfarers brought about by various physical or mental maladies. For Aquinas, the chief expression of the virtue of courage lies in responding bravely to the 'infirmities of the flesh'.
>
> (Aquinas, *ST* II-II 123.1)

Nevertheless, a central element of Berkman's argument is that interpretations of Aquinas according to which physical and mental impairment *per se* prevent the attainment of the human *telos* are misguided, a conclusion with which I agree.

46 One might not think that this is a particular problem. After all, on the privation view of evil, any lack of a good that a thing ought to have according to its nature is an evil. But this broad usage is obviously more expansive than the present concept of evil, which is moral in nature. This situation is relevantly dis-analogous to the suggestion in the text. For in the case involving evil, it can be shown that the contemporary (inherently moral) concept of evil is a species of the broader usage of evil in the privation view of evil. But if we take disability to be coextensive with the medieval concept of defect, then we're no longer talking about what contemporary disability studies recognizes as a disability. While I want to allow for some degree of disagreement regarding the nature of the concept, this suggestion strikes me as too revisionary, particularly if the reason for engaging historical figures is to bring them into discussion with contemporary debates. The more revisionary we go, the more we risk either misinterpreting the historical figures or having them talk past the contemporary debates. Furthermore, elsewhere in

this volume Cross and Ward argue that for some medieval theologians there can be disabilities in heaven, as I've also argued elsewhere (Timpe 2019 and 2020). If this is right, then "fallen, human nature" won't be necessary for having a disability. And it's not sufficient given the plausible claim that some humans are not disabled.
47 It may be that some causes of gastrointestinal bleeding, such as angiodysplasia, do amount to a disability; but not all.
48 Richard Cross, "Disability, Impairment, and Some Medieval Accounts of the Incarnation: Suggestions for a Theology of Personhood," 647.
49 Ibid., 645.
50 Ibid., 646.
51 Ibid., 650.
52 Ibid., 647f.
53 Ibid., 657, note 28; see also 650.
54 Ibid., 648.
55 See, for instance, Ibid., 642–646.
56 I don't deny that our concepts can be revised, but revising the concept of disability so that it *de facto* applies to all humans seems to be replacement rather than revision. Furthermore, going this route would undermine many of the sought interconnections between historical and contemporary discussions.
57 For instance, severe cases of Crohn's disease.
58 Though presumably a failure in basic organic functioning of a certain sort could cause a cognitive impairment.
59 Depending on the details, the failure of having fully developed rational faculties being sufficient for disability would perhaps entail that all children are disabled. One could perhaps attempt to avoid this implication by invoking the capacity/actuality distinction—namely that it's the capacity for fully developed reason that avoids disability, rather than the actualization of that capacity. But this move would mean that temporary disabilities, such as the cognitive impairments that can follow a traumatic brain injury (TBI), would fail to be disabilities.
60 See Kevin Timpe, "Defiant Afterlife: Disability and Uniting Ourselves to God;" Amos Yong *The Bible, Disability, and the Church*; and Nancy Eiesland, *The Disabled God*.
61 If this were the case, how the various concepts can represent the universal would need to be addressed, since for Aquinas "to represent something [just] is to bear the likeness of that thing" (*QDV* 7.5 ad 2).
62 *Resp ad lect. Vercell. de art.* 108, q. 1; as quoted in Klima, "Theory of Language," 374.
63 For a discussion of Aquinas's view of analogy along the lines of similarity and family resemblance, see Drescher, "Analogy in Thomas Aquinas and Ludwig Wittgenstein: A Comparison. According to Drescher," 7: "the attention he [Aquinas] devotes to analogy and the further development of the doctrine of analogy, are not undertaken for their own sake. In fact, they have a thoroughly practical purpose: on the one hand their aim is to present theology as a meaningful discourse about God, and on the other Aquinas's *Summas* are conceived as theological and philosophical textbooks to help the reader follow the teachings explained there and to elucidate the structure of their arguments." If as Drescher suggests analogical predication is needed to have "imprecise, but thoroughly meaningful" (ibid., 7) discourse about God, then I think this gives reason to think something parallel is true regarding disability. Our imprecise but thoroughly meaningful discourse about disability gives some support to thinking that 'disability' should be understood analogically.

Plurality in Medieval Concepts of Disability 45

64 It may be possible that the core concept differs across contexts and purposes the concept is put to, as I argue in Timpe unpublished. My account there bears a number of relationships with Wittgenstein's understanding of language games, which he takes to be "complicated network[s] of similarities overlapping and crisscrossing: sometimes overall similarities, sometimes similarities of detail" are at the heart of 'family resemblances' (Ludwig Wittgenstein, *Philosophical Investigations*, I.66; see also I.67–68).
65 Duns Scotus, *Ordinatio* II, d. 3, p. 1, qq. 5–6, n. 183 as quoted in Paul V. Spade, *Five Texts on the Mediaeval Problem of Universals: Porphyry, Boethius, Abelard, Duns Scotus, Ockham*, 105.
66 See Duns Scotus, *Ordinatio* II, d. 3, p. 1, qq. 5–6, n. 177.
67 Richard Cross, "Duns Scotus on Disability: Teleology, Divine Willing, and Pure Nature," 78.
68 Ibid., 81.
69 It's important to remember that this connection is between disability and original sin, not between disability and individual sins.
70 Richard Cross, "Duns Scotus on Disability: Teleology, Divine Willing, and Pure Nature," 73.
71 This difference is rooted in differences in how Aquinas and Scotus understand divine justice; see Ibid., 81–86.
72 Ibid., 94. Scotus's thought on disability is also more detailed than the discussion of this section indicates, as one should anticipate from the subtle doctor. Even whether an individual with amentia should receive the sacrament of baptism, for Scotus, depends on whether the person's condition is congenital or acquired, and if acquired, whether permanent or temporary. See Vesa Hirvonen, "Mental Disorders in Late Medieval Philosophy and Theology," 181. Duns Scotus also suggests that disability might serve an aesthetic purpose; see Richard Cross, "Duns Scotus on Disability: Teleology, Divine Willing, and Pure Nature," 83f.
73 Joshua Eyler, "Introduction: Breaking Boundaries, Building Bridge," 3; quoting Metzler, *Disability in Medieval Europe*, 3. See also Jennifer Gianfalla, "'Ther Is Moore Mysshapen Amonges Thise Beggeres': Discourse of Disability in *Piers Plowman*," 120. One also finds a growing appreciation for different understandings of disability across the biblical texts. See, for instance, Amos Yong, *The Bible, Disability, and the Church*, 6: "what we call disability today is anachronistic when applied to the Bible, since there is no straightforward biblical notion that captures what the term *disability* has come to mean presently." The most thorough treatment to date appears to be Melcher, Parsons, and Yong, *The Bible and Disability: A Commentary*.
74 Elizabeth Barnes, *The Minority Body*, 2. This is also why Barnes prefers a "ground-up" rather than "top-down" approach.
75 Elizabeth Barnes, *The Minority Body*, 3.
76 We can extrapolate some about how Aquinas and Scotus would think about this distinction given their differing views on the relationship between sin and disability, discussed above.
77 Elizabeth Barnes, *The Minority Body*, 55.
78 Ibid., 60.
79 Whether this neutrality is compatible with the normatively rich metaphysical frameworks of medieval philosophers and theologians is another important question, and one that is addressed at greater length in the chapters by Frost, Romero, Cross, and Ward in this volume.
80 See Cross's chapter in the present volume.

46 Kevin Timpe

81 In fact, Anita Silvers ("An Essay on Modeling: The Social Model of Disability," 23), argues that the idea that the range of disabilities "form a class of 'the disabled' is a 20th century invention …. Only during the first part of the [twentieth] century was the term 'the disabled' introduced to characterize and collectivize" the range of disabilities under a single category.
82 See Christina Van Dyke's and Richard Cross's chapters in the present volume for two such examples.
83 See Irina Metzler, *Disability in Medieval Europe*, and Joshua Eyler, "Introduction: Breaking Boundaries, Building Bridge."
84 As Tom Shakespeare and Nicholas Watson ("The Social Model of Disability: An Outdated Ideology?" 25), put it, "Different societies treat particular groups people with of impairments in different ways. For example, in the medieval period, being unable to read was not a problem, because social processes did not demand literacy."
85 Miguel Romero, "The Goodness and Beauty of Our Fragile Flesh," 223–225.
86 A previous version of this chapter was presented at the 2018 Disability in Medieval Latin Philosophy and Theology at the University of Notre Dame. I am indebted to the other participants not only for their helpful comments and question on my chapter but also for the ways in which their projects have helped me refine the present projects. In particular, I'd like to thank Richard Cross, Miguel Romero, Cheyne Joslin, Mark Spencer, and Jeff Brower for their useful input. Scott Williams in particular gave extended and very useful feedback on the penultimate version of this chapter; his patience as an editor is quite commendable.

References

Primary Sources

Aquinas, Thomas. 1970. *Commentary on the Posterior Analytics of Aristotle*, translated by F. R. Larcher. Albany, NY: Magi Books.
Aquinas, Thomas. 1979. *Responsio de 108 articulis ad magistrum Ioannem de Vercellis*. Editori di San Tommaso.
Aquinas, Thomas. 1981. *Summa Theologiae*, translated by the Fathers of the English Dominican Province. Westminster, MD: Christian Classics.
Aquinas, Thomas. 1999. *Disputed Questions on Virtue*, translated by Ralph McInerny. South Bend: St. Augustine's Press.
Duns Scotus, John. 1994. *Ordinatio*, in Paul Vincent Spade, *Five Texts on the Mediaeval Problem of Universals: Porphyry, Boethius, Abelard, Duns Scotus, Ockham*, Indianapolis: Hackett.

Secondary Sources

Barnes, Elizabeth. *The Minority Body: A Theory of Disability*. Oxford: Oxford University Press, 2016.
Berkman, John. "Are Persons with Profound Intellectual Disabilities Sacramental Icons of Heavenly Life? Aquinas on Impairment." *Studies in Christian Ethics* 26 (1) (2013): 83–96.
Branson, Jan and Don Miller. *Damned for Their Difference: The Cultural Construction of Deaf People as Disabled*. Washington, DC: Gallaudet University Press, 2002.

Brower, Jeffrey E., and Susan Brower-Toland. "Aquinas on Mental Representation: Concepts and Intentionality." *The Philosophical Review* 117 (2) (2008): 193–243.

Creamer, Deborah. *Disability and Christian Theology.* Oxford: Oxford University Press, 2009.

Cross, Richard. "Disability, Impairment, and Some Medieval Accounts of the Incarnation: Suggestions for a Theology of Personhood." *Modern Theology* 27 (4) (2011): 639–658.

——— "Aquinas on Physical Impairment: Human Nature and Original Sin." *Harvard Theological Review* 110 (3) (2017): 317–338.

——— "Duns Scotus on Disability: Teleology, Divine Willing, and Pure Nature." *Theological Studies* 78 (1) (2017): 72–95.

Drescher, Frank. "Analogy in Thomas Aquinas and Ludwig Wittgenstein: A Comparison." *New Blackfriars* (2017): 1–14.

Ehrman, Terrence. "Disability and Resurrection Identity." *New Blackfriars* 96 (1066) (2015): 723–738.

Eiesland, Nancy L. *The Disabled God: Toward a Liberatory Theology of Disability.* Nashville, TN: Abingdon Press, 1994.

Eyler, Joshua R. "Introduction: Breaking Boundaries, Building Bridges." In *Disability in the Middle Ages: Reconsiderations and Reverberations.* Edited by Joshua R. Eyler, New York: Routledge, 2010: 1–8.

Gianfalla, Jennifer M. 2010. "'Ther Is Moore Mysshapen Amonges Thise Beggeres': Discourse of Disability in *Piers Plowman*." In *Disability in the Middle Ages: Reconsiderations and Reverberations.* Edited by Joshua R. Eyler. New York: Routledge, 2010: 119–133.

Hirvonen. Vesa. "Mental Disorders in Late Medieval Philosophy and Theology." In *Mind and Modality: Studies in the History of Philosophy in Honour of Simo Knuuttila.* Edited by Vesa Hirvonen, Toivo Holopainen, and Miira Tuominen. Leiden: Brill, 2006, 171–188.

Kenny, Anthony. *Aquinas on Being.* Oxford: Clarendon Press. 2002.

Klima, Gyula. "Theory of Language." In *The Oxford Handbook of Aquinas.* Edited by Brian Davies and Eleonore Stump. Oxford: Oxford University Press, 2012, 371–389.

Melcher, Sarah J., Mikeal C. Parsons, and Amos Yong (Eds.). *The Bible and Disability: A Commentary.* Waco: Baylor University Press, 2017.

Metzler, Irina. *Disability in Medieval Europe: Thinking about Physical Impairment in the High Middle Ages, c. 1100-c. 1400.* New York: Routledge, 2006.

Pini, Giorgio. "The Development of Aquinas's Thought." In *The Oxford Handbook of Aquinas*, Edited by Brian Davies and Eleonore Stump. Oxford: Oxford University Press, 2012, 491–510.

Romero, Miguel J. "Aquinas on the *corporis infirmitas*: Broken Flesh and the Grammar of Grace." In *Disability in the Christian Tradition: A Reader.* Edited by Brian Brock and John Swinton. Grand Rapids: William B. Eerdmans Publishing Company, 2012, 101–125.

——— "The Happiness of 'Those Who Lack the Use of Reason." *The Thomist* 80 (1) (2016): 49–96.

——— "The Goodness and Beauty of Our Fragile Flesh: Moral Theologians and Our Engagement with 'Disability.'" *Journal of Moral Theology* 6 (2) (2017): 206–253.

Shakespeare, Tom and Nicholas Watson. "The Social Model of Disability: An Outdated Ideology?" *Research in Social Science and Disability* 2 (2002): 9–28.

Silvers, Anita. "An Essay on Modeling: The Social Model of Disability." In *Philosophical Reflections on Disability*. Edited by D. Christopher Ralston and Justin Ho. Dordrecht: Springer, 2010, 19–36.

Spade, Paul Vincent. *Five Texts on the Mediaeval Problem of Universals: Porphyry, Boethius, Abelard, Duns Scotus, Ockham*. Indianapolis: Hackett, 1994.

Stump, Eleonore. *Aquinas*. London: Routledge, 2003.

Te Velde, Rudi. *Aquinas on God: The "Divine Science" of the Summa Theologiae*. London: Ashgate, 2006.

Timpe, Kevin. unpublished "Denying a Unified Concept of Disability."

———. "Defiant Afterlife: Disability and Uniting Ourselves to God." In *Marginalized Identities, Peripheral Theologies: Expanding Conversations in Analytic Theology*. Edited by Michelle Panchuk and Michael Rea. Oxford: Oxford University Press, 2020.

Timpe, Kevin, and Aaron D. Cobb. "Disability and the Theodicy of Defeat." *Journal of Analytic Theology* 5 (2017): 100–120.

Van Dyke, Christina. "Aquinas's Shiny Happy People: Perfect Happiness and the Limits of Human Nature." In *Oxford Studies in Philosophy of Religion Volume 6*. Edited by Jon Kvanvig. Oxford: Oxford University Press, 2014, 269–291.

Wittgenstein, Ludwig. *Philosophical Investigations*, translated by G.E.M. Anscombe. Oxford: Basil Blackwell, 1953.

Yong, Amos. *The Bible, Disability, and the Church*. Grand Rapids, MI: Wm. B. Eerdmans, 2011.

Part II
Disability in This Life

2 Medieval Aristotelians on Congenital Disabilities and Their Early Modern Critics[1]

Gloria Frost

Introduction

This chapter explores medieval Aristotelian perspectives on the phenomenon which we refer to today as "congenital disability." According to the World Health Organization, congenital disorders, also called "birth defects," are "defined as structural or functional anomalies (*e.g.* metabolic disorders) that occur during intrauterine life and can be identified prenatally, at birth or later in life."[2] The contemporary category includes conditions that are the result of genetic inheritance or mutation, as well as those caused by environmental factors during pregnancy. Though we know much about the general causes of congenital impairments, medical professionals are unable to identify the specific causes of an individual child's congenital disability in about 50% of cases.[3] This chapter presents and analyzes medieval theories about the causes of congenital disabilities, as well as medieval views about the humanity and moral status of people born with severe disabilities. The chapter highlights respects in which medieval theories about congenital disabilities are significant for both the history of medicine and the history of philosophy.

The chapter shows that in the medieval period the Aristotelian thinker Albert the Great developed a detailed taxonomy of types of congenital defects and their physical causes. He recognized a distinction between conditions that were caused by defects in the organic material contributed by the parents and those which arose from a defect in the embryo's environment. Though writing long before the modern science of genetics, Albert had a theory about how medical conditions could be inherited from parent to child. In contrast with Albert's focus on the natural causes of congenital disabilities, many in the medieval period believed that the primary causes of congenital disabilities were parental sexual sin or the mother's misuse of her imagination during pregnancy.

In addition to being relevant to the history of medicine, medieval Aristotelian discussions of congenital disabilities are significant for the history of philosophy, particularly with regard to the downfall of Aristotelian metaphysics in the early modern period. Modern thinkers, such as John Locke, claimed that congenital defects disproved the Aristotelian hylomorphic conception of nature. Locke's rejection of Aristotelian forms paved the way for him to reject the humanity of those born with severe cognitive impairments. The chapter discusses this objection and these other aspects of Locke's views in order to further analyze the merits and significance of the Aristotelian account of congenital disabilities. It will be shown that one strength of Aristotelian hylomorphism is that it provided a metaphysical framework for upholding the full humanity and equal moral status of those born with severe disabilities.

The Medieval Concept of the Monster

There have always been people born unable to see, or walk, or with limited cognitive abilities. However, the concept of a "disability" is a fairly recent notion. It was not until the 19th century that the myriad of physical and mental limitations were generalized together under the single class known as "disability."[4] To uncover past ways of thinking about a uniquely modern concept, one must first identify appropriate ancestral concepts.[5] In the case of disability, this task is complicated by the uncertainty that surrounds this concept today. In present discourse, there is disagreement about whether disabilities arise purely from the biological level or also from contemporary social organization. On the medical model, biological impairments are the sole cause of the limitations which those with a disability face. By contrast on the social model, biological impairment is not sufficient for disability. A disability arises through the "poor fit" between an individual body and its environment. On this model, lacking eyesight is not sufficient to be disabled. It is this medical condition *together with* a lack of societal accommodation that disables. The medical model seeks to improve lives through cures and treatments, while the social model seeks to *change society* so that those with disabilities are more able to participate. Both the social and the medical models agree that a biological impairment is *at least a necessary condition* for a disability.[6] In order to produce historical research which is relevant on both models, this chapter focuses on medieval views about the biological impairments involved in disabilities.

While medieval thinkers had no generalized concept of a class of people who were disabled, they had a concept which ranged over all people with atypical bodily conditions, namely the "monstrous." To the contemporary ear, the term "monster" evokes that which is frightful, horrific, or perhaps even morally depraved. To medieval thinkers, however, the term signified merely an organism born with an unusual physical structure.[7] Such conditions include paralysis, blindness, missing limbs, and severe cognitive impairments. The sorts bodily impairments which we today consider to ground disabilities fall under the medieval concept of the monstrous. Yet, the medieval concept also included conditions which we would not consider as grounding disabilities. For instance, twins were considered monstrous since multiparous pregnancies are not the norm for humans. For some medieval figures, the concept also ranged over bodily conditions that we would deem impossible, such as hybrid species.[8] While the medieval concept of a monster is by no means the same concept as the contemporary concept of a disability, it is an appropriate ancestral concept since it includes under its extension the bodily structures that are a necessary feature of disability.

Common Views on the Causes of Monsters: Sin and Maternal Imagination

Two different lines of ancient and patristic sources shaped medieval concepts of the monstrous. In Aristotle's *Generation of Animals*, he explains monstrosities as happenings which are contrary to nature's usual operations. In his view, natural causes sometimes intersect with each other to produce a result which is infrequent or rare.[9] Aristotle's thought also includes the notion that monsters are instances of nature failing to reach its goal. The sense in which Aristotle thought that natural processes intended goals will be explained further on.

Other classical and Patristic sources offered a different perspective on monsters.[10] The Latin roots of the word monster are *monstrare* and *monere*, which respectively mean "to show" and "to warn." Thus, among many Latin authors, monsters were seen as conveying special revelations from God. In his *City of God* (XXI.8) Augustine writes:

> Therefore, just as it was possible for God to make such natural kinds as He wished, so it is possible for him to change those natural kinds into whatever he wishes. From this power comes the wild profusion of those marvels which are called omens, signs, portents, prodigies .... The various names *monstra, ostenta, portenta, prodigia* come from the verbs monstrare "show," because they show something by a sign ... [and] predict the future .... To us these ... *monstra* ... should demonstrate ... that God will do what he has declared he will do ....[11]

For Augustine, monsters both reveal God's power over nature and warn that God is about to do something important. Particular monstrous births in the period were considered as divine warnings of subsequent historical calamities.[12] So, while Aristotle saw monsters the result of nature's failure to achieve its purpose, Christians were inclined to view monsters as fulfilling an extrinsically ordained divine purpose.

Medieval explanations of the more immediate created causes of congenital disabilities frequently appealed to religious and moral phenomena. It was quite common to blame parental sexual sin as the cause of a monstrous birth. Hildegard of Bingen (1098–1180) writes the following:

> often in forgetfulness of God and by the mocking devil, a mixture (*mistio*) is made of the man and the woman and the thing born

therefrom is deformed, for parents who have sinned against me return to me crucified in their children.[13]

A 13th century church synod in France stated that children conceived in illicit sex would be born deformed.[14] A wide range of sexual activities were considered sinful in the medieval period. It was not merely fornication or adultery. Sex between married people was considered sinful if it occurred at the wrong time, such as after childbirth or during menstruation, or in the wrong position, that is, not in the missionary position. All of these actions were seen as a potential cause of an offspring with a bodily defect. "Hybrid species" births were attributed to bestiality.[15]

It was common in the period to lay exclusive blame on the mother for birth defects. Misuse of the maternal imagination was commonly appealed to as a cause of monstrous birth.[16] It was believed that if the mother were to imagine something unusual either during conception or pregnancy, her child would bear a resemblance to that which she had imagined. The 14th century thinker Giles of Rome adopted this theory. He recounts a story of a fair-skinned woman who looked at a picture of an Ethiopian prior to having intercourse with her Caucasian husband. Giles claims that as a result of imaging the Ethiopian at the time of conception, she gave birth to a black child.[17] The origin of the "maternal imagination" theory is the biblical story of Laban and Jacob.[18] In this story, Laban promises to give Jacob all of the striped and spotted sheep from his flocks. Jacob then places striped and spotted rods in the drinking water near where solid-colored sheep mated. Gazing upon these sticks causes the ewes to give birth to striped and spotted offspring. Giles cites this story as evidence that maternal imagination influences fetal development.[19] To a contemporary reader, the proposal that the mother's imagination can impact fetal development sounds fantastical. However, this theory had many supporters up through the modern period in both natural philosophy and medicine. Perhaps one of its most well-known adopters was Rene Descartes, often dubbed the father of modern philosophy and science.[20]

Medieval Aristotelians on the Causes of Monsters: Albert the Great's Taxonomy

Background: Aristotle's Hylomorphism, Theory of the Four Causes, and Human Generation

Medieval Aristotelian approaches to the causes of congenital defects de-emphasized the religious and moral realm and instead focused more on physical causes. Their causal explanations of congenital defects presupposed many Aristotelian theories about the natural world, particularly Aristotle's theory of hylomorphism and the four causes. Hylomorphism is the theory that material substances are composed of two correlative principles: matter and substantial form. A substantial form is that which accounts for a substance's actual existence, its being of a determinate species, and its possession of the attributes that are proper to its species. By contrast, matter is characterized as a mere receptivity or potentiality for taking on form. Matter was conceived of as lacking any actual qualities of itself. Aristotle's motivation for developing the theory of hylomorphism was to provide an account of how one substance could be generated from the corruption of another. In his view, when substance A passes out of existence and substance B comes to be from A, the substantial form of B informs the prime matter which was previously actualized by A's substantial form. Prime matter accounts for the continuity in substantial change, while substantial form accounts for the novelty or difference.[21]

The prime matter which carries over from the corrupted substance into the generated one does not have any actual quality or quantity of itself. Nevertheless, not just any substance can be generated from any other. Forms must be actualized in prime matter according to a certain order. Matter must be prepared by certain forms in order to take on another one.[22] Thus, the forms that matter is actualized by just prior to a substantial change constrains the range of qualities and quantities which can be actual in the newly generated substance. This aspect of the theory will be extremely relevant to understanding how some congenital defects are explained.

Though matter and form are central to explaining change, Aristotle recognized that matter and form alone could not explain why actual changes in the material world begin to be.[23] When one substance changes, this change must be initiated by another substance known as an agent or efficient cause. Efficient causes are the sources of the movements by which matter gains and loses a form. Aristotle thought that even the activities of non-rational, natural substances must be ordered toward a determinate goal known as a final cause. Aristotle thought that without assuming that natural substances act for the sake of a determinate result, there is no explanation for why the same type of natural processes regularly terminate in the same results.

While medieval thinkers generally agreed with Aristotle's account of the four causes (matter, form, agent, and final/end), there was disagreement about which substances played these causal roles in human generation. According to Aristotle, the male alone was an agent or efficient cause of generation. The woman only supplied the matter upon which the male acted. According to this theory, the male sperm acted upon the female menstrual blood until it was gradually changed, eventually passing out of existence, to give way to a series of new substances and finally a new human being. In contrast with Aristotle, the early physician

Galen (c. 130 AD–c. 210 AD) maintained that both the male and the female contributed actively in generation. He thought that both produced sperm.[24] John Duns Scotus and many Franciscans likewise granted active causality to the female.[25] However, Albert and his student Thomas Aquinas followed Aristotle in maintaining that only the male was an active efficient cause in generation.

Albert the Great on the Causes of Congenital Disabilities

With this background in place, we can examine some medieval Aristotelian views on congenital disabilities. I focus on Albert the Great since the comprehensiveness and detail of his account of congenital defects goes far beyond other major scholastic figures. After discussing Albert's views, I will show that his more well-known student Thomas Aquinas adopted the main points of his theory about the possible causes of congenital defects, though he did not go into the level of detail which Albert does.

Albert's fullest and most systematic discussion of the causes of congenital defects is found in his commentary on Book II of Aristotle's *Physics*. This text was a popular locus for medieval Aristotelians to discuss the topic. The text contains Aristotle's response to the ancient thinker Empedocles's rejection of final causality in nature. According Empedocles, the fact that natural processes sometimes have unusual outcomes is supposed to prove that natural processes are not ordered to determinate effects as their goal (i.e., there is no final causality). In his commentary *Physics* II, Albert follows Aristotle in rejecting Empedocles's inference. Albert argues that the reason why natural processes sometimes fail to reach their goals is because of a defect in the particular natural principles which are involved in a particular case. Defects in the efficient cause or material cause can thwart a process from reaching its proper end. He then explains how this applies in cases of human generation.

Before going into the details of his taxonomy of the causes of congenital defects, it is useful to clarify the sense in which Albert and his scholastic counterparts thought that the process of human generation could "fail to reach its goal." They thought that if this process terminated in a live birth, the organism which is born could be nothing other than a human organism. But sometimes the human which was born lacked the usual qualities, size, or abilities which human beings typically have. This is the respect in which the process was thought to have "missed its goal." The male formative power tended toward producing a human being with all of the attributes which *typically* belong to human beings.[26] Sometimes, however, it is impeded from reaching this goal. In such a case, the new organism would have a human substantial form; however, it would be missing some of the attributes which typically belong to human beings.

In his commentary on *Physics* II, Albert describes approximately fifteen different types of atypical bodily structures. He groups these body types into four categories.[27] He then describes the particular causes

Categories of Monster	Bodily condition	Particular Cause
Lack of Matter	1. Atypically small members	Insufficient amount of matter or weakness in the formative power
	2. Missing members or members unable to sustain acts	Defect in matter or weakness in formative power
	3. Both 1 and 2	Lack of matter and weakness in formative power
Superabundance of Matter	4. Entire body is atypically large (with members proportionate to each other in size)	Strength of the formative power and abundance of matter
	5. One or more members are disproportionally large	Abundance of matter
	6. Bodily members arisen before natural time (*e.g.* infants born with teeth, sexual maturity)	Strength of the formative power
	7. Extra bodily members	Abundance of matter
	8. Twins / Conjoined Twins	Division of sperm in mother's womb—complete or incomplete
	9. Either 4 and 7, or 5 and 7	Strength of the formative power and abundance of matter
Disproportionateness of Quality	10. Hermaphrodite	Contrary qualities "conquer" each other and both characterize the embryo (in different material parts)
	11. Excessively lean or fat body	Disproportion between elemental qualities in the forming of the embryo
Defect in that which Surrounds the Embryo	12. Missing, curved, disjointed or separated bodily member	Rupture in amniotic sac (which causes matter to flow out)
	13. Conjoined twins	Ruptured sac with multiple embryos which become fused
	14. Body parts resembling parts of a different species of animal	Defect in the heat which contains the power of the heavenly bodies

Figure 2.1 Albert's taxonomy of monsters and their causes (*In Phys.* II.3).

which explain why the particular bodily structure occurred. Figure 2.1 above summarizes Albert's account of the types of monstrous bodies and their particular causes. Each category is explained in greater detail in the following subsections.

Lack of Matter

1. ATYPICALLY SMALL BODILY MEMBERS

The first type of monstrous body Albert discusses is the body which lacks matter. This type of body can be either atypically small or missing bodily parts. In cases in which all bodily members are present, but they are atypically small, Albert claims that the cause is either that (1) the matter from which the fetus was generated (i.e., the female menstrual blood) was of an insufficient quantity or that (2) the father's formative power was too weak. When the formative power is weak, Albert explains: "[I]t is only able to form a part of the matter and it rejects the rest."[28] The mother supplies enough menstrual blood, but the father's power is too weak to form all of it. With the father's power acting on only a part of the menstrual blood, there is an insufficient quantity of matter transformed, and so, the offspring's body is atypically small.

2. MISSING BODILY MEMBERS

When a child is born missing a bodily member, this can be either because of a defect in the matter provided by the mother or because of weakness in the father's formative power. Albert notes that what he means by those which lack members is both a complete absence of a member "as if it's been cut off" as well those who lack actions performed through a member on account of "weak or curved members which cannot sustain acts."[29] Albert believes that it is possible to discern whether the mother's or father's contribution was responsible in a particular case of a weak or missing member by considering which part of the body is missing. He explains:

> The sign of this [i.e. missing members due to weakness in the formative power] is that they especially lack members far from the heart and distant from the liver in which the power for forming the members is especially located, as for example when they lack a hand or foot or some extrinsic member on their head.[30]

Albert believed that the male's formative power, which continued to act on the developing embryo throughout the pregnancy, was located in the embryo's heart and liver. A weak power cannot extend to form the parts of the organism that are farthest from its own location. Thus, when members are missing far from the liver and heart, Albert reasons that weakness of the formative power was to blame.

3. BOTH MISSING MEMBERS AND THE MEMBERS THAT
ARE PRESENT ARE ATYPICALLY SMALL

When a person is born both with atypically small members and missing members, Albert thinks that both lack of matter and a weakness in the formative power are to blame. The lack of matter explains the body's small size, while it is the weakness in the formative power which explains the missing members.[31] Albert claims lack of matter alone does not cause members to be missing. Even when the mother supplies an insufficient quantity of matter, a strong formative power forms every member of the body in the matter given. So, Albert thinks that when members are missing in addition to atypically small members weakness in the formative power must also be at fault.[32]

Before moving on to discuss the next type of monstrous body and its causes, it is worth considering how it can be that the quantity or quality of the matter out of which the fetus is generated can be causally responsible for a congenital defect. Recall that in Aristotle's theory of hylomorphism the matter which carries over from one substance to the next in generation and corruption is *prime matter*, and it has *no actual qualities and or even quantity of itself*. It is purely a receptivity for form. Given this view of prime matter, it is initially puzzling that Albert thinks that the quantity (and as we will see also the quality) of the woman's menstrual blood can be causally responsible for a congenital defect in the fetus. If that which carries over from the menstrual blood into the new fetus is prime matter and it bears no quality or quantity of itself, how is it that the properties of the menstrual blood can be explanatory of the fetus's properties? The answer to this question lies in the nature of prime matter and how it must be actualized. Though prime matter has no actual properties of itself, it must receive forms of different species according to a determinate order. It must be prepared by lower forms in order to be actualized by higher ones. This is why certain types of substances can only be generated from certain other types. For example, a human cannot be immediately generated from a rock. The prime matter which composes the rock must be actualized by other higher forms before it can eventually be actualized by the form of a human being. The same is true with accidental qualities and quantities. In natural change, prime matter cannot be actualized first by the form of whiteness and then immediately afterward, with no forms intervening, by the form of blackness. It must be gradually and successively actualized by the intermediate forms between whiteness and blackness. Likewise, prime matter cannot be composing a substance which is ten feet tall and then immediately at the next moment composing a substance which is two feet tall without being actualized by intermediate quantitative forms. In natural change, there is a determinate order in which matter must be actualized by form. Given this fact, the substantial and accidental forms of one substance place constraints on the forms which can actualize any substance which is immediately generated from it. Since not just any form can follow upon any other, the qualities and quantity of the mother's menstrual blood constrain the forms that can actualize the new fetus which is generated from it. If the quantity of the menstrual blood is too small, quantities which fall within the typical range for a human body cannot be actualized in the substance which comes to be from the blood. We will see in the next category how it is that an excess of menstrual blood can likewise lead to an atypical bodily structure.

Superabundance of Matter

4–6, 9. EXCESSIVE SIZE OF BODY

Albert notes that sometimes infants are born with a whole body of excessive size, while in other cases the body as a whole is normal in size and only a certain member of the body is excessively large. If the entire body is enormous and all bodily members are proportioned to each other, Albert claims that the cause was both strength of the formative power and abundance of matter. When only one member is large and not proportioned to the rest of the normal sized body, Albert claims that the cause was only an overly strong male formative power. Since the power is not proportionate to the matter (as in the case in which there is an excessively strong formative power and an abundance of matter), Albert claims that the power forms some parts of the matter better than others. It will form the interior organs in normal proportions since these are closer to the site of the power and thus "easier" for it to form and then will err in forming the external members, such as hands and feet, making these of an excessive size.[33]

7–9. EXTRA MEMBERS (INCLUDING CONJOINED TWINS)

There are different ways in which an animal might be born with an extra member. First, it might happen that an infant is born with body parts having arisen before their natural time. He gives the example of infants born with teeth having already descended and an infant girl, who, he claims, was born in his time, with breasts and menstruation. Albert says the cause of such births is excessive strength of the heat (i.e., the formative power) that forms and matures the embryo.[34] Second, a child might be born with more members than usually present in the human body, such as a sixth finger on a hand. The cause of this is an abundance of matter.[35] Albert notes, however, that when there is a case in which there are two heads or two conjoined bodies, the cause is different. This is due to the dividing of the sperm in the mother's womb. When the sperm divides in the womb, there are two instances of the formative power, each forming a distinct embryo. Albert thought that twins were born through a complete division of the sperm and infants born with two bodies or two heads were the result of an incomplete division.[36] He writes:

> [T]here are certain women and certain animals who take much pleasure in sexual intercourse, and in that pleasure the mother moves when the sperm pours over her sensible nerves, and in that motion the sperm is divided. When the division is totally completed, then there will be twins, if the semen coalesces in a fetus. If, however, the division is not completed, but the sperm divides as if into branches,

then there will be a two-bodied animal either in its lower half, upper-half or even in the middle depending upon the way in which the sperm is divided.[37]

Albert says that the incomplete division of the sperm in the mother is likewise the cause of why infants are born with too many openings in their bodies. Presumably when the sperm is divided, the various quantities of sperm act on the developing body in an uncoordinated fashion, each attempting to form the same parts over again. He claims that in his time there was a fetus which died before birth which had eleven mouths and tongues and twenty-two incomplete lips.[38]

Quality Disproportionate to the Matter

10–11. HERMAPHRODITES, AND THOSE WHO ARE LEAN OR FAT

In discussing the category of "disproportionate quality," Albert cites infants born with bodies which are too lean or too fat, as well as hermaphrodites. What these seemingly diverse conditions have in common is that they are caused by either an excessive or a defective proportion of one or more of the elemental qualities (hot, cold, wet, dry) which characterize the forming embryo's body.[39] A body which is too lean is caused by excessive heat, while a body which is too fat is caused by excessive cold.[40] Albert does not explain exactly what it is that causes the body to have disproportionate qualities when it is being formed. Presumably there could be many possible causes since the precise degree of hot, cold, wet, and dry that characterized the various parts of the embryo body would depend both on the qualitative characteristics of the male sperm and on the matter supplied by the female, as well as many environmental factors.[41]

In his *De animalibus*, Albert offers a more detailed account of how hermaphrodites were generated. The general theory of sex differentiation was that sex was determined based on the proportion between the heat of the male formative power and the moisture of the matter it acted upon. If the male formative power was hot enough to dry the moisture, a male was formed. If the moisture was too great for the formative power to dry, then a female resulted. The first condition needed for a hermaphrodite to be generated is an abundance of matter in the genital region. But this was not by itself a sufficient cause. Hermaphrodites were formed when in one part of the matter, the heat of the formative power overcame the moisture of the matter, but yet in a different part of the matter, the moisture overcame the heat.[42] This led to the forming of the genital organs of both sexes. In some cases of hermaphroditism, one sex was the principal sex. But in other cases, Albert claims it is not clear whether one sex is principal.[43]

Defect in that Which Surrounds the Embryo

Albert claimed that there are two categories of monsters which are caused by a defect in the embryo's surrounding environment. The two categories are based on the two different surroundings: first, that which "contains [the fetus] as a skin" (i.e., the amniotic sac) and second, the heat that surrounds the fetus and contains the power of the heavenly bodies.[44] Albert, like other Aristotelians, held that in addition to the male semen, the heat and light of the sun was as a general active cause in the generation of new organisms of any species. In the case of higher species, the celestial bodies needed to be positioned in particular ways favorable to the generation of the species in question.

12-13. DEFECTS IN THE AMNIOTIC SAC

Many sorts of monsters result from a rupture in the amniotic sac. Albert writes: "[S]ometimes matter flows out and so a member is missing or curved or too large or disjointed or separated from those near it."[45] If the sac is ruptured when there are multiple embryos, the bodies of two different embryos can become fused together.[46]

14. DEFECTS IN THE HEAT CONTAINING THE POWER OF THE HEAVENLY BODIES

Albert was influenced by a work attributed to Ptolemy, the *De nativitatibus*, which attributed atypical births to the position of the celestial bodies at the time of conception.[47] Presumably changes in the positions of celestial bodies altered the strength of the light and heat that acted on both the matter involved in generation and on the male semen. Furthermore, Albert claimed that figures of the rays and stars can draw the embryo into a different shape from the one which is the goal of the male semen.[48] Albert claimed that from a defect in the heat surrounding the embryo, there could arise animals born with body parts resembling animals of diverse species. He claims to have seen a human born with truncated arms and legs who lacked a human bodily appearance. He attributed this to the heavenly bodies being positioned in a way that impeded the causal influence of the sun.[49]

Albert discussed the case of pigs and cows born with human-appearing heads.[50] Albert claims that organisms such as these cannot be the result of the two diverse species mating since he says the male and female contributions of such diverse species would destroy each other.[51] According to him, animals of one species which have parts resembling a different species are caused as a result of the sperm deriving a quality from the heavenly bodies. Such a derived quality goes beyond its innate formative power.[52] Albert maintained that the heavenly bodies could be responsible for a non-human animal having the shape of a human being, yet he denies that the heavenly bodies could cause an *actual human being* to be generated from a non-human animal.[53] The heavenly bodies have the power to cause figures and shapes, but they lack the power to cause a new member of the species; only the semen has the power to cause a new member of the species.

According to A.W. Bates, there is a well-known story in which Albert the Great saved the life of a herdsmen accused of bestiality when his cow gave birth to an offspring which appeared human-like. Albert argued that it was through the influence of the power of the heavenly bodies that the cow offspring had a human-like figure.[54] Albert's explanation was so persuasive that the herdsman was spared from the punishment of death.

Albert on the Causes of Intellectual and Sensory Impairments

A question one might have about Albert's taxonomy is whether it offers any explanation of the causes of intellectual or sensory impairments. Most of Albert's attention seems to be focused on classifying the causes of atypical physical structures of the body. However, in his view, both sensory impairments and cognitive impairments are rooted in bodily structures which would fall under the taxonomy above. One such example he gives in his *Quaestiones de Animalibus* is excessive fleshiness of the head which was thought to impair the senses and intellect. Excessive fleshiness would fall under the category of a disproportionate quality since it is an imbalance of qualities that causes more flesh, rather than bone, to form.[55] Ancient philosophers and physicians maintained that animal bodies contained spirits or *pneuma*.[56] These were not thought to be immaterial entities, but rather they were an extremely rarified material substances derived ultimately from breath. The spirits travelled from one bodily organ to another and were responsible for tasks such as bringing about muscle movement and conveying sense information from bodily parts to the brain. They played a role similar to the role of the nervous system in modern physiology. The way in which excessive fleshiness of the head obstructed thought and sensation was by obstructing the spirits' pathway by impeding the body's natural erect posture. As a result of the lack of alignment in the body, the *pneuma* or spirits could not travel directly from the heart to the brain. This, according to Albert, resulted in a weakness of the senses.[57] While Albert, like his medieval Aristotelian counterparts, denied that the intellect used a material organ to operate, he nevertheless claimed that the intellect could be impeded in its operation through weaknesses of the senses. The intellect cannot operate, in the Aristotelian view, apart from a *phantasm* gained through the senses.[58]

Significance of Albert's Views: Decoupling Congenital Defect from Parental Sin and Rejecting Exclusive Blame on the Mother

Many of Albert's theories about the causation of congenital defects were derived from Avicenna's medical works.[59] Nevertheless, Albert played a crucial role in introducing these theories into Latin scholastic philosophy. Against the larger backdrop of theories about monsters on offer in the Middle Ages, Albert's view is significant insofar as it offers an alternative to the widespread view that monsters were caused by the sexual sins of the child's parents. Albert's alternative naturalistic approach to explaining why children were born with impairments no doubt would have lifted the stigma and shame which followed from the other theory.

In Albert's view, it remains the case that some monstrosities are a result of the particular manner in which the parents had intercourse when they conceived the child. For instance, as we have seen, motions of the mother during intercourse can cause the sperm to divide, which in turn can lead to conjoined twins. Furthermore, sex at the "wrong time" with respect to astronomical phenomena can likewise result in a monster through the interference of the heavenly bodies' causality. It is unclear, though, whether Albert would have regarded the couple's ill-times or ill-positioned sexual activity as sinful.[60] Furthermore, Albert recognized other causes of monsters which were not tied to the manner in which the parents had intercourse. Among these causes were defects in the male's formative power. If the male's power were excessively strong or weak, a monstrous offspring would result regardless of how the couple had sex. By recognizing that some monsters simply followed from the state of the male or female's biological contribution to the offspring, Albert separated the causation of monsters from the moral realm of human choice.

In addition to de-coupling monstrosity from sexual sin, Albert's views are significant insofar as he denied that the female parent was exclusively to blame for this phenomenon. Irina Metzler, a leading scholar of medieval views on disability, has claimed that medieval views on the causes of monsters were misogynistic. According to her, even those who took a more naturalistic or medical approach to disability traced all monstrosity in offspring to failures of the mother in her biological contribution to generation.[61] It should be clear that this is not an accurate characterization of Albert's views. As we have seen above, Albert traced several types of atypical bodily structures to the excessive strength or weakness of the male formative power. In his view, even with the female making a perfect contribution to the generation of the new child, a monstrosity may nevertheless follow because of the condition of the male's formative power. In other texts, Albert even offers a theory about how disabling bodily illnesses, such as leprosy, can be passed on from father to child.[62]

Reception of Albert's Views in Aquinas

Aquinas did not have the level of learning or interest which Albert had in biology and medicine. Nevertheless, there are passages in Aquinas's works which show that he adopted the same general range of causes to explain congenital disabilities as his teacher did. Like Albert, Aquinas admits that some birth defects arise through a weakness in the male's formative power. He writes: "A defective operation always proceeds from a defect of some principle just as from a defect in the semen proceeds monstrosity of the offspring."[63] He also acknowledges that birth defects can arise from matter which is not properly disposed to receive a form or from an interfering action of a more powerful agent (e.g., the heavenly bodies).[64]

Aquinas never attributes birth defects to divine punishment for the personal sins of an individual. Yet, in his view had Adam and Eve not committed original sin, nature would have remained in a state of perfection such that no failures of natural causes would have been possible.[65] In the state of innocence (i.e., the state humans were in prior to original sin), there would be no defective formative powers or matter which was ill-disposed to receive a form. Thus, for Aquinas defects in this life arise from biological conditions which are punitive in response to original sin. Nevertheless, Aquinas claims that the failures of biological causes which give rise to various monstrosities fall under God's providence.[66] Aquinas more generally maintains that God only permits causes to fail and defects in their effects because he is able to bring a greater good out of these failures.[67] He never discusses what these greater goods are in the case of monstrosities. He believed that oftentimes we are unable to know how the suffering which we undergo brings a greater good to us.[68]

An Early Modern "Anti-Aristotelian" Perspective on Congenital Disabilities

To further highlight the conceptual and historical significance of medieval Aristotelian views on congenital disabilities, this section considers later developments in thinking about this topic. Though often omitted from narratives about the rise of modernity, congenital disabilities were an important battleground for Aristotelians and their early modern opponents.[69] The congenitally impaired were seen as a vivid counterexample to the Aristotelian world of fixed essences and regular patterns of natural causation. This section will first discuss John Locke's (1632–1704) objection to substantial form based on congenital impairments. It will then analyze the implications of Locke's rejection of real essences for his understanding of the moral status of the congenitally impaired. Comparison with Locke's perspective brings out some significant aspects of the Aristotelian understanding of those with congenital impairments.

Congenital Disabilities and the Challenge to Substantial Form

Medieval Aristotelians had no doubt about the humanity of monsters. Regardless of their outward appearances or differences from other human beings, the fact that they were generated by human parents entailed that they themselves were members of the human species. It was generally accepted in the period that substances which were capable of generating new substances could only generate a substance of the same species.[70] Thus, even those with the severest of disabilities were believed to be, in virtue of their human parentage, substances actualized by a human substantial form and, thus, fully human.

According to John Locke, the belief that monsters are animated by substantial forms specifically the same as individuals with more typical attributes demonstrated the incoherence of the doctrine of substantial form. Substantial forms are supposed to be invariable principles which actualize in a substance all of the attributes which naturally belong to its species. Thus, Locke reasons that if there are substantial forms, then individual members of the same species should not be able to vary with respect to the attributes which are proper to the species. Locke, however, sees monsters as organisms which vary from the attributes standard to the species. Thus, he construes them as disproving substantial form. He writes the following in his *Essay Concerning Human Understanding*:

> [The opinion] which supposes these *Essences*, as a certain number of Forms or Molds, wherein all natural Things, that exist, are cast, and do equally partake, has, I imagine, very much perplexed the Knowledge of natural Things. The frequent Productions of Monsters, in all the Species of Animals, and of Changelings, and other strange Issues of humane Birth, carry with them difficulties, not possible to consist with this *Hypothesis*: Since it is as impossible, that two Things, partaking exactly of the same real *Essence*, should have different Properties, as that two Figures partaking in the same real *Essence* of a Circle, should have different Properties.
>
> (III.iii.17)

In Locke's view it cannot be the case *both* that there are monsters *and* that all human beings are human in virtue of being animated by a human substantial form. This is because the substantial forms, if they did in fact exist, would have guaranteed that any member of the species has all of the attributes proper to the species.

Locke's objection may initially seem quite devastating; however, Aristotelians have some resources that they can draw on to respond. Briefly considering these resources will help further our understanding of the metaphysics underlying atypical bodily structures on the Aristotelian paradigm. It is useful to begin with a distinction medieval Aristotelians made between two different types of attributes which belonged to a substance in virtue of its species: an essential attribute and a necessary accident (*proprium*). An essential attribute is a quality which is included in a substance's essence or nature. Rationality and animality are essential attributes of humans because these qualities are included the very nature or definition of humanity. What it is for a substance to be human just is for it to be a rational animal. Necessary accidents (*propria*), by contrast, are not included in the very nature or definition of a substance. However, these attributes naturally arise or follow from that nature. Put otherwise, the substance's nature is a sufficient explanation for why the substance has the necessary attribute in question. Examples of necessary attributes of humans are the capacity to see or having two legs. These attributes are not the very heart of what it is to be human. However, if a human being has these attributes, they are sufficiently explained by the substance's being human. By contrast a human's black skin color or particular height or weight is not grounded simply in the substance's being human.[71] There will be other particular causes which explain why these accidental features are present in a substance. They do not follow from its very nature.

The distinction between essential attributes and necessary accidents is crucial for thinking about Locke's objection to substantial forms. With regard to essential attributes, it is not logically possible for a substance to be of a particular kind and lacking essential attributes proper to that kind. For instance, what it is to be human just is to exist as a rational animal. So what would an Aristotelian say about human beings with severe cognitive impairments ("changelings") whom Locke judges to be lacking in rationality? Our medieval Aristotelians would likely say that Locke is *simply wrong* in his judgment that they are not rational substances. In the context of considering the question of whether those with severe cognitive impairments ought to be baptized, Aquinas considers an objection which compares humans with severe cognitive impairments to irrational (i.e., non-human) animals. Aquinas writes:

> [T]he mentally ill and cognitively impaired lack the use of reason accidentally, namely on account of some impediment in a bodily organ, not however on account of lacking a rational soul, as brute animals do. Hence the comparison between them does not hold.[72]

Aquinas's point is that humans with severe cognitive impairments are still rational animals with a rational soul. Defects in their bodies impede them from using their intellectual power, but that power is nevertheless present. Those with severe cognitive disabilities are not in fact examples of humans who lack rationality.

Regarding necessary accidents, at least some medieval Aristotelians allow that individual organisms can lack at least some of the attributes which naturally arise from their species. Scotus, for example, explicitly discusses a class of necessary accidents which follow from a nature only *for the most part*.[73] While these attributes are explained by the substance's nature when they are present, they are not logically entailed by the species. But how can it be that substantial forms are invariable *and* that there are some attributes which are proper to a given species but nevertheless missing from some individuals within the species? Shouldn't the substantial form invariably actualize every attribute which is natural to a substance's species? The details we have seen in Albert's taxonomy of the causes of congenital disabilities can help to answer these questions.

In Albert's taxonomy, we saw that the general reasons for why a human being might have an atypical bodily structure is (1) because the matter from which the human being was generated did not have a suitable quality or quantity or (2) because the male formative power which transformed that antecedent substance (i.e., menstrual blood) into a human being was weak or (3) because an extrinsic cause interfered in the process of generation. In each of these cases, it happens that the prime matter which carries over from the corrupted substance into the new human being is suitably prepared to receive the human substantial form. However, it is not suitably prepared to receive some of the accidental forms which naturally follow from that substantial form. The substantial form itself is invariable and perfect. What explains why certain accidental forms which naturally follow from it were not actualized is the fact that the matter which received that substantial form was not adequately prepared to receive these further accidental forms. Though the prime matter which carries over from the substance out of which the human was generated into the new human has no actual quality and quantity of itself, it must be prepared by being actualized by a series of prior forms in order to take on further determinate forms. Through weakness of the efficient cause, interferences by other agents or defects in the original material substance (i.e., the menstrual blood), it happens that the matter is not suitably prepared to receive all of the accidents which naturally follow from the new substantial form. Thus, although the substantial form is itself invariable, there are variations in the accidents which arise from it on account of differences in the preparation of the individual matter of each individual substance. The prime matter which makes up each individual substance varies with regard to its history of which prior forms it was under, and this variability is what accounts for why on occasion some substances lack necessary accidents which are proper to their species.

Rejection of Substantial Form Leads to Rejection of the Humanity of the Severely Disabled

Once Locke rejects substantial forms and real essences, there is nothing left to secure the sameness in kind between those with severe cognitive impairments and other human beings. In Locke's view nothing in the internal constitution of individual beings determines their species. Boundaries between species are not fixed in nature. According to him, the sorting of individuals into species is a system of classification which we as humans actively create. In Locke's view, we form abstract ideas of distinct species, and then we use these abstract ideas to classify individuals into groups.[74] Locke claims that those with severe cognitive disabilities are not rightly classified as human because they cannot reason. The abstract idea of a human being is a rational animal, and in Locke's view, the cognitively impaired do not fit this idea because they do not reason. In his view, the severely cognitively impaired are better represented by the abstract idea of "the shape, motion and life of a man without reason," and he notes that this abstract idea is distinct from the abstract ideas of both "man and beast."[75] Thus, in his view those with severe cognitive disabilities make up their own species different from both human and other species of non-human animals.

Not only does Locke deny that the cognitively impaired belong in the same class or kind as human beings with typical attributes but he also denies that there is any evidence that they have souls as typical human beings do. Locke claims that attributing souls to the cognitively impaired on the basis of their human bodily appearance is like attributing a soul to a human corpse because of its outward appearance. He writes:

> For it may as rationally be concluded, that the dead body of a man, wherein there is to be found no more appearance or action of life than there is in a statue, has yet nevertheless a living soul in it, because of its shape; as that there is a rational soul in a changeling, because he has the outside of a rational creature, when his actions carry far less marks of reason with them, in the whole course of his life, than what are to be found in many a beast.[76]

We saw above that Aquinas explicitly claimed that those with severe cognitive disabilities nevertheless have rational souls. Regardless of whether they can use their power of intellect to actually think, Aquinas would say, we can know they are humans, animated by a rational soul because they were generated by two human parents. Locke, however, goes on from this passage above to urge his reader to abandon the idea that there are species or essences in nature and instead "examine [things] by what our faculties can discover in them as they exist."[77] In Locke's view, if an existing being does not *actually engage in acts of reasoning*, then there is no rationale for placing him in the category of human being since he, as he actually is, does not fit the abstract idea of a rational animal.

We also saw above that Aquinas defended the view that those with severe cognitive disabilities ought to be baptized. He believed that even those who lack the opportunity to cause acts of reasoning nevertheless retained the same moral status as other human beings in virtue of having the same specific type of substantial form, that is, a rational soul.[78]

In Locke's view we find a different account of the criteria which must be met for moral status. Once it is rejected that there is some common nature or essence which secures the metaphysical sameness between all human beings, some other foundation must be sought for securing the moral and political rights. In his *Second Treatise on Government*, Locke claims that human persons are "equal and independent, no-one ought to harm anyone else in his life, health, liberty, or possessions" in part because "we have the same abilities."[79] In Locke's view, beings have moral status and political rights because they are *able to do* certain things. This leaves those with severe disabilities in a dangerous place. The merits of the medieval Aristotelian position are clear when compared with Locke's alternative. Rather than making moral status hinge on one's abilities, the Aristotelian framework makes it possible to hinge moral status on sameness of natural kind. All human beings, regardless of abilities or impairments, have equal moral status because they are all the *same kind of being*.[80]

Of course, any view that maintains that species or essences are real in nature can similarly hinge moral status on sameness of natural kind to secure the equal moral status of both typical humans and those with severe disabilities. Nevertheless, Aristotelian hylomorphism has an explanatory power which may go beyond other forms of essentialism. In order to make essentialism plausible in light of the range of disabilities that individual organisms face, it is necessary to have some account of how essence can be real in nature and yet there can be such a wide of range of diversity among members of the same species. Hylomorphism offers a metaphysic which can meet this challenge. Hylomorphism can explain how it can be the case both that all members of the same species share the same specific essence and, nevertheless, that it is possible for some of them to be impaired with respect to the attributes and powers which naturally follow from this essence. As we have seen, hylomorphism posits that in addition to a principle which confers species (form), there is also a receptive principle in each individual (matter). Positing this receptive principle provides a way of accounting for how there can be variation in individuals even with respect to what is proper to a species. As we have seen, matter can be well- or ill-prepared to receive a given form, and this explains why individuals can be lacking in certain forms which naturally follow from their substantial kind.

Conclusion

As noted in the introduction, even today we do not understand the particular causes which are responsible for half of all cases of congenital birth defects. Studying medieval views on this matter certainly will not help us solve that problem. Yet, there are a number of reasons why medieval views on the causes of congenital disabilities remain important. First and foremost, those who live with congenital disabilities deserve to know their place in history. If we believe that understanding the history of ideas is valuable in and of itself, we should care about how minorities have been understood in the past and how those past concepts influence today's attitudes. Second, studying the views of medieval Aristotelians, particularly Albert the Great, reveal that the Middle Ages may not have been so dark after all. Though it was widespread in his time to attribute congenital disability to religious and moral causes, Albert the Great took a reasoned, scientific approach to explaining the causes of particular congenital disorders. Beginning from the Aristotelian conception of the four causes, he applied logic to determine what particular types of failures of natural causes would give rise to particular types of atypical differences in bodily structure. We have also seen that his theory, contra Metzler, was not misogynistic. Far from laying exclusive blame on women for atypical births, he maintained that congenital disorders could be caused by a weakness in the male's formative power. Lastly, examining the early modern rejection of substantial forms and Locke's alternative views on those with severe cognitive disabilities reveals some of the philosophical merits of the hylomorphic approach to the material world. Aristotelian hylomorphism provides a metaphysical framework which allows for maintaining the humanity and equal moral status of those born with severe impairments. By thinking of substances as composed of an invariable principle which confers species, as well as a receptive principle, hylomorphism can make sense of the individual differences (including impairments) of those with severe disabilities without sacrificing their more important shared humanity.[81]

Notes

1 This chapter is dedicated to the memory of Dr. Karen Chan. The final time I presented this material was at a joint session with her on "Disability" at the 2019 meeting of the American Catholic Philosophical Association. This would also be the last time I saw her before her remarkable life ended far too soon. Eternal rest grant unto her, O Lord, and let perpetual light shine upon her. May she rest in peace.
2 World Health Organization (2019).
3 Ibid.
4 Asch, Adrienne, Jeffrey Blustein, Daniel Putnam, and David Wasserman, "Disability: Definitions, Models, and Experience."
5 Richard Cross makes this point in "Duns Scotus on Disability: Teleology, Divine Willing, and Pure Nature," 72–95.
6 I am using "biological impairment" here to encompass impairments of the brain, and I am assuming that psychological disorders are rooted in such impairments.
7 For a collection essays on various aspects of monsters in medieval religion and culture, see Bettina Bildhauer and Robert Mills (eds.), *The Monstrous Middle Ages*.

8 Isidore of Seville's 7th century taxonomy of monsters in his *Etymologiae* includes animal births of humans and monstrous races. See Isidore of Saville, *The Etymologies*, 243–246. Pliny's *Natural History* (first circulated AD 77) introduced the notion of monstrous races. He describes over fifty races of people which he judged to have anomalous bodies. His list ranges from the extremely short Pygmies to Cynocephali, which are claimed to be humans with dog heads. See Pliny, *Natural History*. Aristotle himself explicitly rejected the possibility of hybrid species. He argued that since different species of animals have different lengths to their gestation periods, it was not possible for a single animal to be born of two species. See Aristotle, *Generation of Animals*, 769b21–25
9 Aristotle, *Generation of Animals*, 770a5–771a15.
10 Cicero's *De Divinatione* was one influential source. He listed the following synonyms for monsters: *monstra, ostenta, portenta, prodigia*, which associated monsters with the fulfillment of a special purpose rather than a failure of purpose. See Cicero *De Divinatione*, 42.
11 Augustine, *The City of God*, 56–58.
12 One very well-known example was the "Monster of Ravenna," who was viewed as warning of the battle of Ravenna in 1512 when the city was overtaken by the French and the citizens massacred. See A.W. Bates, *Emblematic Monsters*, 22–24.
13 Quoted from Joseph Needham, *A History of Embryology*, 85. In other places in her works, Hildegard claims that sexual activity when one is not at a proper age or at the wrong time with respect to the lunar phase can lead to a disability in the offspring. For discussion, see Irina Metzler, *Disability in Medieval Europe*, 84–86.
14 Irina Metzler, "Disabled Children: Birth Defects, Causality, and Guilt," 172.
15 Vincent de Beauvais (c. 1190–1264) writes in his *Speculum Naturale*: "[t]his type of hybrid monstrosity sometimes occurs in this way, that is by means of coitus between two different species" (quoted from Bates, *Emblematic Monsters*, 118).
16 On the theory, see Marie-Héléne Huet, *Monstrous Imagination*.
17 See Anthony Hewson, *Giles of Rome and the Medieval Theory of Conception*, 193. This story was common in the Middle Ages. It originates with Jerome, quoting Quintilian. See Jerome, *Liber quaestionum Hebraicarum in Genesim cap. 30.32–33*, 38. For a discussion of Albert the Great's reference to this story, along with other medieval figures who reference the story and adopt the "maternal imagination theory," see Irven Resnick, *Marks of Distinction*, 296–300.
18 *Genesis* 30: 25–43.
19 Ibid.
20 For a discussion of the texts in which Descartes adopts this theory, see Justin Smith, "Imagination and the Problem of Heredity in Mechanist Embryology," 80–99, esp. 90–91. For a discussion of Malebranche's adoption of the "maternal imagination" theory, see Huet, *Monstrous Imagination*, 45–55.
21 See Aristotle's *Physics*, 189b30–191a22.
22 Aquinas explains this point here: *In XII Meta.*, lec. 2, n. 15:

> Licet enim materia prima sit in potentia ad omnes formas, tamen quodam ordine suscipit eas. Per prius enim est in potentia ad formas elementares, et eis mediantibus secundum diversas proportiones commixtionum est in potentia ad diversas formas: unde non potest ex quolibet immediate fieri quodlibet ....

See also Thomas Aquinas, *ScG* III.22. All Aquinas texts are from Thomas Aquinas, *Opera Omnia*.
23 For Aristotle's general discussion of the four causes, see *Physics*, 194b16–195b30, and *Metaphysics*, 1013a24–1014b25.
24 For an overview and analysis of both the Aristotelian and Galenic theories of reproduction, see Sophia M. Connell, "Aristotle and Galen on Sex Difference and Reproduction: A New Approach to an Ancient Rivalry," 405–427. On medieval theories of reproduction in general, see Joan Cadden, *Meanings of Sex Difference in the Middle Ages: Medicine, Science, and Culture*. Despite initial appearances, Galen's theory was no less misogynistic and no more correct than Aristotle's. Galen conceived of females as inverted males, and he accorded the female sperm the role of nourishing and protecting the male sperm. Galen had mistaken cervical mucous for sperm. We know today that females make an active contribution to generation by way of ovulation (not fluids).
25 On Franciscan views of the active role of the mother in generation, see James Roger Bell, "Conceiving of the Word: Mary's Motherhood in the Oxford Franciscan school 1285–1315," 30–105.
26 More specifically, Aristotle believed that the male formative power tended toward producing a male offspring who resembled the father in its physical characteristics. Both females and males who did not look like their father and earlier ancestors were thought to be the result of a process that failed (to some extent) in reaching its goal. For a discussion of Aristotle's views, see Thomas V. Upton, "Aristotle on Monsters and the Generation of Kinds," 21–36. Aquinas likewise accepts that the male seed tends toward producing a male, but he affirms that with respect to human nature as such and God's intentions, the female is not a failure of purpose. See Aquinas, *ST* I 92.1 ad 1.
27 Albert the Great, *II Phys*. 3.3 (ed. Col. 4.1, p. 136, ll. 55–61):

> Monstra enim sunt peccatum illius quod in natura est propter aliquid. Fiunt autem monstra, ut in genere dici potest, propter quattor causas, quae tamen sub se multas habent particulares causas; aliquando enim fiunt propter materiae diminutionem, aliquando propter materiae superfluitatem, aliquando propter qualitatum improportionabilitatem ad materiam, aliquando autem propter continentis malitiam.

I quote Albert's *Physics* from Albertus Magnus, *Physica*, ed. Coloniensis, vol. 4.1 (Münster: Aschendorf, 1993).
28 Ibid., *II Phys*. 3.3, 136, ll. 70–71: "[N]on potest formare nisi parum de materia et reicit aliam."
29 Ibid., *II Phys*. 3.3, 137, ll. 11–13: "Quae autem deficiunt in membris, vel in toto deficiunt, quasi sint abscisa, vel deficiunt ab actu, eo quod sint curva vel mollia, quae actum sustinere non possunt."
30 Ibid., *II Phys*. 3.3, 137, ll. 7–11: "Et huius signum est, quod praecipue deficiunt membra longe a corde et hepate distantia, in quibus praecipue situm habent virtutes membra formantes, sicut deficient manus vel pedes vel aliquid extrinsecorum membrorum in capite."
31 Ibid., *II Phys*. 3.3, 136–137, ll. 71–03.
32 Ibid.
33 Ibid., *II Phys*. 3.3, 137, ll. 28–35:

> [Q]uando virtus est proportionate et non materia, tunc virtus non potest omnia formare aequaliter et ideo habilem materiam melius format quam inhabilem. Est autem, sicut prius diximus, materia exteriorum, in quibus

minus potest formans virtus quam in interioribus, propterea quia plus distant a membris, in quibus sita est vis formativa.

34 Ibid., *II Phys.* 3.3, 137, ll. 38–51.
35 Ibid., 52–55.
36 On Albert's views on twinning, see J.M. Thijssen, "Twins as Monsters: Albertus Magnus's Theory of the Generation of Twins and Its Philosophical Context," 237–246. Thijssen shows that Albert's theory was adopted from Avicenna.
37 Albert the Great, *II Phys.* 3.3, 137, ll. 65–73:

> ... sunt enim quaedam mulieres et quaedam animalium, quae multum in coitu delectantur, et in delectatione illa movetur matrix, cum sperma infunditur nervis sensibilibus eius, et in motu illo dividitur sperma. Cum ergo divisio tota perficitur, tunc fiunt gemini, si coalescit semen in fetum. Si autem divisio non perficitur, sed sperma quasi ramificatur, tunc fiunt bicorporea animalia subtus vel supra vel etiam in medio secundum modum, per quem dividitur sperma.

38 Ibid., *II Phys.* 3.3, 137–138, ll. 77–04.
39 Ibid., *II Phys.* 3.3, 138, ll. 5–7.
40 Ibid., 7–8.
41 For an overview of how bodily and psychological temperament was both inherited from the parents and influenced by the environment, see Claire Weeda, "The Fixed and the Fluent: Geographical Determinism, Ethnicity and Religion 1100–1300 CE," 93–113. On Albert's views on how illnesses, such as leprosy, and other bodily defects can be inherited from the male parent to child, see Resnick, *Marks of Distinction*, 176–177.
42 Albert the Great, *De animalibus*, Bk. 18, tract. 2, c. 3, 1220–1224.
43 Albert the Great, *II Phys.* 3.3, 138, ll. 10–12.
44 Ibid., *II Phys.* 3.3, 138, ll. 20–24.
45 Ibid., 25–28: "[Q]uandoque enim materia effluit, et sic deficit membrum vel curvatur vel grandescit vel discontinuatur et dislocatur a membro sibi vicino."
46 Ibid., *II Phys.* 3.3, 138, ll. 28–30.
47 B.B. Price, "Physical Astronomy and Astrology," 180–181. Price discusses Albert's own experience of witnessing non-human animals born with human-appearing heads.
48 Luke Demaitre and Anthony A. Travill, "Human Embryology and Development in the Works of Albertus Magnus," 436.
49 Ibid.
50 Albert the Great, *II Phys.* 3.3, 138, ll. 33–34.
51 He says that when the species are close or similar to each other, a middle species of animal can be generated, as with the mule generated from a horse and an ass. See ibid., *II Phys.* 3.3, 138, ll. 43–47. The mule is not understood by Albert as an animal that shares in two distinct species but rather as an animal of its own third species.
52 Ibid., *II Phys.* 3.3, 138, ll. 38–40: "Sed potius fit ad constellationem ad illam formam sperma extra suam qualitatem moventem ...."
53 B.B. Price, "Physical Astronomy and Astrology," 181. For a primary text in Albert, see *VIII Phys.* 2.10, 613, ll. 18–24:

> Id ideo si dispositiones et contemporationes seminis possunt sufficienter haberi per stellas, tunc posset fieri homo de eo semine, quod non est abscisum ab homine, vel capra et esset eiusdem speciei cum aliis, quia

virtutes caelestes, quae inducunt seminis causas specificas, operarentur ad eandem speciem, ad quam dispositum est semen.

54 A.W. Bates, *Emblematic Monsters*, 118.
55 Albert the Great, *QQ. de animalibus* XIV, q. 10. This work, which is a *reportatio* of Albert's teaching, is available in English translation. See Albert the Great, *Albert the Great's Questions Concerning Aristotle's "On Animals."*
56 On Albert's positions on *pneuma* in general and with regard to ancient debates about the organ from which they originated, see Miguel de Asúa, "Medicine and Natural Philosophy in Albert the Great," 277–281.
57 Albert the Great, *QQ. de animalibus* XIV, q. 10.
58 See especially ibid., *QQ. de animalibus* XIV, q. 10, ad 2.
59 On Albert's medical learning and the influence of Avicenna, see N.G. Siraisi, "The Medical Learning of Albertus," 379–404.
60 According to John T. Noonan, Albert's views on sexual morality were non-standard in comparison with his counterparts. See Noonan, *Contraception*, 275–289. In addition to recognizing like other medieval authors that sexual intercourse had the natural end of begetting children, he believed that the act had the end of "recalling the sacramental good of marriage." So there is some question as to whether Albert would have believed that certain acts that other medieval would have regarded as sinful, such as ill-times sex, would be permissible if they helped the couple "recall the sacramental good of marriage." Noonan also cites the following study of Albert's views on sex: Leopold Brandl O.F.M., *Die Sexualethik des heiligen Albertus Magnus*, 171–178.
61 Metzler writes the following in her "Disabled Children: Birth Defects, Causality, and Guilt," 179:

> Since in medieval medical discourse, taken on from classical traditions, the female tended to be viewed purely as a vessel receiving the procreative powers that resided exclusively in the male it was readily assumed that when things went wrong, this was the result of maternal malfunctioning, whether at a purely anatomical or at a moral level, which caused the pristine paternal seed deposited in the maternal body to be corrupted.

62 Albert the Great, *QQ. de animalibus* XV, q. 13.
63 Thomas Aquinas, *De malo* 16.6 co.: "Defectiva autem operatio semper procedit ex defectu alicuius principii, sicut ex aliquo defectu seminis procedit monstruositas partus, ut dicitur in II Physic." See also ibid., *De malo* 1.1 ad 8 & 1.3 co. and *ScG* IV.51. Aristotle seemed to be open to the idea that at least some monstrosities arise through weakness in the male sperm. In *Generation of Animals*, Bk. IV 768b 25–27, Aristotle writes:

> Now that which is acted on escapes and is not mastered, either through deficiency of power in the concocting and moving agent or because what should be concocted and formed into distinct parts is too cold and in too great quantity.

64 Thomas Aquinas, *ScG* III.99:

> multae enim naturalium causarum effectus suos producunt eodem modo ut frequenter, non autem ut semper; nam quandoque, licet ut in paucioribus, aliter accidit, vel propter defectum virtutis agentis, vel propter materiae indispositionem, vel propter aliquod fortius agens; sicut cum natura in homine generat digitum sextum.

76 Gloria Frost

65 Thomas Aquinas, *De veritate* 18.6 co: "Unde, sicut in conceptione humani corporis in statu innocentiae nulla monstruositas accidisset, ita etiam in intellectu eius nulla falsitas esse posset."
66 Thomas Aquinas, *ST* II-II.51.4 co.: "... sicut monstruosi partus animalium sunt praeter ordinem virtutis activae in semine, tamen cadunt sub ordine altioris principii, scilicet caelestis corporis, vel ulterius providentiae divinae."
67 See for instance Thomas Aquinas, *ST* Ia 22.2 ad 2.
68 This is apparent in his commentary on the book of Job. See especially Thomas Aquinas, *In Job* c. 9, lec. 4.
69 In their book *Wonders and the Order of Nature 1150–1750*, 9, Lorraine Daston and Katharine Park write: "Bacon, Hobbes, Leibniz, Locke—all put monsters on the front lines of their campaigns to reform natural philosophy ...."
70 Aquinas expresses this principle as applied to human beings in *ST* Ia 100.1 co.: "Respondeo dicendum quod naturaliter homo generat sibi simile secundum speciem." See also *ST* Ia 98.1.
71 See Colleen McCluskey, "Black on the Outside, White on the Inside: Peter Abelard's Use of Race," 135–163.
72 Thomas Aquinas, *ST* III.68.12 ad 2: "furiosi vel amentes carent usu rationis per accidens, scilicet propter aliquod impedimentum organi corporalis, non autem propter defectum animae rationalis, sicut bruta animalia. Unde non est de eis similis ratio."
73 See Richard Cross, "Duns Scotus on Disability: Teleology, Divine Willing, and Pure Nature," 79–80. Locke and perhaps other early moderns received from their logic textbooks an understanding of the relationship between substantial forms and *propria* that did not accurately capture the scholastics' view. Burgersdijk's logic textbook, which Locke was assigned, states that the relationship between an essence and its propria is logical necessity; one is inconceivable without the other. On these points, see Michael Jacovides, *Locke's Image of the World*, 20–24.
74 John Locke, *An Essay Concerning Human Understanding* Bk. III, c. 4, n. 22 and 30. He goes on to argue that the fact that we can disagree about the species of an individual organism proves that boundaries of species are not set in nature. See Bk. III, c. 4, n. 22.
75 For the full passage, see John Locke, *An Essay Concerning Human Understanding*, Bk. IV, c. 4, n. 13:

> It would possibly be thought a bold paradox, if not a very dangerous falsehood, if I should say that some changelings, who have lived forty years together, without any appearance of reason, are something between a man and a beast: which prejudice is founded upon nothing else but a false supposition, that these two names, man and beast, stand for distinct species so set out by real essences, that there can come no other species between them: whereas if we will abstract from those names, and the supposition of such specific essences made by nature, wherein all things of the same denominations did exactly and equally partake; if we would not fancy that there were a certain number of these essences, wherein all things, as in molds, were cast and formed; we should find that the idea of the shape, motion, and life of a man without reason, is as much a distinct idea, and makes as much a distinct sort of things from man and beast, as the idea of the shape of an ass with reason would be different from either that of man or beast, and be a species of an animal between, or distinct from both.

He goes on to consider and respond to a number of objections against the thesis that "changelings" are a species between man and beast.

76 Ibid., Bk. IV, c. 4, n. 15.
77 Ibid., n. 16.
78 Thomas Aquinas, *ST* Ia.29.3 ad 2: "Et quia magnae dignitatis est in rationali natura subsistere, ideo omne individuum rationalis naturae dicitur persona ...."
79 John Locke, *An Essay Concerning Human Understanding*, Ch. 2, n. 6. https://ebooks.adelaide.edu.au/l/locke/john/l81u/index.html
80 It should be noted, however, that some medieval Aristotelians, including Aquinas, maintained that by sinning a human could *in certain respect* lower his or her dignity. See Thomas Aquinas *ST* II-II 64.2 ad 3: "homo peccando ab ordine rationis recedit, et ideo decidit a dignitate humana, prout scilicet homo est naturaliter liber et propter seipsum existens, et incidit quodammodo in servitutem bestiarum, ut scilicet de ipso ordinetur secundum quod est utile aliis ...." For a discussion of medieval views on dignity, see Bonnie Kent, "In the Image of God? Human Dignity after the Fall," 73–98.
81 I am grateful to Harm Goris and Scott Williams for comments on an earlier draft. Earlier versions of this chapter were presented at the University of Notre Dame, Georgetown University, Universität Bonn, the University of St. Thomas and the 2019 meeting of the American Catholic Philosophical Association. I am grateful to the audiences at these presentations for helpful questions and comments. I am also grateful to the Terrence Murphy Institute at the University of St. Thomas for a summer research fellowship, which supported my work on this project.

References

Primary Sources

Albert the Great. *Physica*, Edited by Paul Hossfeld. *Opera Omnia*, vol. 4.1–4.2, Münster: Aschendorf, 1987–1993.

Albert the Great. *De animalibus*, Edited by Hermann Stadler. Beiträge zur Geschichte des Mittelalters 15–16. Münster: Aschendorff, 1916–1920.

Albert the Great. *Albert the Great's Questions Concerning Aristotle's "On Animals."* Translated by Irven M. Resnick and Kenneth F. Kitchell Jr. *Fathers of the Church, Medieval Continuation 9*. Washington, DC: Catholic University of America Press, 2008.

Aquinas, Thomas. *Opera Omnia*, Edited by R. Busa. <http://www.corpusthomisticum.org/iopera.html>

Aristotle, *Generation of Animals*. Edited by Jonathan Barnes. *The Complete Works of Aristotle*. Princeton: Princeton University Press, 1984.

Aristotle, *Physics*. Edited by Jonathan Barnes. *The Complete Works of Aristotle*. Princeton: Princeton University Press, 1984.

Augustine. *City of God*. Translated by William M. Green. *Loeb Classical Library* 417. Cambridge, MA: Harvard University Press, 1972.

Cicero. *De divinatione*, vol. 1. Edited by Arthur Stanley Pease. Urbana: University of Illinois, 1920.

Isidore of Seville. *The Etymologies*, 243–246. Translated by Stephen A. Barney, W.J. Lewis, J.A. Beach, and Oliver Berghof. Cambridge: Cambridge University Press, 2006.

Jerome. *Liber quaestionum Hebraicarum in Genesim*. CSSL. Turnholt: Brepols, 1959.

Locke, John. *An Essay Concerning Human Understanding.* <https://ebooks.adelaide.edu.au/l/locke/john/l81u/index.html>

Pliny. *Natural History, Volume I: Books 1–2.* Translated by H. Rackham. Loeb Classical Library 330. Cambridge, MA: Harvard University Press, 1938.

Secondary Sources

Asch, Adrienne, Jeffrey Blustein, Daniel Putnam, and David Wasserman. "Disability: Definitions, Models, and Experience." In *Stanford Encyclopedia of Philosophy* (Summer 2016), <https://plato.stanford.edu/entries/disability/>.

de Asúa, Miguel. "Medicine and Natural Philosophy in Albert the Great." In *A Companion to Albert the Great.* Edited by Irven M. Resnick. Leiden: Brill, 2013, 269–297.

Bates, Alan W. *Emblematic Monsters: Unnatural Conceptions and Deformed Births in Early Modern Europe* [*Emblematic Monsters*]. Amsterdam and New York: Rodopi, 2005.

Bell, James Roger. "Conceiving of the Word: Mary's Motherhood in the Oxford Franciscan School 1285–1315." Unpublished PhD dissertation. Washington, DC: The Catholic University of America, 2001.

Bildhauer, Bettina and Robert Mills (eds.). *The Monstrous Middle Ages.* Toronto and Buffalo: University of Toronto Press, 2003.

Brandl, Leopold O.F.M. *Die Sexualethik des heiligen Albertus Magnus.* Regensburg, 1955.

Cadden, Joan. *Meanings of Sex Difference in the Middle Ages: Medicine, Science, and Culture.* Cambridge: Cambridge University Press, 1993.

Connell, Sophia M. "Aristotle and Galen on Sex Difference and Reproduction: A New Approach to an Ancient Rivalry," *Studies in the History and Philosophy of Science* 31:3 (2000): 405–427.

Cross, Richard. "Duns Scotus on Disability: Teleology, Divine Willing, and Pure Nature," *Theological Studies*, 78:1 (2017): 72–95.

Daston, Lorraine and Katharine Park. *Wonders and the Order of Nature 1150–1750.* New York: Zone Books, 1998.

Demaitre, Luke and Anthony A. Travill. "Human Embryology and Development in the Works of Albertus Magnus." In *Albertus Magnus and the Sciences: Commemorative Essays 1980.* Edited by James A. Weisheipl, OP. Toronto: Pontifical Institute of Mediaeval Studies, 1980, 405–440.

Hewson, Anthony. *Giles of Rome and the Medieval Theory of Conception: A Study of the De formatione corporis humani in utero.* London: The University of London, The Athlone Press, 1975.

Huet, Marie-Hélène. *Monstrous Imagination.* Cambridge, MA: Harvard University Press, 1993.

Jacovides, Michael. *Locke's Image of the World.* Oxford: Oxford University Press, 2017.

Kent, Bonnie. "In the Image of God? Human Dignity after the Fall." In *Dignity: Oxford Philosophical Concepts.* Edited by Remy Debes. Oxford: Oxford University Press, 2017, 73–98.

McCluskey, Colleen. "Black on the Outside, White on the Inside: Peter Abelard's Use of Race," *Critical Philosophy of Race* 6:2 (2018): 135–163.

Metzler, Irina. *Disability in Medieval Europe: Thinking about Physical Impairment during the High Middle Ages* [*Disability in Medieval Europe*], c. 1100–1400. London: Routledge, 2006.

——— "Disabled Children: Birth Defects, Causality, and Guilt." In *Medicine, Religion and Gender in Medieval Culture*. Edited by Naoë Kukita Yoshikawa. Boydell & Brewer: D. S. Brewer, 2015, 161–180.

Needham, Joseph. *A History of Embryology*. 2nd edition revised by Arthur Hughes. Cambridge: Cambridge University Press, 1959.

Noonan, John T. *Contraception*. Harvard: Harvard University Press, 1986.

Price, Betsey B. "Physical Astronomy and Astrology." In *Albertus Magnus and the Sciences: Commemorative Essays 1980*. Edited by James A. Weisheipl, OP. Toronto: Pontifical Institute of Mediaeval Studies, 1980, 155–186.

Resnick, Irven. *Marks of Distinction: Christian Perceptions of Jews in the High Middle Ages*. Washington, DC: Catholic University of America Press, 2012.

Siraisi, Nancy G. "The Medical Learning of Albertus." In *Albertus Magnus and the Sciences: Commemorative Essays 1980*. Edited by James A. Weisheipl, OP. Toronto: Pontifical Institute of Mediaeval Studies, 1980, 379–404.

Smith, Justin. "Imagination and the Problem of Heredity in Mechanist Embryology." In *The Problem of Animal Generation in Early Modern Philosophy*. Edited by Justin Smith. Cambridge: Cambridge University Press, 2006, 80–100.

Thijssen, Johan M. "Twins as Monsters: Albertus Magnus's Theory of the Generation of Twins and Its Philosophical Context," *Bulletin of the History of Medicine*, 61:2 (1987): 237–246.

Upton, Thomas V. "Aristotle on Monsters and the Generation of Kinds," *American Catholic Philosophical Quarterly* 77:1 (2003): 21–36.

Weeda, Claire. "The Fixed and The Fluent: Geographical Determinism, Ethnicity and Religion 1100–1300 CE." In *The Routledge Handbook of Identity and the Environment in the Classical and Medieval Worlds*. Edited by Rebecca Futo Kennedy and Molly Jones-Lewis. London and New York: Routledge, 2016, 93–113.

World Health Organization. "Health Topics: Congenital Anomalies," (2019) <http://www.who.int/topics/congenital_anomalies/en/>.

3 Personhood, Ethics, and Disability

A Comparison of Byzantine, Boethian, and Modern Concepts of Personhood

Scott M. Williams

Introduction

The question "Who is an equal member in the moral community, and who has more or less status than others?" arises in contemporary ethics. One answer, at least since Kant, is that personhood gives one equal, and intrinsic, moral status. If one is a person, then one has intrinsic moral status and is equal to others in this regard. If one is not a person, then one's moral status is less than those who are persons. (It is noteworthy that in Terence Irwin's three-volume text, *The Development of Ethics: A Historical and Critical Study*, which totals 2,743 pages, "person" does not appear until the third volume that begins with Kant.) Philosophers disagree, however, on the criteria for personhood. This chapter assumes, for the sake of argument, the stipulation that personhood gives one intrinsic and equal moral status compared to others in the moral community. It then evaluates different accounts of personhood, namely some medieval accounts and some modern accounts, by whether they are supportive of a disability-positive perspective. By a "disability-positive perspective," I mean that all disabled human beings (i.e., physically or cognitively or developmentally disabled human beings) are equal members of the moral community and are intrinsically so. In other words, if we assume (for the sake of argument) that personhood gives one equal and intrinsic moral status, then it would be helpful to know which accounts of personhood are supportive of a disability-positive perspective and which are not. This chapter argues that the medieval accounts of personhood that are discussed are preferable to the modern accounts of personhood on the assumptions that personhood gives one equal and intrinsic moral status and that the disability-positive position is correct. (The historical treatment of disabled individuals, particularly the cognitively disabled, is what partly animates the disability-positive position. The history of violence against disabled human beings – including the eugenics movement of the 19th and 20th centuries that animated state-sanctioned violence and mass murder – should ever be on our minds when theorizing about the moral status of disabled human beings.)[1]

This chapter is divided into three sections. The first section surveys some modern accounts of personhood. The second section surveys early medieval accounts of personhood. I divide these early medieval accounts into Byzantine accounts and Boethian accounts. The Byzantine accounts begin with the Cappadocians (e.g., Gregory of Nyssa), who influence later "scholastic" Greek and Latin theologians (e.g., Leontius of Byzantium, John Maxentius, Maximus the Confessor, and John of Damascus); the Byzantine approach also influenced various Christian ecumenical councils.[2] Further, Boethius initiated a different way of understanding personhood than Byzantine theologians, namely, he stipulated that "rationality" should be added to the definition of "persona." This stipulation is not in Byzantine accounts of personhood (i.e., hypostasis, prosopon). The third section compares the modern accounts of personhood with these early medieval accounts of personhood and argues that the medieval accounts are preferable over the modern accounts if we assume that personhood gives one equal and intrinsic moral status and we assume a disability-positive perspective regarding morality. It is not assumed that personhood in fact gives one equal and intrinsic moral status. The conclusion of this chapter is a conditional: *if* personhood gives one equal and intrinsic moral status and the disability-positive perspective is correct, *then* the medieval accounts of personhood (that are surveyed) are preferable over the modern accounts (that are surveyed).

Before proceeding there is an important caveat to be made regarding methodology. There are different ways for historians of medieval Christian philosophy and theology to engage with the philosophy and theology of disability. Historians of philosophy or theology typically adopt the method of trying to understand the historical texts on their own terms. In hermeneutics this has been called "understanding" a text – aiming to explicate the text's meaning. Another method has been called "overstanding" a text – aiming to explain how a text addresses the contemporary reader's own questions, that is, the significance of the text for the reader's own questions.[3] This chapter aims to explicate the meaning of certain medieval texts (understanding the texts) and then to discuss their significance for questions raised in contemporary philosophy of disability (overstanding the texts). It will be important for understanding what follows to keep this distinction in mind; otherwise, the reader may misinterpret various claims. (Chapter 4 employs a similar methodology by examining different accounts of the image of God and then evaluating whether they can provide a basis for the equal, and intrinsic, moral status of profoundly cognitively disabled human beings.)

Modern Concepts of Person

To be a person, or "a human being in the moral sense," is to be a self-conscious agent. At least, that is what a modern account would stipulate.

Modern and contemporary philosophers disagree on the details of personhood but in general take being a self-conscious and voluntary agent as central. I contend that to posit such a concept of personhood is an expression of ableism when it is taken as the basis for equal membership in the moral community. That is, those who posit it are very likely to discriminate against human beings who are cognitively impeded from self-conscious activities of one sort or another. Why suppose that these concepts of personhood support discrimination against some cognitively disabled human beings? The connection is fairly direct. Assume a modern concept of personhood. Then, assume that personhood is the sole basis on which an entity has intrinsic moral status. Consider a human being that is not a person in this sense. Conclude that such a human being does not have intrinsic moral status. A modern concept of personhood is ableist to the extent that either it is used in an argument to support the conclusion that some human beings do not have intrinsic moral status or it is the basis for treating disabled human beings as morally inferior to non-disabled human beings. (More than this needs to be said in order to establish the conclusion. I give a more extended argument for this conclusion elsewhere.)[4]

I take John Locke as historically significant for such a modern concept of personhood.[5] When Locke considered what a person is, he considered it within the context of moral and legal responsibility. What sort of entity is morally or legally responsible for its actions? Locke's reply is that only an entity that is an "incommunicable consciousness" can be morally and legally responsible.[6] He names this entity a person. This makes some sense. When considering moral or legal responsibility, we ought to suppose that the entity in question is aware of the relevant issues, is aware of one's own deliberating about what to do, is aware of one's doing a particular action, and has chosen to do that particular action.

Kant is well known for distinguishing between persons and things and ascribing intrinsic moral dignity to persons alone.

> Beings whose existence rests not indeed on our will but on nature, if they are non-rational beings, still have only a relative worth, as means, and are therefore called *things*, whereas rational beings are called *persons*, because their nature already marks them out as ends in themselves.[7]

Peter Singer quotes Kant on how non-human animals fit into this ethical framework. "Animals are not self-conscious and are there merely as a means to an end. That is end man." Singer then comments on how this ethical position relates to cognitively impaired human beings, saying:

> Kant's argument for why human beings are ends-in-themselves is that they are autonomous beings, which, in terms of Kantian philosophy,

means that they are capable of reasoning. Note that Kant goes from defending the value of autonomy or self-consciousness to maintaining that "man" is the end. If we really take his argument seriously it means that human beings who are not self-conscious – because perhaps they are so profoundly mentally retarded that they lack self-consciousness or self-awareness – are also merely means to an end, that end being autonomous or self-conscious beings. So the Kantian approach is not going to help those whose objective is to demonstrate that all human beings have superior status to nonhuman animals.[8]

Despite Singer's presentation of Kant, it is important to note that Kant himself conceded that human children have the "seed ofrationality" and should, for practical purposes, be treated as ends in themselves.[9] Still, it is clear from Kant that the expectation of children's future self-consciousness, autonomy, and voluntary choices are the basis for treating children as ends in themselves.

The centrality of conscious reasoning and voluntary choice for personhood is ubiquitous in modern and contemporary discussions of personhood. Consider A.J. Ayer, who says, "it is characteristic of persons in this sense that besides having various physical properties ... they are also credited with various forms of consciousness."[10] Consider Robert Pasnau's use of the term "person" in this modern sense in his book *Thomas Aquinas on Human Nature*. Pasnau discusses modern criticisms of Aquinas on self-knowledge that appeal to the need for one to have a direct awareness of oneself.

> The worry is that Aquinas will be unable to give an account of human beings as persons. Instead of a human person we would have Hume's bundle of experiences; instead of Descartes's *I think* we have Lichtenberg's *It thinks*. ... There is nothing in Aquinas's account to license any sort of direct experiential self-awareness of the self.[11]

Further, while Therese Cory disagrees with Pasnau's claim that for Aquinas, there is no direct experiential self-awareness, we find a similar acknowledgment of modern personhood in Cory's monograph, *Aquinas on Human Self-Knowledge*, in which she has a chapter titled "Self-knowledge and psychological personhood."[12] Further, consider the Protestant theologian Karl Barth, who references modern and premodern notions of personhood in talking about the Christian doctrine of the Trinity – the claim that there is one God and there are three persons who are this God.

> What is called "personality" in the conceptual vocabulary of the 19th century is distinguished from the patristic and medieval *persona* by the addition of the attribute of self-consciousness. This really

complicates the whole issue. One was and is obviously confronted by the choice of either trying to work out the doctrine of the Trinity on the presupposition of the concept of person as thus accentuated or of clinging to the older concept which since the accentuation in usage has become completely obsolete and is now unintelligible outside monastic and a few other studies.[13]

Barth bears witness to a departure from an "older concept" of personhood that is "now unintelligible outside monastic and a few other studies" and to an arrival of a modern trend in thinking of a person as something that is self-conscious. (One may wonder whether Augustine's discussions of self-awareness and the like imply that he has a concept of person that is similar to modern concepts. I strongly doubt this because in his famous discussion of "persona," Augustine says that it is a "generic name" and that what it names can be numbered. There is no mention or use of self-awareness as a condition for persona.)[14]

This preference for self-consciousness as a requirement for personhood as such shows up in expanded form in Mary Anne Warren's five criteria for personhood, all of which she claims are "obvious" and "self-evident."

> I suggest that the traits which are most central to the concept of personhood, or humanity in the moral sense, are, very roughly, the following:
>
> 1 Consciousness (of objects and events external and/or internal to the being), and in particular the capacity to feel pain.
> 2 Reasoning (the *developed* capacity to solve new and relatively complex problems).
> 3 Self-motivated activity (activity which is relatively independent of either genetic or direct external control).
> 4 The capacity to communicate, by whatever means, messages of an indefinite variety of types, that is, not just with an indefinite number of possible contents but on indefinitely many possible topics.
> 5 The presence of self-concepts, and self-awareness, either individual or racial, or both.[15]

Warren applies her criteria for personhood to the case of disabled human beings, saying, "defective human beings, with no appreciable mental capacity, are not and presumably never will be people."[16] I take Warren's analysis of personhood to be morally troubling because it excludes many cognitively disabled human beings from personhood and in turn from having intrinsic moral status. This is ableist at its core.[17]

But suppose someone sympathetic to a modern concept of personhood wondered if the charge of ableism is misguided. One might ask, "Doesn't morality require self-conscious awareness of what one thinks and does? Doesn't morality apply only to self-conscious agents? Why can't we name morally responsible beings by the name 'person'?" My reply is that such a position assumes that intrinsic moral status can only apply to moral agents. Why can't there be moral patients too? That is, beings capable of being morally wronged or harmed whether or not they are also moral agents at some time. (For example, an infant is a moral patient, even if not a moral agent. And, one might suppose, plausibly, that humans can wrong non-human animals and the environment too.) Moreover, why should it be the case that morality construed as exclusive to moral agents alone is the sole context in which we consider personhood? After all, if we look to the history of thinking about personhood, we find that discussion of personhood was not always constrained by considerations of moral and legal responsibility. For over a thousand years, philosophers who were Christians discussed personhood within a different context, namely theological discussion of the Trinity and the Incarnation. The very term "person," from the Latin *persona* rose to philosophical prominence because of Christian theorizing about Jesus of Nazareth, whom they believe is one person with a divine nature and a human nature. They also theorized about personhood in relation to their beliefs that there is one God and there are three persons who are this God.[18]

If modern philosophers must have a name for moral agents, why not stick with "moral agent"? Why add the name "person"? One reason that Locke adopted the name person for the sort of entity that is morally and legally responsible was the Christian belief that there is nobility that comes with being a person, something that is rational or intellectual. (Another reason has to do with personal identity through time in relation to Locke's belief that persons will be resurrected from the dead; that is, the same persons who die will be resurrected.)[19] The association between personhood and dignity is found among scholastic theologians too (and also in Boethius, whom I discuss below). For example, Thomas Aquinas ascribes dignity to human beings because of their being rational and denies that non-rational animals have dignity.[20] Further, Henry of Ghent puts it like this:

> "Person" names something that is simply of dignity in creatures and in the creator. For, it names the feature of [being] incommunicable from its significate ..., which comes from its perfection that it has in itself what cannot be communicated to another .... Moreover, it names this concerning a rational or intellectual nature, each of which is of dignity and nobility.[21]

Note that Henry includes "rational or intellectual nature" in his definition of "person"; as I discuss below, this reflects Boethius's influence on Latin scholastic theologians. Further, Henry claims that to be a person is to be something incommunicable. This is reminiscent of Locke's description of a person: a person is an "incommunicable consciousness."[22] Talk of "incommunicability" is absent from much contemporary discussion of personhood. In its place we find terms like "individual" or "single."[23] This is not a trivial difference of terms. For, when most medieval Christian theologians discussed personhood, they explicitly denied that being an individual or singular and being incommunicable are the same. Duns Scotus, for example, distinguishes something's being communicable by identity, inherence, or division. "Communicable by identity" means that numerically the same thing can be shared among more than one subject (*suppositum*). (Duns Scotus posits that the divine essence is communicable by identity among the divine persons.) "Communicable by inherence" means that an accident, which is a contingent property, can characterize a substance. "Communicable by division" means that a common nature can be multiplied into numerically distinct instances. For example, human nature is divisible such that it can be multiplied into numerically distinct human beings. In contrast to communicability is its negation: incommunicability. Duns Scotus argues that a divine person's personal property (e.g., God the Father's paternity) is incommunicable by identity, inherence, and division; and, that the divine essence is communicable by identity, but not communicable by inherence or division. All this shows that, for example, Duns Scotus distinguishes between singularity and incommunicability in order that "person" is applicable to the kind of cases it was meant to describe, namely how it is that there are three persons who are the same singular God, and that these persons are non-identical with each other on the basis of their incommunicable properties. (This account of "person" is also used in his account of how it is that Jesus is one person with a divine nature and a human nature.)[24] This medieval focus on personhood will be, so I argue, a reason why the medieval accounts are preferable over the modern accounts surveyed above if personhood is the sole basis for intrinsic moral status and the disability-positive perspective is correct.

Early Medieval Concepts of Person

In contrast to modern accounts of personhood, there are Byzantine accounts and Boethian accounts. Later Byzantine accounts of personhood were influenced by Cappadocian theologians like Gregory of Nyssa. The core idea or root intuition among Byzantine accounts is that "hypostasis" or "prosopon" should be understood, in some way, as what names an individual in comparison to a universal or shareable nature, which is named by "ousia" or "phusis." In the 5th–7th centuries

Christian theologians slightly revised the Cappadocian posit because of concerns about the metaphysics of the Incarnation of God the Son. While there are fine-grained details that differentiate these Byzantine theories of the Incarnation,[25] for my purposes what is important is that all of these approaches share something in common: none of these stipulate that hypostasis or prosopon as such require rationality, and all take these terms to refer to what exists in itself or is a complete individual. As Joseph W. Koterski, S.J., puts it, "Even the ancient Greeks, who proverbially had a word for everything, seem not to have had a word for what divine, angelic, and human beings have in common."[26] This is in stark contrast to Boethius, who stipulates that rationality is included in the definition of persona (which Boethius takes to name what prosopon, but not hypostasis, names).

Boethius's definition of a person (*persona*) as "an individual substance of a rational nature" was quite influential in Latin scholastic theology, as is reflected in the quotation from Henry of Ghent above. It will be important to understand that Boethius added "rational" to the definition of "person" and why he did this – especially in the contemporary context of personhood being used as a basis for one's intrinsic moral status.

Boethius discusses persona in the *Treatise against Eutyches and Nestorius*. He reports in the beginning of his treatise that questions were raised about how to understand the union of divine nature and human nature in Jesus Christ. Boethius says that a letter from some Scythian monks to Pope Symmachus (which Boethius heard read aloud) is what prompted him to try to work out for himself what the connection is between nature (*natura*) and person (*persona*).

> But the proper definition of person is a matter of very great perplexity. For if every nature has person, the difference between nature and person is a hard knot to unravel; or if person is not taken as the equivalent of nature but is a term of less scope and range, it is difficult to say to what natures it is may be extended, that is, to what natures the term person may be applied and what natures are dissociate from it. For one thing is clear, namely that nature is a substrate of person, and that person cannot be predicated apart from nature.[27]

Boethius reports the claim that every nature "has person." This claim was shared by Eutychians and Nestorians; one way to put this is that the number of natures is equivalent to the number of persons. This suggests that nature and person have the same extension. (Note that this is a fairly general claim.) But Boethius doubts whether they have the same intension or extension. The next sentence ("if person is not taken as equivalent of nature but is a term of less scope and range ...") suggests the claim that going from the term "nature" to the term "person" is a case of increasing intension. Later he develops a response to this sentence by stipulating which natures are to be associated with person, that is, which natures fall under the extension of the intensional meaning of persona. Boethius concludes this passage by saying what is evident to him is that some, but not all, natures are to be associated with person.

He goes on to distinguish substance and accidents and claims that persona is predicated of substance and not of accidents, "for who can say there is any person of whiteness or blackness or size? It therefore remains that persona is properly predicated of substances."[28] This is a significant claim. Persona is not properly predicated of accidents, for example, qualities (colors) or quantities (size). Further, since he insists that persona is properly predicated of substance and denies that it is properly predicated of accidents, one may wonder whether he allows that persona is predicated of the conjunction of a substance and its accident, for example, an action such as an occurrent thought. But given that he explicitly says that persona is properly predicated of substance to the exclusion of accidents, it is likely that he would deny that persona is properly predicated of the conjunction of a substance characterized by certain accidents.[29] On this reading, persona is not properly predicated of thoughts (whether self-conscious or unconscious) or volitions (whether categorized as actions, passions, qualities, or relations), nor is persona properly predicated of, for example, a substance that is characterized by, for example, an occurrent thought, that is, a thinking substance. A thinking substance goes beyond the scope of persona.

Boethius continues, saying,

> Now from all this it is clear that person cannot be predicated of bodies which have no life (for no one ever says that a stone has a person), nor yet of living things which lack sense (for neither is there any person of a tree), nor finally of that which is bereft of mind and reason (for there is no person of a horse or ox or any other of the animals which dumb and without reason live a life of sense alone), but we say there is a person of a human, we say [there is a person] of God, and we say [there is a person] of an angel.[30]

This is the crucial passage in the treatise where Boethius exclusively associates personhood (*persona*) with rationality. Prior to this passage Boethius stipulated that a reason why the (intensional) meaning of "person" is not equivalent to the (intensional) meaning of (every) 'nature' is that there must be some difference between them. So, in the passage just given, he reports that "no one ever says" there are horse persons, or ox persons, and the like. And, he appeals to what "we say." This shows that he is looking at his examples of when person is associated with a nature.

Boethius continues his investigation into the difference between person and nature by observing that,

> Universals are those which are predicated of individuals, as man, animal, and stone, plank and other things of this kind which are either genera or species; for man is predicated of individual men just as animal is predicated of individual animals, and stone and plank of individual stones and plans. But particulars are those which are never predicated of other things, as Cicero, Plato, ... But in all these things person cannot anywhere be predicated of universals, but only of particulars and individuals; for there is no person of man as animal or a genus; only of Cicero, Plato, or other single individuals are single persons named.[31]

Boethius denies that person is predicated of universals and affirms that it is predicated of "particulars and individuals." Directly after this passage, he gives his definition of a person: a person is an individual substance of a rational nature. This definition evidently shows the difference between nature and person, and so Boethius's initial perplexity is resolved.

However, it is unclear why Boethius felt it necessary to distinguish person and nature by including some natures (rational natures) and excluding others (non-rational natures). He could have found the relevant difference between person and nature by distinguishing, as he and Byzantine theologians do, between universals and particulars, and claiming that a person is an individual substance of a nature. (There are further nuances on the metaphysics of individuality that were debated, but for my purposes, this is sufficient.) While his stipulation makes some sense in itself (i.e., that rational modifies nature in the definition of person), it seems unnecessary for his Christological purposes, especially when we compare his definition with Byzantine Christian theologians' definitions of person (*persona*) (in Greek the terms are "hypostasis" and "prosopon") in the context of Christology or Trinitarian theology.

In what follows I begin discussion of the Byzantine tradition with a contemporary Latin theologian of Boethius, namely John Maxentius, and afterward discuss some Greek theologians (Gregory of Nyssa and Leontius of Byzantium). Contrasting Boethius with a contemporary Latin writer shows that Boethius represents a subgroup in Latin Christian theology in the 6th century. John Maxentius was an influential Scythian monk who adhered to the extant ecumenical councils. Of particular note is the council of Chalcedon that held that Jesus is one person with a divine nature and a human nature. It was of great importance to Catholic Christians (like Maxentius and Boethius) to distinguish person and nature in order to uphold the council and make (some) sense of the mystery of the Incarnation of God the Son. Maxentius wrote a *Dialogue against the Nestorians*. The Nestorians did not distinguish person and nature; they held that Jesus Christ is one human person, and God the Son is a divine person. In a crucial passage he gives his definition of person:

> Person [*persona*] is discerned from nature [*natura*] because person signifies one individual thing of a nature, but nature is known to declare the common material from which many persons are able to subsist. Therefore, every person simultaneously contains a nature, but not every nature equally grasps a person; otherwise, just as there are three persons, so also [there would be] three natures of that holy and ineffable Trinity.[32]

Maxentius takes person to signify what is an individual and nature to signify what is common in individuals. He uses this definition in order to explain to his Nestorian opponent how Christ can be one person yet have two natures: a human nature and the divine nature. The Nestorian opponent denies a difference between nature and person and concludes that if Christ is human, then there is a human person in addition to a divine person. So, by distinguishing nature and person as he does, Maxentius can deny that Christ's human nature is itself a person.

Further, the last sentence above is a *reductio* argument. The absurd (rejected) claim is that the number of divine persons is equivalent to the number of divine natures. Maxentius assumes that the Nestorian agrees with him that there is just one divine nature, even though there are three divine persons. It should be accepted, then, that person and nature are not equivalent and their distinction has to do individuality for person (or what later theologians call incommunicability by identity) and commonality for nature (or what later theologians call communicability by identity in the case of the divine nature, and communicability by division for created natures).

It is important to notice that rational is not included in Maxentius's definition of person.[33] If he supposed that rational should be a part of the definition of person, then he would have included it. But he does not include it. So, it is likely that he does not suppose that rational is a part of the definition of person. Further, there are no passages in Maxentius's writings (of which I am aware) in which he includes rational in his definition of person. So, the burden of proof (it seems to me) is on those who would insist that (i) he assumes that rational is in the definition of person and (ii) he believes that including rational in the definition is not relevant for any of the Christological debates in which he took part.

John Maxentius's definition of person reflects influential Greek-speaking theologians' ways of distinguishing "ousia" and "hypostasis." In Basil of Caesarea's (or Gregory of Nyssa's, the authorship is uncertain) *Letter 38* (c. 369–370 CE), clarification is given on how Christian theologians ought to understand and use the terms "ousia" and "hypostasis."

Those nouns, which are predicated of subjects plural and numerically diverse have a more general meaning, as for example "man." ... Other nouns have a very specific denotation, whereby it is not the common nature that is indicated by the term employed, but rather a limitation to a particular thing, this delimitation implying no participation in the genus so far as the individuality of the object is concerned; for example, "Paul" or "Timothy." For such expressions no longer have reference to the properties common to the nature of the objects, but by setting apart certain delimited objects from the comprehensive term, specify what they are by means of these names.

... This, then, is our statement of the matter; that which is specifically referred to is indicated by the expression "hypostasis." For if you say "man," by the indefiniteness of the term used you have produced in our minds a sort of vague concept, so that, although the nature of the thing is indicated by the noun, yet the thing which subsists in that nature and is specifically indicated by the noun is not made evident to us. But if you say "Paul," you have indicated by the noun the nature subsisting ....

This, then, is subsistence or "hypostasis." It is, however, not the indefinite notion of "ousia," which by reason of the generality of the term employed discloses no "sistence"; it is the conception which, by means of the specific notes that it indicates, restricts and circumscribes in a particular thing what is general and uncircumscribed ....

... [T]ransfer to the divine dogmas that principle of differentiation which you recognize as applying to "ousia" and "hypostasis" in human affairs, you will not go astray. In whatever manner and as whatever thing your mind conceives of the "ousia" of the Father (for it is of no avail to press upon a spiritual thing a definitely prescribed conception, because we are sure that it is beyond all conception), this you will hold for the Son also, and likewise for the Holy Spirit.[34]

In sum, ousia names a common nature, and hypostasis names an individual of some nature – that which subsists. Further, one hypostasis is different from another hypostasis on the basis of unique characteristics (called "idiomata").[35] When these terms are applied to the Trinity, ousia names what is shared by Father, Son, and Holy Spirit, and hypostasis names each separately by reference to their unshared characteristic(s). For my purposes, there are two points to draw from *Letter 38*.

First, the author does not try to differentiate ousia and hypostasis by limiting which specific species (or natures) can be included in the reference of the term "hypostasis." In another text, *To the Greeks: Concerning the Commonality of Concepts*, Gregory of Nyssa uses hypostasis to refer to rational beings and to non-rational beings; he uses it to refer to, for example, God the Father, individual human beings, and to individual horses.[36] This more expansive use of hypostasis was common among

Byzantine theologians. For example, Leontius of Byzantium (a rough contemporary of Boethius) predicates hypostasis of "this horse, this ox, and this man."[37] (John of Damascus even predicates hypostasis of olives, olive trees, and date palms.)[38] Leontius claims that "*hypostasis* does not simply or even primarily signify that which is complete, but that which exists for itself, and secondly that which is complete; while the nature signifies what never exists for itself, but most properly that which is [formally] complete."[39] Given this broad description of hypostasis, Leontius has no problem predicating hypostasis of "this horse, this ox." By contrast, Boethius supposes that he must identify which specific species or natures can be referred to by the term "persona."

Second, the author of *Letter 38* does not distinguish hypostasis and prosopon; there is simply no mention of prosopon. By contrast, Boethius supposes that there must be a difference between hypostasis and prosopon for his theological purposes.[40] Still, we know that in Gregory of Nyssa's *To the Greeks: Concerning the Commonality of Concepts*, he uses prosopon, hypostasis, and ousia. For my purposes there are two observations to make about this text. First, Gregory mentions the difference between rational (*logikos*) natures and non-rational (*alogos*) natures, but this distinction plays no role in how he distinguishes prosopon or hypostasis and ousia. (This is mirrored in John of Damascus's *Institutio Elementaris*.)[41] Second, we know that "prosopon" and "hypostasis" have different Greek etymologies, but it is noteworthy that Gregory uses these terms interchangeably; that is, he uses them as synonyms.[42] Gregory says, for example,

> Therefore it is firmly established for us, rightly and logically, grounded in scientific reasons, that we profess one God, the Creator of the Universe, even if God is contemplated in three *prosopa* or *hypostases*, that of the Father and of the Son and of the Holy Spirit.[43]

(Maximus the Confessor also claims they are equivalent terms and also does not include rationality in his account of hypostasis and prosopon.)[44] Furthermore, this synonymy between hypostasis and prosopon is repeated in all ecumenical councils from the second one in 381 CE to the seventh one in 787 CE.[45]

It is important to recognize that there is evidence of a disagreement about whether rational belongs in the definition of persona in the generation after Boethius. Rusticus the Deacon wrote *Against Acephalos* (553–564 CE) and in it explicitly represented his miaphysite opponent as rejecting his contention that rational should be in the definition of persona. Rusticus claims that "there are many individuals of a nature that are not also persons, for example [individuals] of inanimate natures and irrational natures."[46] By comparison, John Maxentius also wrote a *Response against Acephalos*, but unlike Rusticus, Maxentius does not posit rationality as a requirement for personhood. Rationality is not even mentioned in his discussions of persona. Instead, Maxentius focuses on the difference between common natures and what subsists or is a singular person. For example, he writes, "[I]t is clear that there are two natures in the Son of God after the Incarnation – that is, divinity and humanity – of which and in which the one and singular person [*persona*] of Christ subsists [*subsistit*]."[47] Further, Maxentius gives a *reductio* argument to establish that nature and person are not equivalent. The claim that is to be rejected is that nature and person are equivalent. (That is, if *x* is a person, then *x* is a nature, and, if *x* is a nature, then *x* is a person.) In the following passage Maxentius reports his miaphysite opponent's position and reduces it to absurdity (from an orthodox Catholic point of view).[48]

> If there is no nature without person, how much more is person not able to be without nature. Therefore, there is no nature without person and there is no person without nature; therefore, there are three natures of divinity, not one, because there are three – without a doubt – subsistences or persons, of the Father, of the Son, and of the Holy Spirit. But those who say this [associate with Arians and are known to blaspheme].[49]

Maxentius's way of distinguishing nature and person mirrors the way that the Cappadocians use ousia and hypostasis (and prosopon). It does not reflect Boethius's way of distinguishing these terms to the extent that Boethius stipulates that rational is part of the definition of persona.

All of this suggests that some segment of Latin-speaking theology in the 6th century held that rational belongs in the definition of person (Boethius and his followers, including Rusticus the Deacon) and other segments of Latin-speaking theology did not (e.g., Scythian theologians like John of Maxentius). Why, then, does Boethius feel inclined toward choosing which natures should, and should not, be associated with person? One answer, given above, is that it was his first pass at distinguishing person and nature. But another reason is also significant, and possibly more explanatory of Boethius's proposal to include rational in the definition of person.

Boethius's Latin Roman context suggests an explanation for why he includes rational in his proposed definition of persona and why persona applies only to humans, angels, and God. In Roman Law the term "persona" was used as a synonym for "homo" (human). (While some scholars speculate whether persona was applied to only a subclass of human beings, namely legally free human beings, this is likely not the case.)[50] "Persona" taken as a synonym for "homo" is found in book one of Gaius's *Institutes* (and repeated in Emperor Justinian's *Institutes* and *Digest*).[51] (Gaius was an influential Roman lawyer.) Boethius knew

Gaius's *Institutes*, and so it is a plausible influence on Boethius with regard to the common understanding of "persona" and "homo" as synonyms.[52] Gaius, as quoted by Justinian in Justinian's *Institutes* Chapter 3 "On the Law of Persons," says that:

> [T]he highest division of the rights of persons is that all humans are either free or a slave. Liberty (from which we are called free) is one's natural faculty, which [humans] have of acting, as we please, if not hindered by force or refrained by the law. Slavery is that by which one human is made subject to another according to the law of nations, although contrary to nature.[53]

Roman Civic Law claims that human slaves are persons, because they are human beings, and they are things, because of having no or few rights and no or few obligations.[54] Boethius claimed elsewhere that human beings are "mortal rational animals."[55] Now, if human nature is defined this way, and human nature is associated with personhood, we can begin to understand why Boethius was inclined to associate personhood and rationality. If one of the natures (i.e., human nature) that can be a prerequisite for personhood is a certain rational nature, and if a divine person (God the Son) is also associated with rationality (or maximal rationality, namely omniscience), then for Boethius there is the suggestion that personhood should be associated with rationality. He differentiates person and nature by limiting person to a subclass of natures (the rational ones) and by limiting person to individuals of that subclass of natures. So, it is plausible that Boethius associated personhood and rationality because the examples of persona with which he was familiar were associated with rationality in one way or another.

Boethius's association between person and rationality was influential in Latin philosophy and theology. It is common to find in Latin-speaking scholastic theologians the distinction between an individual that exists in itself (usually named "suppositum") and an individual that exists in itself and is rational (usually named "persona").[56] What is distinctive in comparison with Byzantine theological discussions is the Boethian stipulation of a class of entities called persons that are not only different from universal natures because they are individuals but also because they are rational individuals. And, this class of entities is supposed to be relevant in understanding (at least in part) the Incarnation and the Trinity. Nevertheless, many Latin scholastic theologians recognized that rationality did not do any substantive work in their discussions of persona as such because the details of rationality were not directly relevant to the metaphysics of personhood in the context of discussion of the Trinity and Incarnation. For example, in Duns Scotus's brief narrative of the history of the term "persona", rationality plays a minor role. On this narrative, *persona* begins as a name of theatrical masks of famous human beings, then *persona* is used as the name for an intellectual substance taken as a secondary substance (i.e. a universal or common nature), and lastly *persona* is used as the name for a metaphysically incommunicable suppositum.[57]

It was common among scholastic theologians to accept that the term "rational" had one meaning when referencing God and angels, and another meaning when referencing human beings. Aquinas is representative of this in saying that:

> "Rational" is said in two ways. Sometimes it is taken strictly and properly, according to which "reason" implies a certain shadow of intellectual nature, as Isaac says that reason arises in the shadow of intelligence. It is clear from this that [reason] does not immediately have the truth, but finds [the truth] through investigation by discoursing. And in this way "rational" is a difference of [the genus] animal, and does not belong to God nor to angels. Whenever [rational] is taken commonly for any cognition by a power [*virtute*] that is not impressed in matter, it does apply commonly to God, angels and human beings. Hence even Gregory, calls an angel a rational animal, and Dionysius also says that sensibility and rationality are in angels in a superior way compared to us; and he even includes "rational" among the divine names; and Boethius accepts [rational] in this way.[58]

Aquinas introduces some distinctions in order to identify the sense in which rational is predicated of God, angels, and human beings. First, some rational beings require discursive reasoning in order to gain the truth (true beliefs or knowledge) and others do not. Second, some cognitive powers are "impressed in matter" (i.e., the senses and imagination) and other cognitive powers are not "impressed in matter" (i.e., rational powers (intellect and will)). The commonality between human, angelic, and divine reason is that in each case the rational power is "not impressed in matter." The upshot regarding Boethius's associating personhood and rationality is that it is a way to group together individual entities that have non-material cognitive powers. On the basis of rational or intellectual powers, which are non-material powers, Boethius claims that such entities with these have a higher dignity than irrational individual substances.[59]

One consequence of Boethius's stipulation that persona is not predicated of accidents but rather of an individual rational substance is that debates about the metaphysical details of persona did not occur within the context of philosophy of mind or philosophy of will where various acts (actions, qualities, relations, etc.) were discussed. We do not find debates about whether there can be persons who are unconscious or impeded from making voluntary decisions whether temporarily, for the most part, or always. Instead, we find debates about the metaphysics of individuality or incommunicability. It is typical among Latin scholastics to say that an individual substance that is called a suppositum requires being separate from others and not being a part of something else.[60] Still others argued that a suppositum requires being incommunicable.[61] Details regarding rationality were treated as a separate issue. All that is said about rationality in the context of discussion of personhood is that it implies rational power. The exercising of rational power is not stipulated as a necessary condition for personhood; rather, only the rational power is required. To be a person as such does not imply or require any occurrent rational acts (e.g., thoughts, volitions). It is in other contexts that scholastics claim that rational power implies intellect and will – whether distinct faculties of intellect and will (as for Aquinas and Duns Scotus) or a simple rational soul (as for Ockham) that can cause intellectual acts and volitional acts.[62] Henry of Ghent, for example, claims that all humans are equally rational in the sense that they have specifically the same nature, which entails that each human being is a composite of rational soul and body. Rational *power* is grounded in one's rational soul and not in contingent facts of one's material cognitive organs (e.g., eyes, brain). Further, human beings are more or less rational with regard to their intellectual *acts* because intellectual acts in some way depend on contingent facts of one's material cognitive organs. (I leave aside the details here; let it suffice that for Henry, the intelligible content of most intellectual acts derives from what one has sensed. Sensory impairments have a knock-on effect regarding the content of one's intellectual acts.)[63]

So, a consequence of Boethius's stipulation that a person is a person whether or not they have occurrent or dispositional rational acts is that in Latin scholastic circles personhood is compatible with a wide range of cognitive or volitional activity and inactivity. For, personhood does not depend on rational activity (understood as occurrent acts or as habits) but rather on the metaphysics of individual rational substances.

Comparing and Evaluating Medieval and Modern Concepts of Person

Thus far I have surveyed two traditions within early medieval theology regarding personhood, namely a Byzantine tradition and a Boethian tradition. On the Boethian account, persona as such requires rationality (taken as rational power). On a Byzantine account, persona or hypostasis or prosopon as such does not require rationality in any sense. On both traditions, persona (or hypostasis or prosopon) requires subsistence or being an individual or what exists in itself. Having distinguished these branches of early medieval accounts of personhood, and surveyed some modern accounts of personhood, we can evaluate them by using a disability-positive criterion.

Which of these accounts, the modern ones that I've referenced or the medieval ones, is more supportive of a disability-positive perspective?

Before answering this question, it should be made clear what a disability-positive perspective is. A disability-positive perspective regarding morality holds that disabled human beings have as much moral status as any other non-disabled human beings. It rejects the claim that morality should come in degrees among human beings, according to which the most morally significant human beings are entities associated with higher-order conscious activity and volitions, and the less morally significant human beings are associated with lower-order cognitive activity.[64] (See Chapter 8 for a discussion of differing scholastic theories of sensory, imaginative, and intellectual cognitions.) In the philosophy of disability there is a parallel debate whether disabilities or impairments as such make a bad-difference, mere-difference, or good-difference to one's well-being.[65] Although it may be tempting to say that a disability-positive perspective with regard to morality must endorse either the mere-difference or the good-difference position, this is not necessary. One can have a disability-positive perspective regarding morality and not yet be decided on the general question whether all disabilities make a mere-difference, bad-difference, or good-difference to one's overall well-being. After all, one might be of the mind that not all disabilities or impairments are the same such that some of them might make a bad-difference (or even a horrendous-difference),[66] others a mere-difference, and others a good-difference to one's well-being. All of these views on difference-making to well-being are consistent with upholding the claim that all human beings have equal intrinsic moral status.

Now we can compare the significance of these modern and medieval concepts of personhood in relation to a disability-positive perspective regarding morality. Assume that personhood is the basis on which one has equal intrinsic moral status with others. A modern concept of personhood (at least, the ones I'm considering) implies that human beings who do not have occurrent self-conscious cognitions and volitions do not count as persons. But human beings who have occurrent self-conscious cognitions and volitions count as persons. Consequently, (1) if personhood is the basis on which one has equal and intrinsic moral status and personhood is modern (as understood above), then human beings who are modern-persons have a higher moral status than human beings who are not modern-persons.

On the Boethian account, a human being is a person just in the case he or she is an individual substance of a rational nature. Personhood as such does not require any rational activities (accidents, i.e., actions, qualities, etc.); on this view, human beings with, or without, occurrent self-conscious cognitions and volitions are persons.[67] Individual human beings who do not have occurrent self-conscious cognitions and volitions are persons because each is an individual that is a composite of a human substantial form and body. Moreover, a very common medieval position, including Boethius and most scholastic philosophers and theologians, is that human rational power is grounded in one's immaterial substantial form, and not in a material organ (e.g., the brain).[68] All human beings are Boethian-persons (setting aside complications about the Incarnation). Consequently, (2) if personhood is the basis on which one has equal intrinsic moral status and personhood is Boethian, then all human beings have equal intrinsic moral status.

On a Byzantine account the requirements for personhood are that one is an individual of some nature. (The qualification "of some nature" excludes there being an individual that fails to be some *kind* or *species*. Admittedly, there are fine-grained differences among various Byzantine theologians on how to understand being an individual, but for my purposes these details do not make a relevant difference here.) Given this account, all individual human beings are Byzantine-persons (again, setting aside complications about the Incarnation). Consequently, (3) if personhood is the basis on which one has equal intrinsic moral status and personhood is Byzantine, then all human beings have equal intrinsic moral status.

Further, let the following conditional be the disability-positive criterion by which to evaluate claims (1)–(3): (4) if a definition of person claims or entails that all individual human beings, including disabled human beings, have equal intrinsic moral status, then that position is to be preferred over definitions that exclude any disabled human beings from having equal intrinsic moral status. Given (4) it is evident that the Byzantine and Boethian accounts of personhood are preferable over the modern views that I surveyed. Consequently, (5) *if* personhood gives one equal and intrinsic moral status and the disability-positive perspective is correct, *then* the Byzantine or Boethian accounts of personhood are preferable over the modern accounts that I have surveyed.

Having compared the Byzantine and Boethian accounts of personhood with the modern accounts surveyed, it is informative to ask: which is friendlier to a disability-positive perspective, the Byzantine account or the Boethian account? Recall that a significant difference between these accounts of personhood is rationality: the Byzantine account does not require rationality, but the Boethian account does.

For Boethius, persona requires a rational nature. Further, according to his metaphysics (and many others, including Thomas Aquinas's), rational power is an immaterial cognitive power.[69] This metaphysical claim is a part of scholastic hylomorphism, according to which an individual human being is a composite of an immaterial substantial form (or forms)[70] and matter. (I am speaking roughly here; for my purposes the fine-grained details don't make a difference.) Boethius's account of personhood plus the claim that rational power is immaterial are consistent with a human being having an unexercised rational power. For example, Aquinas (along with many others) holds that in this life, for human beings to exercise their rational power depends on, and is consequent to, exercising their external cognitive powers (e.g., visual power, auditory power) and internal sensory powers (e.g., imagination). External sensory powers require material organs (e.g., eyes, ears), and internal sensory powers (e.g., imagination) also require material organs (i.e., the brain).[71] This is a broadly Aristotelian understanding of the prerequisites for rational activity. A human being obtains information through sensory experiences of material objects and then abstracts from this information so as to have universal concepts applicable to what was sensed. Given all of this, even if a human being were to lose the use of their sensory organs, or lose the use of parts of their brain, or even lose a sensory organ (or organs) altogether, or lose parts of one's brain, it would remain the case that such a human being has (unexercised) rational power. For, rational power is grounded in one's immaterial substantial form and is not grounded in a material organ (e.g., one's brain).

Given the metaphysical distinction between immaterial soul and human body, all human beings are Boethian-persons (again, setting aside the Incarnation) because all have rational power that is grounded in their rational soul and not in any material organs. But what if someone had reason(s) to reject this metaphysical account of rational power? Suppose one is a materialist about human beings; that is, a human being is entirely a material being and has no immaterial parts or immaterial properties. On such a view, a human being could lack rational power if they were missing relevant (material) parts of their brain – assuming that rational power is grounded in parts of one's brain.[72] If one were a materialist about human beings, and one adopted Boethius's definition of person, then one would be open to the possibility that some human beings (namely ones who lack relevant parts of their brain) are not Boethian-persons. Given Boethius's account of personhood, and a materialist metaphysics of human beings, it would follow that some human beings are Boethian-persons and some human beings are not Boethian-persons. So, the conjunction of Boethius's definition of person and the stipulation that rational power itself does not require a material organ implies that all human beings (setting aside the Incarnation) are Boethian-persons. But, the conjunction of Boethius's definition of person plus a materialist metaphysical framework for human beings implies that some human beings are Boethian-persons, and some are not Boethian-persons. These two conjunctions show that Boethius's definition by itself does not secure that all human beings are Boethian-persons. For, this definition is consistent with all human beings counting as Boethian-persons, and it is consistent with some human beings counting as Boethian-persons and some human beings not counting as Boethian-persons.

While Byzantine theologians have much to say about human souls and organic bodies, their discussion of hypostasis, prosopon, and ousia does not depend on these details. For, their way of distinguishing these terms is more general because hypostasis and prosopon are not limited to some natures and excluded from other natures. Hypostasis (and prosopon) names what is an individual of some nature, and ousia names what is common in individuals. Given that this account does not include rationality (*logikos*) as a requirement for hypostasis or prosopon, the question about whether one has a certain kind of (cognitive) power and whether one exercises that power does not directly arise from this account of hypostasis and prosopon. Of course, Byzantine theologians believed that human beings consist of an immaterial soul and human organic body.[73] But given the generality of the Byzantine account of hypostasis or prosopon, the details about human beings are external to personhood as such. Consequently, the Byzantine account by itself implies that all human beings (again, setting aside complications regarding the Incarnation) are Byzantine-persons (i.e., hypostasis or prosopon) – assuming that all human beings are individuals. (Byzantine theologians had different metaphysical analyses of individuality – but all conceded that there are individuals.) The conjunction of a materialist metaphysics of human beings (assuming that there are individual human beings) and the Byzantine account of hypostasis and prosopon also implies that all human beings are Byzantine-persons (setting aside complications regarding the incarnation of God the Son). Likewise, the conjunction of a hylomorphic account of human beings plus the Byzantine account of hypostasis implies that all human beings are Byzantine-persons.

By comparing the Byzantine account and the Boethian account in this way, we have reason to suppose that the Byzantine account is even friendlier to a disability-positive perspective than the Boethian account. For, the requirements for personhood are fewer (and easier) to satisfy on the Byzantine account compared to the Boethian account. In light of this comparison, we can rank these different accounts of personhood according to a disability-positive perspective. The modern accounts surveyed here are the least friendly, the Boethian account is friendlier, and the Byzantine account is the friendliest of these three.

Still, if one were to base moral status on a Byzantine account of personhood, then it would likely be thought to be too inclusive. With that concern in mind, one might suppose that the modern project of basing moral status and equality on some general account of personhood is a dead-end. However, if one insists on personhood, then it would be better to go with a medieval account of personhood (Byzantine or Boethian) so as to avoid ableist assumptions about which human beings have moral status and equality and which do not. The worry about the Byzantine account being too inclusive might begin to be addressed by stipulating that when the Byzantine account is used to refer to, for example, human beings or certain other animal species, then it is not too inclusive. But then another worry arises: why are these species picked out and not others? If they are selected on the basis of higher-order cognitive functioning, then again, we have discrimination against the severely cognitively disabled.[74]

Conclusion

By comparing medieval and modern concepts of personhood, we become aware of the fact that personhood is no innocent or self-evident concept and that whatever it is, it can be used as an explanans for different explananda. For Byzantine Christian theologians and Latin medieval Christian theologians, personhood is an explanans for the miracle of the Incarnation, in addition to the mystery of the Trinity. For modern philosophers like John Locke, personhood is the name for who counts as a moral agent. Some philosophers use personhood in ethics in order to establish who has intrinsic and equal moral status and who does not. This consideration of personhood also has played a role in normative debates in the philosophy of disability. Some philosophers use personhood in order to argue that some human beings, namely severely cognitively impaired human beings, do not have intrinsic moral status or membership in the moral community. Elsewhere I have argued that this use of personhood is a failure. But here I have argued that if one is going to use personhood for this role in normative ethical theorizing, and if one affirms a disability-positive perspective (which I do), then one is better off using a medieval concept of personhood (whether Byzantine or Boethian).

Still, one might have doubts. One concern is whether personhood should be the basis for moral status and equality. Another concern is whether one is open to endorsing a hylomorphic account of human beings (and living beings in general). If one finds hylomorphism, in general, to be less plausible than other general theories (e.g., materialism), then Boethius's account of personhood (i.e., an individual substance of a rational nature) would not be believed to refer to all human beings. Given materialism about human beings, one may doubt whether certain human beings have rational powers if they, for example, lack significant physical parts of their brain that are (believed to be) directly relevant to self-consciousness, abstract reasoning, and decision making. So, given materialism about human beings, Boethius's persona would not be supportive of a disability-positive perspective. But given hylomorphism, Boethius's concept of personhood is supportive of a disability-positive perspective. By contrast, a Byzantine account of personhood is supportive of a disability-positive perspective whether one endorses a materialist account of human beings or a hylomorphic account of human beings. So, the disability-positive advocate may prefer the Byzantine over the Boethian account of personhood because it does not require any debate about the rationality of a particular human being. In Chapter 6 Miguel Romero discusses some debates about the rationality of the Amerindians among 16th century Christian theologians within the context of Spanish colonialism. The stakes were extremely high in these debates. These debates suggest that if we take rationality to be required for a human being's intrinsic moral status, then we may be taking high-stakes moral risks. If one gets it wrong in theorizing about rationality, then there might be (and historically there *were*) profound and extensive moral harm for those deemed – and treated as – non-rational. It may be morally safer to take the Byzantine route over the Boethian route in order to identify the moral community, assuming that one takes personhood as the basis for intrinsic moral status. Of course, if one goes the Byzantine route, then one has no immediate way to distinguish which individuals have equal and intrinsic moral status and which individuals do not. This may be reason, then, to worry whether personhood by itself ought to do the substantive ethical work that some modern and contemporary moral philosophers have assigned to it.

Notes

1 See Eva Feder Kittay, "Deadly Medicine: Project T4, Mental Disability, and Racism," 715–741.
2 On Greek "scholasticism," see Brian Daley, "Boethius' Theological Tracts and Early Byzantine Scholasticism," *Mediaeval Studies* 46 (1984) 158–191; on the Cappadocian influence, see Jean-Claude Larchet, "Hypostasis, Person, and Individual according to St. Maximus the Confessor, with Reference to the Cappadocians and St. John of Damascus," 47–67. Also, see note 45 for references to the ecumenical councils. Also, for discussion of the Cappadocians in general, see R.P.C. Hanson, *The Search for the Christian Doctrine of God: The Arian Controversy, 318–381*, 676–737; and Lewis Ayres, *Nicaea and Its Legacy: An Approach to Fourth-Century Trinitarian Theology*.
3 See Kevin J. Vanhoozer, *The Bible, The Reader, and the Morality of Literary Knowledge: Is There a Meaning in This Text?*, 401–403.
4 Scott M. Williams, "When Personhood Goes Wrong in Ethics and Philosophical Theology: Disability, Ableism and (Modern) Personhood," 264–290.
5 Cf. Antonia Lolordo, "Persons in Seventeenth- and Eighteenth-Century British Philosophy," 160–166, especially 165, where Lolordo reports that Locke excludes "Children, Fooles and Mad-men" from personhood.
6 John Locke, *An Essay Concerning Human Understanding*, 344.
7 Immanuel Kant, *Groundwork of the Metaphysics of Morals*, 40.
8 Peter Singer, "Speciesism and Moral Status," 337.
9 Immanuel Kant, *The Metaphysics of Morals*, 70–71. For more on Kant, cf. Udo Thiel, "The Concept of a Person in Eighteenth-Century German Philosophy: Leibniz-Wolff-Kant," 213–231; Owen Ware, "The Concept of Persons in Kant and Fichte," 232–242.
10 Alfred J. Ayer, *The Concept of a Person*, 82.
11 Robert Pasnau, *Thomas Aquinas on Human Nature*, 349.
12 Therese Cory, *Aquinas on Human Self-Knowledge*, 199–214.
13 Karl Barth, *Church Dogmatics*, vol. I.1, 357.
14 Cf. Augustine, *De Trinitate*, 7, 4, 7–8, 255–259.
15 Mary Anne Warren, "On the Moral and Legal Status of Abortion," 437–438.
16 Ibid., 438.
17 For my response to Warren's argument, see Scott M. Williams, "When Personhood Goes Wrong in Ethics and Philosophical Theology: Disability, Ableism and (Modern) Personhood," 264–290.

18 See Scott M. Williams, "Persons in Patristic and Medieval Christian Theology," 52–84.
19 Cf. Antonia Lolordo, "Persons in Seventeenth- and Eighteenth-Century British Philosophy," 154–156, 160–166.
20 Cf. Thomas Aquinas, *ST* 3, 4, 1, co.
21 Henry of Ghent, *SQO* 53.1, 6, ll. 31–37.
22 Cf. John Locke, *An Essay Concerning Human Understanding*, 344.
23 P.F. Strawson, *Individuals*, 101–102.
24 For a discussion of the metaphysics of "incommunicability," see Richard Cross, *Duns Scotus on God*, 158–163.
25 For an extensive discussion, see Benjamin Gleede, *The Development of the Term 'Enhypostastos' from Origen to John of Damascus*.
26 Cf. Joseph W. Koterski, SJ, "Boethius and the Theological Origins of the Concept of Person," 205.
27 Boethius, *A Treatise against Eutyches and Nestorius*, 83.
28 Ibid., 85.
29 Ibid., 83.
30 Ibid., 85.
31 Ibid.
32 John Maxentius, *Dialogue of John Maxentius, Servant of God, against the Nestorians*, 69:

> Discernitur ergo a natura persona, quia persona unam rem indiuiduam naturae significat; natura uero communem cognoscitur declarare materiem, ex qua plurimae possent personae subsistere. Quapropter omnis quidem persona simul naturam continet, non autem omnis natura personam aeque complectitur; alioquin, sicut tres persona, ita et tres naturas sanctae et ineffabilis illius trinitatis ....

33 Cf. Henry Chadwick, *Boethius*, 187.
34 Basil of Caesarea, *Letter 38*, 197–205.
35 See Basil of Caesarea, *Letter 214*, 234; *Letter 236*, 400, 402.
36 Gregory of Nyssa, *Ad Graecos*, 29, ll. 11–20.
37 Leontius of Byzantium, "Epilyseis," 276, ll. 15–16.
38 John of Damascus, *Institutio Elementaris*, ch. 7. Thanks to Beau Branson for this reference. Also, cf. Joseph W. Koterski, SJ, "Boethius and the Theological Origins of the Concept of Person," 215.
39 Leontius of Byzantium, "Epilyseis," 309.
40 Boethius, *A Treatise against Eutyches and Nestorius*, 88–90.
41 Cf. Gregory of Nyssa, "To the Greeks: Concerning the Commonality of Concepts," 388–389.
42 Ibid. Also, cf. Lucian Turcescu, "'Person' versus 'Individual', and Other Modern Misreadings of Gregory of Nyssa," 533–534.
43 Ibid., 378.
44 For relevant passages and references, see Jean-Claude Larchet, "Hypostasis, Person, and Individual according to St. Maximus the Confessor, with Reference to the Cappadocians and St. John of Damascus," 47–51.
45 Cf. Norman Tanner, *Decrees of the Ecumenical Councils*, 27 ll. 35–37, 54, ll. 11–13, 55, ll. 8–11, 58 ll. 30–31, 86 l. 39, 114 ll. 6–8, 116 ll. 6–7, ll. 16–19, 128 l. 2. This synonymy appears in the 2nd through 6th ecumenical councils and is entailed by the 7th ecumenical council insofar as it endorses the previous six councils.
46 Rusticus the Deacon, *Contra Acephalos*, 39 ll. 1216–1217.
47 John Maxentius, *Responsio Contra Acephalos*, 44 ll. 23–26.

48 I discuss miaphysite metaphysics of the incarnation in my "Persons in Patristic and Medieval Christian Theology," 61–66.
49 John Maxentius, *Responsio Contra Acephalos*, 44 ll. 29–35.
50 Cf. Fritz Schulz, *Classical Roman Law*, 71–73. Also, W.W. Buckland, *The Roman Law of Slavery: The Condition of the Slave in Private Law from Augustus to Justinian*, 1–6.
51 Cf. Gaius, *Institutiones*, 1, 3, 9, 3: "Et quidem summa diuisio de iure personarum haec est, quod omnes homines aut liberi sunt aut servi." Also, cf. Justinian, *Corpus Iuris Civilis: Iustiniani, Institutiones*, 4; Justinian, *Corpus Iuris Civilis: Iustiniani, Digesta*, 35.
52 Boethius discusses Gaius's *Institutes* book one in, "*In Ciceronis Topica*," 89–90. The Latin text is in *Patrologia Latina* vol. 64, 1094–1095.
53 Justinian, *Institutes*, Tit. 3 p. 2. The first sentence from this quotation is also found in Justinian's *Digest*; the section heading for this sentence in the *Digest* is "on the status of humans" (*de statu hominum*).
54 Cf. W.W. Buckland, *The Roman Law of Slavery*, 1–3.
55 Cf. Boethius, "The Consolation of Philosophy," 169, ll. 35–38; also, Boethius, "*In Ciceronis Topica*," 91.
56 Cf. Timothy Pawl, *In Defence of Conciliar Christology*, 30–34.
57 Cf. Duns Scotus, *Reportata* 1, 25, 1, nn. 4–6, 131.
58 Thomas Aquinas, *In Sent.* 1, 25, 1 a 1, ad 4.
59 Boethius, "A Treatise against Eutyches and Nestorius," 91.
60 For discussion, cf. Eleonore Stump, *Aquinas*, 407–410; Richard Cross, *The Metaphysics of the Incarnation*, 246–256.
61 Cf. Richard Cross, *Duns Scotus on God*, 158–163.
62 Cf. William of Ockham, *Reportatio* 2, 20, 441–442.
63 Henry of Ghent, *SQO* 2.5, 228–233.
64 Cf. Jeff McMahan, "Cognitive Disability and Cognitive Enhancement," 345–367, and, "Radical Cognitive Limitations," 240–259. Also, Peter Singer, "Speciesism and Moral Status," 338ff.
65 Elizabeth Barnes casts this in terms of 'well-being.' Cf. Elizabeth Barnes, "Disability, Minority, and Difference," 337–355.
66 Cf. Scott M. Williams, "Horrendous-Difference Disabilities, Resurrected Saints, and the Beatific Vision: A Theodicy," 1–13.
67 Richard Cross discusses this with regard to Duns Scotus. Cf. Richard Cross, "Duns Scotus on Disability: Teleology, Divine Willing, and Pure Nature," 79.
68 For a discussion of medieval theories of the soul's faculties, see Dag Nikolaus Hasse, "The Soul's Faculties," 305–319.
69 See John Marenbon, *Boethius (Great Medieval Thinkers)*, 60; Marenbon references Boethius, *De Differentiis Topicis*, 1196D. For a wide-ranging discussion of soul (as immaterial) and body, cf. John Haldane, "Soul and Body," 293–304 (Boethius is mentioned at 296). For a wide-ranging discussion of medieval discussion of the intellect as immaterial, see Deborah Black, "The Nature of the Intellect," 320–333. Boethius writes of the soul leaving "its earthly prison," in *The Consolation of Philosophy*, 220 ll. 80–86.
70 For a discussion of the debate about the number of substantial forms in human beings, cf. Marilyn McCord Adams, *Some Later Medieval Theories of the Eucharist: Thomas Aquinas, Giles of Rome, Duns Scotus, and William Ockham*, 4–30.
71 See Robert Pasnau, *Thomas Aquinas on Human Nature*, 284ff. Also, see Richard Cross, *Duns Scotus's Theory of Cognition*, 81–101.
72 For a discussion that raises concerns about potentiality and actuality regarding rational power, see Hans S. Reinders, *Receiving the Gift of Friendship*, 91–115.
73 See, for example, Gregory of Nyssa, *On the Soul and the Resurrection*, 37–48.

74 For a contemporary discussion of this worry, see Eva Feder Kittay, "At the Margins of Moral Personhood," 100–131; Eva Feder Kittay, "The Personal Is Philosophical Is Political: A Philosopher and Mother of a Cognitively Disabled Persons Sends Notes from the Battlefield," 393–412; Eva Feder Kittay, "Deadly Medicine: Project T4, Mental Disability, and Racism," 715–741. For a discussion of Christianity and morality, see Terence Irwin, *The Development of Ethics: A Historical and Critical Study, Volume 1: From Socrates to the Reformation*, 360–396.

References

Primary Sources

Aquinas, Thomas. *In Sententia*. Edited by Enrique Alarcón. <http://www.corpusthomisticum.org/iopera.html>

——— *Summa Theologiae*. Edited by Enrique Alarcón. <http://www.corpusthomisticum.org/iopera.html>

Augustine. *De Trinitate Libri XV*. Edited by W.J. Mountain and Fr. Glorie. Turnhout: Brepols, 1968.

Basil of Caesarea. "Letter 38," in *Saint Basil: The Letters (Loeb Classical Library) Volume 1*. Translated by Roy J. Deferrari. Cambridge, MA: Harvard University Press, 1961: 197–226.

——— "Letter 214," "Letter 236," in *Saint Basil: The Letters (Loeb Classical Library) Volume 3*. Translated by Roy J. Deferrari. Cambridge, MA: Harvard University Press, 1962: 226–236, 386–404.

Boethius. "In Ciceronis Topica," and "De Differentiis Topicis." In *Patrologia Latina* vol. 64. Edited by J.-P. Migne. Paris, 1891.

——— "A Treatise against Eutyches and Nestorius." In *The Theological Tractates*. Edited by G.P. Goold; Translated by H.F. Stewart, E.K. Rand, and S.J. Tester. Cambridge, MA: Harvard University Press, 1973: 72–129.

——— "The Consolation of Philosophy." In *The Theological Tractates*. Edited by G.P. Goold; Translated by S.J. Tester. Cambridge, MA: Harvard University Press, 1973: 130–435.

——— *In Ciceronis Topica*. Translated by Eleonore Stump. Ithaca: Cornell University Press, 1988.

Duns Scotus, John. *Reportata Parisiensia*, vol. 11.1. Edited by L. Wadding. Lyon, 1639. Reprinted by Georg Olms in *Johannes Duns Scotus: Opera Omnia XI.I*. Hildesheim, 1969.

Gaius. *Institutiones*. Edited by E. Seckel and B. Kvebler. Stuttgart: B.G. Teubner, 1968.

Gregory of Nyssa. "Ad Graecos ex communibus notionibus." In *Gregorii Nysseni opera*, vol. 3.1. Edited by F. Mueller. Leiden: Brill, 1958: 19–33.

——— *On the Soul and Resurrection*. Translated by Catharine P. Roth. Crestwood, NY: St. Vladimir's Seminary Press, 1993.

——— "To the Greeks: Concerning the Commonality of Concepts." In Daniel F. Stramara, Jr. "Gregory of Nyssa, Ad Graecos "How It Is that We Say There Are Three Persons in the Divinity but Do Not Say There Are Three Gods," *The Greek Orthodox Theological Review* 41:4 (1996) 375–391.

Henry of Ghent. *Summa (Quaestiones ordinariae) art. I-V*. Edited by G.A. Wilson. Leuven: Leuven University Press, 2005.

―――― Summa (Quaestiones ordinariae) art. LIII-LV. Edited by Gordon A. Wilson and Girard J. Etzkorn. Leuven: Leuven University Press, 2014.

John of Damascus. "Institutio Elementaris." In *Die Schriften des Johannes von Damaskos, vol. 1 [Patristische Texte und Studien 7]*. Edited by P.B. Kotter. Berlin: De Gruyter, 1969: 20–26.

Justinian. *Corpus Iuris Civilis: Iustiniani, Institutiones; Iustiniani, Digesta*, vol. 1. Edited by Paulus Krueger and Theodorus Mommsen. Dublin: Apud Weidmannos, 1966.

Kant, Immanuel. *The Metaphysics of Morals*. Edited by Lara Denis. Cambridge: Cambridge University Press, 2017.

Leontius of Byzantium. "Epilyseis." In *Leontius of Byzantium: Theological Writings*. Edited and translated by Brian Daley, SJ. Oxford: Oxford University Press, 2017: 270–335.

Locke, John. *An Essay Concerning Human Understanding*. Edited by Peter H. Nidditch. Oxford: Clarendon Press, 1979.

Maxentius, John. *Dialogue of John Maxentius, Servant of God, against the Nestorians*. Edited by Fr. Glorie. Turnhout: Brepols, 1978.

Rusticus the Deacon. *Rusitici Diaconi Contra Acephalos*. Edited by Sara Petri. Turnhout: Brepols, 2013.

Tanner, Norman. *Decrees of the Ecumenical Councils, Volume One: Nicaea I to Lateran V*. Washington, DC: Georgetown University Press, 1990.

William of Ockham. *Quaestiones in Librum Secundum Sententiarum (Reportatio)*. Edited by Gideon Gal and Rega Wood. St. Bonaventure, NY: Franciscan Institute Publishing, 1981.

Secondary Sources

Adams, Marilyn McCord. *Some Later Medieval Theories of the Eucharist: Thomas Aquinas, Giles of Rome, Duns Scotus, and William Ockham*. Oxford: Oxford University Press, 2012.

Ayer, Alfred J. *The Concept of a Person*. New York: St. Martin's, 1963.

Ayres, Lewis. *Nicaea and Its Legacy: An Approach to Fourth-Century Trinitarian Theology*. Oxford: Oxford University Press, 2006.

Barnes, Elizabeth. "Disability, Minority, and Difference," *Journal of Applied Philosophy* 26:4 (2009) 337–355.

Barth, Karl. *Church Dogmatics: The Doctrine of the Word of God*, vol. I.1. Edited by G.W. Bromiley and T.F. Torrance. London: T&T Clark, 2004.

Black, Deborah L. "The Nature of the Intellect." In *The Cambridge History of Medieval Philosophy*, Vol. 1 Revised Edition. Edited by Robert Pasnau and Christina van Dyke. Cambridge: Cambridge University Press, 2014: 320–333.

Buckland, William W. *The Roman Law of Slavery: The Condition of the Slave in Private Law from Augustus to Justinian*. Cambridge: Cambridge University Press, 1970.

Chadwick, Henry. *Boethius: The Consolations of Music, Logic, Theology, and Philosophy*. Oxford: Clarendon Press, 1983.

Cory, Therese Scarpelli. *Aquinas on Human Self-Knowledge*. Cambridge: Cambridge University Press, 2015.

Cross, Richard. *The Metaphysics of the Incarnation: From Thomas Aquinas to Duns Scotus*. Oxford: Oxford University Press, 1999.

——— *Duns Scotus on God*. Burlington, VT: Ashgate, 2005.

——— *Duns Scotus's Theory of Cognition*. Oxford: Oxford University Press, 2014.

——— "Duns Scotus on Disability: Teleology, Divine Willing, and Pure Nature," *Theological Studies* 78:1 (2017) 72–95.

Daley, Brian E.S.J. "Boethius' Theological Tracts and Early Byzantine Scholasticism," *Mediaeval Studies* 46 (1984) 158–191.

Gleede, Benjamin. *The Development of the Term "Enhupostatos" from Origen to John of Damascus*. Leiden: Brill, 2012.

Haldane, John. "Soul and Body." In *The Cambridge History of Medieval Philosophy, Volume 1, Revised Edition*. Edited by Robert Pasnau and Christina van Dyke. Cambridge: Cambridge University Press, 2014: 293–304.

Hanson, Richard P.C. *The Search for the Christian God: The Arian Controversy, 318–381*. Grand Rapids, MI: Baker Academic, 2007.

Irwin, Terence. *The Development of Ethics: A Historical and Critical Study*, 3 volumes. Oxford: Oxford University Press, 2011.

Kittay, Eva Feder. "At the Margins of Moral Personhood," *Ethics* 116.1 (2005) 100–131.

——— "The Personal Is Philosophical Is Political: A Philosophers Sends Notes from the Battlefield." In *Cognitive Disability and Its Challenge to Moral Philosophy*. Edited by Eva Feder Kittay and Licia Carlson. Oxford: Wiley-Blackwell, 2010: 393–413.

——— "Deadly Medicine: Project T4, Mental Disability, and Racism," *Res Philosophica* 93.4 (2016) 715–741.

Koterski, Joseph W.S.J, "Boethius and the Theological Origins of the Concept of Person," *American Catholic Philosophical Quarterly*, 78.2 (2004) 203–224.

Larchet, Jean-Claude. "Hypostasis, person, and individual according to St. Maximus the Confessor, with reference to the Cappadocians and St. John of Damascus." In *Personhood in the Byzantine Christian Tradition*. Edited by Alexis Torrance and Symeon Paschalidis. London: Routledge, 2018: 47–67.

Lolordo, Antonia. "Persons in Seventeenth- and Eighteenth-Century British Philosophy." In *Persons: A History (Oxford Philosophical Concepts)*. Edited by Antonia Lolordo. Oxford: Oxford University Press, 2019: 154–181.

Marenbon, John. *Boethius (Great Medieval Thinkers)*. Oxford: Oxford University Press, 2003.

McMahan, Jeff. "Radical Cognitive Limitations." In *Disability and Disadvantage*. Edited by Kimberley Brownlee and Adam Cureton. Oxford: Oxford University Press, 2009: 240–259.

——— "Cognitive Disability and Cognitive Enhancement." In *Cognitive Disability and Its Challenge to Moral Philosophy*. Edited by Eva Feder Kittay and Licia Carlson. Oxford: Wiley-Blackwell, 2010: 345–367.

Pasnau, Robert. *Thomas Aquinas on Human Nature*. Cambridge: Cambridge University Press, 2002.

Pawl, Timothy. *In Defence of Conciliar Christology*. Oxford: Oxford University Press, 2016.

Reinders, Hans S. *Receiving the Gift of Friendship: Profound Disability, Theological Anthropology, and Ethics*. Grand Rapids, MI: Eerdmans, 2008.

Schulz, Fritz. *Classical Roman Law*. Oxford: Clarendon Press, 1951.

Singer, Peter. "Speciesism and Moral Status." In *Cognitive Disability and Its Challenge to Moral Philosophy*. Edited by Eva Feder Kittay and Licia Carlson. Oxford: Wiley-Blackwell, 2010: 331–344.

Strawson, Peter F. *Individuals*. London: Methuen, 1959.

Stump, Eleonore. *Aquinas (Arguments of the Philosophers)*. Oxford: Routledge, 2005.

Thiel, Udo. "The Concept of a Person in Eighteenth-Century German Philosophy: Leibniz-Wolff-Kant." In *Persons: A History (Oxford Philosophical Concepts)*. Edited by Antonia Lolordo. Oxford: Oxford University Press, 2019: 187–231.

Turcescu, Lucian. "'Person' versus 'Individual', and Other Modern Misreadings of Gregory of Nyssa," *Modern Theology* 18:4 (2002) 527–539.

Vanhoozer, Kevin J. *The Bible, The Reader, and the Morality of Literary Knowledge: Is There a Meaning in This Text?* Grand Rapids, MI: Zondervan, 1998.

Ware, Owen. "The Concept of Persons in Kant and Fichte." In *Persons: A History (Oxford Philosophical Concepts)*. Edited by Antonia Lolordo. Oxford: Oxford University Press, 2019: 232–259.

Williams, Scott M. "Horrendous-Difference Disabilities, Resurrected Saints, and the Beatific Vision: A Theodicy," *Religions* 9:52 (2018) 1–13.

——— "Persons in Patristic and Medieval Christian Theology." In *Persons: A History (Oxford Philosophical Concepts)*. Edited by Antonia Lolordo. Oxford: Oxford University Press, 2019: 52–84.

——— "When Personhood Goes Wrong in Ethics and Philosophical Theology: Disability, Ableism and (Modern) Personhood." In *The Lost Sheep in Philosophy of Religion: New Perspectives on Disability, Gender, Race, and Animals*. Edited by Blake Hereth and Kevin Timpe. Oxford: Routledge, 2019: 264–290.

4 The *Imago Dei/Trinitatis* and Disabled Persons

The Limitations of Intellectualism in Late Medieval Theology

John T. Slotemaker

Introduction

Christian reflection on Genesis 1:26 throughout the patristic and medieval periods often supported what can be called an intellectualist interpretation of the *imago Dei*: the idea that the image of God in humanity is to be found in human noetic faculties and their proper functioning. This tradition perhaps originated with Origen of Alexandria (†254), who speculated on the relationship of the Father to the Son in psychological terms, such that the Son of God is the will (*thelēma*) proceeding from the divine mind (*nous*).[1] For Origen, there was an analogy between the generation of the Son from the Father and an act of the will proceeding from the human mind: a theological position adopted by Gregory of Nyssa and other theologians in the Greek-speaking East.[2] In the Western Latin tradition it was Augustine of Hippo who developed the most extensive and influential intellectualist account of the *imago Dei*. Augustine explored this theory throughout various writings, but most significantly in the latter books of *De Trinitate*.[3]

The question at the heart of this chapter is whether the intellectualist account of the *imago Dei* that dominated medieval Latin theology provides a useful or an adequate resource for thinking about individuals who have a significant cognitive impairment. I will begin by considering two distinct accounts of the *imago Dei* in Thomas Aquinas (†1274) and William of Ockham (†1347). These accounts are not intended to be representative of the entire medieval tradition but to give two variants of the intellectualist account that were the most influential in the 13th and 14th centuries. This discussion will be followed by a brief consideration of two responses to this intellectualist account: Gregory of Rimini's (†1358) rejection of the models proposed by Thomas and William, and Irenaeus of Lyons's (†c.202) alternative to the intellectualist account. The chapter concludes with some reflections on the value of the intellectualist tradition of the *imago Dei* and whether or not it provides sufficient resources for thinking about persons with severe cognitive impairment.

Augustine and the *Imago*

Augustine's theory of the *imago Dei* – often referred to as the psychological analogy – would come to have a significant influence on the development of medieval trinitarian theology as well as conceptions of the human person made in the image of God.[4] In the present section I will be examining briefly Augustine's account of the *imago Dei* and the reception of this account in Thomas Aquinas.

Augustine's theology of the *imago Dei* is intricately linked to an understanding of the human mind (*mens*).[5] In *De Trinitate* he writes,

> For as not only the most true reason, but also the authority of the Apostle himself declares, man was made to the image of God, not according to the form of the body, but according to the rational mind. For it is a vain and degrading thought which represents God as circumscribed and limited by outlines of corporeal members. … [I]f, therefore, we are renewed in the spirit of our mind, and it is precisely the new man who is renewed unto the knowledge of God, according to the image of Him who created him, then no one can doubt that man has been made to the image of Him who created him, not according to the body, nor according to any part of the mind, but according to the *rational mind* where the knowledge of God can reside.[6]

Here Augustine is clear that the image of God is to be found in the rational mind (*rationalem mentem*), and he rejects any attempt to locate the image in the human body or some other part of the human soul/mind (*quamlibet animi partem*). The image is to be located *secundum rationalem mentem*. But what does this mean?

Throughout the latter books of *De Trinitate*, Augustine attempts to define in what sense the rational mind can be understood to be made in the image of God. He is clear throughout that the image resides not simply in the mind but in the mind when it contemplates eternal things. He writes that "in that part alone, to which belongs the contemplation of eternal things, there is not only a trinity but also an image of God."[7] The image of God, therefore, is not simply the trinitarian structures one finds in the mind – such as *memoria*, *intelligentia*, and *voluntas* – but those faculties eternally contemplating eternal things.

The image, therefore, is not some structural similarity or likeness between the Father emanating the Son and the Father and Son emanating the Holy Spirit, just as *intelligentia* emanates from *memoria*, or *voluntas* from *memoria* and *intelligentia*. In a certain sense this is an image that one can find in the human being – an image of the divine Trinity – but Augustine in the passage noted above argues that while such a structural similarity may be an image of the triune God, the *imago Dei* is actually something quite distinct. The *imago* is the mind contemplating God. Here, we can do no better than to quote Rowan Williams, who writes,

> If we want to find where the image of God really is, we have to think of the mind thinking of itself in relation to the supreme, unique immaterial reality, God. So the image of God in us is not a structure of correspondence between our minds and God's mind; it is the mind completely caught up in contemplating God – aware of itself before God, opening its intelligence to God (though God can never be captured in a concept), directed in love towards God - held by this infinite "object" which is endless awareness, intelligence and love.[8]

The image, therefore, is not some structural analogy based on the similarities between the faculties of *memoria, intelligentia, voluntas* and the Father, Son, and Holy Spirit; the image is, instead, those faculties of the human mind actively knowing and loving God. This basic position would come to have a significant influence on Thomas Aquinas, who works through various interpretations of the *imago* as presented in Augustine.

Thomas Aquinas and the *Imago Dei/Trinitatis*

Thomas Aquinas's account of the *imago Dei/Trinitatis* was worked out over a considerable period of time and is an extensive reflection of Scripture, the Augustinian heritage described above, and Aristotelian psychology. In what follows we will present a brief overview of Thomas's position as it developed between the *Scriptum* and the *Summa theologiae*.[9] We begin, however, with Peter Lombard.

Peter Lombard treats Augustine's noetic triads in distinction 3 of the first book of his *Sentences* and in distinction 16 of the second book.[10] In his account of the *imago Dei*, Peter considers the triads of mind, knowledge, and love (*mens, notitia, amor*) and memory, understanding, and will (*memoria, intelligentia, voluntas*). The second triad – of particular interest to Aquinas – was interpreted by the Lombard as "three properties or powers of the mind itself."[11] This interpretation of memory, understanding, and will as three powers of the mind was initially accepted by Thomas, only to be rejected in his later works. Here we will briefly trace aspects of the development of Thomas's thought through the *Scriptum*, the *Lectura romana*, and the *Summa theologiae*.

The development between the *Scriptum* and the *Lectura romana* – on the question of memory, understanding, and will as powers of the mind – demonstrates Thomas's considerable shift concerning his reading of Augustine. In the *Scriptum*, Thomas considers whether the mind is the subject of the image (*Sent.* I, d. 3, q. 3).[12] Further, in defining memory, understanding, and will, Thomas argues that these three distinct powers of the soul (*in potentiis mentis*) are the image of God.[13]

In his study of Thomas's theology of the *imago Dei/Trinitatis*, Juvenal Merriell argues that in the *Scriptum*, Thomas has interpreted *memoria*, *intelligentia*, and *voluntas* as three powers (*potentiae*), or Aristotelian faculties, of the soul.[14] The problem, as Merriell points out, is that within Aristotelian psychology, understanding (*intelligentia*) and will (*voluntas*) are considered parts of the intellective soul, while *memoria* is not. Memory, instead, "is a capacity of the faculty of intellect to retain the forms or intelligible species of things to which the intellect can recur in order to reactivate its knowledge of those things."[15] In this sense, memory is to be assigned to the faculty of imagination and has more to do with sensation *per se*. Thus, the Aristotelian model of faculties, or powers, interjects a tension into the model because, strictly speaking, memory is not part of the intellective faculty. Further, Thomas understands the image to be active, in the sense that it imitates the divine nature.[16] The mind, when it is actively knowing and loving God, is said to be in the perfect image of God, and the problem, as Thomas notes, is that this seems to demand constant knowing and loving.[17] What happens, on this model, if one is not presently in the act of knowing or loving? Is the image of God permanent or temporary? Is it present when one is first born, asleep, drunk, or in a coma? Thomas responds – with an "uncomfortable answer" in the words of Juvenal Merriell – by arguing that there is an ongoing and a consistent "preconceptual activity of memory, intellect and will" in human beings.[18] This preconceptual activity is what guarantees the permanence of the *imago*.

The *Lectura romana* was written over a decade after the *Scriptum* and originates from Thomas's lectures to the Dominicans at Santa Sabina, Rome.[19] The discussion of the psychological analogy occurs, following Peter Lombard, in distinction 3, questions 2 and 3. Having established in article 1 of question 3 that the essence of the soul (*essentia animae*) consists in memory, understanding, and will, Thomas considers in the second article how precisely these three faculties can be understood both as an image of God and as pertaining to the human mind.[20] The third objection of the second article (*Lectura Romana* I, d. 3, q. 3, a. 2, ob. 3) argues that the three *potentiae* – in particular *memoria*, *intelligentia*, and *voluntas* – are not an image of the Trinity. This is because in God one person is from another (i.e., as the Son is from the Father), whereas when talking about the human mind, it is not proper to talk about one *potentia* being from another.[21] In his response to this objection Thomas makes the distinction between the positions of Peter Lombard and Saint Augustine. Rejecting the opinion of the Lombard, Thomas argues, "It would seem that the Master did not understand the intention of Augustine."[22] The Master – as Thomas understands him – argues that the trinitarian image of memory, understanding, and will are three powers of the soul (*tres vires animae*) or three *potentiae*.[23] The Lombard's reading of Augustine, according to Thomas, is suspect (*sed hoc Augustinus non vult!*):[24] Augustine does not argue that memory, understanding, and will should be understood as three *potentiae* (or powers) but instead as the habitual decision to act and to the acts themselves.[25] In his more mature works – *De veritate*, the *Lectura Romana*, and the *Summa theologiae* – Thomas argues that the image of God is found in the habits corresponding to memory, intellect, and will, such that a person's actual knowledge and love of God in the human soul is the *imago Trinitatis*. It is worth briefly considering Thomas's account of this position in the *Summa*.

Thomas's fullest account of the *imago Dei/Trinitatis* in its mature form is found in *Summa Theologiae* Ia, question 93. Thomas argues that there are three ways in which human beings are created in the image of God: (1) through the capacity or natural aptitude to understand and love God, (2) through habitually knowing and loving God, and (3) through knowing and loving God perfectly.[26] These three "images" move from the least perfect to the most perfect image of the Trinity in human beings but represent Thomas's complete break with his earlier position defended in the *Scriptum*. The emphasis in his later works is not on the *potentiae* of the soul but on the habits of knowing and loving God.

Here it is necessary to say a bit more about the first and second levels described by Thomas. The image of God is linked explicitly to the intellectual nature (*intellectualem naturam*). In article 6 Thomas specifies that the intellect or mind is "that whereby the rational creature excels other creatures" such that the "image of God is not found even in the rational creature except in the mind (*secundum mentem*)."[27] The image, therefore, is only in the human person *secundum mentem* – and, while it is correct here to insist that this is not some accidental property added to the human person, the image is limited to the intellectual nature.[28] This is important in two ways. First, it is correct to insist that for Thomas the intellectual nature is the rational soul. Second, however, it must be insisted that this is only the most basic or limited sense of the *imago*. Thus, if we apply this to the question at hand, one could note that while it would be accurate to state that someone with severe cognitive impairment would participate in the *imago Dei* at this basic level, it is just that, the most basic level. Thomas consistently points out that the image of God is that by which humanity excels other animals and is rational (here, presumably, he is most often talking about not just a bare capacity of the soul, which all human beings have *qua* souls, but human beings actually reasoning and willing).[29] But what are the implications of this position?

Thomas maintains that there are three levels of the image. The first level is the only one, by definition, that would apply to someone with severe mental impairment. A person who does not have the ability to remember, understand, or will (love) only has the image in the most basic sense: as some unactualized power, or ability, latent in the human person. There are several problems that one could level against Thomas's claim, and here I want to focus on just one point. Thomas says that at the first level the person has the image "in so far as a person possess[es] a natural aptitude for understanding and loving." Now, a person with a severe mental impairment would have this level of the *imago*, according to Thomas, because on his philosophical psychology, such a person would have certain capacities that are unactualized because the person's sense organs have been damaged. That is, Thomas thinks that the person's mind in question has the natural aptitude for loving and understanding *per se*; it is just the case that because this person's sense organs are damaged, he or she cannot be said to "actually and habitually know and love God" (to use Thomas's language). But, does this account work given what we know about human cognitive functioning and those who suffer from severe cognitive impairment? Is Thomas right that individuals with severe cognitive impairment are simply lacking the correct sensory data and that with proper functioning eyes, ears, and so on, they would be able to know and will and love? We will return to this question in the concluding section of the chapter, but I think that, in short, there are good reasons to think that Thomas's account remains insufficient, given what we know about individuals with severe cognitive impairment.

William of Ockham and the *Imago/Dei Trinitatis*

William of Ockham treats the *imago Trinitatis* in distinction 3, question 10, of the first book of his commentary on the *Sentences* of Peter Lombard.[30] Ockham divides the material into two distinct questions: (1) In what way can one creature be called an image with respect to another and (2) in what way is anything the image of God?[31]

In the second question Ockham attempts to describe the nature of the *imago Trinitatis* as found in the rational creature, and he begins with a consideration of the common opinion. The common opinion, according to Ockham, asserts that aspects of the image of God (Trinity) are found in the faculties of the rational soul. In particular, he maintains that the common view understands the Augustinian triad of *memoria*, *intelligentia*, and *voluntas* to be powers (or faculties) of the rational soul (*potentiae animae*).[32] Ockham is not clear about who, precisely, he thinks holds this common view; however, the editors are perhaps correct to think that Ockham has in mind Peter Lombard, Bonaventure, Thomas Aquinas (in the *Scriptum*), and Henry of Ghent.[33] Regardless, Ockham simply states that this common view is probably not true. He argues that the three powers under consideration are not distinct in the substance of the rational soul before the distinction of the acts consequently produced.[34] That is, because Ockham denies that there is a real distinction (*distinctio realis*) between memory, understanding, and will in the human soul,[35] this triad understood as three powers of the soul cannot be a strict analogy of the divine Trinity because there is a real distinction between the three divine persons.[36] But, Ockham is not prepared to reject either the authority of sacred Scripture or Saint Augustine, and consequently he develops a slightly modified version of the common opinion.

Ockham's interpretation of the *imago Trinitatis* emphasizes a passage from Augustine – which was also the focus of Peter Lombard[37] – that is centered on the *capax Dei*, the capacity for God. Reflecting on Augustine's argument in book 14 of his *De Trinitate*, Ockham argues that if it is true that "the soul according to its substance is capable of God and can participate in him," it is also true that "the soul according to its substance is the image of God."[38] Thus, Ockham holds that the imperfect image of God (*imago Dei imperfecta*) consists of the soul according to its substance, while the perfection of the image (*perfectio imaginis*) consists of the substance of the soul and its two acts.[39] Thus, the perfect image of God (i.e., the Trinity) is not found in the substance of the soul *simpliciter* but in the substance of the soul and the corresponding acts of the soul: understanding (*intelligere*) and willing (*velle*). Ockham, unlike some of his medieval predecessors,[40] strongly emphasized the corresponding acts of the soul because he denied that there is either a real or a formal distinction between the powers of the soul *per se*. Here it is perhaps useful to expand a bit upon this central intuition.

The Venerable Inceptor argued explicitly that there is not a real or a formal distinction between the powers of the human soul. Unlike Thomas Aquinas and John Duns Scotus – who argued for a real distinction and a formal distinction respectively – Ockham argues that there is no distinction in the powers of the soul *per se*. As Armand Maurer explicates Ockham's position, there are two ways in which Ockham interprets the term "powers of the soul": (1) the term designates the "nominal definition" of the powers in question; and (2) the term designates "that which is named" by the term of the power in question.[41] Considered under the first aspect, the powers of the soul are distinct because they have different nominal definitions. The nominal definitions are "the intellect is the substance of the soul capable of understanding," and "[the will] is the substance of the soul capable of willing." Further, these definitions can be understood in three distinct ways: (1) as referring to words (*voces*), (2) as referring to concepts (*conceptus*), or (3) as referring to things (*res*). When analyzing these definitions as words, concepts, and things, Ockham argues that if the definitions are understood as referring to words, they are really distinct, as concepts they are conceptually distinct, and as things they are really distinct (in part).[42] Thus, for Ockham, when the nominal definitions of the powers of the soul *intelligere* and *velle* are analyzed there are various distinctions that can be made between the corresponding words, concepts, and things. However, when the term "powers of the soul" indicates that which is actually named, Ockham argues that there is neither a real nor a formal distinction between the powers of the soul.[43] The distinction between the powers of the soul is found, therefore, in the acts that correspond to the powers of understanding and willing.

Ockham's argument that there is no distinction between the powers of the soul (understood as that which is named) had significant implications for how he interpreted Augustine's triad of memory, understanding, and willing. If, as other theologians had held, there was a real or formal distinction between the powers of the soul, Augustine's triad of memory, understanding, and willing would qualify as a fitting analogy of the three persons of the Trinity: Father, Son, and Holy Spirit. The analogy would be fitting because there would be both unity and distinction in the two analogates: the divine Trinity and the human mind. However, if Ockham is right that there is no distinction between the powers of the soul (understanding and willing), the analogy threatens to dissipate because of the lack of distinction. Thus, when Ockham discusses the two powers of the soul and their corresponding acts, his emphasis has shifted to the distinction between the two acts. It is, in the end, the distinction between the two acts (and their corresponding habits) of the respective powers that ultimately allows Ockham to retain Augustine's psychological analogy. Thus, it is important here to consider more fully Ockham's understanding of the two acts.

Returning to the notion of the "capacity for God" (*capax Dei*), Ockham argues that the *capax Dei* is intricately related to the perfection of the image of God. This capacity for God is defined by Ockham in the following way: "the complete *ratio* of the image consists in the substance of the soul itself and its two acts."[44] The two acts in question, knowing and willing, and their corresponding habits are therefore the perfection of the image of God and entail the *capax Dei*. For Ockham the *imago Trinitatis* consists both in the substance of the soul and in its two noblest acts, such that the imperfect image (*imperfecta*) found in the substance of the soul is brought to perfection through the habitual acts of right knowing and right loving. The soul, thus ordered, reflects the inner trinitarian life of God as the Father produces (generates) the Son and the Holy Spirit, and communicates the fecundative power of generation to the Son. The act of understanding proceeds from the essence of the soul as the Son proceeds from the Father, and the act of willing proceeds from the essence of the soul and understanding just as the Holy Spirit proceeds from the Father and the Son.[45]

Ockham focuses on how, precisely, the human being is created in the image of God: in particular, Ockham considers the various opinions developed by the Lombard and Thomas Aquinas regarding the powers of the soul and its two acts.[46] Rejecting the position of the Lombard (and the early Thomas), as he understood it, Ockham develops a position that is much closer to that of Aquinas in his later works. The critical difference between Thomas and Ockham is that Ockham's understanding of the *imago* is grounded in a radically different account of human psychology. Because Ockham denies any distinction between the powers of the human soul (pace Aquinas and Scotus), the acts and corresponding habits of the soul are accentuated because it is the only way of retaining the *imago Trinitatis* as an analogy of the divine Trinity.

Here we can glean a couple of lessons with respect to whether the image is in fact the powers in question or their corresponding acts. What is interesting, and what Ockham highlights, is that there is a real problem – depending on one's philosophical psychology – in claiming that the image is found in some latent way in the powers of the soul. Thus, what Ockham points out is that unless one is willing to state that there is some kind of distinction between *memoria*, *intelligentia*, and *voluntas* in the human person (and not just the corresponding acts), the entire discussion of an *imago Trinitatis* must be forced into the arena of the acts themselves. And, well, what this highlights is that to accept Thomas's most basic level of the *imago* – the latent image that is found in the "the capacity or natural aptitude to understand and love God" – is to accept a very particular philosophical psychology.

It is perhaps useful to take stock here: I presented Thomas and Ockham because they represent two basic claims. Thomas, in the *Scriptum*, linking the image with the powers of the soul, and not necessarily the two acts, and the later Thomas and Ockham, insisting that the real image is found in the corresponding acts of the soul (not just the powers). These two views would be discussed by most of the 14th century doctors, with many debating the two options at length. What is interesting, however, is that the latter view – that of the later Thomas and Ockham – certainly was preferred by many of the later scholastics. That is, the true image of God, the complete *ratio* of the image, is understood to consist in the substance of the soul itself and its two acts. This is the dominant medieval heritage and supports explicitly an intellectualist view of the image of God. The true image – the image *perfecta*, not *imperfecta* – is to be found in acts of understanding and willing. This, of course, has serious implications for how one thinks about those with severe cognitive impairment who are not able to understand or rationally will something in a particular way.

Gregory of Rimini, Irenaeus of Lyons, and the *imago Dei/Trinitatis*

The intellectualist account of the *imago Dei/Trinitatis* found in Augustine, Thomas, and Ockham is not, of course, the only way in which

Christians have imagined human beings as bearers of the image of God, and here it is useful to consider two possible alternatives. First, we will consider a response to the intellectualist tradition by the Augustinian theologian Gregory of Rimini, who would take a critical stance toward the theologies of Thomas and Ockham considered above. Second, we will examine briefly an account of the *imago Dei* that predates the origins of the intellectualist account, in the writings of Irenaeus of Lyons. Thus, we will consider both a critique of this tradition and an alternative proposal.

Following the Lombard's treatment of the *imago Trinitatis*, Gregory of Rimini places his own discussion of the triad *memoria, intelligentia,* and *voluntas* in book II, distinction 16/17. However, Gregory does not consider the theological topic addressed by the Lombard (i.e., the *imago*) and instead considers in the first article the distinction between the sensitive soul and intellective soul,[47] and in the second article how one should understand, within the intellective soul, the triad *memoria, intelligentia,* and *voluntas*.[48] The content of the second article analyzes whether or not the intellect and the will are distinct powers of the soul,[49] and Gregory elicits arguments both pro and con from Augustine's *De Trinitate*. Two of the five arguments supporting the contrary opinion are from Anselm and Peter Lombard,[50] but these arguments are not the focus of Gregory's concern: Gregory devotes only a couple of lines to refuting the arguments of Anselm and the Lombard.[51] Thus, the article is really a sustained attempt to explicate the position of Saint Augustine on whether or not the terms *memoria, intelligentia,* and *voluntas* refer to acts of the soul or powers of the soul. His conclusion is that when referring to the human person, the three terms refer to acts of the soul not powers of the soul.[52] However, one reads in vain for any discussion of the *imago Trinitatis*; only occasionally does Gregory relate this discussion of human psychology to the divine nature.[53] In short, Gregory makes it particularly clear that there is no analogy between the divine nature and human nature that warrants a discussion of the *imago Trinitatis* in the form of *memoria, intelligentia,* and *voluntas*.

For Gregory of Rimini there is no clear image of the Trinity found in human cognitive capacities or acts. Gregory,[54] in both of the *loci classici* of the *imago Trinitatis* (*Sent.* I, d.3; *Sent.* II, d.16), argues that there is no strict analogy between the divine nature and the human nature that is particularly informative. This argument of Gregory clearly breaks with the previous tradition of theologians like Henry of Ghent, Thomas Aquinas, and John Duns Scotus, but it is closer to the Oxford tradition that developed in the 1320s and 1330s and followed closely the theology of William of Ockham. Russell Friedman is certainly correct to locate Gregory Rimini alongside both Walter Chatton and Robert Holcot in articulating a trinitarian minimalism that rejects the use of the psychological analogy.[55]

The upshot is that one can chart out three basic positions in the writings of Peter Lombard, Thomas Aquinas, William of Ockham, and Gregory of Rimini. (1) Peter Lombard and the early Thomas (*Scriptum*) held that the *imago Trinitatis* is found in human memory, understanding, and willing understood as three powers of the soul (*tres vires animae*) or three *potentiae*. (2) The later Thomas and Ockham reject this reading (for different reasons) and argue that the *imago* is not three powers of the soul but the corresponding acts and habits associated with memory, understanding, and willing. Finally (3), Gregory of Rimini denies that there is a strong analogous relationship between human noetic faculties and the divine Trinity, arguing that there is more dissimilitude than similitude; in effect, Gregory seems to reject the broader intellectualist tradition of the *imago Trinitatis* found in the Lombard, Thomas, and Ockham.

While Gregory's critique of the previous scholastic tradition is perhaps instructive, he does not provide a positive re-interpretation of how to understand the image of God. Here, therefore, it is perhaps instructive to return to the early Christian theologian, Irenaeus of Lyons, who predates the origins of the intellectualist tradition in either the East or the West. Irenaeus presents a unifying and Christological-Pneumatological reading of how human beings are created in the image and likeness of God.[56] First, throughout his discussion the emphasis is on precisely how the entire human person – not just a part or an aspect – is made in the image and likeness of God. Thus, he is explicit that the body, soul, and spirit are made in the image and likeness of God, in that the soul and spirit are essential to the likeness of God, and the body is essential to the image, such that if a human person were to lack one of the three, he or she would cease to be in the image and likeness of God.[57] To this end, he will employ various biblical passages that justify this reading: for example, I Thessalonians 5:3, "... and may your spirit, and soul, and body be kept sound and blameless at the coming of our Lord Jesus Christ."

Further, as in the biblical passage just cited, Irenaeus links this understanding of the image and likeness with Christ.[58] It is Christ who knows the Father and has seen the Father, and Christ who is the perfect image of the Father; thus, for human beings to be perfected in the image of God, or to return to a perfect image, is to be conformed to the image of Christ.[59] There is also a pneumatological aspect to Irenaeus's reading of the image, in that the *spirit* of humanity refers precisely to the Holy Spirit, such that to truly be made in the image – to be restored to the image of God – is be filled with the Holy Spirit.[60]

The upshot is that for Irenaeus it is precisely the entire human person who is made in the image and likeness of God; rationality has a role to play, for Irenaeus, but it is only part of the person as body, soul, and spirit. This approach has certain advantages, as we will see below, because it provides a way of thinking about human beings with profound cognitive impairments as bearers of the image and likeness of God in ways that the intellectualist account fails to support.

Severe Mental Impairment and the *Imago Dei/Trinitatis*

Trevor Waltrip was born on Christmas Eve 2001 with a rather severe case of hydranencephaly, and his body was able to function with only a brain stem. He lived for twelve years.[61] With a brain stem, individuals such as Trevor can breathe and move, their hearts beat, but they do not have a brain in a strict sense (above the brain stem is cerebrospinal fluid collected in the cranial cavity; both cerebral hemispheres may be completely missing in extreme cases).

I bring up Trevor Waltrip because, in his case, we can get right to the heart of the problems with an intellectualist account of the *imago Dei*. Thomas and William inextricably link the *imago Trinitatis* to human noetic faculties. For both, to be made in the image of God is to have some rational capacity (and to act upon it) that other animals do not have. The problem, however, is that such an account of the *imago Dei* cannot accommodate, in a satisfying sense, what it means for someone with severe mental impairments to be made in the image of God. For, even on Thomas's first level or gradation of the *imago*, it requires a physical mind, a brain. Thus, even at Thomas's most basic level, it would seem that individuals with extreme hydranencephaly simply do not have the image of God by definition: while Thomas can claim that such individuals have a bare *capacity* for willing and loving, such a capacity could not be actualized because intellectual cognition and volition requires acts of sensation and imagination not available to someone without a brain. I think this raises important questions: What are the implications of linking the image of God with rational capacities or mental faculties? What resources can one find in the Christian medieval theological tradition to answer such questions?[62]

First, if we take the writings of Thomas Aquinas as a point of departure, there is no doubt that when his understanding of the *imago* is coupled with everything he had to say about human persons and their life in the Church, one can tease out a satisfying account of Thomas's understanding of those we could describe as having profound cognitive impairments. In his practical theology, in particular, one finds resources for thinking through many of the relevant issues. Further, as both Miguel Romero and John Berkman have argued, for those graced individuals within the Church – that is, those who are baptized – Thomas has quite a bit to say about how such individuals can participate in a graced afterlife.[63] This important work has demonstrated that if one is willing to extend the discussion beyond the *imago*, there are significant resources in Thomas's corpus for thinking about persons with extreme cognitive impairment. But what are we to make of this in relation to the intellectualist tradition of the *imago Trinitatis* described in this chapter?

This brings me to my second point. There is no doubt that for theologians such as Augustine, Peter Lombard, Thomas Aquinas, and William Ockham, the image of God in the human person was intricately tied to human noetic functioning. The idea that rationality was central to being made in the image and likeness of God was assumed by all of the medieval thinkers discussed in this chapter. This intellectual tradition, I would argue, is simply not a useful point of departure for thinking about individuals, such as Trevor Waltrip, who are not capable of rationality because they do not have a brain in a strict sense. If the image of God is about rationality – or the capacity for it, even if unactualized throughout one's entire life – individuals such as Trevor simply lack the image of God described in Genesis 1:26. This is an extremely unfortunate consequence that seems unavoidable given the intellectualist account of the *imago*.[64]

Here I am reminded of the less-than-helpful Irish proverb: *If I were going there, I would not be starting from here.* When I think about the resources in medieval philosophy and theology for addressing questions of disability or impairment, I do not think that medieval theologies of the *imago Dei* are a particularly rich point of departure for discussions of human beings with severe cognitive impairment. The Western-Latin discussion of the *imago Dei*, following Augustine, was focused primarily on the intellectual capacities and abilities of adults who do not suffer from any kind of mental or cognitive impairment. And, while there are points where this is somewhat expanded upon in the tradition – for example, in Augustine's discussion of children in *De Trinitate* 14.5.7–8 – the center of the discussion has always remained focused on able-bodied and able-minded adults.[65] By contrast, for a theologian like Irenaeus, there would be other strategies or possibilities when it comes to analyzing the *imago Dei* in persons with extreme mental impairment. If the *imago* is not linked precisely to human rational faculties but is instead the entire human person, body, soul, and spirit, it is easier to argue that all human persons, regardless of rational capacity, are bearers of the image of God.

In conclusion, therefore, I do not think that medieval theologies of the *imago* are a particularly relevant resource for modern theologians developing a theology of disabled persons.[66] I would argue, instead, that the most fruitful discussions of the *imago* would be those that are not explicitly intellectualist in the ways described in the present chapter, or those that, at the least, couple the intellectualist account with a broader notion of what it means to be a human person made in the image of God.[67]

Notes

1 Origen, *Origenes Vier Bücher von den Prinzipien*, I 2.9. See also, Henri Crouzel, *Théologie de l'image de Dieu chez Origène*; Origen, "Le Dieu d'Origène et le Dieu de Plotin."

2 On Gregory, see Michel René Barnes, "Divine Unity and the Divided Self: Gregory of Nyssa's Trinitarian Theology in its Psychological Context," 45–66; Sarah Coakley, "Introduction – Gender, Trinitarian Analogies, and the Pedagogy of *The Song*," 1–13; David B. Hart, "The Mirror of the Infinite: Gregory of Nyssa on the *Vestigia Trinitatis*," 111–131; and Morwenna Ludlow, *Gregory of Nyssa Ancient and [Post]Modern*. Similar language is also found in Cyril of Alexandria. See Brian E. Daley, "The Fullness of the Saving God: Cyril of Alexandria on the Holy Spirit," 113–148, esp. 146–147.

It should be noted that the intellectualist interpretation of the *imago Dei* was at times defined as something particular to Adam's masculinity. Diodore of Tarsus, John Chrysostom, and Theodoret of Cyr "understood 'image' as being the dominative power that Adam qua male received to rule in God's place over the material universe" such that "women were not created in God's 'image,' at least not in the same sense [as] Adam." See Frederick G. McLeod, *The Image of God in the Antiochene Tradition*, 235, 248.

3 Gerald P. Boersma, *Augustine's Early Theology of Image: A Study in the Development of Pro-Nicene Theology*.

4 Augustine's influence was not always direct but was often mediated by Peter Lombard and other compilers. In fact, there is good reason to think that the influence of Augustine's interpretation of the *imago* is significantly influenced by Peter Lombard's *Sentences*. See John T. Slotemaker, "Reading Augustine in the Fourteenth Century: Gregory of Rimini and Pierre d'Ailly on the *Imago Trinitatis*," 345–358.

5 See Anthony Dupont and Cheuk Yin Yam, "A Mind-Centered Approach of *imago Dei*: A Dynamic Construction in Augustine's De Trinitate XIV," 7–13.

6 Augustine, *De Trinitate* 12.7.12, 366, ll. 70–84. Also, Augustine, *The Trinity*, 353–354.

7 Augustine, *De Trinitate* 12.4.4, 358, ll. 11–13.

8 Rowan Williams, *On Augustine*, 136.

9 The number of studies on the psychological analogy in Thomas is substantial. See in particular: Marie–Joseph Serge de Laugier de Beaurecueil, "L'homme image de Dieu selon saint Thomas d'Aquin," *Études et Recherches* 8 (1952): 45–82; *Études et Recherches* 9 (1955): 37–96; Francis L. B. Cunningham, *The Indwelling of the Trinity: A Historico-Doctrinal Study of the Theory of St. Thomas Aquinas*; Juvenal Merriell, *To the Image of the Trinity: A Study of the Development of Aquinas' Teaching*. Juvenal D. Merriell, "Trinitarian Anthropology," 123–142.

10 Peter Lombard, *Sent.*, I, d. 3, 68–77; Peter Lombard, II, d. 16, 406–409. On the *imago* in Peter Lombard, see Marcia Colish, *Peter Lombard*, 33–77, esp. 245–254. Colish compares the formal structure of the Lombard to that of: Peter Abelard, Gilbert of Poitier, Hugh of St. Victor, the *Summa sententiarum*, Roland of Bologna, Robert Pullen, and Robert of Melun. Colish should be read alongside, Philipp W. Rosemann, *Peter Lombard*.

11 Lombard, *Sent.* I, d. 3, c. 2, 73, ll. 22–28:

> Hic attendendum est diligenter ex quo sensu accipiendum sit quod supra dixit, illa tria, scilicet memoria, intelligentiam et voluntatem esse unum, unam mentem, unam essentiam. Quod utique non videtur esse verum iuxta proprietatem sermonis. Mens enim, id est spiritus rationalis, essentia est spiritualis et incorporeal; illa vero tria naturales proprietates seu vires sunt ipsius mentis, et a se invicem differunt, quia memoria non est intelligentia vel voluntas, nec intelligentia voluntas sive amor.

The Imago Dei/Trinitatis *& Disabled Persons* 123

12 Aquinas, *Scriptum* I, d. 3, q. 3, a. 1, 109–110:

> Respondeo dicendum, quod imago in hoc differt a vestigio: quod vestigium est confusa similitudo alicujus rei et imperfecta; imago autem repraesentat rem magis determinate secundum omnes partes et dispositiones partium, ex quibus etiam aliquid de interioribus rei percipi potest. Et ideo in illis tantum creaturis dicitur esse imago Dei quae propter sui nobilitatem ipsum perfectius imitantur et repraesentant; et ideo in Angelo et homine tantum dicitur imago divinitatis, et in homine secundum id quod est in ipso nobilius. Alia autem, quae plus et minus participant de Dei bonitate, magis accedunt ad rationem imaginis.

13 Aquinas, *Scriptum* I, d. 3, q. 3, a. 1, ad 1, 110:

> Ad primum ergo dicendum, quod Augustinus in multis ostendit similitudinem Trinitatis esse; sed in nullo esse perfectam similitudinem, sicut in potentiis mentis, ubi invenitur distinctio consubstantialis et aequalitas. Constat autem illa tria in visu dicta, non esse consubstantialia, et ideo solum in mente ponit imaginem.

14 Juvenal Merriell, "Trinitarian Anthropology," 128.
15 Ibid.
16 Aquinas, *Scriptum* I, d. 3, q. 4, a. 4, 120: "Servatur etiam ibi actualis imitatio ipsius Trinitatis, inquantum scilicet ipsa anima est imago expresse ducens in Deum. Si autem considerentur respectu hujus objecti quod est Deus, tunc servatur ibi actualis imitatio."
17 Aquinas, *Scriptum* I, d. 3, q. 4, a. 5, 122:

> Respondeo dicendum, quod, secundum Augustinum, De util. credendi, cap. xi, differunt cogitare, discernere et intelligere. Discernere est cognoscere rem per differentiam sui ab aliis. Cogitare autem est considerare rem secundum partes et proprietates suas: unde cogitare dicitur quasi coagitare. Intelligere autem dicit nihil aliud quam simplicem intuitum intellectus in id quod sibi est praesens intelligibile.

18 Aquinas, *Scriptum* I, d. 3, q. 4, a. 5, 122:

> Dico ergo, quod anima non semper cogitat et discernit de Deo, nec de se, quia sic quilibet sciret naturaliter totam naturam animae suae, ad quod vix magno studio pervenitur: ad talem enim cognitionem non sufficit praesentia rei quolibet modo; sed oportet ut sit ibi in ratione objecti, et exigitur intentio cognoscentis. Sed secundum quod intelligere nihil aliud dicit quam intuitum, qui nihil aliud est quam praesentia intelligibilis ad intellectum quocumque modo, sic anima semper intelligit se et Deum indeterminate, et consequitur quidam amor indeterminatus. Alio tamen modo, secundum philosophos, intelligitur quod anima semper se intelligit, eo quod omne quod intelligitur, non intelligitur nisi illustratum lumine intellectus agentis, et receptum in intellectu possibili. Unde sicut in omni colore videtur lumen corporale, ita in omni intelligibili videtur lumen intellectus agentis; non tamen in ratione objecti sed in ratione medii cognoscendi.

See also, Juvenal Merriell, "Trinitarian Anthropology," 129.

19 The work is preserved in one manuscript (Oxford, Lincoln College Ms Lat. 95) and was rediscovered by Hyacinthe François Dondaine just over three decades ago. Leonard Boyle argued this manuscript contains the heretofore lost *Lectura Romana* of Thomas Aquinas, though that position has come under considerable critique as of late. See, in particular, Leonard

E. Boyle, "Alia lectura fratris Thomae," 418–429; Hyacinthe François Dondaine, "'Alia lectura fratris thome'? (*Super 1 Sent.*)," 308–336; Mark F. Johnson, 'Alia lectura fratris thome': A List of the New Texts of St. Thomas Aquinas found in Lincoln College, Oxford, MS. Lat. 95," 34–61; and John F. Boyle, "Introduction," 1–57. A useful summary of the debate can be found in Pasquale Porro, *Thomas Aquinas: A Historical and Philosophical Profile*, 185–188.

In a certain sense, whether or not the *Lectura* belongs to Thomas (or a student/disciple) is somewhat beside the point. One can trace the development of Thomas's account without the *Lectura*; further, if the *Lectura* proves to be inauthentic, then it is simply evidence of a disciple of Thomas rejecting Thomas's earliest position (in the *Scriptum*) in favor of his more mature theology (e.g., in *De veritate* or the *Summa theologiae*). Here I find it useful, however, in framing the debate as one between Augustine and the Lombard's reading of Augustine.

20 Aquinas, *Lectura Romana* I, d. 3, q. 3, a. 1, ad. 1, 114, ll. 38–41:

> Ad primum ergo dicendum quod sicut tota vita hominis dicitur ex eo quod homo est rationalis, eo quod rationale est superius et dignius in homine, ita essentia animae dicitur voluntas et intelligentia et memoria, ex eo quod mens in qua haec sunt est superior et nobilior pars animae.

21 Aquinas, *Lectura Romana* I, d. 3, q. 3, a. 1, ob. 1, 115, ll. 10–13:

> Videtur quod tres potentiae scilicet memoria, intelligentia et voluntas non sint imago Trinitatis. In divinis enim una persona est ex alia, sicut Filius a Patre, et Spiritus Sanctus ab utroque. Sed una potentia non est ex alia. Sed una potentia non est ex alia. Ergo huiusmodi tres potentiae non repraesentant illas tres personas.

22 Aquinas, *Lectura Romana* I, d. 3, q. 3, a. 1, ad. 3, 116, ll. 62–64: "Ad tertiam dicendum quod si recte considerentur verba Magistri et verba Augustini, non videntur sonare idem; et videtur quod Magister non intellexerit intentionem Augustini."

23 Aquinas, *Lectura Romana* I, d. 3, q. 3, a. 1, ad. 3, 116, ll. 64–65: "Magister enim vult quod illa tria, scilicet memoria, intelligentia et voluntas, sint tres vires animae et tres potentiae." On the relationship between the Lombard and Thomas's position, see Marie-Joseph Serge de Laugier de Beaurecueil, "L'homme image de Dieu selon saint Thomas d'Aquin."

24 In support of Thomas's reading of Augustine here, see Walter H. Principe, "The Dynamism of Augustine's Terms for Describing the Highest Trinitarian Image in the Human Person," 1291–1299.

25 Aquinas, *Lectura Romana* I, d. 3, q. 3, a. 1, ad. 3, 116–117, ll. 65–69:

> Sed hoc Augustinus non vult; immo vult quod nullum istorum sit potentia. Ipse enim per memoriam nihil aliud intelligit hic quam habitualem notitiam ad cognoscendum aliquid; per intelligentiam vero actualem cogitationem ex illa notitia procedentem; per voluntatem vero actualem voluntatis motum ex cogitatione procedentem.

See also "Nota 2" as found in the margins of the *Lectura Romana*, 121, ll. 1–6:

> Dicendum est quod huiusmodi assignationes imaginis differunt ab invicem, quia in secunda (secundum Augustinum prima secundo loco ponitur), non dico quod memoria et intelligentia et voluntas sint tres potentiae; sed quod memoria dicit habitualem dispositionem animae secundum quod se habet ad volendum et intelligendum in actu; intelligentia vero dicit actum intelligeni; voluntas vero ipsum actum secundum quod convertitur in obiectum.

The Imago Dei/Trinitatis & Disabled Persons 125

26 Aquinas, *Summa theologiae* Ia, q. 93, a. 4, co., 404–405 (*Opera Omnia*, V):

> Respondeo dicendum quod, cum homo secundum intellectualem naturam ad imaginem Dei esse dicatur, secundum hoc est maxime ad imaginem Dei, secundum quod intellectualis natura Deum maxime imitari potest. Imitatur autem intellectualis natura maxime Deum quantum ad hoc, quod Deus seipsum intelligit et amat. Unde imago Dei tripliciter potest considerari in homine. Uno quidem modo, secundum quod homo habet aptitudinem naturalem ad intelligendum et amandum Deum; et haec aptitudo consistit in ipsa natura mentis, quae est communis omnibus hominibus. Alio modo, secundum quod homo actu vel habitu Deum cognoscit et amat, sed tamen imperfecte; et haec est imago per conformitatem gratiae. Tertio modo, secundum quod homo Deum actu cognoscit et amat perfecte; et sic attenditur imago secundum similitudinem gloriae. Unde super illud Psalmi IV, 'Signatum est super nos lumen vultus tui, Domine', Glossa distinguit triplicem imaginem, scilicet creationis, recreationis et similitudinis. Prima ergo imago invenitur in omnibus hominibus; secunda in iustis tantum; tertia vero solum in beatis.

27 Aquinas, *Summa theologiae* Ia, q. 93, a. 6, co., 407 (*Opera Omnia*, V):

> Respondeo dicendum quod, cum in omnibus creaturis sit aliqualis Dei similitudo, in sola creatura rationali invenitur similitudo Dei per modum imaginis, ut supra dictum est, in aliis autem creaturis per modum vestigii. Id autem in quo creatura rationalis excedit alias creaturas, est intellectus sive mens. Unde relinquitur quod nec in ipsa rationali creatura invenitur Dei imago, nisi secundum mentem.

28 That said, Thomas does speak of the *imago Trinitatis* being "*in mentem*" as something that is in the soul (not as something identical with the soul). See, e.g., q. 93, a. 7, co., 409 (*Opera Omnia*, V):

> Respondeo dicendum quod, sicut supra dictum est, ad rationem imaginis pertinet aliqualis repraesentatio speciei. Si ergo imago Trinitatis divinae debet accipi in anima, oportet quod secundum illud principaliter attendatur, quod maxime accedit, prout possibile est, ad repraesentandum speciem divinarum personarum.

29 It is important to note that what it means for a human being to reason is distinct from what it means for God to "reason." For human beings an act of reason involves deliberation and is, as such, imperfect when compared to God's reason (which is a pure perfection and devoid of learning or deliberation). That said, it is the human acts of reasoning and willing that Thomas thinks are the image of God in the human person, if not a perfect image (Thomas speaks of a more perfect image).

30 The literature on Ockham's trinitarian theology does not contain an extensive discussion of the *imago Trinitatis* or the psychological analogy. The most developed account is found in Pekka Kärkkäinen, "Interpretations of the Psychological Analogy from Aquinas to Biel," 256–279, esp. 264–270. On related issues in Ockham, see Russell L. Friedman, *Medieval Trinitarian Thought from Aquinas to Ockham*, 124–132; Russell L. Friedman, *Intellectual Traditions at the Medieval University: The Use of Philosophical Psychology in Trinitarian Theology among the Franciscans and Dominicans, 1250–1350*, 645–652.

31 Ockham, *Ordinatio* d. 3, q. 10, 552, ll. 15–18 (*Opera Theologica*, II): "Circa istam quaestionem primo videndum est quomodo accipitur imago secundum quod invenitur vel dicatur de una creatura respectu alterius. Secundo, quomodo aliquid est imago Dei."

32 Ockham, *Ordinatio* d. 3, q. 10, 554, ll. 6-10 (*Opera Theologica*, II): "Quantum ad primum est opinio communis quod partes imaginis sunt ipsae potentiae animae, ita quod imago consistit in intelligentia, memoria et voluntate, -vel saltem illa est evidentior assignatio imaginis-, et non est in actibus secundis, saltem principaliter."

33 Steve Brown and Gedeon Gál record the following references: Peter Lombard, I *Sent.*, d.3 c.2 nn. 39-43, 33-36; Bonaventura, I *Sent.*, d.3 p.2 a.1 q.1, 80-82; Thomas Aquinas, I *Sent.* d.3 q.3 a.1, 109-111; Henricus Gandavensis, *Summa Quaestionem*, a.40 q.7, ff. 259^v -262^r; Ioannis Duns Scoti, *Ordinatio*. I, d.3 p.3 q.4 nn.569-604, 338-357.

34 Ockham, *Ordinatio* d. 3, q. 10, 554, l. 18-555, l. 3 (*Opera Theologica*, II):

> Sed ista opinio non videtur esse vera, quia non sunt tales tres potentiae, quia sicut declarabitur in secundo, nulla est distinctio praevia in ipsa substantia animae ante distinctionem actuum secundorum productorum; igitur non sunt ibi talia tria quae repraesentent divinas personas.

35 See Armand Maurer, *The Philosophy of William of Ockham in Light of Its Principles*, 460-470.

36 Ockham, *Ordinatio* d. 3, q. 10, 555, ll. 4-10 (*Opera Theologica*, II):

> Praeterea, quando aliquid ponitur imago alicuius propter distinctionem in imagine correspondentem distinctioni in illo cuius est imago tanta debet esse distinctio inter partes imaginis quanta est in illo cuius est imago; sed inter personas divinas est distinctio realis, et inter potentias animae non est talis distinctio realis; igitur propter distinctionem illarum potentiarum non est ponenda in anima imago.

37 Lombard, *Sent.* I, d. 3, c. 2, n. 1, 71, l. 28-72, l. 8:

> 'Nunc vero ad eam iam perveniamus disputationem, ubi in mente humana, quae novit Deum vel potest nosse, Trinitatis imaginem reperiamus'. Ut enim ait Augustinus in XIV libro De Trinitate, 'licet humana mens non sit eius naturae cuius Deus est, imago tamen illius 'quo nihil melius est' id est in mente. In ipsa enim mente, etiam antequam sit particeps Dei, eius imago reperitur; etsi enim, amissa Dei participatione, deformis sit, imago tamen Dei permanent. Eo enim ipso imago Dei est mens, quo capax eius est eiusque esse particeps potest.' Iam ergo in ea Trinitatem quae Deus est inquiramus.

38 Ockham, *Ordinatio* d. 3, q. 10, 557, ll. 8-14 (*Opera Theologica*, II):

> Primum patet, quia secundum beatum Augustinum, XIV *De Trinitate*, cap. 8: 'eo anima imago Dei est quo capax eius est particepsque esse potest', ita quod de quocumque verificatur hoc quod est capax Dei posseque eius esse particeps, de eo verificatur imago; igitur sicut haec est vera 'anima secundum suam substantiam est capax Dei et potest esse particeps eius' ita haec est vera 'anima secundum suam substantiam est imago Dei.'

39 Ockham, *Ordinatio* d. 3, q. 10, 557, ll. 4-7 (*Opera Theologica*, II): "Circa secundum dico quod imago Dei imperfecta et quasi radicaliter et originaliter consistit in ipsa anima secundum suam substantiam. Verumtamen perfectio imaginis completive consistit in ipsa substantia animae et duobus actibus productis."

40 For a summary of the positions of Thomas Aquinas, Henry of Ghent and John Duns Scotus, see A. Maurer, *The Philosophy of William of Ockham*, 460-462.

41 Maurer, *The Philosophy of William of Ockham*, 463–464. Ockham, *Sent.* II, q. 20, 435, ll. 8–15 (*Opera Theologica*, V):

> Sed distinguo de potentia animae: nam potentia uno modo accipitur pro tota descriptione exprimente quid nominis, alio modo accipitur pro illo quod denominatur ab illo nomine vel conceptu. Primo modo loquendo de intellectu et voluntate, dico quod distinguuntur, nam descriptio exprimens quid nominis intellectus est ista quod 'intellectus est substantia animae potens intelligere'. Descriptio voluntatis est quod est 'substantia animae potens velle'.

42 Ockham, *Sent.* II, q. 20, 435, ll. 17–21 (*Opera Theologica*, V): "Primo modo distinguuntur realiter sicut voces distinguuntur realiter. Secundo modo distinguuntur ratione sicut conceptus. Tertio modo distinguuntur realiter, saltem partialiter, quia licet eadem sit substantia numero quae potest intelligere et velle, tamen intelligere et velle sunt actus distincti realiter."

43 Ockham, *Sent.* II, q. 20, 436, ll. 5–18 (*Opera Theologica*, V):

> Sed loquendo de intellectu et voluntate secundo modo, sic intellectus non plus distinguitur a voluntate quam ab intellectu vel quam Deus a Deo vel Sortes a Sorte, quia nec distinguitur a voluntate nec re nec ratione. Sed sic est una substantia animae potens habere distinctas actus, respectu quorum potest habere diversas denominationes. Quia ut elicit vel elicere potest actum intelligendi dicitur intellectus; ut actum volendi voluntas. Illud patet in divinis, nam Deus habet potentiam gubernativam, reparativam, praedestinativam, reprobativam, quae nullam distinctionem ponunt in Deo, sed quia alius effectus consequitur potentiam Dei creativam, gubernativam, praedestinativam, et propter diversos effectus denominatur Deus diversis denominationibus, et hoc denominatione extrinseca. Sic est in multis, sicut saepe dictum est, et sic est in proposito.

44 Ockham, *Ordinatio* d. 3, q. 10, 558, l. 16–559, l. 1 (*Opera Theologica*, II):

> Praeterea, omnes ponunt imaginem in tribus consistere habentibus ordinem originis inter se; sed potentiae non originantur nec ipsa substantia animae originatur; igitur oportet ponere aliqua accidentia animae originata pertinere ad imaginem. Ideo dico quod completa ratio imaginis consistit in ipsa substantia animae et duobus actibus, scilicet actu intelligendi et volendi, et etiam potest consistere in ipsa substantia animae et in duobus habitibus correspondentibus ipsis actibus.

45 Ockham, *Ordinatio* d. 3, q. 10, 559, ll. 1–20 (*Opera Theologica*, II):

> Et tunc loquendo de actibus naturalibus, iste est ordo: quod sicut Pater in divinis habet fecunditatem ad producendum tam Filium quam Spiritum Sanctum et communicat Filio fecunditatem producendi Spiritum Sanctum, et Pater et Filius producunt Spiritum Sanctum, ita ipsa substantia animae est fecunda et productiva tam actus intelligendi quam volendi; et producit primo actum intelligendi, qui est etiam productivus actus volendi, et tunc illae duae causae, scilicet ipsa substantia animae et actus intelligendi possunt producere actum volendi, ita quod sicut Filius in divinis est tantum ab uno, et Spiritus Sanctus est a Patre producente et a Filio producto, ita actus intelligendi est a sola substantia animae, et actus volendi est a substantia animae et ab actu intelligendi producto, et sic imago potest aliquo modo repraesentare distinctas personas, et ordinem et originem earum. Quod autem actus volendi sit effective ab actu intelligendi, ostendo per illud commune verbum quod 'omne absolutum

necessario praesuppositum alteri habet rationem causae in aliquo genere causae'; sed actus intelligendi necessario tamquam aliquid absolutum praesupponitur actui volendi; igitur habet rationem causae respect illius.

46 Ockham does not discuss Thomas directly in d. 3 of the *Ordinatio*, but he does consider the positions of Thomas Aquinas, Henry of Ghent, and John Duns Scotus (on the distinction between the powers of the soul) in: Ockham, *Sent.* II, q. 20, 427–434 (*Opera Theologica*, V). For more discussion on Scotus, see Richard Cross, *Duns Scotus on God*, 183–222 and Pekka Kärkkäinen, "Interpretations of the Psychological Analogy," 257–270.

47 Gregory of Rimini, *Lectura* II, dd.16 et 17, q. 3, a.1, 354–368, esp. 354, ll. 17–22 (V):

> Et arguo primo quod sic de potentia sensitiva. Nam potentiae sensitivae sunt multae in homine, anima vero tantum una. Igitur aliqua potentia sensitiva hominis distinguitur ab anima, et qua ratione una, et quaelibet. Consequentia patet, quia, si quaelibet esset eadem animae, essent omnes eaedem inter se, et per consequens non essent multae, sed una tantum. Antecedens est notum.

48 Gregory of Rimini, *Lectura* II, dd.16 et 17, q. 3, a.2, 368–373, esp. 354, ll. 23–33 (V):

> Secundo idem probatur de intellectivis, et per idem medium sic: Memoria, intellectus et voluntas in homine sunt tres res distinctae; igitur quaelibet est res alia ab anima. Consequentia probatur sicut praecedens. Antecedens probo auctoritate Augustini 4 De trinitate capitulo ultimo dicentis: 'Cum memoriam meam, intellectum et voluntatem nomino, singular quidem nomina ad res singulas referuntur, sed tamen ab omnibus tribus singular facta sunt. Nullum enim horum trium nominum est quod non et memoria et intellectus et voluntas mea simul operata sint.' Ubi patet quod secundum ipsum illa tria nomina pro tribus rebus distinctis, quae sunt in ipso, supponunt et nullum supponit pro re pro qua aliud supponit. Alias non singula ad res singulas referuntur, ut ait.

49 Gregory of Rimini, *Lectura* II, dd.16 et 17, q. 3, a. 2, 368, ll. 20–22 (V): "De secundo articulo dico consequenter quod ipsa anima rationalis est intellectus et voluntas, ita quod nec intellectus est res distincta ab essentia animae nec etiam voluntas."

50 Gregory of Rimini, *Lectura* II, dd. 16 et 17, q. 3, a. 2, 370, ll. 4–16 (V):

> Quarto, Anselmus De concordia capitulo 29: 'Sicut habemus in corpore membra et quinque sensus, singula ad suos usus apta, quibus quasi instrumentis utimur' etc, 'ita anima habet in se quasdam vires, quibus utitur velut instrumentis ad usus congruos. Est namque ratio in anima, qua sicut suo instrumento utitur ad ratiocinandum, et voluntas, qua utitur ad volendum. Non est enim ratio vel voluntas tota anima, sed est unaquaeque aliquid in anima'. Haec ipse.
>
> Quinto, Magister Sententiarum libro 1 distinctione 3 expresse dicit quod 'illa tria naturales proprietates seu vires sunt ipsius mentis et a se invicem differunt, quia memoria non est intelligentia vel voluntas, nec intelligentia voluntas sive amor'. Et ante praemisit quod dictum Augustini, quo ait quod sunt 'una mens et una essentia', non est 'verum iuxta proprietatem sermonis'.

51 Gregory of Rimini, *Lectura* II, dd. 16 et 17, q. 3, a. 2, 373, ll. 6–10 (V):

> Ad Anselmum et Magistrum simul, quamvis aliqui conentur eos exponere, dico tamen quod mihi apparet eos fuisse illius opinionis sicut et

multi alii sollemnes doctores. Quia tamen Augustinus videtur mihi eis contrarius nec necessitatem video ponendi huiusmodi distinctionem, idcirco oppositum teneo, salva semper aliorum reverentia.

52 Gregory of Rimini, *Lectura* II, dd. 16 et 17, q. 3, a. 2, 373, ll. 13–15 (V): "Ad secundum dico quod Augustinus accipit illa pro actibus, non potentias, et hoc etiam coguntur concedere alii, cum ipsi non ponant quod memoria et intellectus sint duae potentiae realiter distinctae."

53 Gregory of Rimini, *Lectura* II, dd. 16 et 17, q. 3, a. 2, 372, ll. 17–24 (V):

Ad auctoritatem Augustini dico quod illius terminis 'memoria, intelligentia et voluntate' utitur pro actibus, et secundum hoc maxime patet differentia quam intendit, quoniam quaelibet persona divina est sua memoria et intelligentia et voluntas, et memoria est intelligentia seu intellectio et volitio, in nobis autem non sic. Vel potest dici quod, si accipit pro potentia, ponit illas negativas, devitans affirmativas oppositas, non tamquam falsas sed tamquam inartificiales. Mihi tamen prima solutio magis placet, eo quod plene patet ex textu.

54 Gregory is not alone in this judgment. The late 14th century theologian Peter Gracilis wrote in his commentary on the *Sentences* (book I, q. 4) that there is more dissimilarity than similarity between the divine Trinity and human noetic faculties. Like Gregory, Peter was somewhat hesitant in speaking about the *imago Trinitatis* (Gracilis's commentary is found in London, British Library, ms. Royal 10 A 1, f. 23[v]).
55 Russell Friedman, *Medieval Trinitarian Thought*, 146–170.
56 On Irenaeus's reading of the image and likeness distinction in Genesis 1, see Stephen O. Presley, *The Intertextual Reception of Genesis 1–3 in Irenaeus of Lyons*.
57 Irenaeus, *Contre les hérésies*, 5.16.1–2, 212–216.
58 Denis Minns, *Irenaeus*, 83–102.
59 For a modern systematic appropriation of this, see Kathryn Tanner, *Christ the Key*, 20.
60 See Denis Minns, *Irenaeus: An Introduction*, 92–93.
61 See Dana Dovey, "Boy Born without Brain, Trevor Judge Waltrip, Dies after Living for 12 Years with Hydranencephaly."
62 Are there resources in medieval theology to help modern-day theologians or philosophers think about individuals with extreme cognitive impairment? The short answer, I think, is absolutely. The work of Miguel Romero and John Berkman, to take two examples, point to the various ways in which Thomas Aquinas can be understood to address this particular question. See, Miguel J. Romero, "Profound Cognitive Impairment, Moral Virtue, and Our Life in Christ," 79–94. See also, John Berkman, "Are Persons with Profound Intellectual Disabilities Sacramental Icons of Heavenly Life? Aquinas on Impairment," 83–96.

Further, if one looks at the practical aspects of medieval sacramental theology, there is a significant resource both in theological literature and Canon Law for addressing extreme cases that confront a priest administering the sacraments. The harsh realities of the medieval world often presented priests with difficult choices: Does one baptize a still-born baby? What about a monstrous baby (i.e., deformed baby) who appears to not be "totally human"? What about a breech-birth in which an infant's feet emerge and the child is about to die – can one baptize a babies' feet? If one does baptize a babies' feet, does one re-administer the sacrament if the child lives? These sacramental complications regarding just baptism were real and required practical answers. The questions, however, do not end with baptism: Should a priest administer the eucharist to someone with a debilitating cognitive impairment? What about confession, or marriage? These types of questions generated theological discussion that is a useful resource for modern theologians or philosophers thinking about individuals with severe cognitive impairments.

63 See note 62.
64 Again, this is not to say that someone could not soften a given theologian's intellectualist account of the *imago* by reading it in conjunction with other parts of their corpus that allow for a rather distinct picture of human persons.
65 It is important to point out, I think, that the scholastic theologians discussed in the present chapter were not primarily concerned with the questions at the heart of this study. That is, they were not attempting to answer questions of morality but were examining the speculative theological question of what it means for a human person to be a bearer of God's image. As such, the focus of attention was on what properties or attributes in the human persons are most like the triune God, not on questions of relationality (i.e., how a person interacts with God or nature) or morality. Thus, by pressing their discussion of the *imago Dei* in the direction of applied ethics, it must be insisted that we are posing questions to them that they did not deal with directly in their extant writings.
66 Here I agree, for the most part, with the arguments already put forth by Hans Reinders. See his *Receiving the Gift of Friendship: Profound Disability, Theological Anthropology, and Ethics*.
67 See, e.g., the theological anthropology of Herman Bavink, *Reformed Dogmatics. God and Creation, Volume II*, ch. 12. In short, for Bavink the image of God is not something added to humanity such that one can have it or not, or one can more fully participate in it or not; i.e., the image of God is found in each member of the human race. There is no exclusive set of attributes that renders one member of the human race more in the image of God than another. As he writes (554), "a human being does not bear or have the image of God... [H]e or she is the image of God." Here Bavink is closer to the position of Irenaeus described in the previous section.

References

Primary Sources

Aquinas, Thomas. *Sancti Thomae Aquinatis Doctoris Angelici. Opera Omnia. Iussu Leonis XIII*. Civitas Vaticana: Typis Polyglottis Vaticanis, 1882–.
——— *Scriptum super libros Sententiarum*, 4 vols. Edited by P. Mandonnet and F.M. Moos. Paris, 1929–1956.
Augustine. *De Trinitate*. Edited by W.J. Mountain and Fr. Glorie, in *Corpus Christianorum Series Latina*, vols. 50, 50A. Turnhout: Brepols, 1968.
——— *The Trinity*. Translated by Stephen Mckenna. *The Fathers of the Church*, vol. 45. Washington, DC: The Catholic University of America Press, 1963.
Bavink, Herman. *Reformed Dogmatics. God and Creation, Volume II*. Translated by John Vriend. Grand Rapids, MI: Baker Academic, 2004.
Bonaventura. *Commentaria in Quattuor Libros Sententiarum, In Primum Librum Sententiarum*, vol. 1. In *Bonaventurae Opera Omnia*. Quaracchi: Ex Typographia Collegii S. Bonaventurae, 1882.

Duns Scotus, John. *Ordinatio*. Edited by C. Balić and others. In: *Opera Omnia Ioannis Duns Scoti*, vol. 3. Civitas Vaticana: Typis Polyglottis Vaticanis, 1954.

Gregory of Rimini. *Lectura super primum et secundum Sententiarum*, 7 vols. Edited by D. Trapp and others. Spätmittelalter und Reformation: Texte und Untersuchungen, 6–12. Berlin: Walter de Gruyter, 1981–1987.

Henry of Ghent. *Summa Quaestionum Ordinariarum*, 2 vols. Edited by I. Badius. Paris: 1520.

Irenaeus of Lyon. *Contre les hérésies*. Edited by A. Rousseau, L. Doutreleau, C. Mercier. *Source chrétiennes*, vol. 153. Paris, 2013.

Ockham, William. *Opera philosophica et theologica*, 17 vols. Edited by Gedeon Gál and others. St. Bonaventure, NY: Franciscan Institute, 1967–1988.

Origen of Alexandria. *Origenes Vier Bücher von den Prinzipien*. Edited by H. Görgemanns and H. Karpp. Darmstadt: Wissenschaftliche Buchgesellschaft, 1976.

Peter Gracilis. *In Sententiae*. In: London, British Library, ms. Royal 10 A 1, f. 23^v.

Peter Lombard. *Sententiae in IV libros distinctae*, 3 vols. Rome: Grottaferrata, 1971–1981.

———. *The Sentences: Books I–IV*, 4 vols. Translated by Giulio Silano. Toronto: Pontifical Institute of Mediaeval Studies, 2007–2010.

Secondary Sources

Barnes, Michel René. "Divine Unity and the Divided Self: Gregory of Nyssa's Trinitarian Theology in its Psychological Context." In *Re-Thinking Gregory of Nyssa*. Edited by Sarah Coakley. Oxford: Oxford University Press, 2003.

de Beaurecueil, Marie–Joseph Serge de Laugier. "L'homme image de Dieu selon saint Thomas d'Aquin," *Études et Recherches* 8 (1952): 45–82.

———. "L'homme image de Dieu selon saint Thomas d'Aquin," *Études et Recherches* 9 (1955): 37–96.

Berkman, John. "Are Persons with Profound Intellectual Disabilities Sacramental Icons of Heavenly Life? Aquinas on Impairment," *Studies in Christian Ethics* 26.1 (2013): 83–96.

Boersma, Gerald P. *Augustine's Early Theology of Image: A Study in the Development of Pro-Nicene Theology*. Oxford: Oxford University Press, 2016.

Boyle, John F. "Introduction." In *Thomas Aquinas, Lectura romana in primum Sententiarum Petri Lombardi*. Edited by Leonard E. Boyle and John F. Boyle. Toronto: Pontifical Institute of Mediaeval Studies, 2006.

Boyle, Leonard E. "Alia lectura fratris Thome," *Mediaeval Studies* 45 (1983): 418–429.

Coakley, Sarah. "Introduction – Gender, Trinitarian Analogies, and the Pedagogy of *The Song*." In *Re-Thinking Gregory of Nyssa*. Edited by Sarah Coakley. Oxford: Oxford University Press, 2003.

Colish, Marcia. *Peter Lombard*, 2 vols. Leiden: Brill, 1994.

Cross, Richard. *Duns Scotus on God*. Burlington, VT: Ashgate, 2005.

Crouzel, Henri. *Théologie de l'image de Dieu chez Origène*, Études publiées sous la direction de la faculté de théologie S.J. de Lyon-Fourvière 34. Paris: Éditions Aubier-Montaigne, 1956.

———. "Le Dieu d'Origène et le Dieu de Plotin." In *Origeniana Quinta*. Edited by Robert J. Daly. *Bibliotheca Ephemeridum Theologicarum Lovaniensium*, vol. 105. Leuven: Peeters Publishers, 1992.

Cunningham, Francis L. B. *The Indwelling of the Trinity: A Historico-Doctrinal Study of the Theory of St. Thomas Aquinas.* Dubuque, IA: Priory Press, 1955.

Daley, Brian E. "The Fullness of the Saving God: Cyril of Alexandria on the Holy Spirit." In *The Theology of St. Cyril of Alexandria: A Critical Appreciation.* Edited by Thomas G. Weinandy and Daniel A. Keating. London: T&T Clark, 2003.

Dondaine, Hyacinthe François. "'Alia lectura fratris thome'? (*Super 1 Sent.*)," *Mediaeval Studies* 42 (1980): 308–336.

Dovey, Dana. "Boy Born without a Brain, Trevor Judge Waltrip, Dies after Living for 12 Years with Hydranencephaly," *Medical Daily*. <https://www.medicaldaily.com/boy-born-without-brain-trevor-judge-waltrip-dies-after-living-12-years-hydranencephaly-300736> Accessed December 15, 2018.

Dupont, Anthony and Cheuk Yin Yam. "A Mind-Centered Approach of *imago Dei*: A Dynamic Construction in Augustine's *De Trinitate* XIV," *Augustiniana* 62 (2012): 7–13.

Friedman, Russell L. *Medieval Trinitarian Thought from Aquinas to Ockham.* Cambridge: Cambridge University Press, 2010.

——— *Intellectual Traditions at the Medieval University: The Use of Philosophical Psychology in Trinitarian Theology among the Franciscans and Dominicans, 1250–1350.* Leiden: E.J. Brill, 2012.

Hart, David B. "The Mirror of the Infinite: Gregory of Nyssa on the *Vestigia Trinitatis*." In *Re-Thinking Gregory of Nyssa*. Edited by Sarah Coakley. Oxford: Oxford University Press, 2003.

Johnson, Mark F. "'Alia lectura fratris thome': A List of the New Texts of St. Thomas Aquinas found in Lincoln College, Oxford, MS. Lat. 95," *Recherches de théologie ancienne et médiévale* 57 (1990): 34–61.

Kärkkäinen, Pekka. "Interpretations of the Psychological Analogy from Aquinas to Biel." In *Trinitarian Theology in the Medieval West*. Helsinki: Luther-Agricola-Society, 2007.

Ludlow, Morwenna. *Gregory of Nyssa Ancient and [Post]Modern*. Oxford: Oxford University Press, 2007.

Maurer, Armand. *The Philosophy of William of Ockham in Light of Its Principles*. Toronto: Pontifical Institute of Mediaeval Studies, 1999.

McLeod, Frederick G. *The Image of God in the Antiochene Tradition*. Washington, DC: The Catholic University of America Press, 1999.

Merriell, Juvenal. *To the Image of the Trinity: A Study of the Development of Aquinas' Teaching.* Toronto: Pontifical Institute of Mediaeval Studies, 1990.

——— "Trinitarian Anthropology." In *The Theology of Thomas Aquinas*. Edited by Rik Van Nieuwenhove and Joseph Wawrykow. Notre Dame, IN: University of Notre Dame Press, 2005.

Minns, Denis. *Irenaeus*. London: Geoffrey Chapman, 1994.

Porro, Pasquale. *Thomas Aquinas: A Historical and Philosophical Profile.* Translated by Joseph Trabbic and Roger W. Nutt. Washington, DC: Catholic University of America Press, 2016.

Presley, Stephen O. *The Intertextual Reception of Genesis 1–3 in Irenaeus of Lyons*. Leiden: E.J. Brill, 2015.

Reinders, Hans. *Receiving the Gift of Friendship: Profound Disability, Theological Anthropology, and Ethics.* Grand Rapids, MI: William B. Eerdmans Publishing Co., 2008.

Romero, Miguel J. "Profound Cognitive Impairment, Moral Virtue, and Our Life in Christ," *Church Life* 4:4 (2014): 79–94.
Rosemann, Philipp W. *Peter Lombard*. Oxford: Oxford University Press, 2004.
Principe, Walter H. "The Dynamism of Augustine's Terms for Describing the Highest Trinitarian Image in the Human Person." In *Studia Patristica*, vol. 18. Edited by Elizabeth A. Livingston. Oxford: Pergamon Press, 1982.
Slotemaker, John T. "Reading Augustine in the Fourteenth Century: Gregory of Rimini and Pierre d'Ailly on the *Imago Trinitatis*." In *Studia Patristica*, vol. 69. Edited by Markus Vinzent. Leuven: Peeters, 2013.
Williams, Rowan. *On Augustine*. Oxford: Bloomsbury, 2016.

5 Remembering "Mindless" Persons

Intellectual Disability, Spanish Colonialism, and the Disappearance of a Medieval Account of Persons Who Lack the Use of Reason

Miguel J. Romero

Introduction

At the end of the Middle Ages and the beginnings of modernity, there was a subtle shift in the way the Spanish Dominican interpreters of Thomas Aquinas spoke about the significance of our rational faculties. The scope of this chapter is limited to identifying a set of historical and textual markers that indicate both the origin and the development of this interpretive shift. Those markers present amid a whirlwind of questions that were fiercely debated throughout Spain during the first half of the 16th century.

My overarching concern is what happened in the 16th century to Aquinas's 13th century way of thinking about the vulnerability of our rational faculties and, in particular, Aquinas's account of the undiminished intellectual dignity and inalienable contemplative aptitude of persons who "lack the use of reason."[1] Elsewhere I've shown that Aquinas had a nuanced and integrated way of thinking about conditions that we today refer to as an "intellectual disability" or "cognitive impairment."[2] In this chapter I want to provide a summary account of how Aquinas's way of thinking about persons who lack the use of reason, in particular the *amentes* ("mindless" persons), came to be displaced from the main currents of Thomistic theological discourse.

Integral to the present account of what happened in the 16th century are exegetical judgments concerning three basic principles in Aquinas's anthropological outlook. Specifically, (1) Aquinas's view that the creaturely vulnerability of the human being to corporeal defect is integral to human nature and corresponds with the inalienable dignity of the human being as the image of God[3]; (2) Aquinas's distinction between the specifying *act of intellect* and the derivative intellectual act called *the use of reason*[4]; and (3) Aquinas's understanding of the inviolable intellectual nature and contemplative aptitude of every living human being, including persons who have the condition *amentia* ("mindlessness"; i.e., persons who "lack the use of reason" in a way that is profound and severely debilitating).[5]

In light of those judgments about the content of Aquinas's anthropological outlook, the 16th century questions and debates that interest me here concern the legitimacy of the Spanish colonial enterprise in the Americas and focus on the rational status and moral aptitude of the Amerindian peoples. An important distinction needs to be clear from the outset, between the specific topic of the Spanish colonial debates and the, more general, theoretical subject of those debates. On the one hand, *the specific topic* of the Spanish colonial debates was the truth of allegations concerning the rational status and moral aptitude of the Amerindian peoples (and, by extension, the justice or injustice of the Spanish colonial enterprise in the Americas). On the other hand, *the subject* of the Spanish colonial debates was the anthropological status and moral aptitude of persons who seem to lack the use of reason.

Much has been written on the specific topic of the Spanish colonial debates (i.e., the colonialist allegations and activities in the Americas). By contrast, to my knowledge, nothing has been written about the subject of the Spanish colonial debates (i.e., the anthropological and moral questions relevant to persons who seem to lack the use of reason). This lacuna makes sense because, as I intend to show, among the outcomes of those 16th century debates was (1) a theological vigilance against any denial of a particular person's status as *rational or as lacking the requisite faculties for the use of reason*; and (2) a quasi-Thomistic, rationalistic interpretive tendency when interpreting Aquinas's anthropological outlook, a tendency that is ill-equipped to make Christian theological sense of the undiminished intellectual dignity and inalienable contemplative aptitude of persons who seem to lack the use of reason. Bearing in mind the distinction between the topic and subject of the Spanish colonial debates, and the contemporary lacuna, this chapter is focused on persons who actually (and not allegedly) lack the use of reason.

Key philosophical and theological arguments deployed during the Spanish colonial debates hinged on the correct interpretation and application of two Latin medieval sources: the theology of Thomas Aquinas and the philosophy of Aristotle (reintroduced to the West in the 12th century).[6] When these 16th century engagements are compared to the relevant texts from Aquinas and Aristotle, important points of consistency and inconsistency become apparent. What one finds is Spanish colonial interests twisting medieval accounts of persons *who actually lack the use of reason* and then maliciously applying those novel 16th century formulations to the Amerindian peoples. And, then, one finds a vehement Dominican response: first, a moral argument decrying the malicious 16th century abuse and exploitation of the Amerindian peoples; and, second, a philosophical and theological rejection of both the twisted colonialist theories *and* a wary regard toward the speculative outlook on persons who actually lack the use of reason, as represented in the original medieval texts.

In the writings of *Servus Dei*, Bartolomé de las Casas, composed in defense of the Amerindian peoples, we find indications of a shift in the way the Dominican Thomists of Salamanca spoke about the anthropological, moral, and contemplative significance of our rational faculties. For example, in his monumental and morally heroic *In Defense of the Indians*, las Casas draws upon Aquinas and passionately defends the human dignity of the Amerindian peoples, emphatically asserting and forcefully demonstrating that the Amerindians as a group do not lack the use of reason.[7] In doing so, however, las Casas presumes an understanding of the significance of our rational faculties that is not wholly consistent with the outlook of Thomas Aquinas. This is evident, for example, when las Casas claims that persons who do indeed lack the use of reason, as they are occasionally to be found, are "freaks of rational nature ... who cannot seek God, know him, call upon him, or love him."[8] By contrast, in the writings of Francisco de Vitoria, likewise composed in defense of the Amerindian peoples, we find the remnants of a Thomistic outlook on persons who lack the use of reason that may be worth recovering.

The aspect of the debates that concern me could be mapped in relation to a theologically problematic premise, a presumption that is inconsistent with the anthropological and moral outlook of Thomas Aquinas. Specifically, the presumption that posits a direct correlation between *human dignity* and *the use of reason*. So conceived, the most prominent Spanish colonialist argument ran like this:

i   An individual has distinctively human dignity and potential to a degree that is correlative to that individual's ability to reason discursively.
ii The Amerindian peoples, on the whole, have a low aptitude for discursive reasoning.
iii Therefore, the Amerindian peoples, on the whole, lack the fullness of human dignity and potential.

Given that alleged lack of dignity and potential, the colonialists argued, the Amerindians could be forcefully subjugated by Spanish colonizers who supposedly had the full use of reason.

Against that colonialist argument, Spanish Dominicans like las Casas accepted the theologically problematic premise, countering that the Amerindian peoples satisfied the condition of rationality and had a right to be regarded as dignified and fully human subjects. The standard Spanish Dominican counterargument ran like this:

i   An individual has distinctively human dignity and potential to a degree that is correlative to that individual's ability to reason discursively.

ii   There is incontrovertible evidence that the Amerindian peoples, on the whole, have the typically human aptitude for discursive reasoning.
iii Therefore, the Amerindian peoples, on the whole, do not lack the fullness of human dignity and potential.

Given that the Amerindians possess the fullness of human dignity and potential, the Dominicans of Salamanca argued that the Spanish colonialists had no right to subjugate, violently enslave, or commercially exploit the Amerindian peoples.

The theologically problematic premise positing (i) a direct correlation between human dignity and the use of reason was one of the cornerstones of the Dominican defense of the Amerindians. Unfortunately, in adopting the problematic premise, Dominican Thomists like las Casas likewise assumed theological imprecisions that are serious, difficult to recognize, and have far-reaching implications. Considered from the aspect of Aquinas's anthropological and moral outlook, an unnuanced and unqualified presumption of a correlation between the use of reason and human dignity undermines the rationale that undergirds much of what Aquinas has to say about persons who lack the use of reason. For example, Aquinas holds that (1) short of death, no corporeal vulnerability, limitation, or organic impairment of our rational faculties can diminish our innate intellectual dignity and that (2) moral, contemplative, and sacramental entailments follow from that anthropological judgment concerning the lives of persons who lack the use of reason (e.g., sacramental access, inalienable contemplative aptitude, protective care, etc.). Buoyed by the far-reaching efforts and wide diffusion of Las Casa's writings, in the decades that followed the Spanish colonial debates, something important was displaced from the main current of Thomistic theological discourse.

Mapping the Spanish colonial debates by way of the problematic identification of human dignity with the use of reason provides a bird's-eye view of how *the specific topic* of the debates (relevant to the Amerindian peoples) relates to *the more general theological subject* of the debates (relevant to persons who actually lack the use of reason). However, it does not tell us the story of what happened and how it happened. That story requires that we retrace familiar historical and textual markers but do so in a way that remembers persons we often forget because their presence in history is easy to overlook. This is what I mean by the title "Remembering 'Mindless' Persons": as the Dominican Thomists of Salamanca made their worthy arguments in defense of the Amerindian peoples, many of them did not remember what Aquinas had to say about the *amentes* – "mindless" persons who lack the use of reason, persons who are often overlooked, ignored, and forgotten.

The chapter is divided into four sections. The first section introduces the familiar story, figures, and questions of the Spanish colonial debates. In doing so, I introduce uncontroversial elements from the scholarly consensus on the period that will be taken up in later sections. Special attention is given to John Mair's interpretive gloss of Aristotle's *Politics* (1252a 30–1255b 6) in his commentary on distinction 44 in Book II of Lombard's *Sentences*. In particular, I highlight a constellation of 16th century interpretive errors directly related to John Mair's interpretation, and I draw attention to elements in Mair's interpretation that were novel, imprecise, and well-suited to the aims of the theological and philosophical defenders of the Spanish colonial enterprise in the Americas. The second section offers a close reading of Aristotle's account of the *phusei doulon* figure, the so-called "slave by nature." The analysis aims (1) to show the imprecision of Mair's interpretive conflation of barbarism and the *phusei doulon* figure, (2) to provide an account, on Aristotle's terms, of the defective nature of the *phusei doulon* figure, and (3) to outline the exegetical judgments and the argument for an interpretation of the *phusei doulon* figure as a deeply problematic, ancient Greek account of a person who lacks the use of reason. The third section surveys the theological and anthropological principles relevant to Aquinas's way of thinking about persons who lack the use of reason. From there, a close analysis of relevant sections in Aquinas's *Commentary on Aristotle's Politics* shows (1) Aquinas's interpretation of the *phusei doulon* figure as a person who lacks the use of reason and (2) outlines Aquinas's subversive revision of Aristotle's understanding of what has gone wrong in the case of persons who lack the use of reason. The last section retells the story of the Spanish colonial debates, focusing on the understandings of persons who lack the use of reason in the arguments of Bartolomé de las Casas's *En Defensa de los Indios* and Francisco de Vitoria's *Relectio: De Eo ad Quod Tenetur Homo Veniens ad Usum Rationis* (1534) and his treatise *De Indies* (1539). The aim of that final section is to show how Aquinas's understanding of persons who lack the use reason was displaced from the main current of Thomistic theological discourse in the 16th century.

Admittedly, at first sight, the connection between intellectual disability, Spanish colonialism, and the theology of Aquinas is not obvious. I intend to show why understanding that connection is important for historians who have an interest in the way "disability" was understood by medieval philosophers and theologians. And, further, I want to show why that connection is important for contemporary interpreters of Aquinas, especially those who recognize the outlook of St. Thomas as a valuable resource for the enrichment of contemporary Christian theological reflection and discourse.[9]

The Spanish Colonial Debates, John Mair, and a Novel Interpretation of Aristotle

The story of the Spanish colonial debates unfolds during the decades following the first European encounters with the various civilizations and people groups of the Americas. Anyone with more than a passing interest in the history of Western philosophy and theology will be familiar with the key points of disputation during this period in Spain. Among the most prominent questions were the following: (1) What is the nature and rational status of the Amerindian peoples? (2) If the Amerindians lack the use of reason, do they likewise lack the capacity for intellectual development, moral virtue, and Christian holiness? (3) In relating to the Amerindians, what does justice require of the Spanish and what does justice permit?

Arising from those questions, the story most of us learned in high school goes like this: From 1492 to the middle part of the 16th century, Spanish philosophers, theologians, jurists, and missionaries – scholars and academics of all stripes – brought the titanic conceptual and analytic resources of the European Middle Ages to bear upon an unprecedented set of encounters, conflicting interests, inconsistent reports, and sickening justifications of profoundly unjust behavior.

Advocates of the Spanish colonial enterprise – like Gil Gregorio (146?–153?), Bernardo de Mesa (1470–1524), Juan de Quevedo (1450–1519), and Juan Ginés de Sepúlveda (1494–1573) – argued, among other things, that the Amerindians on the whole were congenitally subordinate, quasi-irrational, bestial men, rendered insane by poor climate and inhuman cultural practices. The centerpiece of the colonialist rationale was a novel interpretation of Aristotle's *phusei doulon* figure (i.e., the slave by nature), articulated and then applied for the first time to the Amerindian peoples by the Scottish theologian John Mair in 1510 (Johannes Maior, 1467–1550).[10] Mair's exegetically problematic formulation of the "natural slave" conflated circumstances and conditions that Aristotle was careful to keep distinct. What emerged from Mair's interpretation, in the arguments of the colonialists at the Burjos junta of 1512, was a being that had the condition of the *phusei doulon*, the fixed congenital strangeness of barbarian foreigners, the status of a civil slave, the unruly passions of an incontinent man, and the irrational wildness of the bestial men described in the folk legends and myths of ancient Greece. Given this caricature of the nature and status of the Amerindian peoples, it was presumed by Spanish colonialists that the Amerindians as a group had little potential for intellectual, moral, and spiritual development. Thus, it was argued, justice required very little of the Spanish in the Americas and much was permitted.

In opposition to the advocates of the Spanish colonial enterprise, Dominican theologians and missionaries associated with the School of Salamanca vehemently rejected the claim that the Amerindians lacked the use of reason or that their lives resembled anything like the condition of "natural slavery" that was attributed to them. Among the most prominent were Dominicans like Matías de Paz (1468–1519), Francisco de Vitoria (1483–1546), Domingo de Soto (1497–1560), Anton de Montesinos (1475–1545), Bartolomé de las Casas (1474–1566),

Juan de la Peña (1513–1565), and Domingo Báñez (1528–1604). These scholars held forth concrete evidence of the rational nature and moral aptitude of the Amerindians – and, in that way, carried out a monumental, historically consequential, and decades-long defense of the rationality, human dignity, and human rights of the Amerindian peoples. Dominicans like las Casas, for example, articulated arguments rooted in the complex Amerindian understanding and engagement with the natural world; the contemplative end and devotional rationale of the various Amerindian religious practices; and the principled civility of the unfamiliar Amerindian social mores. Because it could be both demonstrated empirically and argued theologically that the Amerindians possessed the rational nature of the human species, there was no reason to doubt that the Amerindian peoples likewise possessed the requisite faculties for intellectual development, moral virtue, and Christian holiness. For that reason, the Salamancans argued, justice required much of the Spanish in the Americas in relation to the Amerindian peoples and justice imposed radical constraints on what was permitted for the Spanish in the Americas.

Our historical judgment concerning what is historically significant and most consequential about the Spanish colonial debates is liable to uncritically appropriate at least three interpretive errors that came to be firmly embedded in the discourse of the 16th century interlocutors, on both sides. Namely, (1) the view that John Mair's interpretation of the *Politics*, Book I, is accurate; (2) that the 16th century application of Mair's interpretation to the Amerindians is consistent with Aristotle's outlook; and (3) the view that Aquinas taught that the use of reason is what specifies human nature and that the use of reason is the principle of our creaturely dignity as the image of God. We will treat these three interpretive errors in turn.

John Mair and the Spanish Colonial Claims

In 1512, the Spanish king Ferdinand called for a gathering at Burjos in response to pressure from the Dominican order.[11] In the years leading up to that gathering, the Dominican Order had been decrying the violence and injustices being inflicted upon the Amerindian peoples, and the Dominicans actively questioned the legitimacy of the Spanish colonial presence in the Americas.[12] Ferdinand called the meeting at Burjos to settle the question.

The first time Aristotle's account of the slave by nature in Book I of the *Politics* was invoked during the Spanish colonial debates was at the Burjos *junta* in 1512.[13] There is a solid consensus that the Scottish theologian John Mair inadvertently provided the core inspiration for what became the centerpiece of the Spanish colonialist rationale.[14] In 1510, Mair published the first version of his commentary on Lombard's

Sentences.[15] As a philosopher and theologian, Mair had earned a reputation as a versatile scholar who was able to bring the resources of the 14th and 15th centuries into conversation with the concerns, questions, and preoccupations of his contemporaries.[16] For this reason, Mair's works were widely read and consulted across Europe, including at the Burjos *junta*.

In Mair's commentary on distinction 44 in Book II of the *Sentences*, he takes up the question of whether or not it is legitimate for Christians to rule over pagans. In his response, Mair includes a remark that was recognized by the colonialist interests at the Burjos *junta* as a way to solve the philosophical questions and juridical challenges being raised by the Dominican Order. Mair writes,

> These people [found in the Atlantic Ocean] live in a bestial manner. Near either side of the equator and below the poles live human beings who live as wild animals, as Ptolemy says in his *Tetrabiblos*. And this has now been verified by experience. Wherefore, the first person to conquer them, justly rules over them, because, these people are slaves by nature, as is evident. As [Aristotle] says in the third and fourth chapters of the *Politics*, it is manifest that some are by nature slaves, others by nature free. And it is determined that in some individuals there exists that kind of disposition, so that this state of affairs is beneficial to them; and it is just for the one person to be a slave and for the other to be free. And it is fitting that the one person rules, while the other, in accordance with his innate disposition, belongs to this master; and thereby he is ruled. For this reason the Philosopher, in the first chapter of the same book, says that it is on this account that the poets say that it is proper for Greeks to rule over barbarians, because, by nature, a barbarian and a slave are the same thing.[17]

I've included the whole of the relevant section from Mair's commentary. There are four important interpretive claims in Mair's gloss of Book I of the *Politics*. First, the identification of an entire foreign people group: as already noted, this passage is the earliest extant example of the claim that the indigenous inhabitants of the Americas are *en masse* a paradigmatic instance of Aristotle's slave by nature. Second, the cause of the condition of the *phusei doulon*: Mair conflates Aristotle's account of the slave by nature with Ptolemy's astrological account of region-based, racialized difference (*Tetrabiblos*, Book II, Chapter 2). Third, the distinctiveness of the *phusei doulon*: Mair conflates Aristotle's account of the *phusei doulon* figure with Aristotle's discrete accounts of non-Greeks, of bestial men, and persons subjugated through war. Fourth, the life of the *phusei doulon* within the household: Mair claims that the authority of the "natural master" over the "natural slave" is secured and enforced through the violence of war.

Mair's novel account of the slave by nature bears only a superficial resemblance to Aristotle's description of the *phusei doulon* figure in Book I of the *Politics*. In fact, the plain sense of Aristotle's extended account of the relationship between the "natural master" (*phusei despoton*) and the "natural servant" (*phusei doulon*) in the *Politics* (1252a 30–1255b 6) is a systematic deconstruction of the kind of imprecision one finds in John Mair's 16th century theory of natural slavery.[18] The four problematic elements of Mair's brief interpretative gloss are important because they eventually came to set the template for the Spanish colonialist arguments spanning from the Burjos *junta* of 1512 to the arguments of Juan Ginés de Sepúlveda at Valladolid in 1550. Each of the four problematic interpretive claims mentioned above can be interrogated on their own terms. For the purposes of this chapter, it is sufficient to show that Aristotle does not consider the nature of all non-Greeks (i.e., "barbarians") and the slave by nature to be identical.

Aristotle on Natural Slaves, Women ... *and Non-Greeks?*

For Aristotle, the essential nature or form (*eidos*) of Man is correlative, but not identical, to the function (*ergon*) of Man. The purpose of Man (nature's intent of the human species) is to realize its end or *telos* in particular human beings: to stand upright like the gods, with the same rationality and seminal potency by which Prometheus was able to make mud into the first human being.[19] The function of Man is the means by which the purpose of Man is completed or perfected.

There is wide agreement that a spectrum of anthropological outliers is present in Aristotle's thought: for example, women, the slave by nature, barbarians, madmen, the incontinent, and bestial men. These are human beings who are incapable of realizing the *telos* of ordinary human life. In other words, these are Aristotle's anthropological "problem cases" – the exceptions, so to speak, to ordinary adult human life. As Aristotle sees it, there are two kinds of exceptions to ordinary human life. The *unnatural exceptions* are essentially perfectible human beings: well-born males who suffer an unnatural defect that is caused by some intervening force (e.g., barbarians, madmen, the incontinent). By contrast, *the natural exceptions* are essentially defective human beings: their defect is coordinate with "nature's intent" and the *telos* of humanity on the whole (i.e., women and the slave by nature).

For the most part, scholarship concerned with the question of how best to interpret these various outliers centers on the defective or subordinate status of women and the natural slave (*phusei doulon*).[20] Less common are attempts to make sense of barbarism, bestiality, or madness *on Aristotle's own terms* and in relationship to the status of women and natural slaves.[21] When it comes to the *phusei doulon* figure, there are two common interpretive strategies. Some scholars isolate the description as

Remembering "Mindless" Persons

a prejudicial quirk of an ancient culture and ultimately conclude that it has no real significance.[22] Other scholars recognize the implications if Aristotle held a fundamentally flawed conception of human nature and the human good: specifically, questions would follow about the soundness of Aristotelian moral philosophy on the whole.[23]

Beginning of Aristotle's Politics

Aristotle begins the *Politics* with a claim that every community is established for the sake of some good (Politics, 1252a 1–2).[24] His first concern is to treat those things that cannot naturally exist without a relational counterpart. First, he notes the reproductive relation between male and female. Second, he notes the survival-motivated, cooperative relationship between a "master by nature" (*phusei despoton*) and a "slave by nature" (*phusei doulon*).[25]

For Aristotle, these two classes of relationship are common sense and reflect *nature's intent* for the survival of humanity. As Aristotle sees it, women and the "slave by nature" are misbegotten human males (a defective or unactualized *eidos*) – lacking seminal potency and capacity for rational deliberation, respectively.[26] The impaired function of women and natural slaves is indicative of a defective form (this is usually referred to as Aristotle's function argument).[27] According to Aristotle, these defects are natural because the human species would not exist if humans did not reproduce and humans could not survive if they did not cooperate with one another through the orderly differentiation and performance of nature-stipulated roles. Thus, according to Aristotle, the most basic and natural political relations are male-female and ruler-ruled.

Immediately following this opening framework, Aristotle concerns himself with rejecting the claim that these two nature-stipulated relations can be further reduced into a single relational hierarchy – that is, the idea that women and the "slave by nature" are subordinate to the head-of-household in the same way. Aristotle's rejection of that idea and his explanation of why these two household relations must be distinguished include a reference to non-Greeks (*barbaroi*). That reference to non-Greeks can be misleading if interpreted in isolation of its immediate and wider context. Specifically, in a way that runs contrary to the entire argument of Book I of the *Politics*, Aristotle's comment could be mistaken to be a stipulation that every non-Greek is a "slave by nature." This interpretive mistake is the fundamental problem with John Mair's 16th century account of Aristotle's outlook. Aristotle writes,

> it is by nature that a distinction has been made between female and slave. For nature produces nothing skimpily ... but one thing for one purpose; for every tool will be made best if it serves not many tasks but one. Non-Greeks, however, assign to female and slave the same

status. This is because they [non-Greeks] do not have that which naturally rules: their association comes to be that of a male slave and a female slave. Hence, as the poets say, "it is proper that Greeks should rule the non-Greeks (*barbaroi*)" [and they say this] on the assumption that the barbarian and slave are by nature identical. Thus, it was from these two associations [reproductive and cooperative] that a household first arose ... the association formed according to nature, for the satisfaction of the purposes of everyday, is a household ....[28]

I've included this large passage from Aristotle for two reasons. First, a great deal of what Aristotle has to say about the master-slave relation in Book 1 of the *Politics* is an interrogation of the judgments surrounding the poetic line excerpted from *Iphigenia at Aulis* by Euripides.[29] Second, how one interprets the rhetorical function of that poetic line within the natural slave discourse conditions what can count as a plausible description of Aristotle's proper "slave by nature."

So, what is the status of the assumption of the poets that "the barbarian and slave are by nature identical"? *Do we have before us a metaphysically stipulative definition of barbarism and natural slavery? Or, a prefatory description of Athenian common-sense? Or, perhaps, a foil?* The status of that passage and the rhetorical significance of the poetic line can be teased out through a close reading.[30] To summarize: The rhetorical function of the excerpt from *Iphigenia at Aulis* is to illustrate the common-sense status of a particular Greek claim about non-Greek associations. The claim has to do with the order or governance of non-Greek households (i.e., that non-Greeks allegedly make no distinction between the role of females and the role of slaves). The purpose of the poetic illustration is to support the idiomatic reasonableness of the claim about governance as it stands in relation to Aristotle's initial remark "that nature intends and produces a distinction between females and natural slaves" and that nature intends this for the existence and survival of humanity.[31]

There is no way for us to know the accuracy of Aristotle's description of the assignments that take place in non-Greek households. However, we can reasonably presume that the rhetorical significance of the comparison of non-Greeks and slaves is best understood through the conclusion Aristotle seems to draw from it (1252b 9–15). Specifically, Aristotle's conclusion is that the two necessary associations of the household are male-female (for the purpose of reproduction) and ruler-ruled (for the sake of mutual survival and benefit).

For Aristotle, his claim that the two basic associations of everyday household life are ordered toward reproduction and survival does not depend on the poetic illustration or the idea that there are no natural rulers among non-Greeks. Thus, without further explanation, the rhetorical function of the line from *Iphigenia at Aulis* ("it is proper that Greeks should rule non-Greeks") and Aristotle's interpretation of what

Euripides intends to communicate with the line ("that non-Greek and slave are by nature identical") are, at best, ambiguous. Nevertheless, there is no ambiguity about what we do not have in those lines (i.e., 1252b 9–10): Namely, *we do not have a metaphysically stipulative definition of either the barbarian or the natural slave.* All the key words are in the paragraph – "Greeks," "non-Greeks," "rule," "slave, "nature," and so on – but, simply stated, Aristotle is not claiming what John Mair and the 16th century Spanish colonialists took him to be claiming.

From the Conclusion of Aristotle's Account of the "Slave by Nature"

Fortunately, we have more than the immediate context of that one line in 1252b to help us understand the descriptions and distinctions Aristotle is keen to develop through his account of the *phusei doulon* in Book 1 of the *Politics*. Aristotle directly engages the claims of the Euripidean line near the conclusion of his discourse on the "slave by nature." In 1255a 25–31, Aristotle outlines the key difficulties with categorically mapping an undifferentiated state of slavery onto the status of non-Greek "barbarians." Those Greeks, Aristotle explains, who claim that it is natural to enslave non-Greeks after a war simultaneously deny the claim. The central muddle identified by Aristotle is that noble Greeks, like anyone else, can be conquered and enslaved through violent force by non-Greeks.[32] In what seems to be a critique of Athenian bias, Aristotle points out that those who consider all non-Greeks to be slaves by nature are at the same time unwilling to describe a forcibly enslaved Greek noble as a slave by nature (1255a 29). As Aristotle explains, these Greek nobles only want to assign to non-Greeks the status of being a "slave by nature." Note the parallel here between the outlook of these Greek nobles and the interpretation held forth by John Mair. Identifying both the intuition and the critical mistake of the Greek nobles, Aristotle writes,

> And yet when they say this, they are merely seeking for the principles of natural slavery of which we spoke at the outset; for they are compelled to say that there exist certain persons who are slaves everywhere and certain others who are [slaves] nowhere.[33]

The identity of these persons who are dispositionally and permanently servile will be discussed below. For now, we can focus on the conclusion of Aristotle's argument. In the passage just provided, Aristotle is recalling the line from *Iphigenia at Aulis* that he referenced at the outset of his discussion. In response to the false claim that "Greeks should rule non-Greeks" and not the reverse, Aristotle proposes a distinction between "those who are slaves everywhere" and "those who are slaves nowhere." The distinctiveness of those who are "slaves by nature" is *more determinative*, according to Aristotle, than the accidental differences coordinate with non-Greek moral and cultural formation, social standing, or geography.

When the Euripidean line and Aristotle's interpretation of the line at beginning of the discourse (1252b 9–10) are read in light of this trajectory (1255a 29–32), the identification of the *nature-actions of non-Greeks* with *the nature-actions of the slave by nature* is unambiguously a suppositional claim (and not a stipulative metaphysical claim). Moreover, it is a supposition that Aristotle tests and ultimately rejects. That rejection, however, comes with a qualification: according to Aristotle, Iphigenia's claim is true insofar as it illustrates the Greek intuition that there is a metaphysical difference coordinate with the impaired function of the "slave by nature." For Aristotle, the permanence of that difference is what Greeks (who take Iphigenia's line as axiomatic) aim to express in their attribution of natural slavery to stable and identifiably distinct people groups – that is, generically non-Greek, culturally foreign people. Aristotle shows, however, the problem with conflating the essential permanence of the slave by nature with the perspectival strangeness of the barbarian or the circumstance of subjugation slavery (e.g., slavery resulting from war).

Aristotle is keen, nevertheless, to affirm that there is a certain rationale in the association of natural slavery with both slavery through subjugation and whatever it is that makes non-Greeks readily identifiable as foreigners. Specifically, as we will discuss in the next section, for Aristotle, the *natural defect* of the slave by nature is confused with the *unnatural defect* of the barbarian, neither of which are identical to the *bad fortune* of a free-man (Greek or non-Greek) who happens to be enslaved following a war.

Read in this way, the theatrical conflation of the slave by nature and the non-Greek barbarian in the Euripidean line is rejected by Aristotle but likewise reconfigured to affirm the core intuition animating the proverbial appeal of the line to Greek nobles. Specifically, Aristotle affirms the intuition that there is a naturalness and corresponding permanence to the condition of the slave by nature. For Aristotle, barbarians and slaves do not share the same nature, but there are persons who are "slaves by nature" in a way that is natural, stable, obvious, and uncontroversial.

An Ancient Greek Account of Intellectual Disability

According to Aristotle, who are these dispositionally and permanently servile persons? Up to this point in the analysis, what we have seen only indicates what the slave by nature *is not*, on Aristotle's terms – as distinguished from women, non-Greek barbarians, and those who are enslaved due to violent subjugation. What has not been displayed, on Aristotle's terms, is the nature and significance of the naturalness of the condition of the *phusei doulon*: one who "participates in reason so as to apprehend it, but not to possess it."[34] There are, for Aristotle, many ways that a human being can lack the use of reason. It is important to briefly isolate the particular defects Aristotle associates with the *phusei doulon* figure. Moreover, in light of the governing aim of this chapter, it is important to allow Aristotle's description of the *phusei doulon* to speak for itself and to avoid projecting the ways Aristotle's account was used after the 16th century as justification for centuries of European colonial abuses, quintessentially racist social and political arguments, and the American form of chattel slavery.

For Aristotle, there is a class of naturally inferior human beings who are constituted by the rational principle of human nature (*eidos*), who are able to be moved by reason towards properly human ends (*telos*), but who are incapable of independently functioning (*ergon*) in the properly human way due to Nature's intent. Aristotle explains that the slave by nature is anyone who, though human, is not capable of taking responsibility for himself or making choices for himself (1254a 14–15); whose condition is natural and not a corruption of nature (1254a 36–37); whose condition is not the consequence of moral viciousness, injury, or an unnatural corruption (1254a 36–37); and whose difference from other human beings is as wide as the difference between soul and body, human being and irrational animal (1254b 16–17). For Aristotle, the condition of the *phusei doulon* is an *essential defect* – something proper to the form of Man, the deliberative function, is missing from this human-shaped being.[35] Parallel to Aristotle's view of the partially realized form of women (*peperamenon*), the condition of the *phusei doulon* is a natural deficiency that has a purpose for the human species. According to Aristotle, what the slave by nature lacks is the deliberative faculty ("the deliberative part of the soul," 1260a 12), which means this sub-human or quasi-human being lacks the ability to reason discursively about practical ends and the means to ends, insofar as the rational soul does not actualize the *ergon* of properly human deliberation.[36]

With respect to the capabilities of the *phusei doulon*, Aristotle explains that these are persons who "participate in reason" so far as to understand what is reasonable, but who do not have the ability to generate a line of reasoning on their own (1254b 22–23); persons for whom the best things they are capable of doing comes from manual work, in contrast to intellectual work (1254b 17); and they are persons who are capable of belonging to another in the manner that a ward belongs to his or her guardian, and who actually do belong to someone in that way (1254a 14–15, 1254b 20–21).

As for the life and relationships of the *phusei doulon*, Aristotle explains that these are persons for whom the best life circumstance is one where they are guided by a legitimate, morally worthy, familial authority (1254b 19–20; cf., 1254b 6–9, 1255b 10–13); persons for whom being a servant in a household is both beneficial and just, because they cannot survive on their own and they have no desire to live on their own (1255b 1–8); and they are persons for whom their work of service within the household of their morally worthy guardian is consistent with their personal well-being, is beneficial to the whole household, and is characterized by friendship with the head-of-household (1255b 8–13). Finally, and this is important, according to Aristotle, a person is a civil slave (not a *phusei doulon*) if his or her service within the household is defined by law (not an essential defect of nature), enforced through threat of violence, or is inconsistent with his or her personal well-being and intentions (1255b 13–15).

Aristotle's description of the *phusei doulon* is about persons who lack the use of reason in a way that is comparable to what we today would identify as moderate to severe intellectual disability.[37] As Aristotle sees it, sometimes people are born in a condition that renders them incapable of ordinary self-governance and self-care. Given that ordinary happenstance, according to Aristotle, every good and appropriately mature head-of-household will eventually take in one or several *phusei doulon* and forge a mutually beneficial, cooperative relationship. Nevertheless, I do not believe Aristotle was imagining an assisted living group home or anything like a L'Arche community. For Aristotle, the reason the natural head-of-household provides protection, provision, practical guidance, species-derived kindness, and enters into friendship with the slave by nature, is not centered on the benefit or well-being of the *phusei doulon*. Rather, the nature, and purpose of the cooperative relationship is primarily for the good of the "master," the natural head-of-household.

Aristotle's treatise on the *phusei doulon* is not about slavery, nor is it a racialized theoretical justification of slavery. Nevertheless, and this is vitally important, Aristotle's understanding of the essential defect of the *phusei doulon* is the natural phenomena he presupposes in the development of his rationale for the justice of civil slavery within the *polis*. In other words, Aristotle believes the hierarchical, ruler-ruled relationship of civil slavery (enslavement arising from legal convention and war) is justified because he sees a natural hierarchical, ruler-ruled relationship between the unimpaired "natural-master" (*phusei despoton*) and essentially defective "natural-servant" (*phusei doulon*).

My central claim is not that Aristotle's account of the *phusei doulon* is correct or that he offers a moral vision worthy of being imitated. Rather, my only claim is that Aristotle thought deeply and carefully about the natural basis, significance, and moral implications of the fact that some human beings are born without the full use of reason. With respect to understanding what happened to Aquinas's account of "those who lack the use of reason" in the 16th century, what is important is not Aristotle's conclusion. Rather, what is important is that Aristotle's entire discussion of the *phusei doulon* figure is a serious attempt to account for the existence and communal life of persons who lack the use of reason. This is how Aquinas and Francisco de Vitoria interpreted Aristotle, and this is exactly the interpretation of Aristotle's *phusei doulon* figure that was obscured in John Mair's novel formulation in the 16th century.

At least one question follows: *what is wrong with the non-Greek "barbarians," according to Aristotle, such that the barbarian could be so easily confused with a slave by nature?* The answer to this question is important because it will help us recognize Aquinas's subversive revision of Aristotle, further problems with John Mair's novel interpretation of Aristotle, and the way both Aristotle's and Aquinas's engagements with persons who lack the use of reason were navigated in the Spanish colonial debates of the 16th century.

The "Unnatural Defect" of Barbarians and the "Natural Defect" of the Natural Slave

For Aristotle, non-Greek foreigners (e.g., Europeans and Asians) are not slaves by nature. However, he does consider non-Greek barbarians to be defective, and this in a way that effectively impairs what is perfectible in the form of a well-born, adult male. The impetus of Aristotle's view is not based solely on the mere fact that he favored Athenian Greeks, although he obviously did. What is important here is the etiology of the barbarian defect, as Aristotle understands it. As Malcolm Heath has demonstrated, integral to Aristotle's account of the defects of various non-Greek peoples is Aristotle's theory of how variations in climate from region to region influence the faculties of the human body and, as a result, the functional disposition of the human beings who happen to live in the region.[38]

Specifically, Aristotle believes that the climate and food of particular regions stimulate or depress the spirit or "heat" (*thumos*) of the human being, causing individuals to tend toward *unnaturally brutish* or *unnaturally slavish* behavior.[39] In other words, according to Aristotle, there is an intervening force that impairs the proper functioning (*ergon*) of an otherwise-perfectible human being. This region-based etiology of non-Greek defect is shown to be the case in that Aristotle speaks highly of all *Mediterranean barbarians*, in particular, the Egyptians and other North Africans.[40] Likewise, it is not uncommon for Aristotle to speak with admiration about the virtue of various non-Greeks.[41] Aristotle's understanding of how an extreme climate can impact the bodily dispositions of perfectible, well-born males is the principal rationale for Aristotle's low estimation of the barbarian *qua* non-Greek (i.e., not modern notions of race or racism as is often supposed).

This nuance of Aristotle's view is well illustrated in his discussion of the status of the *paroikos*, non-Greek residents of Greece in the *Politics*.

Aristotle writes that the farmers in his ideal city-state should be given land to cultivate and that the farmers themselves "will of necessity be slaves or barbarian *paroikos*."[42] It should be noted that Aristotle makes a distinction between the civil slave and the "resident alien" *paroikos*, neither of which are slaves by nature. Without a doubt Aristotle considers these Mediterranean-born barbarians to be inferior to the Greeks, but the *perioikoi* are not slaves by nature – for a slave by nature would not be capable of a complicated independent task, like the cultivation of land.

For Aristotle, non-Greeks are unnaturally "slavish" or "slave-like" because of an adverse environmental influence (characteristics that he takes to be often, but not necessarily, inheritable), and not because of a naturally weak capacity for practical rationality, as in the case of the natural slave. Aristotle associates these environmentally conditioned tendencies with particular regions and thus the populations *en masse*. However, for Aristotle, these tendencies very often do not express themselves on a case-by-case basis and, as a result, cannot be taken to be necessarily correlative with the *unnaturally brutish* or *unnaturally slavish* behavior of any particular non-Greek barbarian.[43] Understood in this way, on Aristotle's terms, if the non-Greek barbarian is *slave-like*, this condition is an *expected, but unnatural defect*; however, in no way does he consider the non-Greek barbarian to be a slave by nature without qualification. Specifically, on Aristotle's terms, non-Greeks are slavish or slave-like only by transference of the name.[44]

What we are describing here, as a point of comparison, is at variance with Alasdair MacIntyre's understanding of the Aristotelian barbarian and slave. Specifically, MacIntyre maintains that there is a metaphysically stipulative identification in Aristotle's thought between the nature of non-Greeks and the slave.[45] Now it is possible that MacIntyre is grounding his judgment on the basis of the second type of rulership described in Book 3 of the *Politics*.[46] However, it should be noted that the barbarians Aristotle is talking about in that passage are not Asiatic, European, or Egyptian; nor is he discussing all barbarians, but only *some barbarians*. The second thing to note is that the particular barbarians Aristotle is talking about are not slaves by nature; rather, these barbarians are more "slave-like" or "servile" in their regional (or ethnic) nature when compared to Greeks. The similitude (indicated by the term *doulikoteroi*) is stipulated as being geographically contingent.

The better interpretation of Aristotle's view is that the particular barbarians that Aristotle discusses in Book 3 (1285a 16–30) endure despotic rule because of a depressed *thumos* and not because they are slaves by nature. The significant distinction, according to Aristotle's understanding of human physiology, is between the *environmentally caused unnatural defect* of particular "slave-like barbarians" and the *natural defect* of the slave by nature.[47]

Returning to the beginning of Aristotle's discourse on slavery, Aristotle acknowledges that some Greeks claim that the non-Greek barbarian and the slave have an identical nature. I have shown that there are no textual grounds to take that theatrical supposition as a metaphysically stipulative claim. The key concern for Aristotle at the introduction of his treatise on the natural slave (1252a 34–1252b 14) is to establish the distinction between the way women and the "slave by nature" are each distinctively subordinate to the natural head-of-household.

Contrary to John Mair's gloss of *Politics*, Book I, in Mair's commentary on distinction 44 in Book II of the *Sentences*, the impaired use of reason that characterizes Aristotle's slave by nature is not caused by the injurious effect of a poor climate (i.e., like the impairment Aristotle supposes of the non-Greek 'barbarism'); nor is it a consequence of war or forced subjugation (i.e., like the status the civil slave); nor is it a consequence of poor education (i.e., like that of the common Athenian laborer); and neither is it a consequence of poor habituation (i.e., as with the disordered passions of the incontinent). Rather, Aristotle's account of the *phusei doulon* figure is best understood as a serious reflection on the existence and communal life of persons who lack the use of reason.

Whatever we, as contemporary readers, make of Trevor Saunders's "Lennie" comparison and D. Scott Davis's "mentally retarded" interpretation of Aristotle's "natural slave," as noted above,[48] as I show below, this is exactly how Aquinas interprets Aristotle's description of the slave by nature in his *Commentary on Aristotle's Politics*. Aquinas links Aristotle's slave by nature with "those who lack the use of reason" – a comparison exemplified in the condition Aquinas calls *amentia*.[49] And as I argue below, Aquinas subverts and revises Aristotle's contention that natural slavery is an *essential* defect.

Aquinas's Account of Those Who Lack the Use of Reason and His Interpretation of Aristotle

Shortly after completing the *Prima Pars* of his *Summa* (~1268), Aquinas returned to Paris and wrote his *Commentary on Aristotle's Politics* (~1269–1272).[50] Aquinas's commentary on the *Politics* follows in the interpretive wake of the commentary on the *Politics* composed by Albert the Great.[51] The general continuity between the two commentaries allows us to make some reasonable inferences about what Aquinas may have had in mind.[52] Specifically, while preserving Aristotle's designation for the *phusei doulon* figure (slave by nature or person who is dispositionally servile), against Aristotle, Albert's account includes anthropological judgments affirming the full humanity of the *phusei doulon* figure. For example, Albert affirms the dignity and status of the *phusei doulon* as *imago Dei* (Cap 3, i-k [29]). Albert insists on the status of the *phusei doulon* as an intellectual creature, explaining that the condition of those who lack the use of reason in this way is not a naturally occurring defect of the rational soul (as Aristotle claimed); rather, according to Albert, the condition is the consequence of some corporal accident that impairs the use of reason. (Cap 3, g-h [28]). Moreover, Albert identifies the *phusei doulon* figure as a member of the family, wherein the ordinary domestic activity of the *phusei doulon* is ordered toward participation and promotion of the communal well-being of the family (Cap. 1, g [9]). Finally, Aquinas's grammatical argument about the various kinds of "otherness" that can be predicated by the word "barbarian" parallels the interpretive strategy used by Albert (Cap. 1, i-k [10]).[53]

Aristotle's understanding of the slave by nature is rhetorically nuanced and supported by a detailed metaphysical biology. For Aristotle, the *phusei doulon* is an essentially defective human being. At the most basic level, the anthropological outlook supporting Aristotle's account of the *phusei doulon* is irreconcilable with the Christian account of the human being and Aquinas's Augustinian presumption of the unambiguous status of every human being as the image of God. In Aquinas's subversive revision of Aristotle, he interprets the *phusei doulon* figure to be a human being who lacks the use of reason on account of an operational limitation, caused by an accidental impairment of that person's cognitive faculties.[54] Elsewhere I've shown that Aquinas had a nuanced and integrated way of thinking about conditions that we today refer to as an "intellectual disability" or "cognitive impairment."

The condition that Aquinas ordinarily associates with those who lack the use of reason is *amentia* – analogous to what we today refer to as an intellectual disability or cognitive impairment.[55] Central to Aquinas's understanding of the anthropological significance of conditions like *amentia* is his judgment that the vulnerability of the human being to corporeal defect is integral to human nature and corresponds with (i.e., is not opposed to) the inalienable dignity of the human being as the image of God.[56] The key to understanding the anthropological significance of corporeal infirmities that impair the internal sense faculties (e.g., estimation, imagination, and deliberation) is Aquinas's distinction between the specifying *act of intellect* and the derivative intellectual act called *the use of reason*.

For Aquinas, the operation called understanding (*intelligere*) is the specifying act of the human being; it is the innate and inviolable aptitude to apprehend intelligible truth.[57] The operation or use of reason (*ratiocinari*) is a derivative operation of the intellect, that is, to advance from what is understood toward something that is not yet known, so as to apprehend an intelligible truth. For Aquinas, because the activity he calls the use of reason is a derivative act, it does not and cannot specify our intellectual nature, although it certainly manifests our intellectual nature. If this were not the case, according to Aquinas (following Augustine), we would cease to be human whenever we are not actively reasoning, because species cannot be defined by something transient. The use of reason is but one of the distinctively human, transient activities that manifest the absolute difference between human beings and non-human animals.

This is why Aquinas holds forth the immaterial operation of the intellect as the absolute difference coordinate with the human being's status as the image of God (STh I, q. 93, aa. 1-2), which does not belong to a corporeal organ but makes use of corporeal sensory faculties belonging to the body. (See Chapters 4 and 8 in this volume for more discussion.) Certainly, for Aquinas, nothing is in the intellect that was not first in the senses, but the specifying operation of intellect on intelligible things (actual knowledge of intelligible truth and actual love of the goodness that is known) is not the same as the discursive operation that Aquinas identifies as "the use of reason."

For Aquinas, this distinction between the specifying act of the intellect and the derivative act of reasoning is not overly important when it comes to the *definition of human nature*, where the difference is between the human being and brute animals – thus, *reason, intelligence, knowledge, understanding,* and *mind* all belong to the same incorporeal operation and power called intellect.[58] In other words, although the use of reason is certainly indicative of our intellectual nature, according to Aquinas, it is a mistake to regard *the use of reason* as the seat of our status as intellectual creatures. As Aquinas explains, we commonly refer to substantial forms (like the intellectual soul) by way of their observable accidents (like the act of reasoning). So, it is not a problem when Aquinas variously refers to the "rational soul," "intellectual soul," and the "human soul," or our "intellectual nature" and "rational nature." It's all the same thing.

Nevertheless, for Aquinas, the distinction between the various acts of the intellect and the act of reason is very important when the aspect of consideration is the perfection of our specific dignity as intellectual creatures.[59] The aptitude for the perfection of our intellectual nature, by knowledge and by love, is not reducible to the use of reason. Without ambiguity, Aquinas explicitly affirms that every living human being, including someone who "lacks the use of reason," is capable of actual knowledge and actual love of God.[60] On the basis of the above, Aquinas articulates his understanding of the inviolable intellectual nature and contemplative aptitude of every living human being, including persons who have the condition *amentia* (i.e., persons who lack the use of reason in a way that is profound and utterly debilitating).[61]

A lot could be said about the various ways Aquinas appropriates, revises, and subverts Aristotle on the topics of human dignity, slavery, natural slavery, social hierarchy, civil cooperation, justice, and the common good. On the topics of institutional slavery and the notion of natural slavery in Aristotle and Aquinas, an important comparative analysis is provided in an unpublished dissertation entitled *The Theory of Natural Slavery according to Aristotle and St. Thomas*, written by Fr. Benedict Ashley in 1941.[62] Ashley accounts for the material histories relevant to understanding slavery in the thought of Aristotle and Aquinas, and Ashley systematically interrogates and compares everything that Aristotle and Aquinas said on the topics of institutional slavery and natural slavery.[63]

Following the standard clinical nomenclature of the 1930s, Ashley demonstrates that the only way Aristotle's *phusei doulon* figure can make sense on Aquinas's terms is as a human being who is "feeble-minded" or "mentally deficient."[64] Ashley makes it a point to highlight that Aquinas's interpretation of the *phusei doulon* figure (as a person who lacks the use of reason due to an accidental impairment) is wholly inconsistent with the plain sense of what Aristotle says about the "naturalness" of the natural slave's defect.[65] Although Ashley fails to recognize the extent to which Aquinas subverts Aristotle's outlook on the nature of the *phusei doulon* figure, Ashley makes it clear that Aquinas's view is a clean break with Aristotle and that Aquinas's feudalistic revision is wholly incomparable to the chattel slavery of modernity.[66]

Aquinas's Commentary on Aristotle's Politics

In his commentary on Aristotle's *Politics*, Aquinas provides a brief excursus on the word *barbaros* in Book 1, focusing on 1252a 34–1252b 14.[67] In his remark, Aquinas indicates that it is possible to be confused about who Aristotle has in mind when he refers to "foreigners" (*extraneus*). Thomas gives three ways that the referent of the word "foreigners" might be understood. The first way is the circumstance when people do not share a common language. Noting the apostle Paul, Aquinas explains that such people can be called foreigners in relation to each other on account of their inability to communicate linguistically. The second way in which the word "foreigners" is used in Aquinas's context is in reference to any group of people who do not have a written language corresponding to their spoken dialect. To illustrate this second type of foreigner, Aquinas recalls the work of Bede in introducing "literary skills" into the English language – apparently developing a system of script corresponding to the English language. The third way the word "foreigners" is used in Aquinas's context is in regard to individuals or groups who are not governed by a common law. It is unclear with respect to this third way of using the word "foreigner" if those persons being referred to *cannot* be ruled, *resist* being ruled, or by *circumstance* live without the rule of any public law. Passing over that particular ambiguity, in their own way, each of these colloquial uses of the word "foreigner" approach what Aquinas takes to be the truth – apparently, the truth of who Aristotle has in mind when he refers to "foreigners."

Aquinas next moves to articulate the relevant distinctions, noting that the meaning and use of the Latin word for "foreigner" (*extraneus*) does not precisely correspond to the Greek word Aristotle uses to express "not-Greek-in-relation-to-normatively-Greek" (*barbaros*). Aquinas distinguishes between two senses in which the word "foreigner" is used, referring to persons who are called "foreigners" *in the absolute sense* and those who were called "foreigners" *in relation to another*. For Aquinas, Aristotle's use of the word "foreigners" is the absolute sense, which Aquinas identifies as referring to human beings who have an impaired capacity for reason (*deficit ratione*).[68]

By one reading, Aquinas's remark could be interpreted as a claim that the "human beings" described in this absolute sense correspondingly *lack reason in an absolute sense*, insofar as they lack something proper to the definition of the *human being*. However, that cannot be what Aquinas means in this comment. First, it is clear from the preceding sentence that the word "foreigners" is being used by Aquinas specifically in reference to human beings, and not in reference to *human-like* beings. More importantly, as discussed at the beginning of this section, there are clear anchors that limit the interpretive possibilities. Namely, what we find in the *prima pars* concerning those who lack the use of reason and Aquinas's discussion of what, exactly, defines the human being in his *Treatise on Man*. Additionally, we have Albert's commentary on the *Politics*, which Aquinas evidently had on hand. For these reasons, it is implausible that Aquinas was describing a circumstance where a human being lacks the principle by which we understand humans *to be human* – that is, the intellectual soul. Likewise, if Thomas was attempting to specify a use of the word "foreigner" used in reference to a class of human-like irrational animals, he would not have qualified the designation as contingent upon a semblance of absolute difference – insofar as such a class of irrational creatures could not be properly called human beings. Thomas says that those who are called "foreigners" in an absolute sense "*seem* [*videtur*] absolutely foreign to the human race"; he does not say that they in fact *are* absolutely foreign to the human race.

So conceived, according to Aquinas, the use of the word "foreigner" in the absolute sense refers to the class of human beings who merely *seem* absolutely foreign to the human species, while, nevertheless, remaining irreducibly members of the human species. *In what way might a human being be understood to "seem foreign" to the human species?* In this context, Thomas attributes this strange semblance to an accidental impairment of a person's rational faculties (and not a lack of the use of reason for want of an intellectual soul). Thomas writes:

> They lack reason either because they happen to live in a climate so intemperate that it causes most of them to be dimwitted, or because there is an evil custom in certain lands whereby human beings are rendered irrational and brutish.[69]

Aquinas attributes the diseased or defective capacity to reason to two possible causes: the *first possible cause* is an environmental circumstance that renders a disproportionate number of the human beings living in a particular region "dim-witted" [*ex ipsa dispositione regionis hebetes*]. Aquinas does not indicate what sort of unruly climate could so radically impair the physical faculties required for human cognition, but he does seem to consider this a real cause. *The other possibility* he considers are evil customs that habituate human beings *to act as if* they were irrational or half-beasts. Judging from the two speculative causes Aquinas offers, it is clear that he does not take the absolute sense of the word "foreigner" to be the natural disposition of the human being described, thus, breaking with Aristotle. For Aquinas, the environmentally diseased or habituated impairment of the descriptively "absolute foreigner" (*simpliciter barbari*) is accidental.

On the understanding that the designation "absolute foreigner" is an assessment based on the *appearance* of a diseased or defective capacity for the use of reason, Aquinas outlines criteria for the proper application of the description. Specifically, the establishment of reasonable laws and the ability to write words are noted as activities that can only be performed by beings that have the use of reason, and the presence of such practices among a foreign people group would be clear signs that their capacity for reason is not diseased or impaired. Likewise, Aquinas notes that the absence of just laws or the practice of writing could imply that a hostile climate or evil customs had impaired the development of such signs. Aquinas then distinguishes that extreme class of strangeness from the standard class of strangeness arising from the mere lack of a common language and concludes that "Aristotle is speaking here about those who are foreigners absolutely (*simpliciter barbari*)."[70]

The subtlety of Aquinas's subversion of Aristotle's outlook is impressive. Commenting upon the line from Euripides given in 1252b 9–10, against Aristotle, Aquinas uses Aristotle's revised interpretation of the Euripidean line[71] and a play on Aristotle's earlier use of the word "barbarian" in relation to disease-caused bestial states in *Nicomachean Ethics* (1148b 15–1149a 24) to speculate on why the *phusei doulon* in Book I of the *Politics* might seem profoundly different or "strange." Aquinas uses Aristotle's individual-scale, thumos-theory of regional differences (an "unnatural defect" on Aristotle's terms) to account for the condition of the *phusei doulon*. In other words, on Aristotle's terms, Aquinas shifts the condition of the *phusei doulon* from a "natural defect" to an "unnatural defect," from an essential defect to an accidental defect that impairs the actualization of a faculty proper to the human being.

Aquinas makes this argument using the rationale of Aristotle's individual scale, thumos-theory of regional differences – a theory that Aquinas seems to have accepted, on the understanding that the human body is in this life always in passive potency to external effects. However, Aquinas is not saying that all non-Greeks are essentially defective according to Aristotle's sense of the *phusei doulon*; rather, Aquinas is saying the *phusei doulon* figure (a person who lacks the use of reason) is accidently impaired because of some external cause in the same way that Aristotle thinks differences in regional climate can have an effect on the faculties and dispositions of non-Greeks. In other words, Aquinas isn't using the *phusei doulon* figure to question the humanity and rationality of non-Greeks; rather, Aquinas is using the unquestioned humanity of perspectively strange non-Greeks to eliminate the question about the humanity of the *phusei doulon*.

The formulation of Aquinas's rationale parallels Augustine's argument in *City of God*, Book XVI, 8. Augustine, in his discussion of "certain monstrous races of men," argues that no faithful Christian should doubt that anyone who is born anywhere as a human being is a rational and mortal being. And this, Augustine argues, regardless of "however extraordinary such a creature may appear to our senses in bodily shape, in color, in motion, or utterance, or in any natural endowment, or part, or quality."[72] The Augustinian speculation that Aquinas seems to have appropriated as his own is:

> God decided to create some races in this way [i.e. having differences so profound that they seem to be monstrosities], so that we should not suppose that the wisdom with which God fashions the physical being of men has gone astray in the case of [abnormal human infants very unlike most human beings] which are bound to be born among us of human parents.[73]

Thus, in his commentary on *Politics* 1252b9–10, Aquinas interprets the "strange" (*extraneum*) condition of Aristotle's slave by nature as intelligible only if the description is referring to a human being who lacks the use of reason because of a profound accidental impairment of the faculties or capacitates that are ordinarily (but do not always) manifest in particular persons. In that way, Aquinas subverts Aristotle's rationalistic conception of human nature and the human good, reframing the condition of those who lack the use of reason and Aristotle's slave by nature as the privation of a relative corporeal good due to some external cause. That is to say, an external cause analogous to the way climate affects phenotypic and dispositional differences between geographically isolated people groups. Aquinas rejects the anthropological judgments behind Aristotle's construal of human defect (i.e., the natural defects that nature allegedly intends for women and the slave by nature), and, thereby, Aquinas undermines the allegedly natural correlate that Aristotle presupposes in his rationale for the justice of civil slavery. The theological principles and rationale animating Aquinas's subversion of

Aristotle on the point of essential defect is found in *STh* Ia q. 76, a. 5, where Aquinas engages and ultimately rejects Aristotle's presumption that the "rational form of Man" does not fully inhere or actualize the designate matter in the case of the *phusei doulon*.[74]

Thomas Aquinas subverts and revises Aristotle's rationalistic anthropology and then reconfigures Aristotle's account of the *phusei doulon* to cohere with his (Aquinas's) understanding of the intellectual nature and inalienable dignity of the human being. Aquinas does not develop Aristotle's formulation of the mutually beneficial friendship between a cognitively impaired person and his domestic guide; however, elsewhere, Aquinas does indeed have a lot to say about those who lack the use of reason: their intellectual nature, creaturely dignity, contemplative aptitude, and how such persons participate in the sacramental life of the Church.

Remembering Mindless Persons: Retelling the Story of the Debates

Every serious description of those who lack the use of reason and the condition *amentia* within the Thomistic theological tradition must acknowledge the 16th century use of Aristotle and Aquinas to justify the abuse and exploitation of the Amerindian peoples. Specifically, (1) the invention of an unprecedented interpretation and application of Aristotle's account of the *phusei doulon* and (2) the appeal to Aquinas's qualified acceptance of Aristotle's milieu-theory of human behavioral differences.

In defense of the Amerindian peoples, and against the Spanish colonialist arguments, the Dominican Thomists of Salamanca rejected the colonialist use of Aristotle and the appeal to Aquinas. The 16th century Dominican defense of the humanity of the Amerindian peoples should be regarded as one of the great achievements of Salamancan Thomism.[75] Unfortunately, the circumstances led Salamancan Thomists like Bartolomé de Las Casas, at the debate of Valladolid (1550–1551), to articulate an anthropological outlook that amplified the specifying significance of the use of reason in the thought of Aquinas and obscured the place of persons who lack the use of reason in the thought of both Aristotle and Aquinas. It is precisely in these 16th century interpretations and applications of Aristotle and Aquinas that we find remnants of an outlook that has been generally displaced to the periphery of the Thomistic theological tradition. Some of the most significant clues to the vestiges of Aquinas's outlook are found in Francisco de Vitoria's arguments against the theological and philosophical defenders of the Spanish colonial enterprise.

According to Anthony Pagden and Lewis Hanke, during the first decade of the 16th century, the Dominicans of Salamanca began pressuring King Ferdinand to justify the Spanish claim on the Americas.[76]

Ferdinand called the council of Burgos to formulate a response to the Dominicans. At the Burjos *junta* in 1512, John Mair's novel interpretation of Aristotle was first introduced to the Spanish colonial debates and applied to the circumstances of the Amerindian peoples.[77]

The engagement and debate of the Burgos *junta* was abstract and theoretical in nature.[78] Nevertheless, according to the reports of Matías de Paz and Juan Lopez de Palacios Rubios, the Amerindian peoples were identified to the Spanish crown as a concrete instance of Maír's natural slave: wandering herds of congenitally subordinate, quasi-irrational, bestial men, rendered insane by poor climate and inhuman cultural practices.[79] The defenders of the Spanish colonial enterprise took inspiration from Aristotle's *thumos* theory of regional "barbarism" (i.e., the view that extreme climate can influence a particular person's development, amounting to accidental differences), and then the Spanish colonialists amplified Aristotle's person-scaled *thumos* theory into an account of population-scaled, climate-caused congenital impairment: the milieu-theory of racialized difference (i.e., the view that extreme climate can impact human development and that those effects are communicated to subsequent generations).

The Spanish colonialists conflated Ptolemy's population-scale account of racialized regional differences (drawn from Mair) and Aristotle's individual-scale thumos theory of racialized regional difference. So conceived, the philosophical and theological defenders of the Spanish colonial interests alleged that the purported inferiority of the Amerindian peoples was a congenital defect caused by the influence of an adverse climate. In addition to the claim that the Amerindians were congenitally impaired, there was a further argument claiming that they had been habituated into a form of bestial wildness that would take generations to heal – healed, that is, on the assumption that it was legitimate to baptize natural slaves, which was itself a contested matter among theological defenders of the colonialist claims. Based on the allegation that the lives of the Amerindian peoples did not manifest the potential for rational discourse and moral virtue (according to the colonialist caricature), it was argued on a variation of the axiom "agere sequitur esse" (acting follows being) that the irrationality and wildness of the Amerindians was indicative of some profound natural defect (one that had a bearing on the first perfection of the human being).

The vehement Dominican response and arguments against the colonialist claims challenged both the descriptions of the Amerindian peoples and the interpretation of Aristotle held forth by Bernardo de Mesa and Gil Gregorio. According to Hanke, Anton de Montesinos was indignant at the incoherent and "obvious misrepresentation" of Aristotle's account of the *phusei doulon* figure.[80] For his own part, Matías de Paz argued that the Amerindians were "not slaves in the sense that Aristotle uses the term in the *Politics*."[81] The debate at Burjos failed to resolve the matter for the Spanish crown, and in the years that followed, the conflict only grew more complex.[82] Nevertheless, Mair's version of the natural slave theory began to slowly spread after the Burgos *junta*, taking hold slowly by word of mouth.[83]

The next major appearance of Mair's natural slave theory came in the person of Juan de Quevedo. In 1519, after an unplanned confrontation at a noon-time meal, Bartolomé de las Casas and Quevedo were compelled by Charles V to publicly debate the question.[84] According to las Casas, Quevedo wrote a treatise on Aristotle's theory of natural slavery; although the text itself has not survived, the passages quoted by las Casas in his *Historia de las Indias* highlight the same novel interpretive judgments that distinguished Mair's gloss of Book I of the *Politics* in his commentary on Lombard's *Sentences*.[85] Here, it is important to note that this was the first time las Casas encountered the claim that the Amerindian peoples were an instance of Aristotle's slave by nature.[86]

According to the Spanish colonialist argument, because the end (*telos*) of the human being consists in the perfection of reason and will, the "mindless" *barbarian-cum-natural slave* was incapable of living a human life properly so called. Unable to realize the natural human good, it was questionable whether they could attain the ultimate good of rational human nature in relationship to the Creator God. Thus, the colonialists argued that the Amerindians needed the sort of "benevolent" patronage afforded in the *encomienda* system (where an unspecified number of persons were "entrusted" to the protection and instruction of an *encomendero*, or trustee). As Pagden notes, history has judged the *encomienda* system to be a theologically formulated form of institutional slavery.[87]

Against the most common 16th century justifications for the enslavement of the Amerindians by Spanish colonial interests – that is, natural slavery and profound moral depravity – the Dominican Thomistic defense of the Amerindians was formulated around two kinds of argument.[88] On the one hand, a theological argument, affirming that the Amerindian peoples are rational creatures, formed in the image of God and capable of moral virtue. On the other hand, an affirmation of the natural rights of the Amerindian peoples, an argument from political philosophy, demonstrating that Spanish colonial violence in the Americas was indefensible on just-war grounds and the law of nations (*ius gentium*).

The principle target of the Salamancan Thomist response was the colonialist claim that the condition of the Amerindians was an environmentally caused congenital defect of their rational faculties. This was the favored point of rebuttal because this claim in the colonialist argument could be empirically demonstrated as false and because the claim relied on Mair's exegetically imprecise conflation of Aristotelian categories, as discussed above. For the Dominican Thomists, these arguments amounted to a wholesale rejection of the colonialist milieu-theory of racialized difference (and Mair's novel formulation of the slave by nature). So, against the Spanish colonialist "barbarism-as-congenital-intellectual-inferiority-and-racialized-difference," the Thomists pitched Aquinas's "barbarism-as-perspectival-strangeness" (*extraneum*). In doing so – and for good reason, given the Spanish colonialist claims about the Amerindian peoples – the Dominicans tended to avoid Aquinas's association of the accidental condition of those who lack the use of reason with, on Aristotle's terms, the accidental condition of non-Greeks. If one presumes as fact Mair's rationale for the metaphysically essential inferiority of non-Greek foreigners, it is difficult to recognize the positive aim of Aquinas's association of barbarism with those who lack the use of reason (an appeal to the humanity of the former to affirm the humanity of the latter). During the 1520s and 1530s, the lines of disputation radicalized the Salamancan position in a way that obscured Aquinas's theologically subversive revision of Aristotle's *phusei doulon* figure.

Francisco de Vitoria on the phusei doulon and Those Who Lack the Use of Reason

One noteworthy exception among the Salamancan Thomist defense was Francisco de Vitoria, who recognized and appropriated Aquinas's interpretation of Book I. In his *Relectio: De Eo ad Quod Tenetur Homo Veniens ad Usum Rationis* (1534) and treatise *De Indies* (1539),[89] Vitoria presents (1) Aquinas's view that the *amentes* (mindless persons), who lack the use of reason, are capable of meritorious acts of knowledge and love (intellectual acts prior to the use of reason); (2) Aquinas's understanding of *amentia* in relation to the *phusei doulon* figure; and (3) Aquinas's view that the beatific, graced perfection of the human being in a likeness of virtue is not contingent upon the use of reason. These three lines of argument, (1)-(3), are most relevant to Vitoria's discussion of those who lack the use of reason and Aristotle's *phusei doulon* figure. Vitoria's *Relectio* outlines a moral psychology relevant to understanding the key parts of his argument in *De Indis*, especially the much discussed "eighth-title."

In the first part of his *Relectio de eo ad quod tenetur homo veniens ad usum rationis*, Vitoria discusses what it means to have the use of reason and what it is to arrive at the use of reason. Vitoria argues that our first moral obligation, upon arriving at the use of reason, is to deliberate about whatever is known and to freely direct ourselves toward the truth and goodness apprehended (to whatever extent that one is able).[90]

Vitoria begins by reviewing some of Aquinas's more prominent remarks on the intellectual status and moral aptitude of persons who lack the use of reason: in particular, "mindless" persons (*amentibus*), the mentally insane (*furiosus*), children, those who are intoxicated, and those who are asleep (in the ordinary way). Vitoria notes, for example, that although "mindless persons [*amentibus*] do not have free will, nevertheless, they have intellectual acts and voluntary acts."[91] Along those same lines, Vitoria comments that persons who lack the use of reason, such as "mindless persons [*amentes*], children, and those who are asleep, at various times perform sensible acts, sufficient in their alertness and health to be intellectual acts and volitional acts."[92]

Vitoria follows Aquinas in the view that there are intellectual and voluntary acts, proper and distinctive to the human being *qua* intellectual creature, which do not amount to the use of reason (nor can they constitute, thereby, the deliberative exercise of freewill).[93] In outlining Aquinas's position, Vitoria reiterates the standard Thomistic view that the condition of the *amentibus* is caused by an impairment of the bodily faculties required for specifically human cognition (and that the condition is not caused by a corruption of the intellectual soul or a defect in the essential powers of the soul).

This is why, as Vitoria explains, we often see "mindless persons [*amentibus*] perform many acts that brute animals cannot produce."[94] These are *indeliberate* acts of the rational animal that cannot be attributed to the senses. Vitoria follows Aquinas in the judgment that *actual understanding* and *actual willing* are operative in those who lack the use of reason and freewill.[95] Vitoria provides an example of intellectual and voluntary activity, attributable to the *amentibus*, which falls short of the use of reason and yet is absolutely different from the exclusively sensual knowledge of particulars proper to brute animals:

> The mindless [*amentes*] ... have acts concerning spiritual things that do not fall under sensation, as well as desire for spiritual things, as experience shows us from what they do and from what they say. For in point of fact they speak to God, as well as to angels, and wrestle with their choice of words.[96]

Vitoria takes it as common sense that his readers know persons who lack the use of reason and who, nevertheless, display actual knowledge and actual desire concerning properly human goods. Vitoria picks up on these and other nuances in Aquinas's various remarks relevant to understanding the knowledge and desire of persons who lack the use of reason.[97] Vitoria further highlights a constellation of interpretive judgments relevant to happiness that is possible for persons who have lacked the use of reason from birth.

Like Aquinas, Vitoria acknowledges that a person can lack the use of reason in various ways and to various degrees. And Vitoria shows that there is not a clear one-to-one correlation between adults who lack the use of reason (due to any number and combination of external and internal sensory impairments) and the particular way that very young children are said to lack the use of reason (due to general immaturity).[98]

Among the most important aspects of the argument found in *De eo ad quod tenetur*, however, is that Vitoria never entertains the kind of anthropological questions that characterized Aristotle's account of the *phusei doulon* figure and the Spanish colonialist accounts of the Amerindian peoples. That is, both Vitoria and Aquinas presume, without qualification, that persons who lack the use of reason are intellectual creatures, formed in the image of God, and are capable of progressing toward perfection in knowledge and love of God. Vitoria receives as his own and reiterates Aquinas's view that the dignity of every human being, including those who lack the use of reason, is rooted in an inalienable aptitude for knowledge and love of God.[99]

In *De eo ad quod tenetur*, we find a marker in the 16th century of Aquinas's 13th century concern to provide an account of human dignity and human happiness that takes for granted the fact that sometimes human beings lack the use of reason. Among the most important interpretive points of *De eo ad quod tenetur*, relevant to the 16th century Spanish colonial debates, are the following three claims. First, Vitoria's Aquinas-inspired view that the intellectual nature of the human being is not identical to having the use of reason. Second, Vitoria's Aquinas-inspired view that the intellectual acts of the human being, proper to our created nature, are not reducible to the use of reason (i.e., the living human being has pre-rational, non-deliberative intellectual acts). Third, Vitoria's Aquinas-inspired view that those pre-rational, non-deliberative intellectual acts can be perfected by grace, engendering a properly human contemplative happiness in the life of those who lack the use of reason.

In 1537, Pope Paul II promulgated the bull *Sublimus Deus*, affirming the full humanity of the Amerindian peoples, that they could receive Christ, and stipulated that evangelistic intent and merciful regard should characterize any Catholic engagement with the Amerindian peoples.[100] Following in the wake of that formal declaration, Vitoria wrote his treatise *De Indis* (1539), where among other things, he defends the legitimacy of baptizing Amerindian converts to Christianity and argues against the attribution of natural slavery to the Amerindian peoples.[101]

As for its structure, *De Indis* is organized around the presentation of seven Spanish colonialist claims, seven rebuttals, and is followed by one unanswered Spanish colonialist claim (the so-called *eighth title*). In that last reflection, Vitoria engages the topic of natural slavery in relation to the condition *amentia*. After the disclaimer that what follows is an argument that he "does not affirm, but cannot entirely reject," Vitoria outlines a view that he presents as the only possible justification for the Spanish colonial presence in the Americas. Namely, if all of the Amerindians are *amentibus*, the slave by nature as described by Aristotle, then it would be most appropriate for them to be ruled by those who could provide guidance and protective care.[102]

There is a contemporary interpretive disagreement about what, exactly, Vitoria is arguing for in the eighth title, settling into four common interpretive options.[103] First, some suppose that Vitoria was simply being a thorough scholar but didn't believe the argument. Second, some suppose that Vitoria included the argument to appease the colonial ambitions of Charles V (i.e., it's the only argument for just cause without a rebuttal, thus leaving it available for use in Spanish legal arguments). Third, some speculate that Vitoria secretly held a low opinion of the Amerindians and that the eighth title is Vitoria's actual opinion. Fourth, some contend that Vitoria was forced to concede the rhetorical point to the Spanish colonialists, because Vitoria believed colonialist reports about the irrational, brutish status of the Amerindians.

The contemporary mystery centers on why Vitoria would concede this as a legitimate title, after presenting and accepting (earlier in *De Indies*) all the evidence demonstrating the rational status of the Amerindian peoples. There are four interpretive presumptions behind the contemporary interpretive challenge. First, it is presumed that when Vitoria refers to Aristotle's *phusei doulon* figure, he has in mind John Mair's novel interpretative gloss of the Book I of the *Politics*. That is to say, Mair's formulation of the natural slave theory which conflates into one Aristotle's distinct engagements with the "slave by nature," non-Greek barbarians, bestial men, and vicious intemperance – amounting to the caricature of a rootless, semi-rational, man-shaped beast of burden. Second, it is presumed that Vitoria regarded human nature, the human good, and the contemplative aptitude of the human being to hinge on the capacity for the use of reason. Third, it is presumed that for Vitoria (and perhaps as the theological outlook of Thomism) the condition of *amentia* is somehow inconsistent with human nature or a perversion of human nature. Finally, with respect to differences in intellectual competencies and rational faculties, it is presumed that for Vitoria (and perhaps as the theological outlook of Thomism), a relationship of competency and dependency between adults is unnatural.

Against those contemporary presuppositions, the contention of Vitoria's eighth title becomes clear when interpretive work of the preceding sections is taken into account (concerning the novelty of Mair's interpretive gloss of the *Politics* Book I, Aristotle's understanding of the *phusei doulon* figure, Aquinas's understanding of those who lack the use of reason, and Aquinas's subversion of Aristotle's account of the essential defect of *the phusei doulon* figure). Specifically, in the eighth title of *De Indis*, Vitoria presents and develops Aquinas's understanding of the merciful regard that is due to persons who lack the use of reason. In doing so, Vitoria presumes the intellectual status and contemplative aptitude of those who lack the use of reason. On that basis, when Vitoria associates the condition of *amentia* with Aristotle's *phusei doulon* figure, he is outlining the only possible case in which the Spanish presence in the

America's would be legitimate: namely, if there was some unfathomable circumstance where the rational faculties of a large part of the population were found to be in some way impaired.

In other words, having decisively demonstrated that the Amerindian peoples do not suffer from a population-scale congenital impairment of their rational faculties, Vitoria *remembers* that there are still some human beings who lack the use of reason. Vitoria *remembers* that when persons are found who lack the use of reason due to an accidental impairment, the precepts of mercy oblige Christians to offer guidance, care, protection, and comfort. As Vitoria makes his argument in defense of the rational status and ordinary moral aptitude of the Amerindian peoples, he *remembers* that although the use of reason manifests the intellectual dignity of the human being, our creaturely dignity is not founded upon transient and temporary acts like the use of reason.

Despite the arguments of Vitoria and his extension of Aquinas's way of thinking about those who lack the use of reason, his remarks in the eighth title of *De Indis* reflect an outlook that has been displaced from the standard mores of the Thomistic theological tradition. Amid the various engagements and disputes about the justice of the Spanish colonial enterprise in the Americas, a consensus emerged that *the use of reason* is what specifies the human being and that the perfection of human nature, human flourishing, is defined by *rationality* as a formal principle. There was nothing wholly new about that 16th century consensus, of course, as it reflects the common scholastic presumption that the formal cause and the final cause in living things are mutually implicating. What was different, the notion that was displaced, was Aquinas's distinction between the specifying act of the intellect and the use of reason and Aquinas's particular way of understanding the secondary perfection and final perfection of our intellectual nature in contemplation (an act for which the perfection of our rational faculties is dispositive, but not necessary).[104]

The Debate at Valladolid (1550)

In the years leading up to the debate at Valladolid, Juan Ginés de Sepúlveda had revived John Mair's interpretation of the natural slave theory and its application to the Amerindian peoples.[105] In addition to Sepúlveda's promotion of Mair's outlook, the philosophical and theological advocates of the Spanish colonial enterprise began invoking Aquinas's *Commentary on the Politics* as further justification.[106] Specifically, they appealed to Aquinas's qualified acceptance of Aristotle's milieu-theory of human behavioral differences and interpreted Aquinas association of the *phusei doulon* with non-Greeks through the lens of Mair's Aristotle. The result was arguments that used a questionably human figuration of the *phusei doulon* as justification to challenge the humanity and rationality of the Amerindians (the exact opposite of Aquinas's move, which was to use the unquestioned humanity of perspectivally strange non-Greeks to affirm the humanity of the *phusei doulon* figure). On the basis of that rationale, Aristotle and Aquinas were held forth as authorizing Spanish colonial abuse and exploitation of the Amerindian peoples. In 1550, Sepúlveda was commissioned to make just that argument at Valladolid and to justify, on evangelistic grounds, the Spanish colonial enterprise in general and the "benevolent" subjugation of the Amerindian peoples in particular. Toward that end, Sepúlveda presented Mair's theory of natural slavery and claimed the support of Aquinas and Francisco de Vitoria.[107]

Las Casas rightly rejected Sepúlveda's claims about the rational faculties and moral aptitude of the Amerindian peoples. In his *In Defense of the Indians*, las Casas recounts his refutation of Sepúlveda at Valladolid.[108] Las Casas's response is made on Scriptural and normative theological grounds, supplemented by *ad hoc* exegetical engagements with Aristotle and Aquinas on key points. His argument is structured around three points: a theological argument about the equality of human dignity, a stipulative grammatical argument on "barbarism," and an extensive account of Amerindian practices, as proof of their rational status and moral aptitude. The first and second arguments are directly relevant to Aquinas's account of persons who lack the use of reason.

Las Casas's theological argument begins with an affirmation of the providence of God, contending that the goodness of God is recognizable in the rational and moral aptitude of humanity in general. In doing so, las Casas references particular cases of human beings who "lack reason ... like brute animals."[109] These are framed as exceptions that prove the rule of human rationality. From there, las Casas makes his grammatical argument on "barbarism" (foreignness or strangeness). Appealing to Aquinas, las Casas stipulates four ways that the strangeness of others can be understood. The colonialist Mair-inspired version of natural slavery is taken up in las Casas's third classification of barbarism. In his discussion, las Casas takes as his own Aquinas's rhetorical formulation of "absolute barbarism," however, Las Casas breaks with Aquinas and presents persons who lack the use of reason as "despised by God."[110] He holds forth that persons who lack the use of reason are "savage, imperfect, and the worst of men" and that "half-witted or foolish" people "are mistakes of nature or freaks of rational nature."[111] He claims that a more-than-rare regional occurrence of "slow-witted, moronic, foolish, or stupid" individuals would frustrate the beauty and perfection of God's plan for the universe and that those who lack the use of reason are "far removed from what is best in human nature."[112] Las Casas concludes the section by saying that

> barbarians of this kind are rare, because with such [limited] natural endowments they cannot seek God, know him, call upon him, or

love him. They do not have a capacity for doctrine or for performing the acts of faith or love.[113]

In fairness, las Casas makes most of these remarks in the context of stipulating *what is not the case* for the Amerindian peoples; that is, they are not half-wits, they are not despised by God, they are not mistakes of rational nature, they bear the image of God, and they are capable of faith and love. Moreover, las Casas forcefully argues that the Amerindian peoples have the full use of reason, bear the image of God, and are capable of faith and love. Nevertheless, what is clearly illustrated in las Casas's *Defense* is a tendency to presume that what Aquinas has to say about those who lack the use of reason is in continuity with what Sepúlveda has to say about the *barbarian-cum-natural slave*. Specifically, las Casas implicitly (and at points explicitly) accepted Sepúlveda's rationalistic presentation of Aristotle and Aquinas.

One important outcome of the debate was the wide distribution throughout Europe of las Casas's account of the debate at Valladolid. One could speculate that las Casas inadvertently promulgated Mair's interpretation of Aristotle and Sepúlveda's development of Mair and use of Aquinas. One could also speculate that the 17th and 18th century body of literature identified under the heading "The Black Legend" popularized Sepúlveda's readings of Aristotle and Aquinas, which were not directly contested by las Casas in his *In Defense of the Indians*. The claim that the Amerindian peoples were natural slaves was uniformly recognized as false and rejected in the Spanish-Catholic world by the end of the 17th century. Nevertheless, it is reasonable to surmise that the contemporary, widespread presumption that the barbarian-cum-natural slave properly belongs to the Aristotelian-Thomistic tradition has its origin in the Black Legend.

Exemplified in the efforts of las Casas, the Salamancan defense favored formulations geared to oppose colonialist arguments that questioned the rational status of the Amerindian peoples *en masse*. The result was a spectrum of quasi-rationalistic contentions concerning human nature and the human good, which were attributed to Aquinas. In a way that is understandable, rhetorical expedience and an urgent circumstance led well-intentioned figures like las Casas to gloss over distinctions that were integral to Aquinas's theological understanding of persons who lack the use of reason.

Conclusion: The Aftermath

When it comes to Aquinas's account of persons who lack the use of reason, there were at least two consequences of the Spanish colonial debates. (1) Mair's problematic interpretation of Aristotle's *phusei doulon* became the standard interpretation of Book I of the *Politics* and made it difficult for later interpreters to recognize Aquinas's subversive revision of the *phusei doulon* figure. And, (2) the anthropological outlook animating Aquinas's various remarks on the intellectual nature, inalienable dignity, and moral aptitude of those who lack the use of reason was displaced to the outer periphery of the discursive mores that we call the Thomistic theological tradition.

Although the most common and accepted judgment in Spain after Valladolid was to reject Sepúlveda (and Aristotle's theory of natural slavery), there remained an active debate about Sepúlveda and natural slavery.[114] However, and this is absolutely vital, both the majority who sided with las Casas (against Sepúlveda and the notion of natural slavery) and the minority who sided with Sepúlveda and the notion of natural slavery (against las Casas and the Amerindian peoples) presumed that John Mair's and Sepúlveda's formulation of Aristotle's natural slave theory was a correct interpretation of Aristotle.[115] Lewis Hanke shows that no clear-cut decision from the Spanish crown followed the Valladolid debate on whether or not the Amerindians were slaves by nature.[116] However, what is undeniable is that the natural slave theory being applied or rejected was the formulation of the theory originally developed by John Mair in 1510.

There were a number of things that were lost in the wake of the Spanish colonial debates. First, given the animated concern to assert the significance of rational faculties in the case of the Amerindians, we lost Aquinas's account of persons who lack the use of reason and his view concerning their intellectual nature and contemplative aptitude. Second, although woefully incomplete and deeply problematic, we lost Aristotle's attempt to identify and describe persons who lack the use of reason and Aristotle's account of why the virtue of the virtuous head-of-household requires that he welcome, guide, and protect such persons. Third, we lost Aquinas's subversive revision of Aristotle on human defect and, for this reason, persons who lack the use of reason became a real puzzle for interpreters of Aquinas after the 16th century.

With an eye toward "disability" in the Middle Ages, we're capable of reconstructing a whole world of serious theological and philosophical reflections on the fact that our bodies break. However, no amount of tinkering and disputation about what so-and-so really thought about "disability" will be adequate to the realities under consideration if we do not first recognize how the very fact of these Medieval engagements challenges contemporary presumptions about the theological significance of disability. Is disability a special interest, esoteric topic – commendable for occasional focused study, so long as that special inquiry is not confused with the normative, best-case anthropology of any given historical figure? Or, rather, could it be that the various premodern engagements with the ordinary vulnerability of the human body to damage, dysfunction, and decay were not as marginal as we tend to presume? Attending to the way Aquinas's anthropological outlook was navigated in the 16th century suggests that it may be an error to presume that the generic scope of pre-modern theological anthropologies are implicit arguments for the normative, best-case anthropologies that emerged in the modern era.

Notes

1 The possibility that an aspect of Aquinas's anthropological outlook was lost in the 16th century was originally suggested to me by Fr. Gustavo Gutierrez, O.P. For an engagement with these connections in relation to Vitoria's *De Indis*, see Gutiérrez, *Las Casas: In Search of the Poor of Jesus Christ*, 339–341.
2 Romero, "Happiness and Those Who Lack the Use of Reason," 49–96. For a discussion of the historiographic myth that "medieval scholastics did not think about the vulnerability of our rational faculties," see Irina Metzler, *Fools and Idiots?*, 16–18.
3 See *STh* I, q. 76, a. 1 & a. 5, co & ad 1; q. 91, a. 3; q. 97, a. 1, co & ad 3. For a close analysis of the relevant questions, see my essay "The Goodness and Beauty of Our Fragile Flesh," 231–243. For an expanded discussion of these themes in Aquinas's anthropological outlook, see Miguel J. Romero, "Aquinas on the *corporis infirmitas*: Broken Flesh and the Grammar of Grace," 101–151.
4 See Thomas Aquinas, *STh* I, q. 77, a. 1, ad 7 & a. 5; q. 79, a. 4 & a. 8; q. 93, a. 2 & a. 4; *De Veritate*, q. 15, a. 1. For a close analysis of this basic distinction in Aquinas's thought, see my essay "Happiness and Those Who Lack the Use of Reason," 76–88.
5 For a close analysis and discussion of contemplation and those who lack the use of reason, see my essay "Happiness and Those Who Lack the Use of Reason," 88–94.
6 Considered by way of the historical development of the Western intellectual tradition, the reintroduction of Aristotle to Europe in the 12th century and the way Aristotle's texts were received, navigated, and debated makes him more of a medieval figure (and less of a classical Greek figure). This is certainly a dubious claim with respect to the genealogical classification of Aristotle's ideas. However, the characterization of Aristotle's historical significance as primarily medieval is simply unavoidable when the aspect of consideration is the development of Latin medieval philosophy and theology.
7 Bartolomé de las Casas, *In Defense of the Indians*.
8 Ibid., 34–36.
9 See Reinhard Hütter, *Bound for Beatitude: A Thomistic Study in Eschatology and Ethics*, 61–65.
10 John Mair, *Johannes Maior in Secundum Sententiarum*, dist. 44, q. 3. See Anthony Pagden's *Fall of Natural Man*, 38–41, 46–51.
11 Las Casas, *Historia de las Indias* (1527), vol. 2, 452ff, cited by Anthony Pagden, *Fall of Natural Man*, 47, note 88.
12 Anthony Pagden, *Fall of Natural Man*, 47–56.
13 Lewis Hanke, *The Spanish Struggle for Justice in the Americas*, 23; Anthony Pagden, *Fall of Natural Man*, 47.
14 Lewis Hanke, *Aristotle and the American Indians*, 14; Anthony Pagden, 38–41, 47–56.

170 Miguel J. Romero

15 See Kitanov, Slotemaker, and Witt, "John Major's (Mair's) Commentary on the *Sentences* of Peter Lombard: Scholastic Philosophy and Theology in the Early Sixteenth Century," 374.
16 Ibid., 369–373, 384–395.
17 John Mair, *Johannes Maior in Secundum Sententiarum*, dist. 44, q. 3, fol. 96. For a discussion of key translation issues and associated judgments, see Jeroen Willem Joseph Laemers "Invincible ignorance and the discovery of the Americas: The history of an idea from Scotus to Suárez" (Dissertation: University of Iowa, 2011), esp. 248–250.
18 See Aristotle, *NE*, 1149a 21–36.
19 See Stephen Clark, "The Use of 'Man's Function' in Aristotle," 269–283.
20 See Joseph Karbowski, "Slaves, Women, and Aristotle's Natural Teleology," 323–350; Eugene Garver, "Aristotle's Natural Slaves: Incomplete Praxeis and Incomplete Human Beings," 173–195; John M. Cooper, "Political Community and the Highest Good," 212–264; Peter Garnsey, *Ideas of Slavery from Aristotle to Augustine*, 107–127; Charlotte Witt, "Form, Normativity, and Gender," 118–137; and Marguerite Deslauriers, "Sex and Essence in Aristotle's Metaphysics and Biology," 138–167. See also Allen Gotthelf and James Lennox, *Philosophical Issues in Aristotle's Biology*.
21 See Malcolm Heath, "Aristotle on Natural Slavery," 243–270; Josiah Ober, *Political Dissent in Democratic Athens: Intellectual Critics of Popular Rule*, 290–316.
22 For example, Stephen Clark, *Aristotle's Man*, 105–107; Malcolm Schofield, "Ideology and Philosophy in Aristotle's Theory of Natural Slavery," 115–140.
23 See Martha Nussbaum, "Aristotle on Human Nature and the Foundations of Ethics," 86–131; Alasdair MacIntyre, *After Virtue*, 158–160; see also the Introduction to MacIntyre's *Dependent Rational Animals*.
24 Throughout this chapter I use the critical English translation entitled *Aristotle's Politics, Books I and II*, translated by Trevor J. Saunders. I will occasionally opt in favor of translation choices from the W.D. Ross emendation of the Benjamin Jowett English edition (2005) or the Stephen Everson translation of the *Politics* entitled, *Aristotle: The Politics and the Constitution of Athens*. When a particular translation choice is significant, I will make whatever adjustments are called for and provide the original text inline – drawing upon the critical Greek edition of the *Politics* edited by W.D. Ross, *Aristotle's Politica*.
25 Aristotle, *Politics*, 1252a 30–35.
26 Aristotle, *Generation of Animals*, I, 737a 25; *Politics*, 1335b 19–22.
27 Kathleen Wilkes, following Thomas Nagel, provides a concise description of the "function argument" in Aristotle's thought. Wilkes writes:

> The *ergon* of any X is the function that it has; or, if it is the kind of thing which cannot readily be said to have a function, it is its characteristic activity. It is definitionally assigned; it is what X does that makes it just what it is, and if for any reason X becomes unable to perform its *ergon*, it is then no longer genuinely an X at all (cf. *De Anima* 412b 20 ff.). A sheepdog has the *ergon* of herding sheep; a good sheepdog is one that herds sheep well. Correspondingly the good man is the one who performs admirably the activities specific to his kind (see 1098a 11–15).

Kathleen V. Wilkes, "The Good Man and the Good for Man in Aristotle's Ethics," 553–571, esp. 555. Cf. Thomas Nagel's article "Aristotle on

Eudaimonia," 253–259. Wilkes goes on to note the challenge of translating *ergon*, explaining that "function" and "characteristic activity" better express Aristotle's use of the word and helps distinguish it from the purpose or end (*telos*) of the form (*eidos*).
28 *Politics*, 1252a 34–1252b 14.
29 Euripides, *Iphigenia at Aulis*, 1400.
30 For a close reading, see the discussion in my forthcoming book *Destiny of the Wounded Creature: St Thomas Aquinas on Disability*.
31 Aristotle, *Politics* (Reeve translation), 1252a 2–3 "Those who cannot exist without each other necessarily form a couple."
32 Aristotle, *Politics*, 1255a 25–28 (Saunders translation):

> since it is possible for wars to be started unjustly, and in no way could one call someone a slave who does not deserve to be a slave [i.e. an enslaved Greek noble]; otherwise, it will turn out that those considered to be of the noblest birth are slaves and descendants of slaves, should any of them be captured and sold.

Aristotle's Politics, Books I and II. Translation and Commentary by Trevor J. Saunders. Oxford University Press, 1995.
33 Aristotle, *Politics*, 1255a 29–32.
34 Ibid., 1254b 22–23: "τὰ γὰρ ἄλλα ζῷα οὐ λόγῳ αἰσθανόμενα ἀλλὰ παθήμασιν ὑπηρετεῖ."
35 The absence of a faculty or operation proper to the specific nature of a thing. Aristotle has a way to distinguish between the (seminal) rational principle and the proper entailments that follow from that principle. See Aristotle, *Posterior Analytics*, 73a34–5, "what belongs to a thing in respect of itself belongs to it in its essence [ἐν τῷ τί ἐστι]," because we refer to the thing "in the account that states the essence"; *Metaphysics* 1029b 14, "the essence of a thing is what it is said to be in respect of itself." See also *Metaphysics* 1035a 6.
36 Cf. Richard Bodeus "The natural foundations of right and Aristotelian philosophy," 88–92.
37 In that regard, in his commentary on 1254b 16–26, Trevor Saunders makes an important observation about the *phusei doulon*. He writes:

> '*Apprehend but not possess reason*': a good description of Lennie's intellectual range in Steinbeck's *Of Mice and Men*, who can comprehend a train of reasoning but not institute one and work it out for himself. Initiative and independence in reasoning are crucial. The slave's complete lack of deliberative capacity (1260a 12) calls for 'despotic' rule, i.e. of a master.

See Saunders, *Aristotle's Politics, Books I and II*, 78. G. Scott Davis affirms this interpretation of the *phusei doulon* figure, writing:

> To put it bluntly, Aristotle's slave by nature is most closely analogous to the mentally retarded …. What characterizes Aristotle's natural slave is the level of defect we identify with those retarded we consider capable of a supervised life in the mainstream.

See G. Scott Davis "Humanist Ethics and Political Justice: Soto, Sepúlveda, and the 'Affair of the Indies'," 193–212.
38 See Malcolm Heath "Aristotle on Natural Slavery," 243–270, esp. 255–258.
39 Aristotle, *Politics*, 1327b 20–30.
40 Ibid., 1329a.

172   *Miguel J. Romero*

41 E.g., the courage of non-Greek Hector; cf. NE 1116a 17–1117a 29.
42 Aristotle, *Politics*, 1330a 25–35.
43 Ibid., 1255a 38–1255b 8.
44 Aristotle, *NE*, 1149a 21–36.
45 Alasdair MacIntyre, *After Virtue*, 158–160.
46 Aristotle, *Politics: Books III and IV* (translated by Richard Robinson) 1285a 16–30. Aristotle writes:

> there is another sort of monarchy, such as the kingships found among some of the barbarians. These are like tyrannies in their powers, but they are legal and traditional. Because barbarians are more slavish in their regional [or ethnic] nature than Greeks [γὰρ τὸ δουλικώτεροι εἶναι τὰ ἤθη φύσει οἱ μὲν βάρβαροι τῶν Ἑλλήνων], and those in Asia more so than those in Europe, they endure despotic rule without distaste. Thus, these monarchies are tyrannical in this respect, but they are secure because they are traditional and legal.

47 I am grateful for the various conversations and correspondences through which Alasdair MacIntyre has encouraged me to articulate my take on these interpretive questions.
48 See note 37 above.
49 Thomas Aquinas, *Sententia libri Politicorum* I, lect. 1, sec. 15.
50 Thomas Aquinas, *Commentary on Aristotle's Politics*, 4–41. Jean-Pierre Torrell, O.P. *Saint Thomas Aquinas, vol. 1, The Person and His Work*, 146ff. Cf. Richard Regan, "Preface." Some important inferences can be made from the dating of Aquinas's relevant works. For example, the anthropological outlook and distinctions relevant to "those who lack the use of reason" and the condition *amentia* that we find in Aquinas's *Prima Pars* precede Aquinas's *Commentary on the Politics*. Likewise, we can presume the sacramental outlook relevant to "those who lack the use of reason" that we find in Aquinas's *Scriptum super libros Sententiarum* (c.1252–1257), which are restated with few amendments in Aquinas's treatment of the same themes in the *Tertia Pars*.
51 Albert the Great, *Opera Omnia, Commentarii In Octo Libros Politicorum Aristotelis*.
52 Cf. Jean Dunbabin, "The Reception and Interpretation of Aristotle's Politics," 724–726.
53 For a different account of Albert and Aquinas on these themes, see Metzler's *Fools and Idiots?* 117–131.
54 See Thomas Aquinas, *STh*, 2-2.57.3, ad 2; Thomas Aquinas, *Summa Contra Gentiles*, III.81, 1 and 5.
55 Aquinas's technical use of the term *amentia* is roughly equivalent to what we call a "severe cognitive impairment." Aquinas remarks with some regularity on persons who have *amentia*; these references are variously and inconsistently interpreted (in translation) as "imbeciles," "fools," "simpletons," "idiots," and "the feeble-minded" (Miguel Romero, "Happiness and Those Who Lack the Use of Reason," 49). Aquinas uses the term *amentia* in a way that is nosologically precise: it is a class of infirmity associated with persons who lack the use of reason in a way that is severe and seriously debilitating; the condition is understood as the impairment of an internal sense faculty that Aquinas associates with the brain (*STh*, 1.78.4, co; *STh* 1.84.7–8); and *amentia* is clearly distinguished from other internal sense infirmities like madness, insanity, frenzy, and lethargy (Miguel Romero, "Aquinas on the *corporis infirmitas*: Broken Flesh and the Grammar of

Grace," 110–111). Given the etiology and the particular faculties impaired, *amentia* can reasonably be associated with what is commonly referred to as an "intellectual disability" although, strictly speaking, for Aquinas the operation of the intellect cannot be impaired. Thus, a more precise description would be "cognitive impairment."

56 See Thomas Aquinas *STh* I, q. 76, a. 1 & a. 5, co & ad 1; q. 91, a. 3; q. 97, a. 1, co & ad 3.
57 Ibid., q. 77, a. 1, ad 7 & a. 5; q. 79, a. 4 & a. 8; q. 93, a. 2 & a. 4; *De Veritate*, q. 15, a. 1. Intellect is the principle whereby the human being understands, intellect specifies man as man, and it is the form of the human body (*STh* I, 76.1).
58 Ibid., *STh* I, q. 75, a. 2; q. 77, a. 2; q. 79, a. 8; q. 93, aa. 1–3, 6.
59 Ibid., *STh* I, 7q. 9, aa. 4, 8–11; q. 93, aa. 4, 7–8.
60 Ibid., *STh* I, a. 93, a. 8, ad 3.
61 For a close analysis and discussion of this contemplative aptitude, see Miguel Romero, "Happiness and Those Who Lack the Use of Reason," 88–94.
62 Winston Ashley, *The Theory of Natural Slavery According to Aristotle and St. Thomas*. Ashley's primary concern is to manage and minimize the association of Aquinas's theology with the various forms of chattel slavery practiced in Europe and the Americas in the modern era.
63 Ibid., *Theory of Natural Slavery*, 8–34, 50–128.
64 Ibid., 63–74, 114–121; cf. Thomas Aquinas, *STh*, 2-2.57.3, ad 2.
65 It is important to note that in the final chapter, Ashley balks at the idea that Aquinas could allow that some persons might be impaired to a degree that they are dispositionally dependent and functionally incapable of managing their own affairs (126–128). For that reason, Ashley proposes a metaphorical interpretation: for Aquinas, according to Ashley, natural slavery (under the logic of medieval feudalism) is a "dispositional servitude" that is the result of poor education, injustice, and social inequities (140–146). In effect, Ashley swaps climate caused congenital impairment (as proposed by the Spanish colonialists, see Section 5), for a sociopolitically caused failure to flourish.
66 Ibid., *Theory of Natural Slavery*, 129–139. Although Ashley overlooks Aquinas's direct engagement with the anthropological, moral, and sacramental questions relevant to persons who lack the use of reason, his systematic comparison of Aristotle and Aquinas demonstrates the baselessness of Anthony Pagden's claim that Aquinas singlehandedly revived Aristotle's theory of natural slavery in the 13th century (See Anthony Pagden, *The Fall of Natural Man*, 41).
67 Thomas Aquinas, *Sententia Libri Politicorum*, I, sec. 9.
68 Ibid., 11–12. Aquinas writes:

> For we understand the Greek word for non-Greek [*barbaros*] to mean something foreign, and we can call human beings foreigners either absolutely or in relation to someone. Those who lack reason, by which we define human beings, seem absolutely foreign to the human race, and so we call those who lack reason foreigners in an absolute sense.

(In nomine enim barbari extraneum aliquid intelligitur. Potest enim aliquis homo extraneus dici vel simpliciter vel quo ad aliquem. Simpliciter quidem extraneus videtur ab humano genere qui deficit ratione, secundum quam homo dicitur; et ideo simpliciter barbari nominantur illi qui ratione deficient ....) See Thomas Aquinas, *Sententia Libri Politicorum*, I, sec. 9.

174 *Miguel J. Romero*

69 Thomas Aquinas, *Sententia Libri Politicorum* 1, sec. 1, n. 15:

> ... qui ratione deficiunt vel propter plagam caeli quam intemperatam sortiuntur, ut ex ipsa dispositione regionis hebetes ut plurimum inveniantur: vel etiam propter aliquam malam consuetudinem in aliquibus terris existentem; ex qua provenit, ut homines irrationales et quasi brutales reddantur.

70 *Commentary on Aristotle's Politics*, 12.
71 Aristotle, *Politics*, Rackham translation, 1255a 29–32:

> ... when they say this, they are merely seeking for the principles of natural slavery of which we spoke at the outset; for they are compelled to say that there exist certain persons who are slaves everywhere and certain others who are so nowhere.

72 Augustine, *City of God*, Book XVI.8 (translated by Henry Bettenson), 661–664.
73 Ibid., 663.
74 *STh* I q. 76, a. 5, ad 1; Cf. *STh* I, q. 98, a. 2, co.
75 See Thomas F. O'Meara, "The Dominican School of Salamanca and the Spanish Conquest of America: Some Bibliographic Notes," 555–582.
76 Anthony Pagden, *Fall of Natural Man*, 47–50.
77 Ibid., 38–41; Lewis Hanke, *Aristotle and the American Indians*, 14.
78 Anthony Pagden, *Fall of Natural Man*, 50–56.
79 Lewis Hanke, *The Spanish Struggle for Justice in the Americas*, 23.
80 Ibid., 183, n. 2.
81 Ibid., 27–28.
82 Anthony Pagden, *Fall of Natural Man*, 50, 57.
83 Ibid., *Fall of Natural Man*, 57.
84 Lewis Hanke, *Aristotle and the American Indians*, 16–17.
85 Cf. Anthony Pagden, *Fall of Natural Man*, 220, n. 3.
86 Lewis Hanke, *The Spanish Struggle for Justice in the Americas*, 124.
87 Anthony Pagden, *Fall of Natural Man*, 49–50.
88 Thomas F. O'Meara, "The Dominican School of Salamanca and the Spanish Conquest of America: Some Bibliographic Notes," 572.
89 Francisco de Vitoria, *Relectio: de eo, ad quod tenetur homo veniens ad usum rationis* [alt. *Relectio de eo, ad quod tenetur homo cum primum venit ad usum rationis*](1534), 80–99, 311–352. Ibid., *De Indis et De ivre belli relectiones*.
90 *De eo ad quod tenetur*, III.4, 350–352. Cf., Aquinas, *STh*, I-II, q. 89.
91 *De eo ad quod tenetur*, I §4 (315:7–8) [82:326]. For discussion of these issues in Peter John Olivi, Duns Scotus, and William Ockham, see Vesa Hirvonen, "Mental Disorders in Late Medieval Philosophy and Theology," 171–188.
92 Francisco de Vitoria, *De eo ad quod tenetur*, §4 (315:31–33) [82:328].
93 *De eo ad quod tenetur*, I, §4 (315:18–41) [82:327–28]. Vitoria cites *STh* I, q. 84, a. 8, ad 2; II-II, q. 172, a. 1, ad 2; q. 154, a. 5; IV *Sent.*, d. 9, q. 1, a. 4, ad 3 and 4.
94 Ibid., I, §4 (315:38–41) [82:328]: "sed amentes habent multos actus, quos bruta habere non pussunt."
95 Ibid., I, §4 (315:31–34) [82:328].
96 Ibid., I, §4 (315:9–13) [82:327]). "... quia habent actus circa res spirituales, quae non cadunt sub sensu, ut desiderium etiam rerum spiritualium, ut experientia patet ex his, quae tum faciunt, tum dicunt. Loquuntur enim Deo, et angelis, disputant de dialecticis."
97 Cf. *STh* I, q. 84, a. 8.; q. 86, a. 2, ad. 1; III, q. 180, a. 9, ad. 1.

98 Francisco de Vitoria, *De eo ad quod tenetur*, I, §5 (318:2–16) [83:333].
99 Thomas Aquinas, *STh* I, q. 93, a. 4.
100 See Hanke, *The Spanish Struggle for Justice in the Americas*, 72–74; Hanke, *Aristotle*, 84.
101 Hanke, *Aristotle*, 22–23.
102 Francisco de Vitoria, *De Indis*, Vol. 2, 378–379:

> Barbari enim isti, licet (ut supra dictum est) non omnino sint amentes, tamen etiam parum distant ab amentibus; ita videtur quod non sint idonei ad constituendam vel administrandam legirimam Rempublicam etiam inter terminos humanos et civiles .... Hoc, inquam, posset suaderi, quia, si omnes essent amentes, non dubium est quin hoc esset non solum licitum, sed convenientissimum .... In hoc enim est totum periculum animarum et salutis, et ad hoc posset etiam prodesse illud, quod supra dictum est, quod aliqui sunt natura servi; nam tales videntur omnes isti barbari, et sic possent ex parte gubernari ut servi.

103 Gustavo Gutierrez, *Las Casas: In Search of the Poor of Jesus Christ*, 331–348. See Pagden, *The Fall of Natural Man*, 65–68, 79–80, 93–97.
104 Thomas Aquinas, *STh* I-II, q. 3, a. 5; II-II, q. 179, a. 1-2; II-II, q. 180; III, q. 72, a. 1; III, q. 73. a. 1. See Miguel Romero, "Happiness and Those Who Lack the Use of Reason," 90–94.
105 Lewis Hanke, *The Spanish Struggle for Justice in the Americas*, 117.
106 According to Pagden's narrative, Sepúlveda received his formulation from theologians like Juan de Quevedo, Bernardo de Mesa, and Gil Gregorio. By contrast, Lewis Hanke's account of the period sees less conspiracy of political and institutional powers, while placing more of an emphasis on individual failings and agendas.
107 See Pagden, *Fall of Natural Man*, 45–57; Hanke, *Aristotle and the American Indians*, 48–60; Hanke, *The Spanish Struggle for Justice in the Americas*, 117–125.
108 Bartolomé de las Casas, *In Defense of the Indians*.
109 Ibid., 28.
110 Ibid., 28, 35–36.
111 Ibid., 34–35.
112 Ibid., 38.
113 Ibid., 36.
114 Lewis Hanke, *Aristotle and the American Indians*, 88–95.
115 Ibid., 79–84, 88–95.
116 Ibid., 84–88, 96–99, 104–116.

References

Primary Sources

Albert the Great. *Opera Omnia, Commentarii In Octo Libros Politicorum Aristotelis*. Vol 8. Paris: Apud Ludovicum, 1891.
Aquinas, Thomas. *Summa Theologiae* [=*STh*]. Edited by Enrique Alarcón. <http://www.corpusthomisticum.org/iopera.html>.
——— *Sententia libri Politicorum*. Edited by Enrique Alarcón. <http://www.corpusthomisticum.org/iopera.html>.
——— *Summa Contra Gentiles*. Edited by Enrique Alarcón. <http://www.corpusthomisticum.org/iopera.html>.

———— *De Veritate*. Edited by Enrique Alarcón. <http://www.corpusthomisticum.org/iopera.html>.

———— *Aquinas: Commentary on Aristotle's Politics*. Translated by Richard Regan. Indianapolis, IN: Hackett Publishing, 2007.

Aristotle. *Aristotle's Politica*. Edited by W. D. Ross. Oxford: Clarendon Press, 2005.

———— *Aristotle's Politics, Books I and II*. Translation and Commentary by Trevor J. Saunders. Oxford: Oxford University Press, 1995.

———— *Aristotle: The Politics and the Constitution of Athens*. Translated by Steven Everson. Cambridge: Cambridge University Press, 1996.

———— *Aristotle, Politics (Loeb Classical Library)*. Translated by H. Rackham. Cambridge, MA: Harvard University Press, 1944.

———— *Aristotle, Politics*. Translated by C.D.C. Reeve. Indianapolis, IN: Hackett Publishing, 1998.

———— *Aristotle, Politics: Books III and IV*. Translated by Richard Robinson. Oxford: Clarendon Press, 1995.

———— *Generation of Animals* (Loeb Classical Library No. 366). Translated by A.L. Peck. Cambridge, MA: Harvard University Press, 1942.

———— *Nicomachean Ethics*. Translated by Terence Irwin. Indianapolis, IN: Hackett Publishing Company, 1999.

———— *Posterior Analytics*. Translated by Jonathan Barnes. Oxford: Oxford University Press, 2009.

———— *Metaphysics*. Translated by C.D.C. Reeve. Indianapolis, IN: Hackett Publishing Company, 2016.

Augustine. *City of God*. Translated by Henry Bettenson. New York, NY: Penguin Books, 2003.

Bartolomé de las Casas. *In Defense of the Indians*. Translated and edited by Stafford Poole, C.M. DeKalb: Northern Illinois University Press, 1992.

Euripides. *The Plays of Euripides*. Translated by E.P. Coleridge, Vol. II. London: George Bell and Sons, 1891.

Francisco de Vitoria. "Relectio: de eo, ad quod tenetur homo veniens ad usum rationis [alt. Relectio de eo, ad quod tenetur homo cum primum venit ad usum rationis](1534)." In *Relecciones Teologicas del Maestro Fray Francisco de Vitoria*, Volume II. Edited by Luis G. A. Getino. Madrid: Imprenta la Rafa, 1935: 80–99, 311–352.

———— *De Indis et De ivre belli relectiones*. Edited by Ernest Nys, John Pawley Bate, Johann Georg Simon, and Herbert F. Wright. Washington, DC: Carnegie Institution of Washington, 1917.

John Mair. *Johannes Maior in Secundum Sententiarum*. Edited by J. Badius and J. Petit. Paris, 1510.

Secondary Sources

Ashley, Winston. *The Theory of Natural Slavery According to Aristotle and St. Thomas*. Unpublished Ph.D. dissertation. University of Notre Dame, 1941.

Bodeus, Richard. "The Natural Foundations of Right and Aristotelian Philosophy." In *Action and Contemplation: Studies in the Moral and Political Thought of Aristotle*. Translated by Kent Enns. Edited by Robert Bartlett and Susan Collins. Albany: State University of New York Press, 1999: 65–105.

Clark, Stephen. "The Use of 'Man's Function' in Aristotle," *Ethics* 82 (1972) 269–283.

——— *Aristotle's Man: Speculations upon Aristotelian Anthropology.* Oxford: Clarendon Press, 1975.

Cooper, John M. "Political Community and the Highest Good." In *Being, Nature, and Life: Essays in Honor of Allan Gotthelf.* Edited by James Lennox and Robert Bolton. Cambridge: Cambridge University Press, 2008: 212–264.

Davis, G. Scott, "Humanist Ethics and Political Justice: Soto, Sepúlveda, and the 'Affair of the Indies'," *Annual of the Society of Christian Ethics* 19 (1999): 193–212.

Deslauriers, Marguerite. "Sex and Essence in Aristotle's Metaphysics and Biology." In *Feminist Interpretations of Aristotle.* Edited by Cynthia Freeland. University Park: The Pennsylvania State University, 1998: 138–167.

Dunbabin, Jean. "The Reception and Interpretation of Aristotle's Politics." In *The Cambridge History of Later Medieval Philosophy.* Edited by Norman Kretzman, Anthony Kenny, Jan Pinborg, and Eleonor Stump. Cambridge: Cambridge University Press, 1982: 720–737.

Garnsey, Peter. *Ideas of Slavery from Aristotle to Augustine.* Cambridge: Cambridge University Press, 1996.

Garver, Eugene. "Aristotle's Natural Slaves: Incomplete Praxeis and Incomplete Human Beings," *Journal of the History of Philosophy* 32.2 (1994): 173–195.

Gotthelf, Allen and James Lennox. *Philosophical Issues in Aristotle's Biology.* Cambridge: Cambridge Press, 1987.

Gutiérrez, Gustavo. *Las Casas: In Search of the Poor of Jesus Christ.* Maryknoll, NY: Orbis Books, 1993.

Hanke, Lewis. *The Spanish Struggle for Justice in the Conquest of America.* Boston, MA: Little and Brown, 1965.

——— *Aristotle and the American Indians: A Study in Race Prejudice in the Modern World.* Chicago, IL: Indiana University Press, 1970.

Heath, Malcolm. "Aristotle on Natural Slavery," *Phronesis: A Journal for Ancient Philosophy.* 53.3 (2008) 243–270.

Hirvonen, Vesa. "Mental Disorders in Late Medieval Philosophy and Theology." In *Mind and Modality: Studies in the History of Philosophy in Honour of Simo Knuuttila.* Edited by Vesa Hirvonen, Toivo J. Holopainen, and Miira Tuominen. Leiden: Brill, 2006: 171–188.

Hütter, Reinhard. *Bound for Beatitude: A Thomistic Study in Eschatology and Ethics.* Washington, DC: Catholic University of America Press, 2019.

Karbowski, Joseph. "Slaves, Women, and Aristotle's Natural Teleology," *Ancient Philosophy* 32.2 (2012): 323–350.

Kitanov, Severin V., John T. Slotemaker, and Jeffery C. Witt. "John Major's (Mair's) Commentary on the *Sentences* of Peter Lombard: Scholastic Philosophy and Theology in the Early Sixteenth Century." In *Mediaeval Commentaries on the Sentences of Peter Lombard Vol. 3.* Edited by Phillip W. Rosemann. Boston, MA: Brill 2015.

Laemers, Jeroen Willem Joseph. *Invincible ignorance and the discovery of the Americas: the history of an idea from Scotus to Suárez.* Unpublished Ph.D. Dissertation: University of Iowa, 2011.

MacIntyre, Alasdair. *After Virtue.* Notre Dame: Norte Dame Press, 1984.

——— *Dependent Rational Animals. Why Human Beings Need the Virtues.* Peru, IL: Open Court, 1999.
Metzler, Irina. *Fools and Idiots? Intellectual Disability in the Middle Ages (Disability History).* Manchester: Manchester University Press, 2016.
Nagel, Thomas. "Aristotle on *Eudaimonia*," *Phronesis* 17.3 (1972) 253–259.
Nussbaum, Martha. "Aristotle on Human Nature and the Foundations of Ethics." In *World, Mind, and Ethics: Essays in the Ethical Philosophy of Bernard Williams.* Edited by J.E. J. Altham. Cambridge: Cambridge University Press, 1995: 86–131.
Ober, Josiah. *Political Dissent in Democratic Athens: Intellectual Critics of Popular Rule.* Princeton, NJ: Princeton University Press, 1998.
O'Meara, Thomas F. "The Dominican School of Salamanca and the Spanish Conquest of America: Some Bibliographic Notes," *The Thomist* 56 (1992) 555–582.
Pagden, Anthony. *The Fall of Natural Man: The American India and the Origins of Comparative Ethnology (Cambridge Iberian and Latin American Studies).* Cambridge: Cambridge University Press, 1987.
Regan, Richard. "Preface." In *Aquinas: Commentary on Aristotle's Politics.* Translated by Richard Regan. Indianapolis, IN: Hackett Publishing, 2007.
Romero, Miguel. "Aquinas on the *corporis infirmitas*: Broken Flesh and the Grammar of Grace." In *Disability in the Christian Tradition: A Reader.* Edited by Brian Brock and John Swinton. Grand Rapids: Eerdmans, 2012: 101–151.
——— "Happiness and Those Who Lack the Use of Reason," *The Thomist* 80 (2016) 49–96.
——— "The Goodness and Beauty of Our Fragile Flesh," *Journal of Moral Theology*, Vol. 6, Special Issue 2 (2017) 206–253.
Schofield, Malcolm. "Ideology and Philosophy in Aristotle's Theory of Natural Slavery." In *Saving the City: Philosopher-Kings and Other Classical Paradigms.* New York, NY: Routledge, 1999: 115–140.
Torrell, Jean-Pierre O.P. *Saint Thomas Aquinas, vol. 1, The Person and His Work.* Translated by Robert Royal. Washington, DC: Catholic University Press of America, 1996.
Wilkes, Kathleen V. "The Good Man and the Good for Man in Aristotle's Ethics," *Mind*, New Series, 87:348 (1978) 553–571.
Witt, Charlotte. "Form, Normativity, and Gender." In *Feminist Interpretations of Aristotle.* Edited by Cynthia Freeland. University Park: The Pennsylvania State University, 1998: 118–137.

6 Deafness and Pastoral Care in the Middle Ages

Jenni Kuuliala and Reima Välimäki

There are many ways that one could discuss deafness in medieval Christian theology and philosophy. This chapter looks at the influence of medieval theology on how parish priests interpreted, and in turn treated, their deaf parishioners as they performed their duty of pastoral care. The chapter not only describes the intersection between medieval theology, parish priests, and deaf parishioners but also evaluates these intersections from a disability-positive perspective. Before describing these medieval intersections, we begin by describing a disability-positive perspective as it relates to deafness. After this, we will be able to evaluate (to the extent we can based on the existing evidence) how parish priests treated their deaf parishioners.

As a disability that impacts modes of communication, deafness is (and has always been) first and foremost linked with and defined by the social realities and language of the community. Perhaps the most famous demonstration of this is Martha's Vineyard in Massachusetts, settled in the 1640s. Since an exceptionally large percentage of the population was deaf between the 17th and the early 19th centuries, the community developed into one that was fully bilingual. Residents who were deaf, as well as those who were not, used sign language, regardless of the hearing ability of their interlocutor. Although the hearing inhabitants of the island recognized that others could not hear, the deaf were neither singled out nor portrayed as disabled by the other residents; instead, they were fully integrated, active members of the community.[1] Admittedly, the history of Martha's Vineyard is, in many ways, a one-off case; nevertheless, it offers an illuminating point of comparison to the situation in many modern societies, where audism is a predominant mode of oppression. A term comparable with racism, ageism, heterosexism, or ableism, audism suggests that one person is superior to another because of his or her ability to hear. Thus, at least for the past 2 or 3 centuries, deaf people have been forced to culturally and socially adopt hearing norms.[2]

H-Dirksen L. Bauman has traced the origins of audism, finding metaphysics among its most influential roots: the idea that human identity and *being* [our emphasis] are linked with spoken language. There are clear examples of audism in the thinking of Johann Conrad Ammann, the noted Swiss physician and instructor of non-verbal deaf persons, who wrote at the turn of the 18th century that deaf people were "dull" and animal-like. Over time, as the education of deaf people increasingly became an issue, such comparisons between the deaf and animals likewise became more frequent. Education (and oralism) was perceived to be a means by which deaf people's apparent animal-like way of being could be improved and erased. Jacques Derrida has been the most noteworthy critic of this kind of phonocentrism; recent linguistic and neurolinguistic studies have also shown that spoken language is just one of the many ways in which a human being is "coded" to communicate.[3]

Together with the overarching audism of modern, Western societies, recent medical developments (especially the Cochlear implant) and educational normalization have led to the most predominant bioethical question that Deaf Studies – and Deaf communities – are currently facing: that of the right to exist. Writing about the extrinsic value of Deaf communities and sign languages, H-Dirksen L. Bauman and Joseph J. Murray write that "[t]he task of Deaf Studies in the new century is to ask a fundamental question: How does being Deaf reorganize what it means to be human?"[4] These issues do not directly pertain to the Middle Ages, when sign language in the modern sense of the word and practice did not exist[5] and when deafness, although occasionally discussed in medical texts, was largely considered incurable.[6] However, questions about the ability to participate, especially in the religious life that was central to all communities, were prevalent in the case of the deaf. This intermingles with a long-standing discussion – one that had existed since Antiquity – about (congenitally) deaf people's level of intelligence and whether they were somehow lesser humans because of their impairment.[7] Such notions have had long-lasting implications, but, as will be discussed in this chapter, the lived realities of the deaf in the late Middle Ages were far more diverse than one might have imagined.

Throughout the medieval period, deafness appeared as a distinctive type of disability because of the inevitable problems and challenges that it posed to communication in a largely oral society. This pertains especially to congenital/pre-lingual deafness, which prevented a child from learning to speak. Already in Antiquity, views toward deafness and the deaf largely depended on whether the deafness was pre-lingual or was acquired later in life.[8] Medieval canon law and secular law collections imposed several restrictions on deaf people's ability to function in society, especially if the deafness was congenital. These restrictions mostly pertained to those of a higher social standing: law codes, for example, forbade the deaf from acting as judges or plaintiffs, and in many cases from inheriting if they were unable to stipulate – that is, if they could not communicate properly or, according to some lawyers, understand the transaction.[9] Furthermore, as is well known, a priest was supposed to be physically healthy. For minor impairments it was possible to seek dispensation, but the rules were strict and deaf/deaf-mute men were most certainly denied the ability to be ordained.[10]

A note on nomenclature is useful here. The Latin word for a deaf person is *surdus*. However, the mute and deaf-mute were often lumped together, since congenital deafness causes an inability to speak. Therefore *mutus/muta* often refers to someone congenitally deaf-mute, whereas a person described as *surdus/surda* may have retained one's ability to speak, meaning that one's deafness was likely caused by an accident, illness, or old age.[11] Although the term "deaf-mute" is considered highly derogatory in modern society, in this chapter we use it when directly referring to the writings of medieval authors. In modern society, "Deaf" or "Deafness" with an uppercase "D" refer to deaf culture;[12] since this concept did not exist in medieval society, we use the term with a lowercase "d."

Augustine's Legacy

Augustine of Hippo is the most influential theologian to have written about religion and the deaf, and his writings have been most often interpreted to mean that the ability to hear was a prerequisite for religious understanding, and thus for salvation. He states this claim in his *Contra Iulianum*, pointing to those who are born blind, deaf, or feeble-minded (*fatuus*) as examples of original sin passing from parents to their offspring:

> But, since you also deny that an infant is subject to original sin, you must answer why such great innocence is sometimes born blind; sometimes, deaf. Deafness is a hindrance to faith itself, as the Apostle says: "Faith is from hearing." Indeed, if nothing deserving punishment passes from parents to infants, who could bear to see the image of God, which is, you say, adorned with the gift of innocence, sometimes born feeble-minded, since this touches the soul itself?[13]

This reasoning led to the conclusion that the deaf (and especially the congenitally deaf) were doomed to damnation. Such literal interpretation of Romans 10:17 (*Ergo fides ex auditu*) circulated in late Antiquity but was not universally acknowledged. Jerome, in fact, refuted the reading in a passage that has to our knowledge gone unnoticed in disability history. In *Commentaria in Epistolam ad Galatas*, he responds to the claim that from Romans 10:17 it follows that the congenitally deaf (*qui surdi nati sunt*) cannot be Christians. Jerome thought that the Gospel could be taught with sign language:

> Moreover, one who tries to solve this conundrum will first attempt to assert that the deaf are able to learn the Gospel by means of nods,

everyday routines, and the so-called talking gesticulation of the entire body. Then he will point out that the words of God, to which nothing is deaf, speak instead to the ears about which God himself says in the Gospel, 'He who has ears, let him hear.'

Jerome further stresses that learning the word of God does not require physical ears, in other words hearing ability:

> Furthermore, as I have explained on many occasions, the soul, like the body, has its own limbs and sensory faculties, among which are these [figurative] ears. Whoever has these will not need physical ears to apprehend the Gospel of Christ.[14]

Augustine's writing has, however, dominated modern scholarship, and his exposition of Paul's words has for a long time been repeated as a clear example of ancient prejudices against the disabled. Recently, many historians have adopted more diverse views about Augustine's thought. For example, Scott G. Bruce, Leslie A. King, and John Vickrey Van Cleve and Barry A. Crouch deem this interpretation of Augustine's thinking as completely false, proposing instead that Augustine's views were much more inclusive and diverse. In his thinking, they argue, deafness was a *hindrance* for religion, not an inevitable barrier.[15] Irina Metzler, on the other hand, still accepts that Augustine's theological view in the *Contra Iulianum* condemned the deaf to a theologically inferior position.[16]

Augustine's views on deafness were indeed diverse. Two passages in his other writings present a completely different view from that cited above. In the *De quantitate animae liber unus*, written as a dialogue with Evodius of Uzalis, Augustine proposes that the deaf can be educated, that they can learn, and, furthermore, that using signs also pertains to the soul. As an example of the education of the deaf, he tells of a young man in Milan, fair in body and most courteous in demeanor, who was a deaf-mute and could only communicate with signs. In the *De magistro*, Augustine gives sign language used by the deaf as an example of how complex ideas and actions can be discussed without spoken words.[17] Consequently, there would be no intellectual or communicative obstacle to a deaf person learning the Christian doctrine and receiving salvation.

How can we consolidate these two views of Augustine's writings about the deaf, one positive and the other negative? In fact, we cannot, and there is no reason why we should even try. One has to recognize an often-ignored question of timing: Augustine wrote the *De quantitate animae* in Rome in 388 soon after his own baptism, and the *De magistro* followed almost immediately thereafter (388/389). These two early works, which contain the more positive view of deafness, are the musings of a recent convert reflecting on his own liberal arts education as it pertained to Christian doctrine.[18] Especially in the *De magistro*, Augustine was interested in the nature of language and signs and pushed toward the extremes of their definitions. This is the context in which Augustine's interest in sign language should be understood: it was not for emancipating the deaf but rather an intellectual exercise about what constitutes signs, words, and language. The *Contra Iulianum*, by contrast, is the work of a mature theologian who was by then (c. 421) the bishop of Hippo and seeking to counter Julian of Eclanum's attack against his doctrine of original sin.[19] Although some scholars have preferred the more benign view on deafness that appeared in the *De magistro* and the *De quantitate animae*,[20] it was actually the *Contra Iulianum* in which Augustine pronounced an explicit theological statement: the deaf are inferior in their understanding of faith, and the congenitally deaf suffer due to original sin passed through their parents. Above all, one has to recognize that Augustine never tried to formulate a coherent view of deafness: what we have from him are these three passages written over the course of more than thirty years, each used as an example in debates about topics other than disability as such.

Deafness in the Later Medieval Church: Confession, Free Will, and Pastoral Care

Augustine's work does, nevertheless, manage to reflect issues that became of practical importance for the high and late medieval church: the necessity of communicating theological questions to the deaf and the practical difficulty of doing so. Deafness was thus a theological issue, but primarily at the level of pastoral theology, expressed in manuals and catechetical treatises. In what follows, we focus on the normative instructions and regulations contained in confessors' manuals, as well as on the practical, religious consequences arising from the theological views on which they were based. When we think about the everyday life and social status of the deaf, religion and the ability to participate in religious life were critically important. Religious life, or lived religion, was tightly interwoven into social relations at all levels. It offered a way for people to perform themselves and their position within society, and it linked an individual experience to that of the larger community in which he or she lived.[21] The study of pastoral care, above all confession and other sacraments, preaching, and catechesis, is perhaps the best way to examine both lived religion and the ideas of medieval theologians without creating unnecessary binaries between popular and elite religion.[22] This idea is also the basic viewpoint of this chapter, wherein our aim is to explore the interplay between theological views on deafness and their practical implications.

Canon 21 of the Fourth Lateran Council of 1215 famously ordained that every Christian who had attained the age of reason had to confess his sins at least once a year to his parish pastor or, with the latter's permission, to another priest. This resulted in a flood of literature – confessors' manuals (*libri confessionales*) – that focused on pastoral care and that provided the necessary instructions and education for parish priests responsible for confessions.[23] These works appeared especially often in the 13th century and were written mostly by Franciscans and Dominicans.[24] As Jacqueline Murray notes, these manuals "provide us with a window onto the moral universe of the Middle Ages." They offer insight into the questions that the confessor was supposed to ask and the types of values and morals that he was expected to teach his parishioners. Furthermore, as the manuals had a very practical purpose, they not only instructed the confessor in his tasks but also reflected the laity's values.[25] Yet at the same time, there existed a close connection between these manuals for confessors and the works of school theologians and canonists. The manuals were thus a media that facilitated the dissemination of medieval theology at the level of the parish clergy and his flock.[26] Often the manuals were organized according to the Seven Deadly Sins, but some writers also used the Decalogue and the Seven Sacraments for this purpose, or mixed two or three of these together.[27]

We use a representative selection of these texts, from Raymond of Penyafort's fundamental and extremely influential *Summa de casibus poenitentiae* to late medieval "best-sellers" such as Bartholomeus de Sancto Concordio's *Summa pisanella*, to explore both the ways in which the writers of these texts discussed the religious participation of the deaf and the potential implications of their views on the actual religious participation of the deaf in their communities. It is, however, important to highlight from the very beginning that not all manual authors mentioned deafness in their work. There are important, well-known manuals such as Robert of Mannyng's *Handlyng Synne* and Alain de Lille's *Liber poenitentialis* that do not touch the topic at all. Others, such as the *Summa rosella* by the Fransciscan Baptista de Salis, published between 1480 and 1490, use "deaf" (*surdus*) as a separate title and index term.[28] As is always the case with normative sources, deducing exactly how commonly they influenced direct interaction between people is difficult. However, the fact that deafness was a topic frequently discussed in confessors' manuals demonstrates that it held cultural, religious, and societal importance.

When the writers discussed the topic of deafness, they did so through three topics: sexual behavior in marriage, and in relation to two different sacraments, confession and marriage. We will begin with correct versus improper sexual behavior. Confessors' manuals drew heavily on earlier penitentials and reflected the Church Fathers' ideas about the periods during which a married couple should abstain from sex – in particular Church feast days (for the sake of fasting and impurity created by sexual acts) and during the woman's menstrual period, pregnancy, and lactation. The authors of the earlier penitentials shared the views of Pseudo-Gregory and the Fathers that, even in marriage, sex was impure and sinful and that engaging in it was a concession to the need to produce children. Periods of abstinence were needed both to legitimize the marriage and to avoid sin. Periodic abstinence was thus a virtue and separated marital sex from fornication.[29] Some of our writers stated the belief – based on Mosaic law that sex during menstruation resulted in impurity – that many children who had been conceived during menstruation or pregnancy were somehow infirm. Another common idea was that childbirth itself resulted in ritual impurity.[30] Most often, the manuals stated that having sex during menstruation would result in the birth of a "leprous" child. For example, Thomas of Chobham discussed the matter of sex during menstruation under the sin of adultery.[31] According to medieval canon law historian James Brundage, this thinking appears to have originated among Christian writers: despite the existence of "purity laws," such views were expressed neither in Hebrew Scriptures nor in the writings of ancient anatomists.[32]

Deafness and muteness did not often receive specific mention as the result of illicit marital sex, but occasionally the idea was raised. The *Ayembyte of Inwyt*, a Kentish translation of the *Le Somme de Roi*, which was intended for a non-educated audience, stated that a child conceived during menstruation would be crooked, blind, leprous, deaf, or dumb. (Compare this to Gloria Frost's discussion, in Chapter 2, of various causes of congenital disability according to Albert the Great.) In this text, the issue is discussed among the acts that make marriage sinful; the others include being married for the sole sake of satisfying lust and having carnal relations in holy places.[33] However, most writers of the manuals do not mention the issue even in passing; all in all, ritual impurity appears to have been a minor issue for most 13th and 14th century authors.[34] Nevertheless, religious and cultural views did exist holding that parental sins, especially sexual ones, could result in a child's congenital disability,[35] but the extent to which this issue was raised during confession remains unclear.[36] More often and in more detail, deafness appears in relation to two sacraments of the medieval Catholic Church: marriage and confessions. We can give a more thorough treatment to them.

Marriage

As indicated above, confessors' manuals instructed parish priests about the seven sacraments. Of the seven, deafness/muteness was most often connected to marriage, which became a sacrament of the Western church only in the first half of the 12th century. In the thinking of medieval theologians, marriage offered a remedy to lust (one of the seven cardinal sins) and was thus under the church's jurisdiction. There is not space here to examine the development of marriage as a sacrament, but suffice it to say that by the time the confessors' manuals were written, the ritual was well-established. As theological historian Philip L. Reynolds argues, marriage was "a mode of participating in the life of the church," and although inferior to celibacy and religious vocations, it was so "only in degree and not in kind."[37] Deafness/muteness, in turn, appears in the manuals' discussions of the sacrament of marriage because it intertwines with the medieval consent doctrine, whose origins were both theological and legal. Peter Lombard made the definitive statement about this matter in the 1150s, in his *De sententiae*. According to Peter, consent expressed in words is the efficient cause of matrimony. He also writes that if the couple "consent[s] mentally without expressing themselves in words or with other unambiguous signs, then such consent does not make marriage."[38] Although the spoken word was the norm, then, the practicalities of the time meant that customs varied, and partners could follow established customs to "establish the sense and the tense of their signs" as long as such signs were unambiguous.[39] Therefore, the deaf-mute, as well as spouses who did not share a common language, could use non-verbal signs to indicate consent.[40] Gratian's *Decretals* also point in this direction: the mad could not marry as they lacked the understanding (i.e., mental capacity) to do so, but there was no ban against deaf people getting married.[41]

One of the most influential authors of a confessors' manual, Raymond of Penyafort, wrote his *Summa de casibus poenitentiae* between 1224 and 1226 as a guide for his fellow Dominicans who took confessions. He followed the views of Peter Lombard and Gratian (the latter was a known influence on his work). He simply states that anyone who can consent (*consentire*) can marry – he does not even exclude the mad but writes that they can do so if they have lucid moments.[42] Raymond was also a canon lawyer and decretalist. In the great canon law collection that he compiled, the *Liber extra*, commissioned by Pope Gregory IX and completed in 1234, there is a more explicit approval of a deaf-mute joining with someone in marriage: "he cannot or should not be denied, since what he cannot declare with words he is able to do with signs."[43] What mattered is that marriage is based on the free will of the parties involved: if they can express their consent by signs, there is no theological basis on which to deny the marriage.

Other writers followed Raymond's example, some of them in very laconic statements. The English theologian and subdeacon Thomas of Chobham (d. 1233–1236) states in his *Summa Confessorum* that a monastic vow can be completed without words "just like a mute can confirm his consent in marriage with some signs."[44] The Franciscan Monaldus de Iustinopoli (Capodistria) (d. ca 1285) was of the same opinion: "the mute and deaf can well enter into matrimony with signs and nods if not with words."[45] In the early 16th century, Sylvestro da Priorio

(d. 1523) was likewise concise in his *Summa*, referring to the judgment of decretalists Hostiensis (Henry of Segusio, d. 1271) and Panormitanus (Nicholaus de Tudeschis, d. 1445 or 1453):[46]

> whether a deaf or a blind alike can enter into matrimony, according to Hostiensis, as Panormitanus recites in the chapter 'cum apud. de spon.', if he can express his consent to the [marriage] contract, he should be admitted, otherwise he is rejected.[47]

In fact, Sylvestro probably adopted this passage from an earlier confessors' manual, the already mentioned *Summa rosella* by the Franciscan Baptista de Salis, who discussed the question under a specific title "surdus."[48]

Baptista's opinion is worth looking at more closely. He starts with the usual question about whether a deaf or mute can enter into marriage but adds a blind man into the list. First, he offers a rationale in favor of marriage: such a man can know women naturally; therefore, he has "natural reason" (*ratio naturalis*) to marry. Against it, he says that if one has never seen or heard how a marriage contract is made, he cannot know what matrimony is and thus cannot consent to it.[49] Again, the crucial point is free will and consent. After this introduction to the problem, Baptista refers to the authority of the decretalists Hostiensis and Panormitanus, namely that if one can express his consent, he must be permitted to marry. According to Baptista, it is up to a "discreet judge" to consider the intended meaning "from actions and signs" (*ex gestis enim et signis*); when doubt remains, he must consult the secular prince.[50] At the end, Baptista recounts an example of the marriage of a deaf-mute from his own days:

> In the present times we have seen deaf and mute to enter into marriage. And above all we have [an example] of a woman deaf and mute since her birth, who entered into marriage with a man through signs and nods and stayed with him for forty years and more, and they both still live and she very well knows the forces and nature of matrimony, as it is clear first with regards to inseparability, of which she lived with him for so many years. Secondly with regards to good faith, because she is of such virtue and continence that she would not permit anyone but her husband to touch or kiss her. Which is indeed a miracle, for her husband was an adulterer and he desired that a divorce happen between them.[51]

Baptista's account has too much flavor of a moral *exemplum* to be regarded as the life story of a real deaf woman in the 15th century.[52] Yet even if the story is partly or mostly fictional, it is noteworthy that a deaf-mute woman takes the role of a humble, pious, and virtuous wife who patiently suffered her adulterous husband. There is a bitter tone in Baptista's story: not only did the deaf woman understand the ideal of a Christian wife but she also came to understand the true nature of married life in this world. One should ask if she was an entirely positive character after all: yes, she was the humble and suffering protagonist, but at the same time, the reader can picture an easily misled deaf wife staying at home while her husband entertained lovers around the village.

How often deaf people actually married is, of course, difficult to know. In hagiographic material there are sporadic examples of deafness mentioned as a hindrance to a young woman's attempts to marry.[53] At the same time, there are equally sporadic examples of deaf people marrying. One set of English administrative records known as Patent Rolls (*Rotuli litterarum patentium*) includes an ordination that the brother-in-law of a congenitally deaf man, John de Orleton, must keep his promises and out of his income maintain not just John but also his wife and children.[54] Another English legal document discusses the marriage of a woman called Margaret, who was the daughter and heir of Nicholas de Layburn. The document states that her guardians were supposed to ensure that she was not married against her will and that if she were to be married, she would not be "disparaged."[55] The legal case is related to the shift in the English law after the mid-13th century. Both mentally incapacitated and deaf-mute heirs were appointed a custodian. Before the shift, these custodians were typically family members or representatives of their lords; later, control over their inheritances was transferred to the king and the custodians that he chose.[56]

The deaf in the Middle Ages certainly faced challenges when they wanted to marry, but the evidence shows that they did marry and that they were permitted to do so according to theologians and canon lawyers. The confessors' manuals, when discussing the deaf and matrimony, did not speculate about the possibility of a deaf parent having deaf children. Their main concern was securing unambiguous consent for the marriage itself. One can easily imagine this being a real problem during a time without systematic sign language. Above all, it is worth stressing that medieval canon law was more permissive toward the deaf than 20th-century legislation in many Western countries: in Finland, for example, marriage laws prohibited a congenitally deaf person from marrying another congenitally deaf person between 1929 and 1969.[57]

Confession

If consent to marry someone was difficult to express with signs and nods to a priest who likely had little or no knowledge of sign language, even more challenging was the sacrament of penance. If contrition of the heart was to be followed by confession of the mouth,[58] what to do when the confessant was unable to speak or hear the confessor's instructions?

Again, Raymond of Penyafort set the example that others then followed, at times quoting his work almost verbatim. The deaf and mute are mentioned under other "doubtful" (*dubitabilia*) cases, such as the blind, the mad, and the possessed (*demonicacos*),[59] and Raymond asks what a priest should do if he knows that he has such a parishioner living in mortal sin. He proclaims: "if he (the priest) calls a deaf [person] to make penitence, it does not help, because he cannot hear. If a mute, he cannot confess." He also notes that "others cannot understand anything due to infirmity."[60] The last comment is difficult to interpret: Raymond may mean either those in the last stages of a serious illness or someone suffering from a mental defect that impedes understanding. Nevertheless, for all cases Raymond proposes the following solution:

> The priest must do what he can to introduce them to contrition and full penitence, according to what is possible, namely with words, texts, gestures and signs and in other ways he can. If he cannot accomplish it, he should pray to the Lord and have his people pray, so that the Lord may enlighten their hearts to penitence. And when he would have omitted nothing of those things belonging to him, it is not accounted to his fault.[61]

Raymond's solution was still being repeated, in a summary form, in late-15th century confessors' manuals.[62] It can thus be regarded as a standard medieval response to the quandary of how to take confession from the deaf. There are several points to consider in Raymond's response. First and foremost, the parish priest was expected to do *what he could* in order to induce the deaf to confession and penance. This was, without doubt, the preferred solution, and at least in theory a priest who was charged with deaf, mute, or mentally unstable people was to do all in his power to make them understand their sins and to repent them. When all else failed, he should pray to the Lord along with his entire parish, so that God could reach the sinner with whom the priest was unable to communicate. This adds a communal and social element to the religious life of the deaf and other disabled and ill people mentioned in Raymond's example: participation in the yearly confession and the communion at Easter was, in the late medieval church, one of the most significant moments of the year. Participating meant belonging to the community of faithful and, at the same time, to one's local community. Avoiding the communion was considered extremely suspicious; even the late medieval Waldensians habitually confessed to their parish priests to avoid suspicion of heresy, although they deemed such confessions invalid.[63] Consequently, if a disabled person was excluded from confession, penance, and communion due to his or her disability, he or she was denied not only salvation but also social participation. Therefore, it is understandable that Raymond instructs the priest to do his best to avoid that kind of situation and, should this fail, to integrate the person into the community through common prayer for his or her soul. This is, of course, an ideal picture; nevertheless, it demonstrates an attempt to include as many people in religious life as possible.

There is, however, a condescending undertone in Raymond's instruction. Although he depicts the challenge as a problem of communication, the comparison to mad and possessed persons conveys an ancient connotation of the deaf as dumb and mentally defected. The inability to hear and speak was perceived as a lesser ability to think.[64] In contemporary disability studies, this phenomenon is called "disability spread," which occurs when one makes a hasty generalization on the basis of a particular disability. Although Raymond considered that deaf people had the ability to be contrite and penitent, if somehow instructed to it, he apparently had no great expectations about their intellectual abilities. However, at least one medieval author of a confessors' manual had higher regard for the intelligence of the mute. The already mentioned 13th century theologian Thomas of Chobham proposed that if a mute person (*mutus*) could write, he should write down his sins. Although *mutus* often referred to the congenitally deaf-mute, here Thomas obviously meant a person who was able to hear, as he also proposed that when the priest read the written sins, the mute should show with some signs that he confessed the sins and felt contrition.[65]

Devotion and Religious Participation

Although meant for very practical purposes, the manuals primarily show one side of the story: that of a priest and theologian. Ordinary deaf parishioners and their religious experiences and views, or even the views of their community members, are mostly missing from our sources. One very particular miracle case may, however, shed light on the matter, raising illuminating questions about the relationship between hearing ability and faith. Although not a very common type of a miracle, cures of the deaf had been recorded in different kinds of hagiographic texts since Antiquity – healing the deaf and the mute is, after all, one of the fundamental types of miracle performed by Christ.[66]

The cure of a young man of deaf-muteness was investigated during the canonization inquest of St. Louis of France, conducted in Saint-Denis in 1282–1283. The records of the process are now lost, but Franciscan friar Guillaume de Saint-Pathus, who was the confessor of Louis's widow Queen Margaret of Provence, compiled his *Vie et miracles* based on the documents. Especially in the case of miracles, the text is deemed to be a faithful representation of the original source.[67] It is not possible to reconstruct the actual witness accounts, but it is clear that the youth himself had testified in front of the papal commissaries managing the inquest.

As a child, the youth had been "found" outside the castle of Orgelet, owned by the count and countess of Auxerre, and taken in by the castle's smith named Gauchier. He first worked for the smith and later in the countess' kitchen, where he communicated with others using signs. In his early twenties, he left the castle following an argument with the chamberlain and joined the royal entourage that was carrying Louis's bones from the Holy Land to the Church of Saint-Denis. Upon kneeling down at Louis's grave, the youth began to hear. The sudden voices shocked him greatly and made him flee. Eventually he returned to Orgelet, where Gauchier and others taught him to speak. To honor the saint who had cured him, the youth took the name Loÿs.

Loÿs's extraordinary story has been analyzed in several studies,[68] and it is indeed an exceptionally detailed account of the socialization of and working opportunities available to an (apparently) congenitally deaf boy. It also speaks to the identity crisis faced by someone who regains his hearing later in life. For our current discussion, its religious dimensions are particularly consequential. The narrative states:

> When he was with Gauchier and his wife and with the said countess, he had often seen them go to church and pray there and have devotion, and kneel and raise their eyes with their hands joined together and raised to the sky. For that reason he now went to the church [of Saint Denis] but not because he knew what a church was or what devotion was. ... And thus it happened that when the blessed king was entombed, because he saw the other men kneeling and praying at the tomb, he too knelt and joined his hands without knowing what he was doing.[69]

Loÿs's lack of devotion at the time of his miracle was a theological problem for those conducting the canonization inquiry. Personal devotion was considered crucial for obtaining a miracle, but in this particular case, there was none since Loÿs's understanding of religion was completely insufficient. The commissioners inquired how Loÿs could be sure that his cure was due to the saintly king's merits, to which he replied that he saw no other possible explanation.[70] Apparently the commissioners were satisfied with the response – perhaps other evidence was convincing enough. In the end, the text records Loÿs's ability to say Ave Maria and the Lord's Prayer as the final proofs of his cured state. The miracle thus did not simply give him his hearing, but it gave him religious understanding.

Loÿs's story was also recorded in an earlier list of St. Louis's miracles, compiled at the royal court by the Franciscan historian Guillaume de Chartres before the canonization inquest. In his much shorter and more conventional version of the miracle, Guillaume narrates that Loÿs's decision to go to Saint-Denis was not accidental but rather taken after he had been told by signs about the saintly king's miracles.[71] This version better suited the court's intentions to have Louis canonized, as it was far less controversial. What is interesting here, however, is that Guillaume de Chartres considered it credible that Loÿs could have been taught about miracles, even if that was not the case in real life. Similarly, in the long and detailed testimonies about the miraculous cure of another congenitally deaf-mute youth (Jacobus de Venetiis, recorded in the mid-15th century canonization process of St. Bernardino of Siena), it seems that the young man had travelled from Venice to L'Aquila on purpose. At least none of the educated, critical witnesses questioned him being there; after finding proof that he really had been deaf and mute and that his cure was no hoax, they accepted his story. Particularly illuminating in this sense is the testimony of *frater* Andreas. He explained that Johannes had wanted to go to the chapel where Bernardino's grave was, so his journey clearly had a purpose. He too had communicated his wishes by signs.[72]

Both confessors' manuals and the hagiography discussed above repeatedly mention signs such as nods and gestures. They do not explicate what is meant by these, but the general atmosphere of difficult communication of abstract matters implies that none of the authors assumed a shared sign language. This seems to confirm the existing view that systematic sign languages in Europe emerged only from the early modern period onward. There existed several highly advanced sign languages in medieval monastic communities vowed to silence, but scholars have been skeptical about their use in deaf laypeople's lives.[73] The texts analyzed here do not alter this picture: none of the confessors' manuals refer to the possibility of monastic sign language as a means of communicating with a deaf person.

That understanding was a prerequisite of true devotion is in itself a sign of the theological development that took place in the high and late medieval church. From the annual confession to pastoral education on the Creed, Ave Maria, the Lord's Prayer, and basic articles of faith, the laity was required to know the fundamentals of Christian theology.[74] Deafness, muteness, and mental disabilities now caused new problems: how to ascertain that a person confessed and actually understood what and why they confessed? Both the manuals of confession and the miracle of Loÿs reflect this uncertainty from the clergy's perspective. It was no longer enough to be a blessed fool more pious than erudite men, whom Augustine had once described and praised (adding yet another layer to the complexity of his views on disability).[75] No miracle case can be read as a description of the "actual" course of the events, not even those recorded in canonization inquests (which were juridical procedures). Nevertheless, they reflect cultural and theological ideas about lay piety and devotion. When it comes to deafness and deaf persons, they can also be interpreted as examples of what was expected of their religious socialization and communication. Given the limits of the sign language of the time, the level of religious understanding among the pre-lingually deaf was most likely left incomplete, at least usually. This did not make it a trivial matter, however, but a question that was important for theologians, parish priests, and communities alike.

Deafness and Religious Understanding

The high and late medieval church expanded its pastoral obligations and directed its gaze to the souls of individual believers through confession, penance, and increased catechesis. Some minds were harder to reach than others: the authors and compilers of confessors' manuals soon realized certain "dubious" cases, as Raymond of Penyafort expressed. The congenitally or pre-lingually deaf were one of the most challenging confessants a medieval parish priest would encounter. Relying on signs, nods, and expressions, the priest remained uncertain both whether he had understood the confessants' intentions and whether or not the penitent had understood his guidance – or if he or she had understood the concepts of sin, contrition, absolution, and satisfaction at all. The same problem appeared with regard to marriage, a sacrament for which medieval canon law stressed the free will and consent of the parties involved. Confessors' manuals' approach to these problems was above all practical and tried to solve the fundamental problem of communication. The confessor should do his best to introduce a deaf person to confession and penitence. If the intention and consent to marry could be safely inferred from the signs and nods of a deaf person, there were no grounds to deny the marriage. There was a genuine will to ascertain at least minimum participation in the sacraments.

Below this practical layer there was also a lingering uncertainty about the intellectual abilities of the deaf and mute. When a priest was unable to communicate little beyond concrete things and simple yes or no questions, he had no means to be certain what a deaf person thought about the Church's teachings. Therefore, the attitude of the confessors' manuals is also condescending toward the deaf: they are sometimes bundled together with the mad and mentally defected. It is very difficult to reach an average medieval opinion about the mental capabilities of the deaf, but there were a few thinkers who were able to separate between a disorder in a person's sensory organs and his or her intelligence. Irina Metzler mentions Jean de Jandun, a French scholastic in the early 14th century, who was able to determine that a congenitally deaf person's inability to speak was caused by the lack of exposure to speech, not by the lack of neural connection between the ear and vocal organs. This distinction, in theory, allowed him to perceive deafness simply as an inability to hear, not as a more comprehensive neural or mental defect. However, as Metzler herself proclaims, it took until the 17th century before such ideas were developed enough for the deaf to be seen as intelligent like the rest of humanity.[76] Jean de Jandun was an exception, and there is no reason to assume that the authors of the confessors' manuals harbored any great expectations about the deaf's capacity for religious understanding. Of course, it is worth asking if they thought any better of some of the hearing laypeople.

One should neither idealize nor have an overly pessimistic view of the opportunities for religious life among the deaf in the Middle Ages. On the one hand, in the absence of a systematic sign language, their participation in devotional life and especially their ability to attain a deeper understanding of theology must have remained quite limited. On the other hand, the deaf were not systematically excluded from marriage, and the parish priests were instructed to do their best so that they could somehow participate in the yearly confession and receive absolution. From the perspective of human rights, the bare minimum is not enough. Yet in some ways the medieval church made more effort toward the deaf than did many societies in the following centuries.

Notes

1 Groce, *Everyone Here Spoke Sign Language*, 2–5; Dresser, *Martha's Vineyard*, esp. 46–51.
2 Bauman, "Audism: Exploring the Metaphysics of Oppression," 239–241.
3 Derrida's work *On Grammatology* is the main work on this; for citation and discussion about Derrida, see Bauman, "Audism: Exploring the Metaphysics of Oppression," 242–245. See also Baynton, *Forbidden Signs*, esp. 51–56; Bauman, "Listening to Phonocentrism with Deaf Eyes."
4 Bauman and Murray, "Deaf Studies in the 21st Century," 243.
5 Metzler, "Perceptions of Deafness," 86; Bragg, "Visual-Kinetic Communication in Europe before 1600."
6 Metzler, *Disability in Medieval Europe*, 102; Metzler, "Perceptions of Deafness," 89–90; Laes, "Silent Witnesses," 472.
7 Laes, "Silent Witnesses"; Metzler, "Perceptions of Deafness," 94–95.
8 On Antiquity, see Laes, "Silent Witnesses," 460–473.
9 See Metzler, "Reflections on Disability," 22; Pfau, *Madness in the Realm*, 106–107, and Turner, *Care and Custody*, 37–38, who writes that those born deaf-mute were likely to be skipped in the line of inheritance. For original texts concerning the inheritance of the deaf-mute, see *Corpus Iuris Civilis*, ed. by Mommsen and Krüger, *Dig.* 37,3,2; *Dig.* 45,1,1; *Dig.* 44,7,1; *Cod.* 6,22,10; Henrici de Bracton, *De Legibus et Consuetudinibus Angliæ*, Vol. 3, 300, Vol. 4, 178; *Britton*, ed. and trans. by Nichols, chapter 22, cap. 11, 456; *Fleta*, vol. 4, ed. and trans. by Richardson and Sayles, book VI, cap. 40. The English collection *"Bracton"* directly differentiates between congenital deafness and that acquired later in life, as it states that those who were naturally deaf and dumb are classed as unable to stipulate: Henrici de Bracton, *De Legibus et Consuetudinibus Angliæ*, Vol. 4, 178, 309. On the legal restrictions placed on the deaf-mute in Antiquity, see Laes, "Silent Witnesses," 465–467.
10 Salonen, *The Penitentiary as a Well of Grace*, 156, 179–180, 341–343; Salonen and Hanska, *Entering a Clerical Career*, 9, 12, 103, 115–117, 122–129.

11 Metzler, "Perceptions of Deafness," 80–81.
12 See, e.g., Ladd, *Understanding Deaf Culture*, 32–35.
13 Augustine, *Contra Iulianum*, III, cap. 4. PL 44, col. 707. Translated in Fathers of the Church, vol. 35, 115.
14 Jerome, *Commentaria in Epistolam ad Galatas*, I, cap 3, vers 2. PL 26, col. 349B–349D. Translated in Fathers of the Church, vol. 121, 122.
15 Van Cleve and Crouch, *A Place of Their Own*, 4–6; Bruce, *Silence and Sign Language in Medieval Monasticism*, 174–175; King, "*Surditas*: The Understandings of the Deaf and Deafness in the Writings of Augustine, Jerome, and Bede," cited in Bruce, *Silence and Sign Language*, 174.
16 Metzler, "Perceptions of Deafness," 79–80, 85.
17 Augustine, *De quantitate animae*, cap 18, PL 32, col 1052–1053; *De magistro*, cap. 3, PL 32, col 1197; see also Van Cleve and Crouch, *A Place of Their Own*, 4–5; Bruce, *Silence and Sign Language in Medieval Monasticism*, 174; Metzler, "Perceptions of Deafness," 85.
18 Peter Brown has characterized Augustine's life from September 386 to his ordination as a priest in 391 as "Christian otium," meaning retirement from public life to pursue creative leisure in serious pursuits. See Brown, *Augustine of Hippo. A Biography*, 115–127, cf. 134, where Brown states that this intellectual program started to fade around the time Augustine finished the *De magistro*.
19 Datings according to Allan Fitzgerald and John C. Cavadini, ed., *Augustine through the Ages: An Encyclopedia*.
20 See n. 15 above.
21 See Katajala-Peltomaa and Toivo, "Religion as Experience." See also Biller, "Confession," for the relevance of this term for the study of medieval confession.
22 Reeves, "'The Cure of Souls Is the Art of Arts': Preaching, Confession, and Catechesis in the Middle Ages," 373.
23 Manuals for confessors had existed earlier, but their production picked up in the 13th century. For the earlier texts, see Meens, *Penance in Medieval Europe, 600–1200*. A classic survey of the manuals for confessors between the 12th and 16th centuries is Michaud-Quantin, *Sommes de casuistique et manuels de confession au Moyen Âge*.
24 For these developments, see Biller, "Confession," esp. 7–9.
25 Murray, "Gendered Souls in Sexed Bodies," 82.
26 Boyle, "The Fourth Lateran Council and Manuals of Popular Theology"; Reeves, "The Cure of Souls Is the Art of Arts," 374–375.
27 Murray, "Gendered Souls in Sexed Bodies," 83.
28 Baptista de Salis, *Summa rosella*, 488: "Surdus. Utrum surdus mutus et cecus si[mu]l possint contrahere matrimonium." On Baptista's *Summa*, see Michaud-Quantin, *Sommes de casuistique et manuels de confession au Moyen Âge*, 98–99.
29 Brundage, *Law, Sex and Christian Society*, 90–92, 155–158, 198–199, 242–243.
30 Brundage, *Law, Sex and Christian Society*, 156–157; Murray, "Gendered Souls," 87–88; see also Metzler, *Disability in Medieval Europe*, 87.
31 Thomas of Chobham, *Summa confessorum*, 365: "Item, debet interdici mulieribus ne reddant viris debitum in tempore menstruo, quia ex tali concubitu nascitur partus leprosus."
32 Brundage, *Law, Sex and Christian Society*, 156.
33 Dan Michel, *Ayenbyte of Inwyth*, 223–224.
34 Brundage, *Law, Sex and Christian Society*, 451.
35 For an overview of the topic, see Metzler, "Birth Defects, Causality, and Guilt."

196 *Jenni Kuuliala and Reima Välimäki*

36 Although some disabilities were thought to be caused by one's own or one's parents' sins, not all disabilities were thought to be so. Instead, all illnesses and impairments resulted from the Fall and were caused by God's will; therefore they were the shared burden of humankind. For a discussion about causality between sin and disability, see Metzler, *Disability in Medieval Europe*; Kuuliala, *Childhood Disability and Social Integration*; Frohne, *Leben mit "kranckheit."*
37 Reynolds, *How Marriage Became One of the Sacraments*, 29–31.
38 Peter Lombard, *Sent.* IV. 27.3: "Efficiens autem causa Matrimonii est consensus, non quilibet, sed per verba expressus, nec de futuro sed de praesenti. ... Item si consentiat mente, et non exprimant verbis vel aliis certis signis; nec talis consensus efficit matrimonium."
39 Reynolds, *How Marriage Became One of the Sacraments*, 157–158; Brundage, *Law, Sex, and Christian Society*, 264.
40 Ibid.
41 Gratian, *Decretum*, C. 32 q. 7 c. 26, cited from *Corpus Juris Canonici*, ed. by Friedberg. See also Brundage, *Law, Sex, and Christian Society*, 195, 243.
42 Raymond of Penyafort, *Summa de casibus poenitentiae*, 514.
43 Raymond of Penyafort, X 4.1 "De sponsalibus et matrimoniis":

> Sane, consuluisti nos per nuncios et literas tuas, utrum mutus et surdus alicui possint matrimonialiter copulari. Ad quod fraternitati tuae taliter respondemus, quod, quum prohibitorium sit edictum de matrimonio contrahendo, ut, quicunque non prohibetur, per consequentiam admittatur, et sufficiat ad matrimonium solus consensus illorum, de quorum quarumque coniunctionibus agitur, videtur, quod, si talis velit contrahere, sibi non possit vel debeat denegari, quum quod verbis non potest signis valeat declarare.

44 Thomas of Chobham, *Summa confessorum*, 155: "Ideo autem dico voce vel opere firmata, quia licet aliquis nihil dicat ad susceptionem ordinis vel habitus, potest votum confirmare: sicut mutus per aliqua indicia potest confirmare consensum suum in matrimonio."
45 Monaldus de Capodistria, *Summa aurea*, fol. 133rb: "quod mutus et surdus bene possunt matrimonium contrahere signis et nutibus, licet non verbis."
46 On these decretalists, see Helmholz, *The Spirit of Classical Canon Law*, 24–25.
47 Sylvestro da Prierio, *Summa sylvestrina*, 450: "Surdus simul et caecus vtrum possit contrahere matrimonium, secundum Hosti. vt recitat Pan. in cap. cum apud. de spon. si potest exprimere suum consensum in contrahendo, debet admitti: aliàs repellitur"; see also p. 242 on how the mute could ask for sacraments and enter into matrimony using signs.
48 Cf. similar reference to Hostiensis and Panormitanus in Baptista de Salis, *Summa rosella*, 488.
49 Baptista de Salis, *Summa rosella*, 488.
50 Ibid.
51 Ibid.

> Hodiernis tamen temporibus vidimus surdos et mutos contraxisse matrimonium. Et maxime habemus de vna muliere surda et muta a natiuitate que contraxit matrimonium cum vno viro per signa et nutus et stetit cum eo per xl annos et plus: et adhuc ambo viuunt et optime cognoscit vires matrimonii et naturam eius: vt patet primo quo ad inseparabilitatem ex quo [sic] cohabitauit secum per tot annos. Secundo quo ad bonum fidei, quia est tante virtutis et continentis quod nec etiam ab alio quem viro suo permitteret se tangi vel osculari. Immo quod mirum est, quia vir eius adulter erat quesiuit vt fieret diuortium inter eos.

52 Much has been written about the *exempla* in medieval literature. Bremond, Le Goff, and Schmitt, *L'"Exemplum"* is a comprehensive overview of the genre.
53 See Kuuliala, *Childhood Disability and Social Integration*, 114–117.
54 CPR, Edward II, vol. 5, 62–63.
55 CPR, Edward III, vol. 16, 181, 284.
56 Turner, *Care and Custody*, 100–118.
57 Mattila, *Kansamme parhaaksi*, 272.
58 The tripartite condition of a successful penance since Gratian's *Decretum* had been *contritio cordis, confessio oris* and *satisfactio operis*. See, e.g., D. 1 de pen. c. 87 § 3. See also Larson, *Master of Penance*, 465.
59 In medieval thinking, possession was not a sin, as the possessed were innocent victims. Furthermore, the demon did not enter the victim's soul, which explains the possibility that a possessed person could confess. Then again, a typical symptom of a demoniac was to detest holy places and the company of clerics, but they could also have lucid moments. See, e.g., Katajala-Peltomaa, "A Good Wife," esp. 74. For a discussion of mental disorders and the role of demonic interference according to Peter John Olivi, John Duns Scotus, and William Ockham, see Hirvonen, "Mental Disorders in Late Medieval Philosophy and Theology," 171–188.
60 Raymond of Penyafort, *Summa de casibus poenitentiae*, § 48, 479: "si enim vocat surdum ad paenitentiam, non prodest, quia non audit; si mutum, non potest confiteri [–] Alii propter infirmitatem nihili intelligunt."
61 Ibid.:

> Solutio, debet sacerdos facere posse suum, vt inducat eos ad contritionem, et paenitentiam plenariam, secundum quod est possibile, scilicet verbis, vel scriptis, nutibus, et signis, et alijs modis, quibus possit. Si non potest proficere, oret ad Dominum, et faciat orare populum suum, vt Dominus illustret corda ipsorum ad penitentiam, et cum nil omiserit de contingentibus, tunc non imputabitur sibi.

62 See, e.g., Angelus Carletus, *Summa angelica*, fol. 51r; Nicolaus de Ausmo, *Supplementum Summae Pisanellae*, title "Confessor II." The Franciscan Nicolaus de Ausmo's manual (1444) is a supplement to an extremely popular 14th century confessors' manual by the Dominican Bartholomeus de Sancto Concordio (or Bartolommeo Pisano, d. 1347), the *Summa pisanella*.
63 Välimäki, *Heresy in Late Medieval Germany*, 186–188.
64 Metzler, "Perceptions of Deafness," 80–81.
65 Thomas of Chobham, *Summa Confessorum*, 220:

> Sciendum est tamen quod mutus si sciat scribere bene potest confiteri peccata sua per scripturam, quia non habet aliud os per quod loqui possit. Ita tamen debet hoc fieri quod cum sacerdos legerit peccata illa scripta, debet mutus aliquo signo ostendere quod ipse confitetur peccata illa et corde dolet de illis.

66 Mark 7:32–37:

> et adducunt ei surdum et mutum et deprecantur eum ut inponat illi manum et adprehendens eum de turba seorsum misit digitos suos in auriculas et expuens tetigit linguam eius et suspiciens in caelum ingemuit et ait illi eppheta quod est adaperire et suspiciens in caelum ingemuit et statim apertae sunt aures eius et solutum est vinculum linguae eius et loquebatur recte et praecepit illis ne cui dicerent quanto autem eis praecipiebat tanto magis plus praedicabant.

67 Farmer, *Surviving Poverty*, 7–9; Gaposchkin, *The Making of Saint Louis*, 37–39.
68 Farmer, *Surviving Poverty*, 74–78, 89–90; Farmer, "A Deaf-mute's Story"; Kuuliala, *Childhood Disability and Social Integration*, 57–58, 139–140, 249–251, 254–258; Metzler, *A Social History of Disability*, 200–203; Wittmer-Butsch and Rendtel, *Miracula: Wunderheilungen im Mittelalter*, 272.
69 Guillaume de Saint-Pathus, *Les Miracles de Saint Louis*, 53:

> il estoit avec le dit Gauchier et avecques sa femme et avecques la dite contesse, les avoit veuz souvent aler au mostier et ilecques proier et estre en devocion et agenoillier et lever eus, leur mains jointes au ciel, le dit Loÿs estoit alé a l'eglise, non pas por ce que il seust qu'estoit eglise ne devocion mes por ce que il veoit les autres en l'egelise agenoillier et lever les mains jointes au ciel et fere teles manieres de choses, il fesoit ausi .... Et de ce avint que comme le benoiet roi fust enseveli, por ce que il veoit les autres hommes agenoillier et proier au tombel, ensement il s'agenoilloit et joignoit ses mains sanz ce que il seust que il fesoit, fors pour fer comme les autres, ne ne le fesoit por nule devocion.

A full English translation of the narrative is in Farmer, "A Deaf-Mute's Story."
70 Guillaume de Saint-Pathus, *Les Miracles de Saint Louis*, 55:

> Et comme l'en demandast au dit Loÿs se il creoit que il eust recue oïe et parole par les prieres et par les merites du benoiet saint Loÿs, et il eust respondu 'oïl', l'en li demanda aprés: 'Pour quoi le crois tu, comme en toi n'eust creance adonques ne foi ne devocion vers lui, fors que tu estoies au tombel vuen par cas d'aventure?' Il respondi que il ne set nule autre cause de sa creance fors que tant que il avoit besoing de ce bienfet. De quoi il croit que pour sa misericorde le benoiet mon seigneur saint Loÿs proia Dieu por lui, et einsi reçut l'oïe, si comme il croit.

71 Guillaume de Chartres, *De vita et actibus inclytatae recordationis regis Francorum*, 38: "comperto per signa, quod apud sepulcrum gloriosi regis Franciae Ludovici fiebant miracula, virtute operante divina, adjunxit se quibusdam peditibus venientibus Parisius."
72 *Il Processo di canonizzazione di Bernardino da Siena*, 82–87, 196–197.
73 Metzler, "Perceptions of Deafness," 86; Bruce, *Silence and Sign Language in Medieval Monasticism*, 175–176.
74 French, *The People of the Parish*, 177; Tanner and Watson, "Least of the Laity."
75 *De peccatorum meritis*, cap. 32. Cited and translated in Metzler, *Fools and Idiots?* 106.
76 Metzler, "Perceptions of Deafness," 83–85.

Bibliography

Primary Sources

Angelus Carletus. *Summa angelica de casibus conscientiae*. Speyer: Peter Drach, 1488.

Augustine. *Against Julian*. Translated by Matthew A. Schumacher. Fathers of the Church 35. New York: Fathers of the Church, 1957.

Augustine. *Contra Iulianum*. Patrologia Latina 44. (*Patrologiae: cursus completus series Latina*). Edited by J.-P. Migne, 221 vols. Paris, 1844–1864. *Corpus*

Corporum repositorum operum Latinorum apud universitatem Turicensem. University of Zürich, <http://www.mlat.uzh.ch/MLS/index.php?lang=0>).
Augustine. *De magistro.* Patrologia Latina 32.
Augustine. *De quantitate animae.* Patrologia Latina 32.
Baptista de Salis. *Summa rosella.* Venice: Georgius Arrivabeni Mantuanus, 1495.
Britton. Edited and translated by Francis Morgan Nichols. Washington D.C.: John Byrne & co., 1901.
Calendar of the Patent Rolls Preserved in the Public Record Office, 1272–1582 [CPR] 68 vols, London 1893–2002.
Corpus iuris civilis. Edited by Theodor Mommsen and Paul Krüger. Berlin: Auflage, 1954.
Dan Michel. *Ayenbite of inwyt.* Edited by Richard Morris. London: Early English Text Society, 1866.
Fleta. Edited and translated by Henry G. Richardson and George O. Sayles, Selden Society, 72, 89, 99, 3 vols [vols II, III, IV]. London: Quaritch, 1955–1984.
Guillaume de Chartres. *De vita et actibus inclytatae recordationis regis Francorum,* in *Recueil des historiens des Gaules et de la France,* 20. Edited by Martin Bouquet. Paris: L'imprimerie Royale, 1806, 27–44.
Guillaume de Saint-Pathus. *Les Miracles de Saint Louis.* Edited by Percival B. Fay. Paris: Librairie Ancienne Honoré Champion, 1931.
Henrici de Bracton. *De Legibus et Consuetudinibus Angliæ.* Edited by George Woodbine. New Haven and London: Yale University Press, 1922–1942.
Il Processo di canonizzazione di Bernardino da Siena (1445–1450). Edited by Letizia Pellegrini, Analecta Franciscana, XVI. Nova series, Documenta et studia 4. Grottaferrata: Frati editori di Quaracchi, 2009.
Jerome. *Commentaria in Epistolam ad Galatas.* Patrologia Latina 26.
Jerome. *Commentary on Galatians.* Translated by Andrew Cain. Fathers of the Church 121. Baltimore: Catholic University of America Press, 2010.
Monaldus de Capodistria. *Summa aurea ... in utroque jure tam civili quam canonico fundata etc.* Österr. Nationalbibliothek, 25.X.16.
Nicolaus de Ausmo. *Supplementum Summae Pisanellae.* Venice: cura ac dilige[n]tia Bartholomei de Alexa[n]dria, Andree de Asula [et] Maphei de Salo socio[rum], 1481. University of Turku Library, Feeniks Genera Ai.II.85.
Peter Lombard. *De sententiae.* In *Patrologia latina* 192, col. 519–964. Edited by J. P. Migne. Paris, 1845.
Raymond of Penyafort. *Summa Sancti Raymundi de Peniafort ... De poenitentia, et matrimonio [Summa poenitentia].* Rome: Sumptibus Ioannis Tallini, 1603.
Sylvestro da Prierio. *Sylvestrina Summa, qua summa summarum merito nuncupatur. Pars Secunda.* Lyon: Ioannes Frellonius, 1554.
Thomas of Chobham, *Summa confessorum.* Edited by F. Broomfield. Louvain: Editions Nauwelaerts, 1968.

Secondary Sources

Bauman, H-Dirksen L. "Audism: Exploring the Metaphysics of Oppression." *Journal of Deaf Studies and Deaf Education* 9 (2004): 239–246.
Bauman, H-Dirksen L. "Listening to Phonocentrism with Deaf Eyes. Derrida's Mute Philosophy of (Sign) Language." *Essays in Philosophy* 9 (2008): Article 2.

Bauman, H-Dirksen L. and Murray, Joseph J. "Deaf Studies in the 21st Century. "Deaf-Gain" and the Future of Human Diversity." In *The Disability Studies Reader*, ed. Lennard J. Davis. London & New York: Routledge, 2017, 242–255.

Baynton, Douglas C. *Forbidden Signs: American Culture and the Campaign against Sign Language*. Chicago & London: University of Chicago Press, 1996.

Biller, Peter. "Confession in the Middle Ages: Introduction." In *Handling Sin. Confession in the Middle Ages*, eds. Peter Biller and A. J. Minnis. York: York Medieval Press, 1998, 1–34.

Boyle, Leonard E. "The Fourth Lateran Council and Manuals of Popular Theology." In *The Popular Literature of Medieval England*, ed. Thomas J. Heffernan, Tennessee Studies in Literature 28. Knoxville: University of Tennessee Press, 1985, 30–43.

Bragg, Lois. "Visual-Kinetic Communication in Europe before 1600: A Survey of Sign Lexicons and Finger Alphabets prior to the Rise of Deaf Education." *Journal of Deaf Studies and Deaf Education* 2 (1997): 1–25.

Bremond, Claude, Jacques Le Goff, and Jean-Claude Schmitt. *L'"Exemplum"*. Typologie des sources du Moyen Age occidental, fasc. 40. Turnhout: Brepols, 1982.

Brown, Peter. *Augustine of Hippo: A Biography, Revised Edition with a New Epilogue*. Berkeley and Los Angeles: University of California Press, 2000.

Bruce, Scott G. *Silence and Sign Language in Medieval Monasticism: The Cluniac Tradition, c. 900–1200*. Cambridge: Cambridge University Press, 2007.

Brundage, James A. *Law, Sex and Christian Society in Medieval Europe*. Chicago and London: The University of Chicago Press, 1987.

Derrida, Jacques. *Of Grammatology*, trans. Gayatri Spivak. Baltimore: Johns Hopkins University Press, 1976.

Dresser, Thomas. *Martha's Vineyard: A History*. Charleston: History Press, 2015.

Farmer, Sharon. "A Deaf-Mute's Story." In *Medieval Christianity in Practice*, ed. Miri Rubin. Princeton: Princeton University Press, 2009, 203–208.

Farmer, Sharon. *Surviving Poverty in Medieval Paris. Gender, Ideology, and the Daily Lives of the Poor*, Conjunctions of Religion and Power in the Medieval Past. Ithaca and London: Cornell University Press, 2005.

Fitzgerald, Allan, and John C. Cavadini, eds. *Augustine through the Ages: An Encyclopedia*. Grand Rapids: William B. Eerdmans, 1999.

French, Katherine L. *The People of the Parish: Community Life in a Late Medieval English Diocese*. Philadelphia: University of Pennsylvania Press, 2001.

Frohne, Bianca. *Leben mit "kranckhait". Der gebrechliche Körper in der häuslichen Überlieferung des 15. und 16. Jahrhunderts. Überlegungen zu einer Disability History der Vormoderne*. Affalterbach: Didymos-Verlag, 2014.

Gaposchkin, M. Cecilia. *The Making of Saint Louis. Kingship, Sanctity, and Crusade in the Later Middle Ages*. Ithaca and London: Cornell University Press, 2006.

Groce, Nora Ellen. *Everyone Here Spoke Sign Language. Hereditary Deafness on Martha's Vineyard*. Harvard: Harvard University Press, 1985.

Helmholz, Richard H. *The Spirit of Classical Canon Law*. Athens & London: The University of Georgia Press, 2010.

Hirvonen, Vesa. "Mental Disorders in Late Medieval Philosophy and Theology." In *Mind and Modality: Studies in the History of Philosophy in Honour of Simo Knuuttila*, eds. Vesa Hirvonen, Toivo J. Holopainen, and Miira Tuominen. London: Brill, 2006, 171–188.

Katajala-Peltomaa, Sari. "A Good Wife? Demonic Possession and Discourses of Gender in Late Medieval Culture." In *Gender in Late Medieval and Early Modern Europe*, Routledge Research in Gender and History, eds. Marianna Muravyeva and Raisa Maria Toivo. London and New York: Routledge, 2013, 73–88.

Katajala-Peltomaa, Sari and Raisa Maria Toivo. "Religion as an Experience." In *Lived Religion and the Long Reformation in Northern Europe c. 1300–1700*, eds. Sari Katajala-Peltomaa and Raisa Maria Toivo. Leiden: Brill, 2016, 1–19.

Kuuliala, Jenni. *Childhood Disability and Social Integration in the Middle Ages. Constructions of Impairments in Thirteenth- and Fourteenth-Century Canonization Processes*, Studies in the History of Daily Life 4. Turnhout: Brepols, 2016.

Ladd, Paddy. *Understanding Deaf Culture. In Search of Deafhood*. Clevedon: Multilingual Matters Ltd, 2003.

Laes, Christian. "Silent Witnesses. Deaf-mutes in Greco-Roman Antiquity." *Classical World* 104 (2011): 451–473.

Larson, Atria A. *Master of Penance*. Studies in Medieval and Early Modern Canon Law 11. Washington, D.C.: CUA Press, 2014.

Mattila, Markku. *Kansamme parhaaksi. Rotuhygienia Suomessa vuoden 1935 sterilointilakiin asti*. Helsinki: Suomen Historiallinen Seura, 1999.

Metzler, Irina. "Disabled Children: Birth Defects, Causality and Guilt." In *Medicine, Religion and Gender in Medieval Culture*, ed. Naoë Kukita Yoshikawa. Cambridge: D. S. Brewer, 2015, 161–180.

Metzler, Irina. *Disability in Medieval Europe. Thinking about Physical Impairment during the High Middle Ages, C.1100–1400*, Routledge Studies in Medieval Religion and Culture. London and New York: Routledge, 2006.

Metzler, Irina. *Fools and Idiots? Intellectual Disability in the Middle Ages*. Manchester: Manchester University Press, 2016.

Metzler, Irina. "Perceptions of Deafness in the Central Middle Ages." In *Homo debilis. Behinderte – Kranke – Versehrte in der Gesellschaft des Mittelalters*, ed. Cordula Nolte. Affalterbach: Didymos-Verlag, 2009, 79–97.

Metzler, Irina. "Reflections on Disability in Medieval Legal Texts: Exclusion – Protection – Compensation." In *Disability and Medieval Law. History, Literature, Society*, ed. Cory James Rushton. Newcastle upon Tyne: Cambridge Scholars Publishing, 2013, 19–53.

Metzler, Irina. *A Social History of Disability. Cultural Considerations of Physical Impairment*, Routledge Studies in Cultural History. London and New York: Routledge, 2013.

Michaud-Quantin, Pierre. *Sommes de casuistique et manuels de confession au Moyen Age (XII-XVI siècles)*, Analecta mediaevalia Namurcensia 13. Louvain: Nauwelaerts, 1962.

Murray, Jacqueline. "Gendered Souls in Sexed Bodies. The Male Construction of Female Sexuality in Some Medieval Confessors' Manuals." In *Handling Sin. Confession in the Middle Ages*, eds. Peter Biller and A. J. Minnis. York: York Medieval Press, 1998, 79–94.

Pfau, Alexandra. *Madness in the Realm. Narratives of Mental Illness in Late Medieval France.* Unpublished doctoral thesis, University of Michigan, 2008.

Reeves, Andrew. "'The Cure of Souls Is the Art of Arts:' Preaching, Confession, and Catechesis in the Middle Ages: Preaching, Confession, and Catechesis." *Religion Compass* 7, no. 9 (September 2013): 372–384, doi: 10.1111/rec3.12058.

Reynolds, Philip L. *How Marriage Became One of the Sacraments*, Cambridge Studies in Law and Christianity. Cambridge: Cambridge University Press, 2016.

Salonen, Kirsi. *The Penitentiary as a Well of Grace in the Late Middle Ages. The Example of the Province of Uppsala 1448–1527*, Humaniora 313. Helsinki: Suomalainen tiedeakatemia, 2001.

Salonen, Kirsi, and Jussi Hanska. *Entering a Clerical Career at the Roman Curia 1458–1471*, Church, Faith and Culture in the Medieval West. Aldershot: Ashgate, 2013.

Tanner, Norman, and Sethina Watson. "Least of the Laity: The Minimum Requirements for a Medieval Christian." *Journal of Medieval History* 32 (2006): 395–423.

Turner, Wendy J. *Care and Custody of the Mentally Ill, Incompetent, and Disabled in Medieval England*, Cursor Mundi 16. Turnhout: Brepols, 2012.

Van Cleve, John V., and Barry A. Crouch. *A Place of Their Own: Creating the Deaf Community in America*. Washington D.C.: Gallaudet University Press, 1989.

Välimäki, Reima. *Heresy in Late Medieval Germany. The Inquisitor Petrus Zwicker and the Waldensians*. York: York Medieval Press, 2019.

Wittmer-Butsch, Maria and Constanze Rendtel. *Miracula. Wunderheilungen im Mittelalter. Eine historisch-psychologische Annäherung.* Cologne: Böhlau, 2003.

7 Taking the "Dis" Out of Disability

Martyrs, Mothers, and Mystics in the Middle Ages[1]

Christina Van Dyke

Introduction

The Middles Ages are often portrayed as a time in which people with physical disabilities in the Latin West were ostracized, on the grounds that such conditions demonstrated personal sin and/or God's judgment. This was undoubtedly the dominant response to disability in various times and places during the 5th–15th centuries, but the total range of medieval responses is much broader and more interesting. In particular, the 13th–15th century treatment of three groups – martyrs, mothers, and mystics – whose physical "defects" were often understood as signs of special connection to God in this life (and who were often represented as retaining these signs in the life to come) challenges both medieval and modern notions of beauty, disfigurement, and bodily perfection, particularly as the notion is applied to our (everlasting) final end.

Monsters, Hierarchies, and Social Norms

Contemporary concepts of disability as they appear in legal, medical, educational, philosophical, and activist contexts were not, of course, operative in the Middle Ages.[2] As Douglas Baynton has observed, there has been a significant shift in attitudes since then toward human beings and their place in the world – a shift that can be roughly characterized as a move from comparing subjects against a standard of the "natural" to a standard of the "normal."[3]

The medieval emphasis on nature, function, and hierarchy had two primary sources. On the one hand, it stems from an inherited Platonic and Aristotelian worldview centered on forms as eternal templates against which all particulars could be measured; form was closely linked to function, and so the division of all living and non-living things into ranked genera and species also attributed particular functions to each of those species. By the 13th century, this worldview was, in turn, combined with the belief – widely accepted in Christian, Islamic, and Jewish communities – that there existed a God who created the world according to a divine plan, in which all things had a proper place (and, thus, a proper function), and who expected human beings to respect and maintain this created order.

Complex hierarchies within creation were understood to be part of this divine plan, both within and across species and genera. Thus, men were seen as superior in nature to women, human beings as superior in nature to cows, and horses as superior in nature to grass.[4] Comparative rankings like "superior to" or "lower than" were derived both from the sets of capacities a given species or genera was understood to possess and, within a species, from individuals' relative abilities to exercise those capacities. Thus, cows were considered better or higher than grass insofar as they were understood to possess sensory capacities such as locomotion, sight, and hearing in addition to the vegetative capacities (ability to reproduce, take in nutrition, and grow) they had in common with grass; men were considered superior in nature to women insofar as they were perceived as better able to exercise the rational capacities common to all human beings.[5]

In this context, the sorts of physical, emotional, and mental conditions we today discuss under the umbrella term of "disability" were understood primarily as a deviation from the (God-given) natural order. A calf born with two heads might be called "monstrous" or a "mistake of nature"; an unusually intelligent or articulate woman might be called a false or "pseudo-woman," as Margeurite of Porete was at her trial in 1310.[6] Deviations from the natural order could also be viewed as miraculous and observed with varying degrees of fascination and alarm: literature from this period is rife with characters whose monstrous natures make them objects of special interest.[7] Nature "herself" also appears personified in the literature of this period, as in Alan of Lille's famous *Plaint of Nature* and *Anticlaudianus*.

Importantly, this natural order was seen as fixed and stable. The species-form of cow or human being or grass is an unchanging template that accounts for both what a thing is and what it should be. In this context, perfection is a matter of activating the various potentialities natural to a species and thus performing the function of that sort of species well.[8] Individuals who lacked some of the potentialities seen as natural to their species, who were somehow impaired in their ability to actualize them, or who possessed abilities not natural to their species were considered defective or unnatural.[9]

This perception famously changes in the transition to the early modern period, as forms (and with them, function and teleology) lose popularity as a key explanatory feature of philosophical, theological, and scientific accounts.[10] The fixed nature of such forms is given up when the publication of Darwin's *Origin of the Species* ushers in the age of evolutionary theory. In its place, new statistical and economic measurements for populations (human, bovine, etc.) combine with social optimism to create a worldview in which human beings are seen not as occupying a God-given role in a fixed order but rather as an evolving species with unlimited potential for improvement. Nature-with-a-capital-N ceases to set the standard for either individuals within a species or a species itself; in its place arises the statistical norm and the concept of the "normal."[11] On this view, various physical, emotional, and mental conditions were judged as more or less favorable for the survival – and improvement – of the species. Those conditions seen as less adaptive or beneficial were termed "subnormal" or "abnormal" and viewed as dispositions that should be eliminated (if possible) for the sake of the human race as a whole.[12] Although virtually all current scholarship in disability studies challenges this view, the conception of the statistical norm and "the normal" remains the dominant paradigm in which contemporary discussions take place.

One of the central differences between 13th–15th century attitudes and modern attitudes toward disability, then, is that contemporary discussions often assume a broadly social, changeable framework, as opposed to the earlier "natural" perspective. Contemporary discussions focus, for example, on the extent to which disabilities are socially constructed; they address how these constructions impact the lives of those subsequently labeled as disabled; they argue about what action should be taken in response.[13] Throughout, they accept that social equality is a good for which we should strive. This perspective differs significantly from the medieval emphasis on fixed hierarchies and the portrayal of defects and monsters as (potentially fascinating) exceptions to the natural order.[14]

At the same time, the conditions labeled as defective and monstrous in the Middle Ages overlap extensively with the ones labeled as disabilities today. This is in large part because the (sometimes spoken, sometimes unspoken) paradigm in Western culture for both the "natural" and the "normal" is the able-bodied white male, against whom all others are judged and found wanting. Tradition assigns positive characteristics such as rationality, self-control, independence, and physical and emotional strength to people who fit this paradigm, while those who fall short of fitting the physical model (by, say, lacking a penis or pale skin or physical strength) are typically seen as falling short of the emotional and mental model as well.[15] When medieval scholastics follow Aristotle, for instance, in defining human beings as rational animals, they also adopt the Aristotelian assumption that the best-functioning version of such a creature is one who actualizes rational, sensory, and vegetative capacities to their fullest extent – by, among other things, possessing the semen from which other such animals are generated. The lack of such semen is seen as indicating a more passive, incomplete, or unfinished nature that is unable to actualize other potentialities as well, most crucially the capacities of intellect and will.[16]

Judged against this paradigm, irrationality, overwhelming passions, emotional or physical dependence on others, mental or physical suffering, and/or infirmity (blindness, deafness, chronic illness, etc.) become mental, emotional, and physical disabilities in precisely the same way that conditions that impede or prevent "normal" functioning are constructed as disabilities today. As Baynton observes,

> The natural and the normal both are ways of establishing the universal, unquestionable good and right .... Both are constituted in large part by being set in opposition to culturally variable notions of disability – just as the natural was meaningful in relation to the monstrous and the deformed, so are the cultural meanings of the normal produced in tandem with disability.[17]

The widespread acceptance of these beliefs about human nature and proper function testifies to the deep-rooted and intrinsically linked systems of misogyny, racism, and ableism that still dominate Western culture today. At the same time, as I demonstrate in the following sections, these are not the only attitudes present in the 13th–15th centuries toward people who violate "natural" physical, mental, and emotional ideals. The devotional emphasis in this time on the humanity of the incarnate Christ creates a space in which three distinct groups – martyrs, mothers, and mystics – experience aberrations from the "natural" not as distancing them from perfection but as connecting them more closely with God. These groups may be the exception to the general rule, but they are widespread and (in the case of mothers) extremely common exceptions that fundamentally challenge the superiority of the presumed paradigm and present a world (namely, heaven!) in which perfection is not tied to ideal function.

Christ and the Martyrs: Glorified "Defects" and Alternative Embodiment

In the 13th–15th centuries, an increased emphasis on the humanity (vs. the divinity) of Christ combines with a stress on *imitatio Christi* to undergird a devotional piety that portrays human beings as gaining access to God through shared human experiences – which importantly include mental, emotional, and physical suffering.[18] Because the incarnate Second Person of the Trinity is understood to be both fully human and fully divine, Christ's body becomes a subject of intense interest. Among other things, Christ's body is portrayed as the exemplar for human bodies (since to redeem the human race, Christ had to have a body that was subject to all sorts of conditions that human bodies generally undergo, including hunger, thirst, illness, and pain). Thus, both the general state of his body during his earthly life and the particular state of his body post-resurrection prove of keen interest. As we'll see in the remainder of this section, discussions of Christ's body both pre- and post-death also serve as important templates for speculations about the resurrected bodies of the martyrs. What emerges is a picture where being impaired in various ways (such as being blinded, crippled, flayed, or even decapitated) forms no impediment to carrying out the activities that constitute a happy life for human beings. Defects that were seen as stemming from or caused by sin are barred from being part of the afterlife, but Christ's and the martyrs' eternally 'broken' bodies are held up as more glorious than their "whole" counterparts insofar as they testify to their lived experiences. This opens the door to a philosophical theology of disability that is sensitive to the experiences and desires of those who experience them and that does not necessarily require disabilities being "fixed" to participate in the highest form of eternal life.

One of the most striking features of 13th–15th century Latin Christian piety is its devotion to the human, suffering Jesus. The Savior whom 13th–15th century Christians are counseled to emulate is not the *Christ Victorix* of the Renaissance and early modern period – an attractive and strongly muscled white man who has conquered death and rises into the air in glory, placed above the human subjects who cower beneath him in fear and awe (Figure 7.1).

Figure 7.1 Resurrection of Christ by Michele Ridolfi (1793–1854), in Cathedral of St. Martin in Lucca, Italy.

Instead, artistic representations of the pre-passion Christ from the late medieval period portray him as an ordinary-looking figure generally indistinguishable from those around him (apart from the position he occupies as central figure in healing, teaching, etc.). The most common images of the adult Christ in this period portray him during the Passion, suffering humiliation, flagellation, crucifixion, and finally death. In these representations, Christ is often emaciated and bleeding profusely from his side, as in Figure 7.2, where the blood spurting from the wound in his breast runs all the way through a crack in the earth and onto a human skull (thus representing Christ's victory over death and redemption of both the living and the dead).

Figure 7.2 Christ crucified with the Virgin and John, Jacobello Alberegno (1375–1397) in Gallerie dell'Accademia, Venice, Italy.

Taking the "Dis" Out of Disability 209

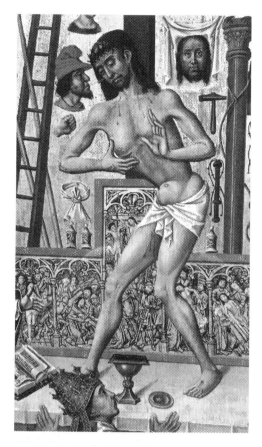

Figure 7.3 Special Exhibit at Museum Catharijneconvent, Utrecht, Netherlands, April 2014.

Even representations of the risen Savior in this period typically show him bleeding from his wounds, particularly the wound in his side – which is usually quite prominent and often displayed by Christ to the viewer(s) both within and without the scene. The risen Christ is also often portrayed with the symbols of his suffering: flagellum, crown of thorns, blindfold, hammer that pounded in the nails into his hands and feet, and (as we see particularly clearly in Figure 7.3) even men spitting on his face. By contrast, Christ's wounds are barely visible in many later representations (see Figure 7.4).

The importance of Christ's suffering *as* one of us while suffering *for* all of us is enormous in the 13th–15th centuries, as philosophical and theological discussions as well as devotional texts and artistic representations attest. As Catherine of Siena writes in her Dialogue: "When my

Figure 7.4 Statue in east transept, Cathédrale Notre-Dame de Chartres, France.

Son was lifted up on the wood of the most holy cross, he did not cut off his divinity from the lowly earth of your humanity. So, though he was raised so high he was not raised off the earth. In fact, his divinity is kneaded into the clay of your humanity like one bread."[19]

Thomas Aquinas also argues in his treatise on Christ's nature in Part Three of the *Summa theologiae* [=ST] that Christ's "infirmities" – both before his Passion and after – serve as a greater link with human beings than his perfections; he also stresses the importance of Christ's spiritual over physical strength and beauty. In ST IIIa.14, Aquinas spends the entire question addressing the "defects" Christ was subject to in becoming Incarnate. He argues that insofar as God became fully human, the body that God assumed needed to be subject to the whole range of defects and infirmities to which human beings are generally subject.[20] The doctrine of original sin entails that no post-lapsarian human being can possess ideal human physiology: hunger, thirst, pain, disease, and dying are inescapable realities of life until the Second Coming. The incarnate Christ must thus experience a natural share of these defects.

The question of exactly how many and what sort of defects and infirmities the incarnate Christ should be subject to, however, was the subject of hot debate. On one line of thinking, in order to redeem all the suffering caused by human sin, the Man of Sorrows needs to experience every single type of defect and sort of suffering of which human beings are capable.[21] On another line of thinking, since he is sinless, Christ should be maximally free from the consequences of sin (both natural or moral).[22] Not surprisingly, Aquinas takes a middle view: he maintains that because Christ assumes human nature in order to save it, he must have been subject to the sorts of defects post-lapsarian human beings are naturally subject to (e.g., hunger, thirst, disease, death); at the same time, because Christ was both born sinless and needed to be able to resist sin, he could not have suffered from any condition that would have been caused directly by sin or that would lead someone to commit a sin (such as certain sorts of ignorance or a lack of grace). Aquinas's conclusion is that Christ assumed a representative sample of the range of defects common to fallen human nature and that he assumed them "economically" (*dispensative*), in the appropriate amount and degree to satisfy for the sin of the human race, without going above and beyond.[23]

In this period, then, Christ is portrayed as having a typical human body, rather than one either superior to or worse than those around him. (He is not shown as particularly tall; or particularly short; he is represented as neither particularly beautiful nor unattractive; he is not possessed of superpowers; he is not blind or lame or deaf. In fact, in many representations, he is identifiable from those around him only by his specific halo.)

The nature of Christ's body after its death and resurrection, on the other hand, is much more remarkable, in part because its wounds remain. Between his rising from the dead and ascending to heaven, Christ is understood to possess a glorified body – incorruptible, capable of crossing great distances in a short time, able to walk through walls, and yet solid enough to be touched and to consume food. At the same time, Scripture depicts the risen Christ as appearing to various groups of people bearing the marks of his passion: a head wounded by thorns, hands and feet pierced by nails, and a side open from having a spear thrust into it. (The last two famously feature in the gospel of John's story of "doubting Thomas," whose claim that he will believe only when he has put his finger in the nail holes and hand in Christ's side is met by Christ's challenge to do exactly that when he appears to him later.)

Importantly, in the 13th–15th centuries, these features are seen not as deforming or disabling Christ but as prefiguring what the rest of the human race can expect for their own glorified bodies in the life to come. From at least Augustine onward, the particular features Christ's resurrected body possessed were taken as the basic template for all glorified human bodies post-resurrection.[24] These include not only the four "dotes" or gifts – clarity, agility, impassibility, and greater dignity of human nature[25] – but also the marks of martyrdom. In his discussion of Christ's resurrected body in ST IIIa 54, 4, for instance, Thomas Aquinas presents no fewer than five reasons for why it was appropriate for Christ's body to be resurrected complete with the scars from his crucifixion.[26] In the context of his triumph over death, not even what would have been fatal wounds constitute defects. Thus, Aquinas meets the worry that Christ's possessing open wounds "interrupts the continuity of his tissues" and that it would be sufficient for merely scars or traces of those wounds to remain, with the response that although the openings of Christ's wounds do mean that he doesn't have perfect physical integrity, he doesn't *need* physical integrity, because "the greater beauty of glory compensates for all this."[27] Not only does the fact that Christ doesn't possess smooth, unbroken skin, muscles, and tissue not entail that his body is less perfect – Aquinas claims that it is actually *more* perfect because of his wounds.

The retention of Christ's open wounds in his resurrected body is particularly significant for the medievals because they held that Christ's ascension to heaven was physical as well as spiritual, and that the body that the risen Christ showed his disciples is the same body that Christ possesses now in heaven, and which he will possess eternally. The thought of Christ's embodied presence in heaven delighted a number of contemplatives and mystics, such as Mechthild of Magdeburg, who wrote, "When I reflect that divine nature now includes bone and flesh, body and soul, then I become elated in great joy, far beyond what I am worth."

On the common medieval view, Christ brings human nature to its highest point with his embodied ascension into heaven – and the doctrine of the bodily resurrection entails that the rest of the human race will someday join him. As Mechthild goes on to describe that state: "The soul with its flesh is mistress of the house in heaven, sits next to the eternal Master of the house, and is most like him. There, eye reflects in eye, spirit flows in spirit, there, hand touches hand, there, mouth speaks to mouth, and there, heart greets heart."[28] In short, our resurrected bodies will be like Christ's in all important respects.

One consequence of this was taken to be that those who suffered and/or died for Christ's sake would rise with bodies that still displayed the marks of their martyrdom. The commonly referenced source-text here was (again) Augustine's discussion of the bodily resurrection in *City of God*.

So, for instance, Aquinas approvingly quotes Augustine's speculation that: "Perhaps in that kingdom we will see on the bodies of the martyrs the scars of the wounds which they underwent for the name of Christ, for [such scars] will not be deformity but dignity in them; and a certain beauty of virtue will shine in them."[29] In other words, conditions that would typically be considered defects – blindness, missing limbs, and so on – need not be removed or healed in the afterlife in order for the martyrs to participate in perfect happiness. This also fits with claims about Christ's wounds being beautiful rather than monstrous.

Of course, one can't conclude too much from these cases about general medieval reactions to disability in the afterlife: attitudes toward physical defects or conditions directly related to suffering for God's sake differ sharply from attitudes toward conditions understood to be caused by fallen human nature or culpable lacks in knowledge or grace. One of the most commonly accepted beliefs about the life to come was that resurrected human bodies would finally be free from the effects of sin, and so the default assumption was that those bodies would be immortal and incorruptible: "perfected" to reach the full measure of human potential without suffering from original-sin-caused distractions like hunger, thirst, or pain.

At the same time, the heavenly example of Christ's and the martyrs' eternally scarred and "imperfect" bodies offers a paradigm where the non-natural can not only remain but in which it has a place of honor. For our purposes, one of the most significant features of 13th–15th century discussions of these permanent marks is its suggestion that God need not fix us up when we get to heaven. God can glorify any sort of body, in any sort of condition.[30]

A more serious worry about Christ's wounds remaining open and martyrs like St. Denis (who was beheaded), St. Lucia (whose eyes were gouged out), and St. Bartholomew (who was flayed alive) retaining their wounds in the afterlife was the question of pain. As I will discuss more in the next two sections, the pain Christ suffers on the cross was understood to be an important element of the redemption of humanity, and the pain various martyrs suffered was a sign of their devotion and likeness to Christ. Yet the afterlife is described as a place where pain and sorrow will be no more, a place where all suffering – mental, emotional, and physical – will end. If Christ's side remains gaping open, Denis continues to carry his own head around (see Figure 7.5), and Bartholomew holds his skin like a coat,[31] these states must somehow be separated from the excruciating pain they would naturally involve.

And indeed, Aquinas is repeating a commonly offered solution when he writes that Christ could have prevented himself from experiencing pain by letting his divine beatitude overflow into his human body (although he, of course, didn't).[32] Post-resurrection, however, Christ can retain his wounds without feeling pain by allowing that overflow. More generally,

Figure 7.5 Late Gothic statue of St. Denis, limestone, formerly polychromed, Cluny Museum, Paris, France.

all glorified human beings will experience an overflow of beatitude in the life to come, from their souls to their bodies – an overflow that is the source of their bodies' new qualities and that will prevent those bodies from experiencing physical (or mental or emotional) pain.[33]

Such claims appear to challenge the "functional" view of human nature described in the previous section, *Monsters, Hierarchies, and Social Norms*. If human happiness depends on maximizing the actualization of particular sets of capacities peculiar to human beings, and given that human nature on this view demands a certain kind of body that can actualize those capacities, it seems as though human bodies would count as perfect (or perfected) only insofar as they were able to carry out those activities perfectly. Yet if Christ's hands and feet are permanently mangled by the nails pounded through them and the subsequent weight of his body bearing down on them on the cross, and if St. Lucia's eyes remain permanently removed from their sockets, then those parts of their glorified bodies are not able to perform their "natural" functions. And yet, they count as the paradigm of perfected bodies in the afterlife!

What this demonstrates, I believe, is that although the default conception of human beings in this period involves their fully actualizing the physical potentialities associated with being a rational animal, the increased emphasis on Christ's humanity and passion in the 13th–15th centuries also inspires portrayals of an afterlife in which brokenness becomes beautiful, and open wounds become portals of grace. The true final end of all rational creatures is to know and love God; in the life to come, we will have opportunities for loving and ways of knowing in which functioning sense modalities are neither central nor required. Rather than causing pain or drawing attention to the pernicious effects of sin, conditions that differ radically from "ideal" human physicality can positively glorify the Creator.

Furthermore, as we will see in the section *Mothers: Bleeding, Leaking God-Bearers and Models of Christ's Humanity*, 13th–15th century authors represent Christ's experiences as further challenging conceptions of ideal human physicality insofar as he suffers patiently and bleeds (activities associated more with women), rather than waging war and siring children (activities prototypical of men, whose bodies were supposed to set the norm for humanity). Indeed, Christ is often portrayed as positively maternal – particularly insofar as he feeds his followers with his own body and suffers (and even dies) to give them life.

Mothers: Bleeding, Leaking God-Bearers and Models of Christ's Humanity

The later medieval emphasis on the humanity of Christ also reaches out to envelop Mary, the human mother of the incarnate God. Mary's experiences of suffering and bleeding in childbirth and then breastfeeding the infant Jesus are compared to her child's suffering and bleeding on the cross and then his feeding the world with the blood from his side. This leads to common representations of Christ and Mary interceding with God the Father for humanity, he indicating the wound in his side and she indicating the breast with which she fed him (see Figure 7.6).

Many representations of Christ from this time emphasize ways in which his body is like a mother's;[34] Jesus often has blood on his thighs as well as his side, and the wound in his side is traditionally placed where a woman's breast would be (see Figure 7.3). For our purposes, one of the most significant consequences of this trend is that it creates a space (artistic, theological, and philosophical) in which mothers' – and more generally women's – bodies are like God's. This forms an important counter to the traditional medieval assumption that women's bodies were defective and/or disabled (taken as a bad-difference). As in the case of the martyrs, it also provides an example of bodies judged imperfect against the measure of then-standard accounts of human nature being

Figure 7.6 The Intercession of Christ and the Virgin, Lorenzo Monaco (act. 1390–1423), the Cloisters Collection of the Metropolitan Museum of Art, New York City.

held up as not just non-deficient but actually *better* (insofar as more God-like) than their able-bodied counterparts.

As mentioned in the section, *Monsters, Hierarchies, and Social Norms*, the 13th–15th centuries inherited the Aristotelian and Galenic conception of human nature, according to which the paradigm of human physiology is the able-bodied, cis-gendered, white male. The ideal human being excelled at both theoretical and practical reasoning; had control over his emotions; exercised willpower over his "baser" appetites for food, drink, and sex; and produced semen – the active seed required for generating more human beings. He had a strong body that was still sensitive to sense-data; Aristotle's concept of the "natural slave" was understood as referring to those human beings who were better suited to manual labor than study or power because of their physiology: rough skin, thick limbs, and so on. Natural rulers were sensitive enough to sense-impressions but also possessed the strength of will and mind not to be overwhelmed by them, and thus they appropriately governed those who either lacked such abilities or were less proficient in their exercise.[35]

On this Goldilocks version of human nature, where natural rulers were the "just right" version of human beings, women were seen as too susceptible to emotions and passions to fall into that category. Insofar as all human beings were understood to be rational animals created in God's image, women were viewed as having the same general make-up as men, both mentally and physically. Yet in women this general nature was viewed as being incomplete and/or "misbegotten" (*mas occasionatus*). Indeed, the Aristotelian biology widely accepted in the 13th–15th centuries portrayed women as possessing a defective version of the human form – one that left their bodies more passive (which is why their contribution to reproduction was limited to providing the matter that nourishes the active seed the man contributes), softer (and thus more susceptible to being overwhelmed by sensory stimuli and passions), and less rational (because the power of rationality could not be fully received in the matter that makes up the woman's body).[36] The main competitor to Aristotelian medical science, Galenic biology, gave women a more active role in reproduction, but even here the man's role is primary: the father serves as the principal active cause and the woman as the secondary active cause.[37] This received "wisdom" about the relative reproductive roles of men and women in turn grounded countless arguments for the natural subjection of women to men.[38]

This assumption about women being essentially disabled men, and medieval understandings of exactly what this entails for women's final end, is put in stark relief in a question that Augustine poses in *City of God* XXII.17, which is picked up by Peter Lombard and then everyone who writes commentaries on Lombard's *Sentences* (which is to say, everyone who receives a master's degree in theology from the University of Paris in the 12th–15th centuries) – namely, "In the bodily resurrection, will women be raised with male bodies?" The standard answer from Augustine onward is "No, women will be raised with female bodies," but there is a real tension present in many of the discussions of this question. On the one hand, as we've seen, women's bodies were viewed as inherently defective in ways that impact their functioning as human beings (particularly with respect to cognition); on the other hand, God created woman as part of the divine plan, and God's plan does not include mistakes.

This tension caused many scholastic theologians to claim that the continued "infirmity" (*infirmitas*) of the female sex was compatible with the glorification of the human body in the afterlife.[39] In other words, it constitutes another case (this one involving half the human race) in which features understood as somehow defective were still argued to be present in perfected human bodies. And again, the reasoning is that God can glorify any condition of the human body God chooses to.

The general infirmities associated with women's bodies are taken to their logical extreme in the particular features of mothers' bodies; childbearing bodies display their incompleteness by leaking all sorts of fluids, with blood, tears, and milk being the paradigmatic examples.[40] And yet the late medieval surge of interest in the Virgin Mother and Christ emphasizes precisely these non-ideal experiences. The most popular devotional literature in this period encourages its readers to imagine and then focus on everyday events in Christ's life, beginning with the childhood of Mary and continuing through Christ's death and resurrection. This form of meditation was encouraged as a spiritual exercise crucial for generating appropriate emotional attitudes toward God, developing virtues, and shaping the will's love toward its proper object (Christ). It was also a form of devotion aimed particularly at women, using their greater emotionality and imagination to generate a closer connection to God.[41]

The most notable example of this genre is the late 13th-century *Meditationes vitae Christi* (commonly but erroneously attributed to Bonaventure), which is translated into a number of vernacular languages (including Nicholas Love's influential English version, the *Mirror of the Blessed Life of Jesus Christ*) and remains wildly popular into the 16th century.[42] The *Meditations* inspires countless homely representations of the Holy Family (e.g., Figure 7.7, where Jesus tugs on Joseph's beard while Mary quietly reads a book) in addition to influencing theological and contemplative treatises.[43]

It explicitly instructs its readers to place themselves at various moments in the life of Mary and of Christ and to imagine what it would have been like to experience those moments with them. To help with this spiritual exercise, the text presents a number of vivid and engaging scenes and suggests ways in which readers can engage the episode.[44] (In the chapter on the Return from Egypt, for instance, the reader is asked to think of how tired the young Jesus's legs and feet must be from trotting behind the donkey and to imagine picking him up and carrying him for a way down the road. Later, after the Temptation, the reader is told to imagine an exhausted Christ asking the angels who attend him for his mother's cooking, and the angels flying to Mary to pick up a meal.)[45]

Use of this sort of meditation is described as enflaming the heart to imitate Mary's and Christ's virtuous examples, increasing knowledge of

Figure 7.7 Relief of the Holy Family, attributed to Lux Maurus, active in Kempton from 1517 to 1527, Cluny Museum in Paris.

the truth and allowing even non-educated people to understand God on a deep level:

> From frequent meditation one's heart is set on fire and animated to imitate and lay hold of these virtues. Then she is illuminated by divine virtue in such a way that she both clothes herself with virtue and distinguishes what is false from what is true: so much so that there have been many unlettered and simple persons who have come to know about the great and puzzling truths of God in this way.[46]

The devotional model of the 13th–15th centuries portrayed the spiritual practices of listening to or reading Scripture, meditation, and prayer (*lectio, meditatio, oratio*) as disciplines that contribute toward the higher goal of contemplation (*contemplatio*) of God in God's own essence and then, finally, union with God – either in a transient mystical state here on earth or everlastingly in the life to come. Thus, this passage from the *Meditations* continues: "You see then, to what an exalted height meditation on the life of Christ leads. Like a sturdy platform, it lifts one to greater heights of contemplation." In other words, formal education and even basic literacy were not required to reach the heights of union with God.

It's worth noting that the most popular devotional manual over these three centuries thus provides a model for human perfection that does not require meeting the ideal of the educated male. It's further worth noting that it is hardly alone in this respect. As we'll see in the section *Mystics: Non-Standard Embodiment and Union with God*, female contemplatives frequently describe direct experiential contact with God as perfecting their intellects and making them figures worth listening to.[47] As with martyrs and mothers, what are typically portrayed as "defects" in body and mind ground the source of greater perfection.[48]

The *Meditation*'s focus on Christ's human experiences is part of a larger tradition: one that emphasizes respects in which Jesus suffers, bleeds, and dies like a mother – that is, for the sake of his children.[49] Figures as varied as the 12th century Benedictine Bernard of Clairvaux, the 13th century Carthusian Marguerite of Oingt, and the 14th century anchorite Julian of Norwich describe Christ's role as one of mothering. Bernard of Clairvaux's discussions of Christ as mother establish the groundwork for later medieval portrayals. He often calls for spiritual leaders to take Christ as their example in this respect as well, instructing his fellow abbots in one particularly memorable injunction in his *Sermons on the Song of Songs* to "Be mild, avoid ferocity, suspend the whip, bring forth your breasts; let them fatten with breastmilk, not swell with passion."[50]

In the late 13th century, Marguerite d'Oingt – an extremely rare example of a female Carthusian author – muses on God's role as mother in her *Pagina meditationum*:[51]

> Are you not my mother and more than mother? The mother who bore me labored at my birth for one day or one night, but you, my sweet and lovely Lord, were in pain for me not just one day, but you were in labor for more than thirty years. Oh, sweet and lovely Lord, how bitterly were you in labor for me all through your life! But when the time approached when you had to give birth, the labor was such that your holy sweat was like drops of blood which poured out of your body onto the ground.[52]

Christ's crucifixion is depicted here as the end of a labor that has been going on for his entire life, and his sweating and bleeding as experiences common to mothers. Marguerite emphasizes the extent of Christ's suffering by portraying him as a woman in labor who isn't even allowed to move around to relieve her discomfort, and who gives birth not just to one child but to the whole world:

> When the hour of birth came, you were placed on the hard bed of the cross where you could not move or turn around or stretch your limbs as someone who suffers much pain should be able to do .... And surely it was no wonder that your veins were broken when you gave birth to the world all in one day.[53]

Julian of Norwich's *Showings* famously also contains a lengthy discussion of Christ as Mother. She begins, like Marguerite, by comparing Christ's suffering on the cross with childbirth:

> In love, [our true Mother Jesus] labors to carry us inside himself, until we come to full term. Then he suffers the most painful blows and excruciating birth pangs that ever have been or ever shall be endured, only to die in the end.[54]

Christ's service as mother does not end with his death, however. Instead, Jesus is resurrected in order to feed us with his own body and blood in the Eucharist, as a mother feeds her child with her milk:

> And when he had finished dying, and birthed us into endless bliss, still all this could not satisfy his wondrous love .... And so now he must nourish us, which is what a mother does. The human mother can suckle the child with her milk, but our beloved Mother Jesus can feed us with himself. This is what he does when he tenderly and graciously offers us the blessed sacrament, which is the precious food of true life.[55]

The wound in Christ's side takes on special significance here, indicating how Christ can literally incorporate us into himself, going beyond what even a mother can do when she snuggles her child to herself: "The human mother can tenderly lay the child on her breast, but our tender Mother Jesus can lead us directly into his own tender breast through his sweet broken-open side."[56] This harks back to an earlier passage, in which Christ invites Julian and the rest of humanity to enter into him via this wound:

> Then, with a cheerful expression, our Beloved looked into his side and gazed into his wound with joy. With his sweet gazing he directed the mind of this creature to enter through that wound in his side. There he revealed to me a beautiful and delicious place, ample enough for all humanity to rest in peace and love. This made me think of his dear blood and the precious water that he allowed to be poured out for love.[57]

Julian's vivid imagery here is entirely in line with standard 13th–15th century representations of the broken, wounded Christ. Countless images of the crucifixion from this period depict blood pouring from Christ's side into a cup – blood which is then offered to his children in the Eucharist (see Figure 7.8).

Women's and mothers' bodies are not generally viewed today as disabled, and yet insurance companies often label pregnancy as a coverable

Figure 7.8 Framed reliquary, Crucifixion with Arma Christi, Paris (?), mid-14th c., Cluny Museum, Paris.

"illness" and birth a "short-term disability" – labels which continue to take able-bodied males as the norm. Furthermore, the conditions that the medieval figures discussed above – bleeding, suffering intense pain, having open wounds, and so on – are still seen as signs of infirmity and imperfection. Yet here they prove central to God's plan for human salvation. The incarnate Christ's experiences are shown as paralleling those of women and mothers in ways that present those forms of embodiment as legitimate in their own right, despite the fact that they fall short of what would typically be portrayed as the Aristotelian "ideal." In so doing, they present a model of "disabilities" that enhance rather than impair their bearer's ability to fulfill their final end.

Mystics: Non-Standard Embodiment and Union with God

This model – in which conditions typically assumed to impair a subject's ability to actualize their natural human capacities are instead experienced as enhancing that subject's connection to God – is also employed by many mystics in this period, including Hildegard of Bingen, Mechthild of Magdeburg, Margret Ebner, Birgitta of Sweden, Angela of Foligno, Catherine of Siena, and Julian of Norwich. As the sweating, bleeding, dying Christ becomes the paradigm of divinity in the 12th–13th centuries, religious sensibilities change, and there is a marked increase in reports of mystic experiences that involve suffering, illness, bleeding, tears, and even (temporary) death.[58] These mystics value such experiences insofar as they mirror Christ's Passion and serve as sources of immediate connection to God. Such experiences are also often described as conferring special spiritual gifts, no doubt because of their relation to the incarnate God's; medieval mystics thus weave their experiences of infirmity into a complex theology that challenges traditional models of human perfection and opens up new possibilities for a theology of disability.[59]

Before continuing, it is important to stress that I do not mean in any way to advocate a theology of disability that sees suffering as inherently valuable or as a necessary source of purification from sin. Such a view has often been pushed on marginalized people, particularly women, as a way of convincing them that patiently bearing with the horrible consequences of institutionalized injustice is a virtue and a way of getting closer to God. As Simone de Beauvoir comments in the *Second Sex*, religion has long been preached to women as a "mirage of transcendence" when actually it "confirms the social order, it justifies her resignation, by giving her the hope of a better future in a sexless heaven."[60] I offer what follows as another way (together with the case of martyrs and mothers) in which the dominant view of human nature that takes the able-bodied man as its standard is challenged in the 13th–15th centuries by people who were widely believed when they reported that they had experiences that perfected human nature while deviating in marked ways from that standard measure.

Marguerite d'Oingt, for instance, explains to her confessor why she has taken the unusual (for a Carthusian nun) step of writing down her revelations in terms of its being necessary to relieve suffering she was experiencing following an intense mystical experience. Describing herself in the third person, she reports, "When she came back to her senses, she had all these things written in her heart in such a way that she could think of nothing else, and her heart was so full that she could not eat, drink, or sleep until she was so weak that the doctors thought she was on the point of death." As a result, she resolved to write down what she had experienced:

> She thought that if she put these things into writing in the same way that our Lord had put them into her heart, her heart would be unburdened. She began to write everything that is in this book, in the order that it was in her heart .... And when she had written everything down, she was all cured. I firmly believe that if she had not put all this down in writing, she would have died or gone mad, because for seven days she had neither slept nor eaten and she had never before done anything to get herself into such a state.[61]

In Marguerite's case, her suffering results from trying to keep God's revelation to her inside herself. More often, however, contemplatives depict intense suffering as preceding or accompanying visions, auditions, and/or other mystical experiences. Julian of Norwich, for instance, specifically asks God for an illness that will bring her near death; in her *Showings*, she reports that God grants her request: her vision of the bleeding Christ occurs as she believes she is dying and is instead brought back to full health.[62]

One of the most interesting cases in this respect comes from Margaret Ebner, an early 14th century Dominican nun at the Monastery of Maria Medingen near Dillingen (in Germany). In her *Revelations*, Ebner reports an experience that begins with great pain but leaves her with a gift of divine understanding:

> The next day I was very sick and began to wonder about what was happening to me. I perceived well what it was. It came from my heart and I feared for my senses now and then whenever it was so intense. But I was answered by the presence of God with sweet delight, "I am no robber of the senses, I am the enlightener of the senses." I received a great grace from the inner goodness of God; the light of truth of divine understanding. Also, my mind became more rational than before, so that I had the grace to be able to phrase all my speech better and also to understand better all speech according to the truth. Since then I am often talked about.[63]

In this context, when Ebner says that she is much talked about, she is not bragging about her new spiritual prowess – she is inviting the reader to verify what she is saying by asking around.

Medieval mystics often report receiving divine understanding directly, and in a way that provides a foretaste of what all human beings will experience in the life to come.[64] Insofar as the ultimate end of human nature is knowing and loving God, human beings can fulfil their potentialities in any way that does this. Moreover, as we saw in the sections *Christ and the*

Martyrs: Glorified "Defects" and Alternative Embodiment, and *Mothers: Bleeding, Leaking God-Bearers and Models of Christ's Humanity*, martyrs imitating Christ by retaining their wounds in the afterlife (without pain) and mothers' bodies mirroring Christ's body in their bleeding (and feeding) also present examples in which God is understood as able to glorify any sort of embodiment, whether standardly able-bodied or not.

One final feature that medieval representations of these three "disabled" groups share is being enclosed in community. Although I here lack the space to expand on this sufficiently, I close with Julian's injunction to avoid the sort of independent-minded self-sufficiency that so often isolate the human beings who do meet the measure of the "natural" and the "normal":

> God would like for us to cultivate our faith through spiritual community and seek our beloved Mother in the solace of true understanding, among the communion of the blessed. For although a single person might often break himself, the whole body of spiritual community can never be broken. And so it is a sure thing – a good and gracious thing – to humbly and powerfully bind ourselves to our Mother, to Holy Church, and to Christ.[65]

Notes

1. I would like to thank Elizabeth Barnes, Kevin Timpe, and Scott Williams for valuable discussion on this topic; a grant from the Calvin Alumni Association Fund made much of the research for this chapter possible, particularly by supporting travel to various museums.
2. Contemporary work in the philosophy of disability and disability studies offers a variety of working definitions, often motivated by broader ideology and/or context-sensitive. For an overview of influential definitions and the larger frameworks in which they function, see Elizabeth Barnes's *The Minority Body: A Theory of Disability*, particularly Chapter 1, "Constructing Disability."
3. Douglas Baynton "Disability and the Justification of Inequality in American History," 33–57.
4. See Sister Prudence Allen's three-volume work *The Concept of Woman*, particularly volumes one and two, respectively subtitled *The Aristotelian Revolution, 750 BC–AD 1250* and *The Early Humanist Reformation, 1250–1500*, for an extensive discussion and an exhaustive list of authors and texts that discuss this "natural order," in particular as it pertains to men and women. Both biological and theological arguments were leveled in favor of this order, which evolves into the Great Chain of Being by the time of Lovejoy.
5. Again, for extensive references, see Sister Prudence Allen, *The Concept of Woman*. Aristotle, Augustine, and Aquinas all agree on this score.
6. The term is recorded in the court records of Porete's trial by the Continuer of William of Nangis.
7. Caliban from Shakespeare's *The Tempest* is a well-known example of this trope.

8 For a more detailed discussion of this notion of perfection, including both its relation to Aristotle's *Nicomachean Ethics* and its application in Thomas Aquinas, see the "metaphysical foundations" chapters in Rebecca Konyndyk DeYoung, Colleen McCluskey, and Christina VanDyke *Aquinas's Ethics: Metaphysical Foundations, Moral Theory, and Theological Context*.

9 A talking cow, for instance, would have been considered defective and a monster, even if a particularly interesting one, as opposed to an advance in or outlier of the species.

10 See Robert Pasnau's *Metaphysical Themes 1274–1671* for a detailed (if controversial) discussion on this shift.

11 For a detailed discussion of the social consequences of this movement, particularly with respect to its effects on punishment and "corrective" treatment of populations, see Michele Foucault's *Discipline and Punish: The Birth of the Prison*, particularly Part Three: Discipline.

12 For this reason, religious and social movements of the time (including Margaret Sanger's Planned Parenthood) often involved eugenics in their missions. For a detailed and distressing history of this connection, see Christine Rosen's *Preaching Eugenics: Religious Leaders and the American Eugenics Movement*.

13 Again, see Elizabeth Barnes *The Minority Body*, Chapter 1, especially 38, 46, and 50, in which she canvasses a number of different current definitions of disability; Barnes argues for what she calls a "moderate social constructionism," on which disability involves someone in a bodily state x such that "the rules for making judgments about solidarity employed by the disability rights movement classify x in context C as among the physical conditions that they are seeking to promote justice for." Barnes argues that this concept of disability "travels" and can be retroactively applied to cases in, say, the Middle Ages and before.

14 Monsters functioned in a variety of ways in medieval society and included virtually everything and everyone portrayed as outside the typical natural and social order, such as dragons, sirens, demons, saints, and martyrs. See Sherry Lindquist and Asa Mittman's *Medieval Monsters: Terrors, Aliens, Wonders* and David Williams's *Deformed Discourse: The Function of the Monster in Mediaeval Thought and Literature*

15 See the Introduction to Susan Bordo's *Unbearable Weight: Feminism, Western Culture, and the Body* for a discussion of both the philosophical history of these characteristics' association with Western European men and the consequences of this construction for contemporary culture. Carol Cohn's "Wars, Wimps, and Women: Talking Gender and Thinking War," also provides an excellent discussion of this topic.

16 See the section, *Mothers: Bleeding, Leaking God-Bearers and Models of Christ's Humanity*, for a more detailed discussion of this phenomenon.

17 Baynton, "Disability and the Justification of Inequality in American History," 35.

18 This shift in devotional piety has been the subject of much scholarship and is often associated with a move towards a distinctively 'feminine' piety. The locus classicus of this view is Herbert Grundmann's 1935 German monograph, translated into English as *Religious Movements in the Middle Ages: The Historical Links between Heresy, the Mendicant Orders, and the Women's Religious Movement in the Twelfth and Thirteenth Century, with the Historical Foundations of German Mysticism*; the view was popularized by Caroline Walker Bynum's work in the 1980s and 90s (see particularly the essays in *Fragmentation and Redemption: Essays on Gender and the Human Body in Medieval Religion*). Recent scholarship has challenged the notion

that the affective piety focused on Christ's humanity and suffering should be viewed as particularly feminine or even as an invention of the 12th and later centuries: see, e.g., Lauren Mancia's *Emotional Monasticism: Affective Piety in the Eleventh-Century Monastery of John of Fécamp*. Regardless, the emphasis on Christ's humanity over his divinity is marked and has a profound impact on religious and aesthetic sensibilities for much of the later Middle Ages.

19 Catherine of Siena *The Dialogue*, 26, 65.
20 See particularly Thomas Aquinas, ST IIIa, 1.
21 Ibid., ST IIIa 14, 4, obj. 1.
22 Ibid., obj. 2.
23 See particularly ibid., ST IIIa 14, 4, co. and ad 2.
24 Augustine's *City of God* determines the shape of the debate over the features of Christ's resurrection and the general resurrection of the dead throughout the Middle Ages.
25 For further discussion of these features and their role in the Beatific Vision, see Christina Van Dyke "Aquinas's Shiny Happy People: Perfect Happiness and the Limits of Human Nature," 269–291.
26 These reasons for Christ's retaining his scars are that they are signs of Christ's triumph over death, to convince the disciples of the truth of the resurrection, to show God when Christ intercedes for us, solidarity with the martyrs, and to rebuke the unrepentant.
27 Thomas Aquinas, ST, IIIa 54, 4, ad 2.
28 Mechthild of Magdeburg *Flowing Light of the Godhead* IV, 14.
29 Thomas Aquinas, ST IIIa 54, 4, co. I've here omitted "*quamvis in corpore, non corporis*" from the final clause for clarity: literally this translates as "although in the body, not of the body" – the idea seems to be that the wounds of the martyrs appear in their bodies but are not caused by physical conditions, and thus it's appropriate for them to remain because they weren't caused by sin.
30 It's worth noting that the Roman Catholic patron saint of the disabled comes from just the time and place I'm focusing on: Margaret of Citta di Castello (1287-12 April 1320) had severe spinal curvature and was barely four feet tall; according to some stories, she was also blind. Yet she became a Dominican tertiary in 1303 and is remembered for her service to her community, including teaching at a small school. In other words, her physical conditions are an important part of her story, but what she is primarily remembered for is service to her community.
31 Sculptures of Bartholomew holding his own skin become popular in the Renaissance and are often clearly meant to display both the artistic prowess and advanced anatomical knowledge of the artist. Probably the most famous of these is the statue in the south transept of the Milan Duomo, carved in 1562 by Marco d'Agrate.
32 See, e.g., Thomas Aquinas, ST, IIIa 54, 5, on whether Christ experienced pain, particularly the response to the third objection.
33 See, e.g., Thomas Aquinas, ST IaIIae 4, 6.
34 For discussions of such representations and how they fit into the general ideology of their age, see, Caroline Walker Bynum *Fragmentation and Redemption*, 151–179, and Barbara Newman's *From Virile Woman to Woman Christ: Studies in Medieval Religion and Literature*.
35 Thomas Aquinas's discussion of these topics in his *Treatise on Human Nature* (ST Ia 75–89) presents a very standard account of this view.
36 See Thomas Aquinas, ST Ia 92, for a question-long discussion of the nature of women and women's bodies.

228 *Christina Van Dyke*

37 This difference causes John Duns Scotus to side with Galen versus Aristotle. Scotus is deeply devoted to the Virgin Mother, and he believes that for her to serve as a true mother to God, she must have played a somewhat active rather than merely passive physical role. Scotus thus places a great deal of emphasis on the sense in which women are secondary active causes of their children. See Marilyn McCord Adams's "Duns Scotus on the Female Gender," 255–270.
38 See, e.g., Aquinas's ST Ia 92.1, particularly the body of the article and the response to the second objection. Christine de Pizan's *Book of the City of Ladies*, published in 1405, is a systematic response to these sorts of arguments.
39 See, e.g., Thomas Aquinas, ScG IV, 88.
40 The blood that men shed is the exception rather than, say, the menstrual rule; men's seminal contribution to reproduction was also portrayed as an active, intentional emission rather than a passive leaking.
41 Women were said to be of a more watery (and cold) constitution and thus able to form images more easily than men – but then also retain them less perfectly. For these general physiological principles, see Thomas Aquinas, ST Ia 78, 4, co.
42 Its enduring popularity is attested to by the survival of over 200 manuscript copies, as is the fact that it was a subject of early printing editions.
43 Its influence on scholastic works has long been overlooked, in part because very few people actually read the *Meditations* today. The number of extant manuscripts made compiling a definitive Latin edition daunting, and the work itself is long, disjointed (the text goes back and forth between vignettes in the life of Christ and sermons by Bernard of Clairvaux), and rather tedious. The first definitive Latin edition of the *Meditations* was produced only in 1997, by Mary Stallings-Taney (*Meditationes Vitae Christi*).
44 The marked contrast between these highly engaging scenes and the interpolation of lengthy passages from Bernard of Clairvaux's sermons has led Sarah McNamer to argue that the longer Latin text is a later version of a much shorter one written by an Italian Franciscan nun in the mid-1300s, most notably in "The Origins of the *Meditationes Vitae Christi*," 905–955. See her *Meditations on the Life of Christ: The Short Italian Text* for a translation and commentary of the Italian text she has reconstructed. McNamer's work has been the subject of intense criticism by her contemporaries in medieval history; Michelle Karnes, for instance, has been quite vocal in arguing in favor of the longer Latin text as the original. See "Exercising the Imagination: The Meditationes vitae Christi and Stimulus amoris" in her *Imagination, Meditation, and Cognition in the Middle Ages*.
45 The pictures from a wonderfully illustrated Italian manuscript of the first two thirds of the text are well worth a look; they are published, along with an English translation of the extant manuscript, in *Meditations on the Life of Christ: An Illustrated Manuscript of the Fourteenth Century*.
46 The text here continues to reference the life of Francis of Assisi: "How do you think blessed Francis arrived at so great an abundance of virtues and so lucid an understanding of the Scriptures? ... He was so ardently drawn toward that life that his own life became a mirror resemblance of Christ's life." Prologue to the *Meditations*, 3. Here and elsewhere I follow Stallings-Taney's Latin edition, translated as *Meditations on the Life of Christ*.
47 For an extended discussion of this topic, see Christina Van Dyke "The Will and Love" in my forthcoming *A Hidden Wisdom: Self-Knowledge, Reason, Love, Persons, and Immortality in Medieval Contemplatives*.

48 A number of feminist scholars have argued that these exceptions actually uphold rather than subvert patriarchal norms. See, e.g., Mary Daly's *The Church and the Second Sex* and Rosemary Radford Ruether's *Sexism and God-talk: Towards a Feminist Theology*.
49 Caroline Walker Bynum's groundbreaking and exhaustive study of this topic remains a classic: "Jesus as Mother" in *Jesus as Mother: Studies in the Spirituality of the High Middle Ages*.
50 Bernard of Clairvaux *Sermones in Cantica Canticorum*, 23.2. For an extensive discussion of Bernard's views on the topic, see Walker Bynum's 1977 "Jesus as Mother and Abbot as Mother: Some Themes in Twelfth-Century Cistercian Writing," 257–284, which forms the basis for her 1982 study.
51 The *Pagina* is written in Latin, although we have other works of Marguerite d'Oingt in which she writes in Franco-Provençal.
52 Margaret of Oingt *The Writings of Margaret of Oingt, Medieval Prioress and Mystic (d. 1310)*, 31.
53 Ibid., 31.
54 Julian of Norwich *The Showings of Julian of Norwich: A New Translation*, 165–166.
55 Ibid., 166. For a discussion of the respects in which Christ's blood is taken to resemble breastmilk (and vice versa), see Elizabeth Robertson's "Medieval Medical Views of Women and Female Spirituality in the *Ancrene Wisse* and Julian of Norwich's *Showings*," 142–167.
56 Julian of Norwich *The Showings of Julian of Norwich: A New Translation*, 166.
57 Ibid., 59.
58 See, e.g., the so-called "Sister Catherine Treatise" for an influential description of mystical death and its consequences; Catherine of Siena is also described by her confessor, Raymond of Capua, as having suffered a mystic death.
59 See Grace Jantzen's *Power, Gender, and Christian Mysticism* for one of the most influential modern discussions of this topic.
60 Simone de Beauvoir *The Second Sex*, 624.
61 Marguerite d'Oingt *Letters*, 64–65.
62 For a discussion of this request and its significance in its own time, see Elizabeth Robertson "Medieval Medical Views of Women and Female Spirituality in the *Ancrene Wisse* and Julian of Norwich's *Showings*."
63 Margaret Ebner *Major Works*, 100.
64 See, for instance, Angela of Foligno *Memorial*, Book IX.
65 Julian of Norwich *The Showings of Julian of Norwich: A New Translation*, 168.

References

Primary Sources

Angela of Foligno. "Memorial." In *Angela of Foligno: Complete Works (Classics of Western Spirituality)*. Translated by Paul Lachance. Mahwah: Paulist Press, 1993.

Aquinas, Thomas. *Summa Theologiae*. http://www.corpusthomisticum.org/iopera.html [=ST]

———. *Summa contra gentiles*. http://www.corpusthomisticum.org/iopera.html [=ScG]

Augustine. *The City of God*. https://www.thelatinlibrary.com/august.html
Bernard of Clairvaux. *Meditations on the Life of Christ: An Illustrated Manuscript of the Fourteenth Century: Paris, Bibliothèque Nationale, MS. ITAL. 115*. Princeton, NJ: Princeton University Press, 1961.
———. *Sermones in Cantica Canticorum*, in *Patrologiae Cursus Completus*, Vol. 183. Edited by J.-P. Minge. Turnhout: Brepols, 1969.
———. *Meditationes Vitae Christi. Corpus Christianorum Continuatio Mediaevalis* (CCCM 153). Edited by Mary Stallings-Taney. Turnhout: Brepols, 1997.
———. *Meditations on the Life of Christ*. Translated by Francis X Taney, Anne Miller and C. Mary Stallings-Taney. Asheville, NC: Pegasus Press, 2000.
Catherine of Siena. *The Dialogue (Classics of Western Spirituality)*. Translated by Suzanne Noffke. Mahwah: Paulist Press, 1980.
Christine de Pizan. "The Book of the City of Ladies." In *The Book of the City of Ladies and Other Writings*. Edited by Rebecca Kingston and Sophie Bourgault. Translated by Ineke Hardy. Indianapolis, IN: Hackett Publishing Co., 2018.
Julian of Norwich. *The Showings of Julian of Norwich: A New Translation*. Translated by Mirabai Starr. Charlottesville, VA: Hampton Roads Publishing Company, Inc., 2013.
Margaret Ebner. *Major Works (Classics of Western Spirituality)*. Translated and Edited by Leonard Hindsely. Mahwah: Paulist Press, 1993.
Margaret of Oingt. "Letters." In *The Writings of Margaret of Oingt, Medieval Prioress and Mystic (d. 1310)*, Translated and with an introduction, essay, and notes by Renate Blumenfeld-Kosinski. Cambridge: D.S. Brewer, 1990.
Mechthild of Magdeburg. *Flowing Light of the Godhead*. Translated by Frank Tobin. Mahwah: Paulist Press, 1998.

Secondary Sources

Adams, Marilyn McCord. "Duns Scotus on the Female Gender." In *The Oxford Handbook of Theology, Sexuality, and Gender*. Edited by Adrian Thatcher. Oxford: Oxford University Press, 2014, 255–270.
Allen, Sister Prudence. *The Concept of Woman: The Aristotelian Revolution, 750 BC–AD 1250*, vol. 1. Grand Rapids: Wm. B. Eerdmans Publishing Co, 1997.
———. *The Concept of Woman: The Early Humanist Reformation, 1250–1500*, vol. 2. Grand Rapids: Wm. B. Eerdmans Publishing Co., 2002.
———. *The Concept of Woman: The Search for Communion of Persons, 1500–2015*, vol. 3. Grand Rapids: Wm. B. Eerdmans Publishing Co., 2016.
Barnes, Elizabeth. *The Minority Body: A Theory of Disability*. Oxford: Oxford University Press, 2016.
Baynton, Douglas. "Disability and the Justification of Inequality in American History." In *The New Disability History: American Perspectives*. Edited by P. Longmore and L. Umansky. New York: New York University Press, 2001.
Bordo, Susan. *Unbearable Weight: Feminism, Western Culture, and the Body*. Berkeley: University of California Press, 1993.

Bynum, Caroline Walker. "Jesus as Mother and Abbot as Mother: Some Themes in Twelfth-Century Cistercian Writing." *Harvard Theological Review* 70: 3-4 (1977): 257-284.

———. *Jesus as Mother: Studies in the Spirituality of the High Middle Ages.* Berkeley: University of California Press, 1982.

———. *Fragmentation and Redemption: Essays on Gender and the Human Body in Medieval Religion.* New York: Zone Books, 1992.

Cohn, Carol. "Wars, Wimps, and Women: Talking Gender and Thinking War." In *The Gendered Society Reader.* Edited by M. Kimmel. New York: Oxford University Press, 2000, 362-374.

Daly, Mary. *The Church and the Second Sex.* Boston: Beacon Press, 1985.

De Beauvoir, Simone. *The Second Sex.* Translated by H.M. Parshley. New York: Vintage Books, 1989.

DeYoung, Rebecca Konyndyk, Colleen McCluskey, and Christina Van Dyke. *Aquinas's Ethics: Metaphysical Foundations, Moral Theory, and Theological Context.* Notre Dame, IN: University of Notre Dame Press, 2009.

Foucault, Michele. *Discipline and Punish: The Birth of the Prison.* Translated by Alan Sheridan. New York: Random House Inc, Second Vintage Books Edition, 1995.

Grundmann, Herbert. *Religious Movements in the Middle Ages: The Historical Links Between Heresy, the Mendicant Orders, and the Women's Religious Movement in the Twelfth and Thirteenth Century, with the Historical Foundations of German Mysticism.* Translated by Steven Rowan. Notre Dame, IN: University of Notre Dame Press, 1995.

Jantzen, Grace. *Power, Gender, and Christian Mysticism.* Cambridge: Cambridge University Press, 1995.

Karnes, Michelle. "Exercising the Imagination: The *Meditationes vitae Christi* and *Stimulus amoris.*" In *Imagination, Meditation, and Cognition in the Middle Ages.* Chicago: University of Chicago Press, 2011, 141-178.

Lindquist, Sherry and Asa Mittman. *Medieval Monsters: Terrors, Aliens, Wonders.* New York: Morgan Library and Museum, 2018.

Mancia, Lauren. *Emotional Monasticism: Affective Piety in the Eleventh-century Monastery of John of Fécamp.* Manchester: Manchester University Press, 2019.

McNamer, Sarah. "The Origins of the *Meditationes Vitae Christi.*" *Speculum* 84 (2009): 905-955.

———. *Meditations on the Life of Christ: The Short Italian Text.* Notre Dame, IN: Notre Dame University Press, 2018.

Newman, Barbara. *From Virile Woman to Woman Christ: Studies in Medieval Religion and Literature.* Philadelphia: University of Pennsylvania Press, 1995.

Pasnau, Robert. *Metaphysical Themes 1274-1671.* Oxford: Oxford University Press, 2011.

Robertson, Elizabeth. "Medieval Medical Views of Women and Female Spirituality in the *Ancrene Wisse* and Julian of Norwich's *Showings.*" In *Feminist Approaches to the Body in Medieval Literature.* Edited by L. Lomperis and S. Stanbury. Philadelphia: University of Pennsylvania Press, 1993, 142-167.

Rosen, Christine. *Preaching Eugenics: Religious Leaders and the American Eugenics Movement.* New York: Oxford University Press, 2004.

Ruether, Rosemary Radford. *Sexism and God-talk: Towards a Feminist Theology.* Boston: Beacon Press, 1993.

Van Dyke, Christina. "Aquinas's Shiny Happy People: Perfect Happiness and the Limits of Human Nature." *Oxford Studies in the Philosophy of Religion* 6 (2014): 269–291.

———. "The Will and Love." In *A Hidden Wisdom: Self-Knowledge, Reason, Love, Persons, and Immortality in Medieval Contemplatives.* Oxford: Oxford University Press, forthcoming.

Williams, David. *Deformed Discourse: The Function of the Monster in Mediaeval Thought and Literature.* Montreal: McGill-Queen's University Press, 1996.

Part III
Disability in the Afterlife

8 Separated Souls
Disability in the Intermediate State

Mark K. Spencer

Introduction

While contemporary accounts of impairment and disability deal with bodily and cognitive impairments and disabilities, medieval treatments had a wider scope. They considered how impairment and disability would be found in the separated soul, the human soul separated from the body during the intermediate state, the period after death and prior to the resurrection.[1] In this chapter, I first consider medieval treatments of cognitive impairments and disabilities in the separated soul; for example, on some views, separated souls are unable to draw new knowledge from material things. Second, I consider treatments of impairments and disabilities that result from the separated soul's relations to the body; for example, on some views, separated souls are lacking in well-being due to the lack of the body. For both sets of treatments, souls are considered impaired or disabled if they lack some ability had by a soul in the natural, embodied state or if they lack some ability that human souls ought to have by nature. I follow contemporary models in distinguishing impairment (an abnormality, a lack, or dysfunction that is internal to a subject and that diminishes functioning relative to some end) from disability (a loss of opportunity to take part in a typical human life).[2]

In some ways, as we shall see, medieval treatments of the separated soul parallel contemporary models of disability and treatments of the relation between disability and well-being. By examining these parallels, we can better understand how medievals thought about disability, human nature, flourishing, cognition, autonomy, and dependence. The medievals largely held normative accounts of human functioning that, in many respects, appear false or discriminatory in light of contemporary disability theory. In order to understand medieval views on disability and their parallels to contemporary thinking about disability, without the false or discriminatory aspects of their theories intruding too much on our attention, we need an application outside the areas covered by contemporary thinking about disability. This is provided by discussions of the separated soul.

This chapter considers three broad contemporary models. First is the medical model, on which disability is constituted only by an impairment internal to the subject, a view generally rejected by contemporary thinkers as potentially discriminatory and as failing to attend to key features of the lives and experiences of persons with impairments. Second is the social model, on which disability is constituted not by physical or cognitive impairment alone but by the impaired subject being situated in a social setting that fails to accommodate or aid him or her in taking part in the typical course of social life. Third is the cultural model, on which disabilities or impairments are to be celebrated as the grounding for new cultures and cultural identities, and as challenges to narrow conceptions of normality – and, hence, on which terms like "impairment" and "disability" lose their standard negative connotations and uses. Generally, in the contemporary literature, the latter two models are generally taken as opposed to the view of disability found in the medical model.

In this chapter, I contrast two groups of views of disability in the separated soul, which follow from two metaphysics of the person and the soul. First are the views of some Dominicans and Jesuits, with a special focus on Thomas Aquinas, but also including Albert the Great, Bernard of Trilia, and Francisco Suárez, who argue that there are disabilities in separated souls, regardless of the aids provided to them. Second are the views of some Franciscans, especially Bonaventure, Matthew of Aquasparta, and John Duns Scotus, who argue for fewer impairments in the soul than the first view posits. Despite their differences, both views emphasize how consideration of the intermediate state reveals abilities of the human soul that could not be discovered through an examination of this life – that is, what appears to be impairment or disability in the loss of the body reveals what is truly natural to us. Especially in the first section, I restrict my attention mostly to the natural abilities of the soul, which the soul has apart from grace or glory, beatitude or damnation.

Cognitive Disability and Impairment in the Separated Soul

Thomas Aquinas and His Followers

On Aquinas's view, like most medieval views, human death is a result of original sin. Due to oppositions among the elements from which they are composed, human bodies, if left to themselves, break down, leading to bodily defects and death. Human persons were created in a state of original justice, in which a divine gift prevented this breakdown from occurring. With original sin, this gift was removed, and nature took its course. Hence, existing in a separated state is part of the punishment for sin.[3]

On Aquinas's view, the separated soul is impaired because it cannot exercise all the functions it has by nature. He thinks that we need to know the correct metaphysics of the person and the soul before we can know what its impairments or disabilities are; hence, in the next few paragraphs, I discuss some key aspects of his metaphysics of human persons and souls. On Aquinas's view, the separated soul is not a human person.[4] A *person* is a rational substance with a complete nature, unable to become part of another.[5] (See Chapter 3, by Scott M. Williams, for more discussion of what it is to be a person.) But a soul is a form, a mere part of the whole human person, who is essentially composed of form and matter, and it lacks a complete nature. A "form" is a non-material aspect of a being in virtue of which it has some structure or content. By our human soul or form, we have the structure of being human. One of Aquinas's fundamental principles is that action follows being: one acts on the basis of one's nature, that is, on the basis of what one is.[6] Since I experience myself as able to act both in the body (e.g., by sensing) and in the soul (e.g., by thinking), my nature includes both soul and matter,[7] and so my separated soul will not be me. Though it is not actually a part of a larger whole when separated, it retains an aptitude to inform matter and it retains its nature of being a part.[8] The soul has an orientation toward being part of a person that is thwarted in the separated state; this lack of actualization of a basic tendency of the soul is the basis for many of the soul's disabilities, on Aquinas's view.

Aquinas distinguishes two principles in creatures, essence or nature, by which a being is of some kind, and act of existence (*esse*), the actuality by which it exists. In creatures lower than us, *esse* directly actualizes the whole being. But in us, *esse* first (in an ontological, not temporal, sense of priority) actualizes the soul, and then the soul gives existence to the body.[9] There is a sense, then, in which human souls exist in a more primary sense than human persons. Because the soul has existence in itself, it subsists, it is not dependent on the body for its existence, and it continues to exist after death.[10]

On this view, the separated soul is impaired fundamentally because it lacks the whole of which it is a part and to which it is ordered to give its *esse*; all other impairments follow on this one. This view parallels the contemporary medical model of disability, according to which impairment constitutes disability, regardless of the subject's environment.[11] On Aquinas's principles, our activity (or lack thereof) follows our nature, and so all we need to know in order to determine if a being is disabled is whether it can fully actualize all the potencies of its nature. Since the separated soul cannot, it is disabled. Just as the medical model is generally criticized in contemporary disability literature for its failure to attend to lived experience in its actual context, so we might think of Aquinas's view as failing to attend adequately to the environment and community in which the separated soul lives – something that is better attended to by Franciscan thinkers, as we shall see.

All powers that had an organ as their subject are lacking to the separated soul. The subject of a power is what performs its action or is affected in virtue of the power.[12] Sensitive powers, including external senses, common sense, imagination, and memory (the ability to store and remember past sensible events); cogitative power (the ability to consider particular features of sensible beings); and sensitive appetites all have organs as their subjects. Accordingly, the separated soul cannot perform the acts of these powers. The soul retains the disposition to give rise to these powers should it again inform matter – in Aquinas's terminology, these powers remain in the separated soul "virtually" or "in root," but not "actually."[13] Aquinas contrasts his view to the Platonic view that sense perception involves one act in the body and one in the soul, the latter remaining in the separated soul.[14] All sensitive acts involve receiving forms of particular material things, known as "sensible species," that are carried by material media. For example, hearing involves receiving forms carried by sound waves, and seeing involves receiving forms carried by light waves. Since sensitive acts always involve material interactions, they require material organs.[15]

Strictly speaking, the inability to perform sensory acts is not an impairment for the soul, since these acts never belong to the soul, but rather to bodily organs. But this inability leads to an impairment. On Aquinas's view, with the intellect, a power belonging to the soul, we think about universal concepts, concepts that apply to many things. We form concepts on the basis of what we sense. Our brains join together the forms taken in through the senses into a composite sense image or "phantasm." We intellectually draw out of this image everything that can be considered universally about the kind of thing we are considering. Without phantasms, we could not gain new intellectual knowledge. We also need to picture phantasms as examples to aid us in intellectual thinking. Since the separated soul lacks union with a brain, it cannot do any of those things.

For the content of intellectual knowledge to be drawn from material things, the forms of those material things have to be rendered intelligible. On Aquinas's view, this requires that they be separated from matter and so rendered immaterial. This can only occur in stages. Material things are only sensible, not even potentially intelligible or able to be understood universally. The intellect can only draw information from what is potentially intelligible. Forms (or "species") received in the senses and phantasms are progressively more immaterial, more separated from a basis in matter, than forms in material thing exterior to the human person. Phantasms, the compilations of sensory information in our brains, are potentially intelligible. Aquinas does not posit a sharp division between material and immaterial things, but rather he posits a series of grades of immateriality. The separated intellect does not have these intermediate grades of immateriality at its disposal and so has no way to draw information from material beings. It would seem to follow that the separated soul cannot understand or gain new knowledge at all.[16]

But, since action follows being, no being can exist and be deprived of its natural activity.[17] Since it can naturally exist without the body, the separated soul must be able to act. Aquinas argues that action follows not only upon the nature of a being but on its "mode" of being. Our souls can exist in two modes: our *esse* can either actualize the whole composite through the soul or it can just actualize the soul. Two modes of action follow upon these modes of being, although the soul retains the same nature in either mode. When embodied, the soul gains new knowledge by turning to phantasms and abstracting intelligible species, which allow it to know the natures of sensible things. But when separated and so not directed toward bodies in its being, it gains new knowledge by turning to separate substances, that is, the angels and God.[18] Angels know lower beings, on Aquinas's view, by receiving forms infused into their intellects by God or by higher angels. God understands creatures practically, as things to be made; his ideas represent everything in beings that are to be made. God causes likenesses or species of these ideas in angels' and separated souls' intellects. Since these species represent everything about lower creatures, including their singularity and materiality, immaterial intellects can, through these species, understand individual beings, not just their natures.[19]

Some Thomists like Francis Sylvester of Ferrara argued that while there is a sense in which the separated state is natural to the soul in that no being can be without its natural act, strictly speaking, the separated soul's mode of knowing is contrary to its natural ordering toward phantasms.[20] This view again parallels the medical model: the soul's impairments constitute its disability, even though it has entered into a society that provides it with the aid it needs to perform its natural act.

But Ferrara's view is not Aquinas's. Rather, for Aquinas, there is a deeper sense in which the new mode of gaining knowledge is natural to the soul.[21] The human soul is essentially the border between the corporeal and incorporeal realms. When in the body, it naturally turns toward the corporeal world for knowledge, and when separated, it naturally turns to the incorporeal world.[22] As Bernard of Trilia explains in defending this view, when the soul is in the body, the agent intellect (the power by which we draw information from the senses and form concepts) is turned towards the body, actualizing the intelligibility potentially contained in phantasms and the potential intellect (the power by which we receive intelligible species). But when separated from the body, this light just actualizes the potential intellect, rendering it prepared to receive influence from above.[23] The agent intellect also activates species and habits retained in the soul from embodied life.[24]

Aquinas, following Albert, gives an experience-based defense for the claim that the separated soul naturally receives concepts from higher beings when it is separated from the body. When our minds are not attending to our bodies, as when we are dreaming or are temperate, then we more readily receive knowledge of higher things: dreamers receive prophecies, and temperate persons more readily attend to concepts. Extrapolating from this, when entirely separated from the body, the soul will entirely be able to attend to what is higher.[25] It will have perfect self-knowledge; the body obscures intellectual self-awareness, and since the body will not be present, nothing will distract the soul from knowing itself.[26] Some contemporary disability theorists argue that the impairment of certain abilities leads to the heightening of others or to alternative abilities.[27] Aquinas affirms this for the separated soul but goes further: while the separated soul is in a worse condition than the embodied soul with regard to being a mere part, it is in a better and freer condition with regard to its intellectual nature.[28] We see this further in Bernard of Trilia's argument that the separated soul cannot engage in discursive reasoning, since that requires turning to phantasms, but this is an improvement in the soul's understanding: it directly and intuitively understands things, without needing to move from premises to conclusions.[29] By calling this cognition "intuitive," he means that that the soul grasps beings in themselves, rather than just knowing *about* beings or knowing *that* certain things are the case about those beings.

One might object that a single power cannot both turn to phantasms and to infused intelligible species, since there seems to be nothing in common between these two kinds of understanding. But Bernard argues that in both cases, the intellect aims at immaterial objects; the phantasm in the former case is just the "terminus" of its gaze, not its essential object.[30] This resembles a key claim of the contemporary cultural theory of disability: what appears to be an impairment sometimes shows that what we often take to be normative is not normative at all.[31]

The new mode of cognition in the separated soul is outside the soul's nature (*praeter naturam*) insofar as the soul is oriented to be a part of a soul-matter composite.[32] But, as Francisco Suárez argues in explaining Aquinas's view, God's infusion of intelligible species is *due* to the separated soul, since no being can be deprived of its natural act.[33] Impaired with respect to its natural embodied state, the separated soul enters a new social environment where it is aided by other persons, and so its impairment is partially overcome, and it is at least less disabled. This resembles contemporary social models of disability.[34] On Aquinas' view, God gives to each being those aids necessary for it to be able perform its natural act, so long as it exists. In the separated state, this requires a sort of "prosthesis," infused species. Aquinas in particular argues for this prosthesis for the sake of the souls of infants. If separated souls only knew through species acquired in this life (as the Franciscan Richard of

Middleton held), then those souls would know nothing and so could not join in community with other separated souls and angels. This would deprive them of their natural act. For their sake, God must infuse species into souls after death.[35]

Despite these social aids, Aquinas insisted, increasingly over his career, on the cognitive disability of the separated soul. One of his fundamental principles is that whatever is received is received in the manner of the recipient. So, even though God infuses species into the soul, the soul can only receive those species in a confused and obscure manner, due to its weakness and natural need to turn to phantasms to cognize perfectly. Separated cognition, while better in itself as compared to embodied cognition, is not better for the human soul.[36] Still, it is not bad for us to have this higher cognition, even if it exceeds our typical embodied cognitive capacity. The separated state reveals what is actually natural to us: we are not just material beings but also participate in spiritual being. Although the Thomistic account has limited parallels to the contemporary social model of disability, it includes the caution that while aids must be provided to prevent impairments from becoming disabilities, these aids will be received by those who are disabled in their own manner. On Aquinas's view, impairments always constitute disabilities to some extent.

Although, on Aquinas's view, infused species allow the soul to think about material singulars directly, the soul can only use infused species to think about those singulars to which it had some connection during embodied life or those to which it is directed by God's revelation.[37] As we have seen, it is unable to investigate the physical world and come to cognize new singular beings under its own power. The soul gains connection to material singulars during this life in the following way. Although with the intellect we primarily grasp universals, we also grasp our acts of applying these universals to singular-sensed beings and phantasms and our acts of willing particular actions. By grasping these acts, we can intellectually think about the individual material beings we encounter.[38] Like universal knowledge and habits of intellect and will, this knowledge of individuals can be retained in the human soul while in the separated state. On this basis, the separated soul would be able to think about people, places, things, and experiences that it thought about during embodied life. But, lacking sensory powers like imagination, it would be unable to picture them. Furthermore, while in infused species, souls have the "prostheses" necessary to not only think about material singulars but also directly grasp them, separated souls are too weak to grasp currently existing material singulars (say, to grasp what is going on right now with their loved ones) without divine aid. This is because, on Aquinas's view, we can naturally use intellectual ideas to understand really existing material things only through the mediation of phantasms and senses.[39] Union with the body is for the good of the soul, and phantasms are not just occasions for understanding or a starting point for gaining knowledge[40] but are needed for perfect natural use of our intellectual knowledge. If we are essentially embodied, then the separated soul is lacking a key good for its well-being, and no aid provided by prostheses or society can remedy this.

Despite these disabilities, Aquinas insists that separated souls enjoy many cognitive benefits. One such benefit is a last point of comparison with contemporary disability theory. As we have seen, separated souls have perfect self-knowledge. Since each human soul is of the same species as other human souls, each images the others. So, by considering itself, it can thereby consider all others. Furthermore, each soul can receive intelligible species from and thereby directly consider other souls.[41] On this view, these species do not just allow thinking *about* other human souls but mediate direct awareness of those human souls. As a result, the separated human souls can enter into perfect community with one another. Some cultural disability theorists argue that some disabilities are to be celebrated for the cultures they produce.[42] There is cause for such celebration among separated souls. Suárez emphasizes this point: most of his arguments regarding the separated soul's cognition are based on the claim that souls require whatever will allow them to enter into more perfect society with one another, since this is most fitting for intellectual agents. On this view, in a way that somewhat anticipates contemporary concerns, those persons with cognitive impairments are always intellectual agents, and are always capable of entering society in some way, and so require what is necessary for doing so.[43] "Entering into society" need not involve actually cognitively contributing to society but involves being recognized, accepted, and assisted as a person with a nature capable of participating in spiritual goods.

Suárez agrees with Aquinas that separated souls receive infused species but contends against Aquinas that God can make species adapted to our weakness, through which we can perfectly cognize angels and material singulars, since this would allow us to enter into more perfect community with others, thereby overcoming our cognitive impairments.[44] He draws reasons for this from the Franciscans, to whom I now turn.

The Franciscans

Franciscan thinkers of the late thirteenth and early 14th centuries agree with Aquinas that the separated soul is not a person, though their metaphysics of the soul differs from his, as do the consequences they draw regarding the soul's impairment and disability. Most of them argue that the separated soul is capable of directly grasping and drawing new knowledge from material singulars, engaging in discursive reasoning, and remembering material singulars from embodied life, and they reject the view that the soul must receive infused intelligible species to engage in cognition. This tradition of thinking was initiated by John of

La Rochelle's mid-13th century *Summa de anima* and by the *Summa Halensis*, begun by Alexander of Hales and completed by others. These texts follow the pseudo-Augustinian text *De spiritu et anima* in arguing that while external senses like vision and hearing are not in the separated soul, the interior senses are in the separated soul insofar as they have a part belonging to the rational part of the soul, although their part belonging to the sensitive part of the soul is lost at death.[45] This view, as we saw, was rejected by Aquinas.

Subsequent Franciscan thinkers continue the claim that the separated soul has cognitive powers for gaining knowledge from material singulars. Among the Franciscans, a guiding principle is that a higher power, like the intellect, is capable of everything of which a lower power, like the senses, is capable, but in a more excellent way.[46] On this view, the soul is not impaired by lacking powers that require organs, though, as we shall see further in the next part of the chapter, the soul *is* impaired by lacking the body altogether, and the separated soul's impairments and disabilities all result from that lack, rather than from lacking sensory and other bodily powers. In a way similar to the parallel drawn to contemporary concerns at the end of the last section, this Franciscan principle invites us to consider that even in the cognitively impaired, apparently absent lower capabilities can still be regarded as present in some sense in higher cognitive powers, and ways must be found to treat such persons in accord with this.

The Franciscans generally reject Aquinas's views that the human intellect naturally requires phantasms and that soul and body are united for the soul's good. Rather, soul and body are united for the good of the whole composite person. The lack of phantasms in the separated soul is not a cognitive impairment for the separated soul itself or its cognition. Rather, it just implies a lack of interconnections among sensory and intellectual powers. These interconnections are goods for the composite, not for the soul in itself.[47] Once again, considering the separated state reveals things about the soul that would not otherwise be known. Just by looking at embodied life, we might (like Aquinas) have thought that these interconnections are essential to the soul or to cognition. But reflecting further on the separated state shows that they are not essential.

In general, as Richard Cross has suggested, Franciscan thinking about impairment and disability has some limited parallels to the contemporary social model of disability.[48] I have mentioned (and will discuss further below) that the Franciscans hold that the soul's lack of a body is an impairment. On their view (and on the social model), an impairment like this would only constitute a disability if the separated soul were in a milieu that rendered it incapable of performing cognitive acts. But on their view the separated soul always fits with any environment in which it finds itself, including with other persons, such that it can effectively cognize on its own, and so it is never disabled. All environments and societies in which the separated soul can exist provide it with what it needs to perform acts of cognition.

Bonaventure is typical of Franciscan views on the separated soul's cognition. On his view, the separated soul's intellect can perceive material singulars present to it, as the external senses did during embodied life. The intellect can remember absent material things, including with images, as the internal senses did during embodied life. And it can consider universals abstractly, as it did during embodied life. The separated intellect is freer in its activity than the embodied intellect. While it lacks benefits such as those it had by ordering and using bodily powers, Bonaventure insists this is not an imperfection (*imperfectio*) in the soul in itself – it is not, in contemporary language, an impairment to the soul's activity.[49] This is all affirmed by other Franciscans, such as John Pecham and Roger Marston. They explain how the intellect can perceive material things without the senses: material things do not act upon it, but the separated soul forms intelligible species in itself when it is in the presence of a material thing.[50]

These views are developed by Matthew of Aquasparta in his *Quaestiones disputatae de anima separata*, which defended what he held was the traditional Augustinian and biblical view on the soul, and which supported the condemnations of Thomistic and Averroistic views made by the bishop of Paris in 1277.[51] Like most of his contemporaries (except Richard of Middleton),[52] Matthew holds that the separated soul can gain new knowledge, again on the grounds that were matters otherwise, the souls of infants would not know anything and would not have society with others. Matthew presumes that the separated soul is not disabled in a social sense and so must be able to gain knowledge.

But he rejects Aquinas's view that the separated soul gains new knowledge through infused species. First, he thinks that view is contrary to Scripture, especially the parable of Dives and Lazarus (Lk. 16:19–31), which he contends represents souls gaining new knowledge from other creatures, not by infusion. Second, he finds Aquinas's view *unfitting* for several reasons. First, the separated state is a punishment, and so no new powers or modes of cognition should be able to come to be in it. Everything in the separated soul must have already been in the embodied soul, though some powers manifested in the separated soul, like being able to cognize angels directly, are obscured in the embodied state because our attention is absorbed by the body and phantasms. Second, if all souls received infused species, then the damned would receive gifts from God. Third, the blessed would be unable to gain their own knowledge but would be entirely dependent on others; this would make them worse off than demons, who he says can gain knowledge directly from material singulars.[53] This last argument fails to address Aquinas's view that cognition through infused species and through aid from others is natural and even a better form of cognition than embodied cognition.

On Matthew's view, material beings act upon the soul only in a certain respect. He explains this claim by drawing on the tradition of positing spiritual senses in the soul, a tradition that includes, among his contemporaries, the Franciscans Alexander of Hales and Bonaventure, and the Victorine Thomas Gallus.[54] These spiritual senses are powers in the soul in itself whereby it experiences material things in a quasi-sensory, non-abstractive way. By these senses, on Matthew's view, it "coheres" with and draws sensible species from physical media. On this basis, the intellect forms in itself intelligible species of these sensed objects.[55] The initial experiential, quasi-sensory step of being "excited" by species of material things, prior to the intellect forming species in itself, ensures that the separated soul's knowledge corresponds to what is around. This step was missing in the views of Bonaventure and Pecham.[56] Matthew insists on the soul's ability to gain new knowledge from things present to it for a reason consonant with the social model of disability: the soul should be able, despite the loss of the body, to cohere with its environment.

John Duns Scotus does not take up the spiritual senses tradition. Rather, he, along with the Franciscan William of Ockham, holds that the human intellect, both in the embodied and in the separated states, can intuitively grasp material singulars, that is, grasp them as present and existing, by grasping contingent propositions about existing individuals. Furthermore, the intellect retains memories of material singulars from embodied life, not by retaining images of them but by grasping and retaining propositions about one's sensory acts and their objects.[57] As we have seen, Scotus thinks that needing and using phantasms is a perfection of the composite, not the soul. The soul lacks this perfection of embodied cognition. While there is a kind of perfection in separated knowing insofar as it is like superior, angelic cognition, it is not, contrary to Aquinas, a positive perfection. Rather, separated cognition is only a "permissive perfection," that is, a necessary condition for a positive perfection, though the positive perfection of superior cognition is found only in the angels. For Scotus, no cognitive impairment or disability accrues to the separated soul, but also no new perfections or modes of cognition accrue to it.[58]

Differences between Scotus and Aquinas are rooted in their different metaphysics of the soul. As we have seen, Aquinas holds that the separated soul's *esse* is also the composite's *esse*; hence, in its being and in the action that follows upon its being, the soul is oriented to the body and impaired without it. For Scotus, the *esse* of a being is really identical to that being. The human soul's *esse* is not the same as the human composite's *esse* but is part of the composite's *esse*. On Scotus's view, as opposed to Aquinas's, the soul in its own being is independent of and really distinct from the composite. Since the human soul's mode of being is the same whether it is embodied or separated, human operations of thinking and willing (which follow upon the soul's being) belong to it in either state.[59] On Aquinas's view, given that action follows being, if the soul leaves the embodied mode of being and knowing, then it enters the angels' mode of being and of knowing. Scotus rejects any entailment between claims about something's mode of being and claims about its mode of action; he allows that the separated soul becomes like the angels in being, but he sees no reason to think that this entails anything about how it knows.[60] What these views have in common is an implicit recognition that in order to know what is an impairment or a disability, we must know not only about how a subject fits into the environment but also about the being of the immediate subject (either an organ or the soul) of the posited disability and how it relates to the whole person.

Like other Franciscans, Scotus rejects Aquinas's view that separated souls gain knowledge about material singulars through infused intelligible species. Like Matthew, Scotus sees Aquinas's view as debasing the nature of the soul: he holds that Aquinas's view makes the separated soul worse off than a rock, since rocks can, without special assistance from God or angels, perform their natural operation, but the separated soul on Aquinas's view can only perform its operation with the prosthesis of infused species. All the scholastics in this debate agree that any existing being can perform its natural acts, but Scotus sees Aquinas's view as entailing the denial of this principle.[61] For Aquinas, prostheses – aids from other persons – can make an act more perfect than an act performed under one's own power. For Scotus, this seems to not be the case, at least with regard to the separated soul.[62] Aquinas's account of our nature entails that prostheses like infused species perfect us or open up aspects of our nature otherwise inaccessible, while Scotus's account of our nature entails that they do not perfect us, nor are they necessary for perfect cognitive activity.

Scotus argues that since the separated soul retains species and propositions acquired during embodied life, and since it can acquire new species under its own power, then species infused by God would be superfluous.[63] He rejects Aquinas's response to such an objection that infused species, coming as they do from God's creative ideas rather than acquired from material things, are a different kind of species from those gained from singulars. He furthermore rejects Aquinas's claim that species in material things must be gradually rendered more immaterial, such that only the phantasm has the requisite grade of immateriality for the intellect to use for abstraction. Phantasms, he reasons, are material things, so if our agent intellect can abstract from them, then it can also abstract from material things directly. On Scotus's view, the intellect can naturally grasp any creature. If there is an intelligible object present to the intellect, then these are jointly sufficient conditions for intuitive cognition, whether in the embodied or in the separated states. Intuitive cognition produces intelligible species in the intellect, and these, along with agent and possible intellect, are sufficient for later abstractive cognition – that is, cognition that prescinds from presence and existence.[64]

William of Ockham agrees with these basic claims but rejects the need for species. Rather, the presence of the object to a functioning intellect is sufficient for intuitive cognition and simultaneous abstractive cognition. These generate a disposition (*habitus*) for later cognition, and this allows later abstractive thinking about the object when it is no longer present.[65] In these ways, the Franciscans affirm that every cognitive act that soul can perform in the embodied state can also be performed when separated.

The Separated Soul's Desire for the Body and Its Well-Being

So far, we have considered cognitive impairments and disabilities in the separated soul. But on many medieval views, the separated soul is more fundamentally impaired or disabled because it lacks the body. In this section, I consider these views, which parallel aspects of some contemporary thinking about relations between disability and well-being. Current disability theorists draw on dominant contemporary theories of well-being, especially *experience-based theories*, on which well-being is determined by experiential quality; *desire-based theories*, on which well-being is determined by fulfillment of desires; and *objective list theories*, on which well-being is determined by whether certain objective goods have been attained.[66] Even more than in considerations of cognitive disabilities, accounts of the separated soul to the body show how the medievals thought of flourishing and impairment as entirely dependent on our nature – a view challenged by social and cultural models of disability, and thus perhaps in tension with aspects of medievals' own views that parallel those models.

Thomas Aquinas

As we have seen, Aquinas holds that the soul is naturally ordered to give its *esse* to the body, an ordering that grounds its need to use sensory phantasms in cognition. On Aquinas's view, these orderings toward the body are for the soul's good. Hence, lack of a body constitutes a disability in itself and not just as grounding cognitive impairments. Why this is can be understood by considering the beatific vision. For Aquinas (and other Dominicans, including Albert), seeing God fulfills the intellect's desire in the sense that everything that belongs to the "substance" (*esse*) of happiness is present in the beatified separated soul. However, not all that belongs to the full well-being (*bene esse*) of its happiness is present there. Certain accidents proper to happiness are missing in the separated state. Full human happiness requires the body. For this reason, the soul experiences the lack of the body as a disability.

On Aquinas's view, even beatified separated souls fall short of full well-being on all three contemporary standards of well-being. However, the separated soul can have greater well-being than it had when it was embodied. Though the beatified soul could not receive more happiness from God than it has received, this happiness could be had to a greater extent if it were shared with the body – that is, happiness could be had in more ways if it were not merely intellectual happiness but also sensory happiness. The beatified soul longs to share its happiness with the body; while it is entirely fulfilled insofar as it is an intellectual entity, it is not entirely fulfilled insofar as it is intrinsically oriented to inform the body. When the medievals discuss what the separated soul longs to do, they mean both a natural orientation of the soul toward the body and a conscious desire. While Aquinas recognizes that not all impairments, such as blindness, necessarily involve an awareness of or missing of what one lacks, in the case of the separated soul, one misses and desires what one lacks. Prostheses like infused species and the presence of God to the intellect cannot overcome its intrinsic disabilities. The separated soul cannot attend as well as it could to the good present to it because it longs to give happiness to the body. While it has the sum of all goods, it does not have those goods in every way that it can. It lacks an objective good and something that it desires and so, as a result of its disability, is lacking in well-being.[67]

The Franciscans

Multiple theories about the separated soul's well-being can result from the Franciscans' metaphysics of the soul. As we have seen, on these views, the soul does not strive to give its own *esse* to the body. Joining with the body is good for the soul only insofar as the soul is part of a whole person. Bonaventure argues that it is more dignified to be actually a part of a person than separated from that whole, especially since separation is a punishment. Nevertheless, when in the beatific vision, the separated soul does not have a disabled condition (*conditionem deteriorem*) with regard to its well-being (*bene esse*), since it enjoys God. This is the case even though the soul essentially does desire to unite to the body, since not being in a whole person is a disabled condition with regard to its natural being (*esse naturae*). This view is an analogue of contemporary disability theories that hold that, even when a good on an objective list is absent, a subject can be fulfilled subjectively or by desire fulfillment.[68]

Matthew of Aquasparta, by contrast to Bonaventure, holds that the lack of a body leads to a defect in the soul's well-being. On Matthew's view, the soul longs for the body, not because lacking the body results in cognitive impairments but because it longs to administer or rule the body, and also, as on Bonaventure's view, because it longs to be a part of a whole person and human nature. Unlike on Bonaventure's view, this lack affects the soul's well-being; unlike on Aquinas's view, something essential, and not merely something accidental for happiness, is missing even in the beatific vision.[69] The soul's longing for the body distracts the soul from fully attending to that vision. When the body is attained again in the resurrection, this will not change the object that is seen (i.e., God), nor will the body share essentially in that seeing (for we cannot see the immaterial God with material eyes). Rather, having the body will allow the soul to participate in and attend to its act of seeing God more and receive God more completely, because it will no longer be distracted by longing for the body. The body is thus a *sine qua non* cause of perfect happiness. Furthermore, the whole person's happiness will be greater with the body than the soul's happiness is in itself, since, as on Aquinas's view, happiness overflows from the soul into lower powers like sensitive appetites. Well-being, on this view, can be impeded by a disability, not because overcoming the disability itself increases happiness but because, the claim is made, disability renders one less capable of enjoyment.[70]

On Scotus's view, the union of soul and body is again for the perfection of the composite, not the soul. On his view, the soul can be perfected without the body. This does not mean that union is merely accidental, as Aquinas feared would result from such a claim. Rather, union is essential to the whole and for its good.[71] On this basis, Suárez wrongly says that Scotus denies that the soul has an appetite for the body.[72] But the 17th century Scotists Bartholomaeus Mastrius and Bonaventura Belluto clarify this point: the soul longs for a perfect, glorified body, not the flawed body it once had, but it does have a natural desire for the body since it is by nature a form.[73] Scotus's position on the separated soul's well-being resembles Bonaventure's.

Conclusion

For the medievals, questions about impairment and disability apply not only to human bodies but also to separated human souls. These applications lead to some distinctive views about disability and impairment, which have some limited parallels to contemporary disability theory, but largely draw on principles quite different from those used in contemporary debates. For example, based on the principle that whatever is received is received in the manner of the recipient, the view was drawn that aids given to impaired and disabled subjects will often be received in ways that cannot overcome impairment but at times may bestow new perfection. The principle that higher powers are capable of everything of which lower powers are capable in a more excellent way led to the view that impaired and disabled persons must be regarded, then, as always capable in some sense of higher cognitive powers, and ways must be found to treat them in accord with this. Most importantly, the medievals involved in this debate generally held that to know what is a genuine disability and to tell whether a given aid will perfect the subject or open up aspects of human nature otherwise inaccessible, we must know the nature of the human person, the way that the person in question fits into the environment, and the nature of the immediate subject of the disability. We must keep such principles in mind in order to understand medieval views of disability in themselves, to see the parallels between medieval and contemporary thinking about disability, and to allow medieval theories to open up new possibilities for thinking about these important issues.

Notes

1 Current discussion of the separated soul centers on two questions, neither of which are my concern here. First, there is the question of whether the separated soul is a person; see my "The Personhood of the Separated Soul," 863–912. Second, there is the question of whether a separated state should be posited at all, or, rather, whether the soul gains a new, glorified body immediately after death; see Matthew Levering, *Mary's Bodily Assumption*, ch. 3.
2 Barbara Altman, "Disability Definitions, Models, Classifications, and Applications," 104–105.
3 Thomas Aquinas, *Summa theologiae* (hereafter, *ST*) I q. 85 a. 5 and 6. Unless otherwise indicated, citations from Thomas Aquinas are from www.corpusthomisticum.org.
4 Thomas Aquinas, *Scriptum super Sententiis* (hereafter, *In Sent.*) III d. 5 q. 3 a. 2; *ST* I, q. 29 a. 1 ad 5.
5 Thomas Aquinas, *In III Sent.* d. 5, q. 2, a. 1 ad 2; *ST* I, q. 29, a. 3 ad 4; III q. 3 a. 1 ad 2.
6 Thomas Aquinas, *ST* I q. 89, a. 1; *Quaestio disputata de anima* (hereafter, *QDA*), a. 19.
7 Thomas Aquinas, *ST* I q. 75, a. 4.
8 Thomas Aquinas, *In III Sent* d. 5 q. 3 a. 2.
9 Thomas Aquinas, *QDA*, a. 1; *ST* I q. 76 a. 1; *Summa contra gentiles* (hereafter, *SCG*), II c. 81.
10 Thomas Aquinas, *ST* I, q.75, a. 6.
11 This coheres with what Richard Cross has observed about Aquinas's accounts of disability; see "Baptism, Faith and Severe Cognitive Impairment in Some Medieval Theologies," 431–432.
12 Thomas Aquinas, *QDA* a. 19.
13 Thomas Aquinas, *ST* I q. 77 a. 8; *QDA* a. 19; *Quaestio disputata de virtutibus* q. 1, a. 4 ad3.
14 Thomas Aquinas, *Quaestiones de quolibet* (hereafter, *QQ*) X a. 4, a. 2.
15 On sensible species, see throughout Robert Pasnau, *Theories of Cognition in the Later Middle Ages*.
16 Thomas Aquinas, *Quaestiones disputatae de veritate* (hereafter, *DV*), q. 19, a. 1. According to the editors of the Leonine edition (pp. 565–566) this is directed against Bonaventure, who held that the separated intellect can draw species directly from material things, and against William of Auvergne, *De universo* I, p. 2, c. 13, who held that the separated soul could gain new knowledge by conforming itself to things. For more on these views, see the next section.
17 Thomas Aquinas, *QQ* III q. 9 a. 1.

18 Thomas Aquinas, *ST* I q. 89, a. 1; *QDA* a. 15; *SCG* II c. 81; *DV* q. 19, a. 1; *In IV Sent* d. 50, q. 1, a. 1.
19 See sources in previous note and Thomas Aquinas, *ST* I q. 55; q. 89, a. 3-4; *QDA* a. 18, 20. In angels, species are infused into them at their creation; Aquinas rejects views, like that of Avicenna or Albert (*In IV Sent* d. 45 a. 12, 621), on which human souls have innate species from their origins. This view is based on an account of embodied cognitive disability: if everyone had innate species, then the blind would have the species needed to understand colors, but they do not. See *ST* I q. 89 a. 1 ad 3; *QQ* III q. 9 a. 1; *DV* q. 19, a. 2.
20 Francis Sylvester of Ferrara, *Commentary on Summa contra Gentiles*, II, c. 83, n. 9.2 ad 2, 527. See Serge-Thomas Bonino, "L'âme séparée: le paradox de l'anthropologie thomiste," 77–78, and Mary Rousseau's, *Toward a Thomistic Philosophy of Death: The Natural Cognition of the Separated Soul*.
21 Thomas Aquinas, *QDA* a.18 ad 11. Some, like Anton Pegis, have argued that Aquinas moved from a more positive view of the separated soul's cognition in *In Sent* to a more negative view in *ST* and *QDA*. See Anton Pegis, "The Separated Soul and Its Nature in St. Thomas Aquinas." Against this view, see Jun Inoue's, *On the Development of St. Thomas Aquinas' Theory of the Knowledge of the Separated Human Soul*. The text cited here supports Inoue's view to the extent that elements of the positive view remain in Aquinas's later texts, but Pegis is correct that there is a move toward positing more disability in the separated soul.
22 Thomas Aquinas, *SCG* II c. 81. cf. Albert, *Summa theologiae* II, t. 12, q. 69, a. 2, 15–16.
23 Bernard of Trilia, *Quaestiones de cognitio animae separatae a corpore* [= *Quaestiones*], a. 1, ad 5, 46–47; a. 2 ad 14, 82–83. cf. Thomas Aquinas, *QDA*, a. 15; *DV* q. 19 a. 1.
24 Thomas Aquinas, *ST* I, q. 89 a.5&6; *In IV Sent* d. 50, q. 1, a. 2.
25 Thomas Aquinas, *SCG* II c. 81; *QDA* a. 15; *In IV Sent* d. 50 q. 1 a. 1; Albert the Great, *De homine, De natura animae rationalis*, 2, ad 3, in *Opera Omnia*, v. 27:2 (Aschendorff, 2008), 473. Aquinas thinks that we can know basically what it's like to be a separated soul on the basis of reasoning from our current state. He is opposed to the contention of many contemporary disability theorists that only (or primarily) the disabled subject is a position to express his or her own situation; see Adrienne Asch and others, "Disability: Health, Well-Being, and Personal Relationships," section 3.4. William of Ockham (*Quaestiones in librum quartum Sententiarum (Reportatio)*, q. 14, 282) agrees with contemporary theorists: on the basis of our current state, we can only know probabilistically what it is like and what disabilities are present in the separated soul; only those souls know these things first-hand.
26 Thomas Aquinas, *ST* I q. 89, a. 2.
27 Ronald Berger, *Introducing Disability Studies*, 29–31.
28 Thomas Aquinas, *ST* I q. 89, a. 2, ad 1; Bernard, *Quaestiones*, a. 1 ad 7–8, 48–49; Francisco Suárez, *Disputationes metaphysicae*, d. 35, s. 2, n. 7.
29 Bernard, *Quaestiones*, a. 4, 141–145. cf. Thomas Aquinas, *QDA* a. 7 ad 1.
30 Bernard, *Quaestiones*, a. 1 ad 3, 44.
31 Berger, *Introducing Disability Studies*, 29–31.
32 Thomas Aquinas, *ST* I q. 89 a. 1. See Bonino, "L'âme séparée," 78–82 on how most later Thomists, e.g., Cajetan and Bañez, recognized that Aquinas makes this point.

33 Francisco Suárez, *Quaestiones in De anima* (hereafter, *QDA*), d. 14, q. 4, n. 5.
34 Altman, "Disability Definitions, Models, Classifications, and Applications," 103–104; Berger, *Introducing Disability Studies*, 27–30; Adrienne Asch and others, "Disability: Health, Well-Being, and Personal Relationships," section 2.
35 Thomas Aquinas, *ST* I, q. 89, a. 1, ad 3. See Richard of Middleton, *In IV Sent* d. 50 a. 1 q. 2. Others argued in a similar way, e.g., Matthew of Aquasparta (*Quaestiones disputatae de anima separata* (hereafter, *QDAS*), q. 4, Henry of Ghent (*Quodlibet* 6 q. 8), and Scotus. See Jerome V. Brown, "The Knowledge Proper to the Separated Soul: Henry of Ghent and John Duns Scotus," 322–323.
36 Thomas Aquinas, *ST* I, q. 89, a. 3; *QDA* a. 18. See Pegis, "The Separated Soul and Its Nature in St. Thomas Aquinas."
37 Thomas Aquinas, *ST* I q. 89, a. 4. Some later Dominicans, such as Durandus of St. Pourçain (*In IV Sent* d. 45 q. 4), held that the separated soul only cognizes individuals when directed to do so by God.
38 Thomas Aquinas, *ST* I q. 86, a. 1. On this basis, Thomas Cajetan (*In I ST* q. 89, a. 4, n. 7, 379) holds that even sensible memories remain in the separated soul in disposition and effect.
39 Thomas Aquinas, *ST* I q. 89, a. 8.
40 This is against the Platonic view of Macrobius and Boethius and against Avicenna. See Bazan's notes to Leonine edition of Thomas Aquinas, *QDA* a. 19, 133.
41 Thomas Aquinas, *ST* I q. 89, a. 2.
42 Berger, *Introducing Disability Studies*, 29.
43 See similar arguments on a Thomistic basis in Miguel J. Romero, "Aquinas on the *corporis infirmitas*: Broken Flesh and the Grammar of Grace"; ibid., "The Happiness of 'Those Who Lack Reason'," 49–96.
44 Francisco Suárez, *QDA*, d. 14, q. 2, n. 10; q. 6, n. 9–10; q. 7, n. 2–9.
45 John of La Rochelle, *Summa de anima*, 7, c. 44, 143; Alexander of Hales, *Doctoris irrefragabilis Alexandri de Hales Ordinis minorum Summa theologica*, v. 2, q. 70, mem. 3, c. 3, 462. See Coloman Viola, "Jugements de Dieu et Jugemnet Dernier," 263–268.
46 See, e.g., Matthew of Aquasparta, *QDAS*, q. 4, 65–73; Duns Scotus, *Ordinatio* IV d. 45, q. 2, II ad 2, 160–161. This principle is used by Aquinas (e.g., *QDA* a. 18), but he denies this application of it. The principle is used by Suárez in his revision of Aquinas along Franciscan lines at *QDA* d. 9 q. 3 n. 3.
47 Bonaventure, *Commentaria in quatuor libros Sententiarum* (hereafter, *In Sent*) IV, d. 50, p. 2, a. 1, q. 1, ad 4–7, 1046–1047; Scotus, *Ordinatio* IV, d. 45, q. 1, ad 3, 143–144.
48 Richard Cross has linked Scotus's views to the social theory of disability in "Disability, Impairment, and Some Medieval Accounts of the Incarnation: Suggestions for a Theology of Personhood," 650–651.
49 Bonaventure, *In IV Sent*, d. 50, p. 2, a. 1, q. 1, 1045–1047.
50 John Pecham, *Quaestiones tractantes de anima*, q. 10, 95–96. See François-Xavier Putallaz, "L'âme et le feu: notes franciscaines sur le feu de l'enfer après 1277," 889–901.
51 R.E. Houser, "Matthew of Aquasparta," 424–426. See references to the condemnations at, e.g., *QDAS*, q. 1, 9–11; q. 3, 46–47. cf. Putallaz, "L'âme et le feu: notes franciscaines sur le feu de l'enfer après 1277," 889–901.
52 Richard of Middleton, *In IV Sent* d. 50, a. 1, q. 2, cited and objected to at Thomas Aquinas, *QDAS*, q. 4, 60.

Separated Souls 253

53 Thomas Aquinas, *QDA* a. 4, 62–64.
54 Boyd Taylor Coolman, "Alexander of Hales" and "Thomas Gallus"; and Gregory LaNave, "Bonaventure."
55 Thomas Aquinas, *QDA* a. 4, 65–71.
56 See Putallaz, "L'âme et le feu: notes franciscaines sur le feu de l'enfer après 1277," 889–901.
57 John Duns Scotus, *Ordinatio* IV, d. 45, q. 3, (Vatican 14:180–184); William of Ockham, *Reportatio* II q. 14, 316321. See Brown, "Knowledge Proper," 330–333.
58 John Duns Scotus, *Ordinatio* IV, d. 45, q. 1, 142–143.
59 Ibid., 144–145.
60 John Duns Scotus, *Ordinatio* IV, d. 45, q. 2, 154.
61 John Duns Scotus, *Ordinatio* IV, d. 45, q. 1, 150–151.
62 It is instructive to compare their views of the gifts of the Holy Spirit. On Aquinas's view, the gifts are dispositions to be moved by divine inspiration such that God, not oneself, is the principle of one's motion, and this constitutes a higher perfection in us than the virtues, which are exercised under our own power (*ST* I-II q. 68 a. 1). On Scotus's view, the gifts just are virtues, performed under our own power (*Ordinatio* III d. 34, q.un., 208–210).
63 John Duns Scotus, *Ordinatio* IV, d. 45, q. 2, 151–152). Suárez agrees with Scotus on the ability of the intellect to cognize singulars, but he sides with Aquinas on the need for infused species (*QDA* d. 9, q. 3; d. 14, q. 4).
64 John Duns Scotus, *Ordinatio* IV, d. 45, q. 2, 153–158. This view is shared by some later, non-Franciscan thinkers, e.g., the fifteenth-century Gabriel Biel (*In Canone*, lect. 32), cited at Suárez, *QDA* d. 14, q. 4, n. 2.
65 William of Ockham, *Reportatio* II, q. 12, 276–277; q. 14, 316–321.
66 Asch and others, "Disability: Health, Well-Being, and Personal Relationships," sections 1.1, 1.2.
67 Thomas Aquinas, *ST* I-II q. 4, a. 5–6; Albert, *In II Sent* d. 17, a. 2 ad 3, 300; *In IV Sent*, d. 49, a. 11–12, 684–685. See Irina Metzler, *Disability in Medieval Europe*, 59–61. It further follows that since the soul is apt to inform just one body, which will not occur until the resurrection, separated souls cannot move, act upon, or be acted upon by a body. Nevertheless, souls can be present in physical places, such as hell, limbo, purgatory, and heaven. But since they cognize through infused species, not through presence to material beings, local distance from material beings does not affect their cognition. Suárez explains that they are not contained in places but substantially present there as befits them for reward or punishment, and they can move themselves around; were they not able to do so, they would not be able to achieve the social goods necessary for a rational being, and they would be as badly off as lower beings like rocks, which cannot move themselves. By divine power, they can even be confined to physical fire in hell, which tortures the soul not as producing pain in it, but because the soul knows itself to be confined to fire. Fire does not affect souls by its own nature but by its being used as an instrument of punishment by divine justice. All scholastics inherited the view from Gregory the Great that physical fire can affect the soul, and in 1270 Stephen Tempier, bishop of Paris, condemned the view that the separated soul could not suffer from fire. See Thomas Aquinas, *QDA*, a. 21; *DV* q. 26, a. 1; *QQ* II q. 7, a. 1; *ST* I, q. 89, a. 7; Suárez, *QDA* d. 14, q. 2. cf. Putallaz, "L'âme et le feu: notes franciscaines sur le feu de l'enfer après 1277," 889–901.
68 Bonaventure, *In III Sent.*, d. 5, a. 2, q. 3, 136–137. cf. Asch and others, "Disability: Health, Well-Being, and Personal Relationships." On Bonaventure's

view, as on Aquinas's, external bodies cannot act directly on the separated soul. But unlike Aquinas, since he thinks we draw knowledge from material beings, Bonaventure holds that being locally distant from material beings impedes knowledge of them. His view of how fire causes damned souls to suffer resembles that of Aquinas — they suffer from being confined to fire and impeded by it — with the addition that the souls see the fire as harmful and so have the pain of fearing it; this pain is particularly great since the separated soul has livelier passions than the embodied soul. The pain of being impeded is explained by a comparison to bodily disability: suffering from being impeded in one's activity is much greater than suffering from being wounded, as can be seen from the experience of paralytics, who suffer at being impeded in moving their bodies. See *In IV Sent.*, d. 20, p. 1, a.un., q. 2, 520–521; *In IV Sent*, d. 44, p. 2, a. 3, q. 2, 933–934; d. 50, p. 2, a. 1, q. 2, 1048.

69 Similar views are held by later Franciscans, e.g., Bernardine of Siena. See Franco Mormando, "What Happens to Us When We Die? Bernardine of Siena on the Four Last Things," 126–129.

70 Matthew of Aquasparta, *Quaestiones disputatae de anima beata* q. 2, 209–223. On Matthew's view, souls are in places distant from earth, as a result of which they cannot see what happens here. They can, contrary to Bonaventure and Aquinas, be affected by material things, and so fire can directly affect the soul and, by divine causality, harm it. Souls can move from place to place, and to do so, they must pass through the intervening places. But separated souls cannot move bodies; in order for the soul to move a body, it has to inform it. He argues for this on an analogy to embodied disability: a paralytic's soul cannot move parts of his or her body because that soul no longer informs those parts. The soul cannot enter bodies at will according to the condemnations of 1277; to think otherwise is close to positing reincarnation. See Matthew of Aquasparta, *QDAS* a. 5, 80–87; q. 6, 102–107. Matthew's view on the soul's relation to fire is the opposite of Henry of Ghent's. On Matthew's view, fire is altered by divine causality to be able to affect the soul; on Henry's, the soul is altered to be able to be affected by fire. These views contrast to those of Scotus and Giles of Rome, on which the soul is just intentionally affected by fire. See Henry, *Quodlibet* 2 q.9, explained in Thomas Jeschke, "... *Per Virtutem Divinam Assistentem*. Scotus and Durandus on the Impassibility of the Glorified Bodies. Aristotelian Philosophy Revisited?" 139–167.

71 John Duns Scotus, *Ordinatio*, IV, d. 45, q. 2, ad 1–2, 159–161.

72 Francisco Suárez, *QDA*, d. 14, q. 10, n. 1.

73 Bartholomaeus Mastrius and Bonaventura Belluto, *Philosophiae ad mentem Scoti cursus integer*, d. 8, q. 1, 250–252. According to some Scotist texts, separated souls can move bodies without informing them. Since the soul will be able to move the resurrected body as a whole, not through the mediation of organs, and since the soul has all the same powers whether embodied or separated, the separated soul can move bodies without the mediation of organs. See *In IV Sent*, d. 49, q. 14 (Vives 21:476–479). These texts are not included in the Vatican edition of the *Ordinatio*; the Vatican editors (at 14: xii–xiii) cite a manuscript according to which some of these texts are drawn from a *reportatio* of Scotus. A similar view is in Dante, on which the separated soul can fashion a temporary body out of air; see Michael Potts, "Catholic Hylomorphism and Temporary Bodies," *Proceedings of the American Catholic Philosophical Association* 91 (2017), forthcoming.

References

Primary Sources

Albert the Great. "In II Sententiarum." In *B. Alberti Magni, Opera Omnia*. Edited by Vives. Volume 27. Paris, 1894.

———. "In IV Sententiarum." In *B. Alberti Magni, Opera Omnia*. Edited by Vives. Volume 30. Paris, 1894.

———. "Summa Theologiae." In *B. Alberti Magni, Opera Omnia*. Edited by Vives. Volume 33. Paris, 1895.

———. "De homine, De natura animae rationalis." In *Opera Omnia*. Edited by Henryk Anzulewicz and others. Volume 27:2. Münster: Aschendorff, 2008.

Alexander of Hales. *Doctoris irrefragabilis Alexandri de Hales Ordinis minorum Summa theologica*. Edited by Bernardin Klumper. Volume 2. Quaracchi, 1924.

Bernard of Trilia. *Quaestiones de cognitio animae separatae a corpore*. Edited by Stuart Martin. Toronto: PIMS, 1965.

Bonaventure. "In Tertium Librum Sententiarum." In *Commentaria in quatuor libros Sententiarum, Opera omnia*. Volume 3. Quaracchi, 1887.

——— "In Quartum Librum Sententiarium." In *Commentaria in quatuor libros Sententiarum, Opera omnia*. Volume 4. Quaracchi, 1889.

Francis Sylvester of Ferrara. *Commentary on Summa contra Gentiles*. In *Sancti Thomae Aquinatis doctoris angelici opera omnia*. Edited by Leonine Commission. Volume 13. Rome, 1918.

Francisco Suárez. *Disputationes metaphysicae*. In *Opera Omnia*. Edited by Vives. Volume 26. Paris, 1866.

———. *Quaestiones in De anima*. Edited by Salvador Castellote. Madrid, 1978–1992. <http://www.salvadorcastellote.com/investigacion.htm>

Durandus a Sancto Portiano. *In Sententias theologicas Petri Lombardi commentariorum*. Volume 4. Lyon, 1563.

Henry of Ghent. *Quodlibet 2*. In *Henrici de Gandavo Opera Omnia*. Edited by R. Wielockx. Leuven: Leuven University Press, 1983.

———. *Quodlibet 6*. In *Henrici de Gandavo Opera Omnia*. Edited by G.A. Wilson. Leuven: Leuven University Press, 1987.

John Duns Scotus. *In IV Sent*. In *Opera Omnia*. Edited by Vives. Volume 21. Paris, 1891. <https://archive.org/details/operaomnia21duns/page/n6>

———. *Ordinatio III, Distinctiones 26–40*. In *Opera Omnia*. Edited by C. Balic and others. Volume 10. Vatican, 2007.

———. *Ordinatio IV, Distinctiones 14–42*. In *Opera omnia*. Edited by C. Balic and others. Volume 13. Vatican, 2011.

———. *Ordinatio IV, Distinctiones 43–49*. In *Opera omnia*. Edited by C. Balic and others. Volume 14. Vatican, 2014.

John of La Rochelle. *Summa de anima*. Edited by Jacques Guy Bourgerol. Paris: Vrin, 1995.

John Pecham. *Quaestiones tractantes de anima*. Monasterii Guestfalorum: Aschendorff, 1916.

Matthew of Aquasparta. *Quaestiones disputatae de anima separata, de anima beata, de ieiunio et de legibus*. In *Bibliotheca Franciscana Scholastica Medii Aevi*. Volume 18. Florence: Quaracchi, 1959.

Richard of Middleton. *In IV Sententia*. In *Super Quatuor Libros Sententiarium*. Edited by M.A. Gonzaga. Volume 4. Brescia, 1591; reprint, Frankfurt am Main, 1963.

Thomas Aquinas. *Opera Omnia*. Edited by R. Busa. <http://www.corpusthomisticum.org>. [=ST]

———. *Opera Omnia*. Volume 24:1. Edited by B.C. Bazán, Rome – Paris: Commissio Leonina, 1996.

Thomas de Vio Cajetan, *Commentary on Summa theologiae*. Edited by Leonine commission. In *Sancti Thomae Aquinatis doctoris angelici opera omnia*. Volume 5. Rome, 1889.

William of Ockham. *Scriptum in librum primum sententiarum Ordinatio*. Edited by Stephen Brown, OFM and others. Volume 2. St. Bonaventure, NY: Franciscan Institutes Publications, 1970.

———. *Quaestiones in librum quartum Sententiarum (Reportatio)*. Edited by Gideon Gal and others. Volume 7. St. Bonaventure: Franciscan Institute Publications, 1984.

Secondary Sources

Altman, Barbara. "Disability Definitions, Models, Classifications, and Applications." In *Handbook of Disability Studies*. Edited by Gary Albrecht and others. Thousand Oaks: Sage, 2001.

Asche, Adrienne, Jeffrey Blustein, Daniel Putnam, and David Wasserman. "Disability: Health, Well-Being, and Personal Relationships," *The Stanford Encyclopedia of Philosophy* (Winter 2016). Edited by Edward N. Zalta. <https://plato.stanford.edu/archives/win2016/entries/disability-health>.

Berger, Ronald J. *Introducing Disability Studies*. Boulder, CO: Lynne Rienner Publishers, 2013.

Bonino, Serge-Thomas. "L'âme séparée: le paradox de l'anthropologie thomiste," *Revue thomiste* 116 (2016): 77–78.

Brown, Jerome V. "The Knowledge Proper to the Separated Soul: Henry of Ghent and John Duns Scotus," *Franziskanische Studien* 66 (1984): 316–334.

Coolman, Boyd Taylor. "Alexander of Hales" and "Thomas Gallus." In *The Spiritual Senses*. Edited by Paul Gavrilyuk and Sarah Coakley. Cambridge: Cambridge University Press, 2012.

Cross, Richard. "Disability, Impairment, and Some Medieval Accounts of the Incarnation: Suggestions for a Theology of Personhood," *Modern Theology* 27 (2011): 639–658.

———. "Baptism, Faith and Severe Cognitive Impairment in Some Medieval Theologies," *International Journal of Systematic Theology* 14 (2012): 420–438.

Houser, R.E. "Matthew of Aquasparta." In *A Companion to Philosophy in the Middle Ages*. Edited by Jorge J.E. Gracia and Timothy B. Noone. Malden, MA: Blackwell, 2006.

Inoue, Jun. *On the Development of St. Thomas Aquinas' Theory of the Knowledge of the Separated Human Soul*. Unpublished Ph.D. Dissertation. Washington, DC: Catholic University of America, 2000.

Jeschke, Thomas. "… *Per Virtutem Divinam Assistentem*. Scotus and Durandus on the Impassibility of the Glorified Bodies. Aristotelian Philosophy Revisited?" *Philosophia* 1 (2012): 139–167.

LaNave, Gregory. "Bonaventure." In *The Spiritual Senses*. Edited by Paul Gavrilyuk and Sarah Coakley. Cambridge: Cambridge University Press, 2012.
Levering, Matthew. *Mary's Bodily Assumption*. Notre Dame: University of Notre Dame Press, 2016.
Mastrius, Bartholomaeus and Bonaventura Belluto. *Philosophiae ad mentem Scoti cursus integer*. Venice: Nicolaum Pezzana, 1727.
Metzler, Irina. *Disability in Medieval Europe*. New York: Routledge, 2006.
Mormando, Franco. "What Happens to Us When We Die? Bernardine of Siena on the Four Last Things." In *Death and Dying in the Middle Ages*. Edited by Edelgard DuBruck and Barbara Gusick New York: Peter Lang, 1999.
Pasnau, Robert. *Theories of Cognition in the Later Middle Ages*. Cambridge: Cambridge University Press, 1997.
Pegis, Anton. "The Separated Soul and Its Nature in St. Thomas Aquinas." In *St. Thomas Aquinas, 1274–1974. Commemorative Studies*. Edited by Armaund Maurer. Toronto: PIMS, 1974.
Potts, Michael. "Catholic Hylomorphism and Temporary Bodies," *Proceedings of the American Catholic Philosophical Association* 91 (2017): 171–183.
Putallaz, François-Xavier. "L'âme et le feu: notes franciscaines sur le feu de l'enfer après 1277." In *Nach der Veruteilung von 1277: Philosophie und Theologie an der Universität von Paris im letzten Viertel de 13. Jahrhunderts. Studien und Texte*. Edited by Jan A. Aertsen and others. Berlin: Walter de Gruyter, 2001.
Romero, Miguel J. "Aquinas on the *corporis infirmitas*: Broken Flesh and the Grammar of Grace." In *Disability in the Christian Tradition: A Reader*. Edited by Brian Bock and John Swinton. Grand Rapids, MI: Eerdmans, 2012.
———. "The Happiness of 'Those Who Lack Reason'," *The Thomist* 80 (2016): 49–96.
Rousseau, Mary. *Toward a Thomistic Philosophy of Death: The Natural Cognition of the Separated Soul*. Unpublished Ph.D. Dissertation. Marquette University, 1977.
Spencer, Mark K. "The Personhood of the Separated Soul," *Nova et Vetera* 12 (2014): 863–912.
Viola, Coloman. "Jugements de Dieu et Jugemnet Dernier." In *The Use and Abuse of Eschatology in the Middle Ages*. Edited by Werner Verbeke and others. Leuven: Leuven University Press, 1988.

9 Disability and Resurrection
Richard Cross

Introduction

In relation to the condition of an ideal human body – Christ's body exalted in heaven – the 16th century Lutheran theologian Johannes Brenz says the following:

> To walk from place to place does not belong to divine excellence but to corporeal weakness; not to heavenly majesty but to earthly insignificance; not to spiritual beauty but (if it is compared to heavenly attractiveness (*venustatem*)) to bodily deformity.[1]

Brenz is not supposing that the ideal condition is to need to be carried around in a sedan chair, like some kind of superannuated aristocrat in a novel by Smollett. He is ruling out from the ideal condition any variety of self-motion that requires limbs. He has complex theological reasons for this, which I will return to at the end of this chapter. For now I want to focus on the following thought: that there may be reasons for supposing that normative views of the body resultant from ableist presuppositions are alien to at least some traditional theological reasoning about the resurrected body. It is this thought that I intend to explore in what follows, focusing on medieval debates on the nature of the resurrected body.

There is one thing that arises from Brenz's text on which I am not going to comment further: Brenz's claim that what we might for convenience think of as typical functionality is *aesthetically* displeasing – that it is a deformity. My concern here is just with function, not with beauty – not because there is not much that could be said, but because it would extend my chapter both thematically and structurally beyond reasonable bounds.

I intend to focus on two issues: questions of sensation – what senses might a resurrected body have, and which of these might it need to use – and the question of mobility – what kinds of capacities for movement might be available to a resurrected body, and what might explain the presence and function of these capacities. Medieval theologians discussed these two questions under the headings of the impassibility and agility of the resurrected body, two of the four supernatural gifts held to be conferred on such bodies. (The remaining two gifts – clarity and subtlety – would take us yet further into the realms of the esoteric, and I will not look at them here.) I do not know who first introduced this classification.[2] We can find it in the late 12th century in Praepositinus of Cremona,[3] and in the 1220s and 1230s in Alexander of Hales,[4] Hugh of St. Cher,[5] Roger Grosseteste,[6] and Richard Fishacre.[7]

Impassibility and super-mobility may make us think of the superpowers associated with transhumanism. But, as we shall see, there are profound differences between transhumanism and medieval accounts of the resurrection. For one thing, according to my thinkers the ideal or perfected body is not understood prosthetically. If such powers belong to bodies as such, it is in virtue of their internal dispositions that they receive the kinds of superpowers that they do. Some theologians worried about the possibility that a body with such-and-such a structure – with such-and-such categorical properties – could be susceptible of dispositional properties quite unlike those standardly associated with it; or that a body of such-and-such a kind could be reconfigured with a set of categorical properties sufficient to explain the presence of the supercharged dispositional properties. Such thinkers tended, at least on occasion, to locate the relevant alteration in the environment, not in the body itself. One important thing to keep in mind about the various speculations, whether they be connected with the body or its environment, is that they are not arbitrary: they always have theoretical motivations, be they philosophical or theological.

Impassibility and Sensation

Medieval theologians from the mid-13th century onward followed Aristotle in supposing that sensation is fundamentally something passive: something *done* to the body. A resurrected body is supposed to be impassible, and this might suggest that a perfected body cannot sense. Aquinas raises the objection in a typically clear way: "As the Philosopher says, in *De anima* II, 'sensing is a certain kind of undergoing (*pati*).' But glorious bodies will be impassible. Therefore, they will not actually sense."[8]

The Aristotelian idea – at least as developed in the high middle ages – is that sensation involves the reception of what were known as species: representational intermediaries somehow originating from the object of sensation, and coming to inhere first in the medium between the perceiver and the object and then in the sense organ itself. On some views, the reception of a species in an appropriate organ was sufficient for sensation. On others, this view looked a bit too much like magic (since it is hard to specify what it is that makes some recipients – organs – capable of sensation and others – the intervening medium – not so capable).

This second kind of view generally posited some additional kind of *act* of sensation, caused jointly by the object or species and the sense-organ. In either case, of course, sensation requires passivity, even if that is not all it requires.

Aquinas reports two attempts (other than his own) to answer the passivity objection. Both involve the thought that resurrected sensation occurs in radically different ways from that in which it standardly occurs. According to the first, impassibility does indeed prevent any form of passivity, and thus that, if an impassible body is to sense, the process cannot involve the reception of species. Rather, sensation consists in the extromission of species, not their reception. The idea – following Augustine and ultimately Galen and others – is that the senses, paradigmatically the eyes, send out species (luminosity in the case of sight) to the objects of sensation and thereby sense them.[9] On the first theory, this account is true, but only for the resurrected body. Bodies pre-resurrection sense in the standard Aristotelian way.

The second theory considered by Aquinas explains perception by supposing that the species required for sensation is received in the sense organ but is caused not by the external object but by the higher intellectual powers of the person. This theory is Albert the Great's. Here is what Albert says about the sense perception of the damned:

> There is one way of receiving cognition before death, and another after. Before death, cognition is received by the sense and rises up, through imagination, into the intellect. But after death it will be the other way round: sense cognition will come down from the intelligible. And according to this way all the senses of the impious will perceive the species of the contrary that afflicts them .... And I say that sense consists in these acts, not in things received from outside. According to this way there will be taste of the bitter, and smell of the fetid, and sight of something disgusting and awful, and hearing of a mournful sound, and touch of the cold and hot.[10]

When talking about the happier fate of the blessed, Albert explains in a bit more detail how the process is supposed to work:

> The object of sense, which characterizes (*distinguit*) a sense, comes down from the intellect. For just as in the current order the universal, which characterizes the intellect, rises up to the intellect through the stripping of sensible forms, so in the future case the sensible will come down from the intelligible, distinguishing (*distinguens*) the sense by clothing it and adding to it sensible forms in relation to it.[11]

In standard cases we form ideas of universals by taking the sense representation and "stripping away" the particularizing conditions – contingent or accidental features – to uncover the essential features of the object. In the resurrected case we perform the opposite operation: we start from a representation of the universal and "clothe" it with particularizing conditions to form in the sense organs a representation of the particular.

Albert raises and replies to an obvious objection that this theory seems to suggest:

> If it is perhaps objected to this that the punishments of hell will be the visions of a dream and not the truth of punishment (for in a dream someone reflects on an image as they do on a real thing, and for this reason even though there is some bodily change [in the dreamer], nevertheless there is a deception, since the thing is not there), I say that if in the sensory cognition, and in the imagination, there were nothing other than the unreal image, then the objection would follow, since it is this way in a dream. But we say that there [viz. in the case of the sensation of the damned] is the reality of the thing. The image is not determined to the reality of the external object prior to sense – as is now the case in a dream – but is determined to the reality of the thing that is in the intellect: for the intellect receives the realities of things.[12]

The idea is that a sensation is veridical if it has its object present, irrespective of the causal story that we tell about the way in which the sensation was formed.

Aquinas rejects both of these theories. The first he rejects on the grounds that the proposed transformation of the senses is so radical that a sense power "would not be specifically the same as it is now, but would be some other sense power given" to the resurrected body. The reason for positing this shift in species is that, according to Aquinas, sense powers are essentially merely passive, and nothing essentially merely passive could become active.[13]

Albert's theory is rejected on different grounds. As Aquinas sees it, it is a virtue of Albert's theory that sensation is still something essentially passive: impassibility is preserved on the grounds that the passivity is wholly internal to the body or at least the human person: sensation is caused in the body by the activity of the person's intellect. But Aquinas does not think that Albert has a sufficient answer to his own dreaming objection:

> Every passive power, according to the kind of its species, is determined to some specific kind of active object: because a power, as such, has an order to that thing with respect to which it is said. So, since the proper active object in external sense is a thing existing outside the soul, and not one existing in the imagination or reason, [it follows that], if the organ of sensing is not moved by exterior

things, but by the imagination or other higher powers, there will not be genuine sensation there [viz. in the case of the resurrected body]. So we do not say that the mad, or others who are mentally ill (*mente capti*) – in whom there is (on account of the victory of the imaginative power) this kind of downward flow of species to the organ of sensing, genuinely sense – but that it seems to them that they sense.[14]

To see the point, imagine a situation in which a person had a hallucination of an object – that is to say, that the apparent perception of the object was generated internally, not as a consequence of the presence of the object – in the case that the object was genuinely present. More generally, there is on Albert's view no way of securing the connection between the act and its object. In this respect, Albert's view seems worse off than the first one.

Aquinas proposes a different account, following Aristotle's account of sensation in *De anima* II: the reception involved in all sensation – even in a non-glorified body – is essentially not a "natural" one but a "spiritual" one. According to Aristotle, all changes involve the reception of a form. In a natural change the patient is made to be an instance of the received form – heat, for instance, when received in a patient in this way, makes that patient hot. In a spiritual change, this condition is not satisfied, and the reception of the form is identified as the patient's coming to cognize the object in some way or another. Heat, when received in this way, gives rise to a feeling or perception of heat.[15] In some cases – for example, touch – Aquinas is clear that these two changes standardly go along with each other and talks of the first of these changes as a "disposition" for the second.[16] Aquinas states that these two kinds of change can nevertheless be detached from each other: "this reception [viz. the natural reception] will not be in glorious bodies; but the second [viz. the spiritual reception], which of itself actualizes a sense and does not change the nature of the recipient [will be]."[17] Presumably, the worry is that the first change is potentially damaging to the body. It is this kind of passivity that Aquinas identifies as passibility: as he puts it, "in a glorious body there will not be able to be any change against the disposition by which it is perfected by the soul."[18]

How might this separation of the natural and spiritual change be effected? As Aquinas understands the resurrected state, it involves the complete subjection of the body to the soul, so that the soul can simply ensure that the body is not damaged by anything against its nature. The soul is supposed to be (among other things) the, or a, substantial form of the human body, structuring that body such that it is a human body with certain natural functions, powers, and capacities.

> Every passion is brought about by the victory of the agent over the patient, otherwise it would not bring the patient to its own end

> terms. But it is impossible that something should dominate over a patient other than to the extent that the dominion of its proper form over the matter of the patient is weakened (speaking of a passion that is against nature, about which we are now speaking), for matter cannot be made subject to one of two contraries without the dominion over it of the other being removed or at least diminished. But the human body, and whatever is in it, will be perfectly subject to the rational soul, just as the soul will be perfectly subject to God. And thus there will not be able to be in the glorified body any mutation against the disposition by which it is perfected by the soul. And thus those bodies will be impassible.[19]

So here the idea is that the soul gains some kind of superpower, enabling it to protect the body from damage: it can thus touch without undergoing any of the physical changes that touch involves. (I will return briefly to Aquinas's strikingly hegemonic language in my conclusion.)

It is not clear just how this might work, however, and we can see what is wrong if we look at the different cases of the blessed and the damned. In the former case, as we have seen, the soul is empowered to protect the body from damage, whatever the environment. (Aquinas's claim here is too strong, incidentally, since it would mean that the soul could ward off even divine hostility to the body: as a result of the soul's power, "here will not be able to be *any* change in the glorified body against the disposition by which it is perfected by the soul.") In the latter, "the fire does not alter bodies materially, but acts in them, for the sake of punishment, only by a certain spiritual action":[20] which is to say that the bodies will feel the heat of the fire without being destroyed by it. Presumably a glorified body, encountering this fire, would have just the same reaction as a damned body: it would feel the pain, just as the damned body does. But it would not be destroyed because of its supercharged soul. On this account, then, the failure of the body of the damned to be destroyed by the fire is left unexplained, since such a body does not have a supercharged soul in the way that the glorified body does.

Duns Scotus agrees with Aquinas that the natural and spiritual changes are detachable. But he proposes a mechanism to explain how this might be and also solves the problem about the indestructibility of the bodies of the damned that Aquinas left unresolved. According to Scotus, what happens in these kinds of case is that God, as the primary cause of every effect, fails to cooperate with the causal powers of secondary causes in cases in which his so cooperating would result in an effect harmful to the human body. He considers the case of the three boys in the furnace in Daniel 3.24:

> There is an example in the case of the fire in the furnace, which did not act to bring about the destruction of the three boys – not because

of some impassibility intrinsic to the boys, or because of some lack of passive potency [in the boys], or because of some intrinsic contrary impediment, but because God, through his will, did not cooperate with the fire in its action.[21]

Aquinas's view is the third rejected view – that the boys were impassible "because of some intrinsic contrary impediment": according to Aquinas, the supercharged power of the soul.

Scotus uses this account to explore the interrelations of passivity and sensation too. Like Aquinas, he supposes that the real and intentional components of sensation are separable, and he uses this to explain how it is that the bodies of the damned can perceive the object surrounding them – specifically fire, with which they are in immediate contact – without being destroyed by it:

> The one can be there without the other [viz. the intentional effect without the real one] ... because neither depends essentially on the other, and they are indeed here and now separable if something is susceptive of a form really but not intentionally, and another thing vice versa. But there, one will not be able to inhere without the other except on account of some impediment – either because God does not act along with the fire in that action, or because some created agent impedes one action but not the other.[22]

Here the idea is that it is possible to sense something that one is in contact with without undergoing any real change – without being harmed by the object that one is in contact with. God is the primary cause of the intentional change but fails to be the primary cause of a real change, which is accordingly absent. In the case of the boys in the fire in Daniel, God simply refrained from being the primary cause of either kind of change, at least for the case of touch. (I suppose the boys could see and hear the fire, but they could not feel the heat. It is not clear to me whether or not Scotus in this context would want to assert that there are physical changes associated with sight and hearing. He associates the sensible species with the intentional change.[23] So there is apparently no other change in the organ. But "intentional" might be ambiguous.)

Other things are worth noting too. Should we, for example, suppose that resurrected bodies have or need all their senses? We might regard loss of taste as something undesirable, but Aquinas is seemingly unmoved by the thought that, since in heaven there will be no food, there will be no tasting. It is not that the sense is absent, but that it is never used, "unless perhaps there will be actual tasting by the change of the tongue by a certain added humidity":[24] the idea being, I assume, that humidity in the air might allow us to taste gases that we will be able to smell in heaven. (And smell is affirmed on the grounds that "the Church sings that the bodies of the saints will have a very sweet smell.")[25]

Bonaventure is more restrictive:

> Being able to sense comes from the conjunction of a power with a well-disposed organ, and sensing comes from the conjunction of that with the object. Since therefore there will there [viz. in heaven] be powers joined to well-disposed organs, there will there be all the powers for sensing.
>
> But because the objects of all the senses will not be in glory, but only some, it follows that some will be in their acts, and others not. For the objects of some senses are absolute properties which will be found in a body that is to be glorified, for example color [as the object] of sight, and lightness [as the object] of touch. And because a glorified body will rise with luminosity and lightness, there will there be the objects of two senses, and for this reason these senses will be in their acts. But the objects of other senses are not properties of a body that is to be glorified, or absolute properties, but emanations from bodies, like smell and sound and taste. And because those things will not be in heaven, therefore [these senses will not be in their acts].
>
> Another argument is taken from the part of the medium: because the medium in sight can be everything that has the feature of translucent, and the medium in touch is flesh joined to it [viz. touch], it follows that, because these two media will be present in heaven, these two senses will be in the acts, but the others minimally [so], given that their media are lacking – unless perhaps someone should insist on hearing, about which a doubt remains, just as in the case of vocal praise in heaven, which it seems neither necessary nor obviously false to posit.[26]

There are two arguments here, though they turn out to be very similar. The first is that the only objects of sensation in heaven will be other glorified bodies (and, perhaps, the bodies of the damned and the fire that surrounds them – but Bonaventure does not mention that possibility here). Now, for a body to be sensed, certain conditions must be satisfied. In the case of sight, the objects require "luminosity," and in the case of touch, they require "lightness." According to Bonaventure resurrected bodies have both features. These are absolute or non-relational features of bodies. But the remaining senses do not sense their objects in virtue of non-relational features of those objects. Rather, they sense them in virtue of "emanations" arising from the bodies: perhaps gases in the case of smell and taste, and sound-waves in the case of hearing. But no such things will be in heaven. So these three senses will not exist in conditions appropriate for their activities.

The second argument is that there are no appropriate media for sensation in these last three cases. The medium of sight is translucence, and of touch contact. The heavenly atmosphere is translucent (air, I suppose), and heavenly bodies can certainly be in contact with each other. But, as in the first argument, the required media for the remaining senses do not exist – unless, Bonaventure speculates, we should understand biblical talk of heavenly singing literally and not metaphorically (see, e.g., Rev. 19.1–7).

Bonaventure goes on to explain that some of the changes associated with sensing are intrinsically imperfections:

> Some acts are perfect, but some have imperfection conjoined. And since the act of tasting has an imperfection attached to it by reason of its status, and likewise [an act] of smelling because of its object (which is not glorified, and has to take place through a medium that is receptive simply of an alien impression), therefore [taste and smell will not be in their acts in heaven].[27]

The thought is that taste involves eating and digestion: and these things are, or involve, *ceteris paribus*, imperfection – the production of waste products. And smell involves some kind of gaseous emission – something that cannot be glorified and thus will not be in heaven. Here, the idea is not that the body is deprived of something it should have. Rather, in ideal conditions it is not a good to be able to taste or smell, because these things are associated with other imperfections.

So in all of these discussions we find that things that someone, given ableism, might be inclined to value are not the things that medieval theologians prized. Other theoretical considerations trump any kind of worth or desirability that might have been ascribed to these functions.

Agility and Mobility

Albert the Great takes a view on agility rather like the one Bonaventure takes on the senses:

> If a glorious body is mobile, it will not be mobile other than by forward (*processivo*) motion, that is, by a motion which is from the appetite of the will or of desire to be in the different parts of place. But it is not mobile by forward motion, which I will prove. Therefore it is utterly immobile. Proof: everything that is mobile by forward motion has something outside itself which is desirable or which is desired by it. But every such thing [viz. that which desires things external to itself] is imperfect in relation to what is willed, because it wills something that it does not have. But the glorified have

everything which they will; therefore they do not desire anything external, and thus do not move in order to achieve that thing.[28]

This, admittedly, is an objection to Albert's own view that "a glorious body has a power for perfect forward motion."[29] But the reply more or less concedes the point: "there will be motion to demonstrate the motive power,"[30] "just like the body of the Lord was moved to show the resurrection to the disciples."[31]

Albert holds too that any such motion – undertaken for revelatory or divine purposes, not to satisfy any need or desire of ours – would be non-organic, not involving organs or limbs. He considers a bipartite objection to the effect that the only kind of motion available to a resurrected body would be organic:

> What does not belong to a nature according to the truth of the nature before the resurrection will not belong to the nature after resurrection. So we do not say that a human being will then have wings to fly. Since therefore before the resurrection a human being does not have the power of leaving the place owed to mortal nature – for they cannot be lifted up into the air or fire when they will – therefore also after the resurrection they will not have the power of leaving the place that is owed to glorified bodies, that is, the empyrean heaven. And so they will not move to us in apparitions.
>
> If perhaps it is said that it is the result of weakness, and not from the truth of the nature, that bodies cannot move outside their place, against this: if it is from the truth of nature, then we have in the soul some power to that act (as is clear from particular cases, such that we have [the power] to speak and walk, and such-like). But to each power there corresponds an organ in the body, which is the power to an organic act. Therefore, to these powers there would correspond an organ, which does not seem to be the case.[32]

Underlying this discussion is a biblical verse: "But they that wait upon the Lord shall renew their strength; they shall soar with wings as eagles; they shall run, and not be weary; and they shall walk, and not faint" (Is. 40.31). The objection basically argues that we shall not be able to "soar like eagles" because we shall not have wings. Here are the details. What is "owed to mortal nature" is what is natural to it, and one example of something natural to a human body in the current life is to exist on or in close proximity to the surface of the earth. And in the current life we do not have the power to exist anywhere else – at least, in the absence of the kinds of artificial aids that Albert had never encountered. But the principle that we lack the unaided power not to exist in whatever is our natural place obtains for the resurrected body too. The natural place of the resurrected body is the empyrean heaven. So resurrected bodies lack the power of leaving that place.

A possible reply proposes that the principle that "bodies cannot move outside their place" is not the result of the nature of the body but from some non-natural weakness of the non-resurrected body. But this is rejected by the objector: the powers of the soul over the body correspond on a one-one basis with bodily organs. There is no organ that enables us to fly. So, we cannot fly, whatever the other intrinsic conditions of our bodies.

Albert replies to the two parts in turn:

> As Avicenna says, lassitude in forward motion is brought about from the contrariety of the elemental nature, which dominates over forward motion in a body. But then [viz. in heaven] the contrariety is removed, and there will not be [this] kind of contrariety by which it impedes motion to every part [of the universe].
>
> To that which is objected, that then that power should be manifested to us in some organ, I say that the powers of the sensible soul are manifested in organs, but not [the powers] of the rational soul, because it [viz. the rational soul] is not the perfection of any part of the body as of an organ (I mean a perfection conjoined to an organ). And for this reason, since forward motion with respect to every difference of place will be immediately from the will, there will be obedience of the body to every difference of place. Neither should it be conceded that then it [viz. the soul] makes use of the feet as an organ in that motion, because, as has been said, it is not a potency to a determinate organ, but its power is with respect to the whole body. And thus it does not follow that we would need to have wings. For the power of flying is a power affixed to a special organ, and not with respect to the whole body.[33]

The point here is that, in the natural human condition, motion of different types corresponds to – is individuated by – various bodily organs. The reply concedes what was assumed in the objection – that resurrected bodies are not the kinds of thing that can have wings. But it articulates a principle that explains the non-organic nature of the resurrected body's motion – namely, that the powers of the rational soul range over the whole body and are not restricted to organic activity. This is consistent with the principle that we do not need wings to "soar like eagles." On Albert's analysis, we would soar without flying – without using wings, which of course we will not have in this story.

The notion that the motion of a resurrected body will be non-organic was commonplace. We find it in Scotus, in a passage I have discussed extensively elsewhere.

> Glorified bodies after the resurrection will be moved by the soul non-organically. The whole body will be moved simultaneously,

not such that one part is moved while another is at rest, because "they shall run and not be weary." But this simultaneous motion of the whole body is not by means of an organ.[34] ... The same power by which [the soul] now moves the body organically is the same [as the power by which] it will move it non-organically after the resurrection.[35]

Note here that Scotus is clear that the relevant power is not a power of a supercharged soul: it is a power of a regular soul given a fully responsive body.

Other thinkers were not so sure about either the non-organic nature of the motion or its being in the power of the soul to bring such motion about. On the first of these, Aquinas, for example, affirms that, given the total subjection of the body to the soul, all that follows is that the body is "prompt and apt to obey the spirit in all motion and action of the soul,"[36] adding merely that this motion will involve no effort.

> The more the power of the moving soul dominates the body the less is the effort in a motion which is even brought about against the nature of the body. So those in whom the motive power is stronger, or who have, from exercise, a body more habituated to obeying the moving spirit, expend less effort in motion. And because after the resurrection the soul will perfectly dominate the body (both because of the perfection of the particular power, and because of the habituation of the glorified body from the redounding of glory from the soul to it), there will not be any effort in the motion of the saints. And in this way, it will be possible to call the bodies of the saints agile.[37]

A different line of objection was taken by the early 14th century Dominican Durand of St. Pourçain. Augustine had maintained that what explains the capacity of the risen body to move at all is God's taking away the weight (*pondus*) from a body that has a disposition to fall or sink (i.e., a body that is *grave*).[38] Durand follows Augustine and maintains that agility consists in weightlessness and that this is sufficient to explain the free motion of the resurrected body.[39] In particular, Durand cannot see how the powers of the pre-resurrected body could ever be such as to allow a body to move non-organically, whatever the circumstances.

> It is clear that every motive power which the soul now has can move the body in one way alone, namely organically, on account of which nature also gave to the body determinate organic parts for this motion, differing according to the differences of motion, just as there are some parts in animals that walk, and others in birds. But it gave no disposition to some other motion which belongs to the whole body in itself. On account of this it seems to be a fiction that a power of the soul should extend itself in some way to that motion.[40]

Durand cannot be right about this. Think about a weightless environment – something like that experienced by astronauts in space. Controlling motion in such environments is not at all a straightforward matter. But still, this gives us a different way of thinking about agility: not in terms of a power of the soul (whether a particular power proper to a supercharged soul or a regular power of the soul in the absence of an organic or bodily impediment) but in terms of a difference in the way the body relates to its environment – since all that weightlessness posits, for a medieval theologian, is a privation, not an intrinsic property. (Though, recall that medieval accounts of course have no notion of Newtonian or relativistic gravity.) In either case, we have theories that would allow for non-organic motion: we would not need to use legs (or wings!) in order to move ourselves around.

Scholastic Ableism

Evidently, the discussion thus far has focused on particular abilities and disabilities. None of this should give the impression that the standard scholastic assumptions were not profoundly ableist, whatever the treatment of particular kinds of bodily configurations. There are many issues on which one could focus to uncover these assumptions. I shall consider one: the debate about corporeal defects and the bodies of the damned. The starting point of the discussion is Augustine's speculations about the resurrected body in *Enchiridion* c. 23:

> The bodies of the saints, then, shall rise again free from blemish and deformity, just as they will be also free from corruption, encumbrance, or hardship. Their facility (*facilitas*) will be as complete as their felicity (*felicitas*). This is why their bodies are called "spiritual (*animale*)," though undoubtedly they will be bodies and not spirits (*anima*). For just as now the body is called "animate," though it is a body and not a "spirit," so then it will be a "spiritual body," but still a body and not a spirit ....[41]
>
> But whoever are not liberated from that mass of perdition (brought to pass through the first man) by the one Mediator between God and humanity, they will also rise again, each in his own flesh, but only that they may be punished together with the devil and his angels. Whether these will rise again with all their faults and deformities, with their diseased and deformed members – is there any reason for us to labor such a question? For obviously the uncertainty about their bodily form and beauty need not weary us, since their damnation is certain and eternal.[42]

Augustine's refraining from discussion was – rather typically – taken by the Schoolmen not as an exhortation to silence but as a provocation to further speculation.

Aquinas makes a distinction:

> Deformity can be in the human body in two ways. In one way, from a defect of some member, as we call the mutilated ugly, because there lacks in them a required proportion of parts to whole. And about this deformity, there is no doubt that it will not be in bodies of the damned, because all bodies, as much of the good as of the wicked, will rise whole. In another way, deformity arises from the undue disposition of parts, whether of quality or position, which is incompatible with the required proportion of parts to whole. And about these deformities and similar defects (such as fevers and illnesses, which are sometimes the cause of deformity), Augustine left indeterminate and subject to doubt in *Enchiridion*.

In relation to the second group, Aquinas reports the view of Bonaventure that damnation requires "maximal misery" and that a result of this is that "nothing of misfortune should be taken away from" the damned.[43] Albert takes a different view:

> The general resurrection corrects two things in nature, namely error and defect: error in the monstrosity of members, defect in the diminished stature of a body. And for this reason the damned will rise in the fullness of their members and fullness of stature.[44]

Aquinas follows Albert:

> Others say, more rationally, that the author who created nature will repair the nature of the body to integrity in the resurrection. So whatever defect or ugliness, following from the corruption or weakness of nature or of the principles of nature were in the body – such as fever, partial-sightedness, and such like – will be removed wholly in the resurrection. But defects which naturally follow the natural principles of a human body – such as weight, passibility, and such like – will be in the bodies of the damned, which defects the glory of the resurrection will exclude from the bodies of the elect.[45]

The point I wish to make is that *both* sides, however much they disagree with each other on the substantive question, share the same ableist assumption that disability and deformity are bad things: they are either a punishment for sin (the first view) or at least not part of perfected nature (the second view). One lesson – rather obvious – is that the disabilities sketched in my first two sections turn out not to be defects at all on these medieval accounts.

A Spiritualized Body?

While it is true that the bodies I have been describing lack certain kinds of capacities that we associated with the able body, it might be thought that they more than compensate for this lack by having their own superpowers, so to speak: they are not recognizable as human bodies because their very bodiliness has been transcended or spiritualized. To this extent, they might not be as friendly to theories of disability as I have been suggesting – they might, as I briefly considered in my introduction, be more akin to transhumanism, which is generally not thought amenable to a positive disability-theoretic assessment. As Fiona Kumari Campbell rather trenchantly puts it:

> Whilst the movement towards transhumanism may bring gifts for the contemporary "needy," the transhuman project, as it is founded on an unbridled form of ableism combined with an "obsessive technological compulsion," will involve a meagre shuffling of the deckchairs .... The rankings remain the same (albeit with new labels that tell us and others who we are). Transhumanism reasserts systems of ranking bodies.[46]

And the claims about impassibility, from this perspective, raise further issues of their own. Here again is Campbell:

> Possibilities of posthumanism developed within the context of technologies of ableism may provide a "new deal" for some – but on closer examination the tentacles of ableism reassert [themselves] through the ... dominant trend in the literature and research to propose a virile style of transhumanism that despises vulnerability.[47]

To begin with bodiliness in general, Brenz, for example, believes that the ideal body is not spatial at all: for him, it is not only walking "from place to place" that is excluded from the ideal body; it is being "circumscribed by place," being spatial at all, that is excluded.[48] Understandably, his opponents thought that what he was describing was simply incompatible with bodiliness altogether.

As the medieval theologians saw it, what is most characteristic of the resurrected body is that it is fully under the control of the soul: as we might say, it is fully under our own personal control – hence Aquinas's powerful language of "dominion" noted above.[49] The medieval accounts are akin to transhumanism in the sense that they posit some radically new powers for the resurrected body and mechanisms by which those powers might be instantiated. They are not formally transhumanist, of course, since a fundamental *desideratum* of the medieval theories is that what is resurrected is a human body, not something of an altogether

Disability and Resurrection 273

different kind. Equally, transhumanism by and large adapts the body for its more successful survival in the kinds of environment in which we currently find ourselves. Medieval accounts are different. They adapt the body for a very different kind of environment: existence in the empyrean heaven (or the fires of hell). Any such view perhaps "despises vulnerability," but that is because it values bodily responsiveness and (ultimately) autonomy over other features. Part of the point is that resurrected bodies will be able to encounter one another. But another part of the view is each human person will depend wholly and immediately on God, and not on other human persons.

Notes

1 Johannes Brenz, *Recognitio propheticae et apostolicae doctrinae de vera maiestate Domini nostri Jesu Christi, de dextera Dei Patri omnipotentis*, 58.
2 For a general history, see Nikolaus Wicki, *Die Lehre von der himmlischen Seligkeit in der mittelalterlichen Scholastik von Petrus Lombardus bis Thomas von Aquin*.
3 See Praepositinus, *De sacramentis et novissimis*, 121.
4 See Alexander of Hales, *Glossa in quattuor libros sententiarum*, IV, d. 11, n. 17, 4:181.8; Alexander of Hales, *Quaestiones disputatae 'antequam esset frater'*, q. 65, 3:1322.24; 1328.7; 1331.12.
5 Hugh of St. Cher, *Quaestio de dotibus resurgentium*, quoted in the apparatus of Albert, *De resurrection*, 26:336, n. 33. For Hugh on the *dotes* of the soul in general, see Magdalena Bieniak, "Hugh of St. Cher (†1263) on the *dotes* of the Soul: A Question from Douai, BM, MS 464," 67–90.
6 See Joseph Goering, "The *De dotibus* of Robert Grosseteste," 83–109.
7 See the text quoted in the apparatus of Albert, *De res.*, n. 56, 339.
8 Aquinas, *Scriptum super sententiis*, IV, d. 44, q. 2, a. 1, qc. 3, obj 1, referring to Aristotle, *De an.*, l. 2, c. 2 (403b25-7). I use the edition of Aquinas's works edited by R. Busa, at http://www.corpusthomisticum.org/iopera.html. Some of the issues I deal with in this section are discussed in Alastair Minnis, *From Eden to Eternity: Creations of Paradise in the Later Middle Ages*, 197–207. To judge by Minnis's appraisal of the theoretical adequacy of the various views he discusses, he tends to view bodily wholeness as the relevant theological *desideratum* and does not approach the issues from a disability-theoretic perspective in the way that I attempt to here. Minnis's discussion contains, nevertheless, a great deal of interest and relevance to my treatment of the matter.
9 See, e.g., Augustine, *De trinitate* IX, c. 3, § 3, 296, ll. 8–15.
10 Albert, *De res.*, tr. III, q. 4, n. 112, 311b.
11 Albert, *De res.*, tr. IV, q. 2, a. 4, n. 159, 343a–b.
12 Albert, *De res.*, tr. IV, q. 4, n. 1112, 312a.
13 Aquinas, *Super sent.* IV, d. 44, q. 2, a. 1, qc. 3, co.
14 Aquinas, *Super sent.* IV, d. 44, q. 2, a. 1, qc. 3, co.
15 Aquinas, *Super sent.* IV, d. 44, q. 2, a. 1, qc. 3, co.
16 There are more complex cases – such as sight. In the early text I am discussing here, he claims that in such cases we find a spiritual change without a natural one – "the pupil receives the species of whiteness without being made white" (Aquinas, *Super sent.* IV, d. 44, q. 2, a. 1, qc. 3, co). Elsewhere he seems to think that there is some kind of bodily change in sight, presupposed

to the spiritual change: but not a natural change in the sense just outlined, according to which the recipient becomes an instance of the received form: for instance,

> sensing and the consequent operations of the sensory soul manifestly occur along with some alteration of the body – as, in the case of seeing, the pupil is altered through the species of a color, and the same is evident for the other [senses]

(Aquinas, *Summa theologiae* I. q, 75, a. 2, co, trans. Robert Pasnau, *Theories of Cognition in the Later Middle Ages*, 43). Understanding the nature of this bodily but non-natural change has been the subject of a vast controversy in the literature.

17 Aquinas, *Super sent.* IV, d. 44, q. 2, a. 1, qc. 3, co.
18 Aquinas, *Super sent.* IV, d. 44, q. 2, a. 1, qc. 1, co.
19 Aquinas, *Super sent.* IV, d. 44, q. 2, a. 1, qc. 1, co.
20 Aquinas, *Super sent.* IV, d. 44, q. 3, a. 2, qc. 2, ad 1.
21 Scotus, *Ordinatio* IV, d. 49, p. 2, q. un., n. 437, 14:404.
22 Scotus, *Ord.* IV, d. 44, p. 2, q. 2, n. 127, 14:127.
23 Scotus, *Ord.* IV, d. 44, p. 2, q. 2, n. 125, 14:126.
24 Aquinas, *Super sent.* IV, d. 44, q. 2, a. 1, qc. 4, co.
25 Aquinas, *Super sent.* IV, d. 44, q. 2, a. 1, qc. 4, co. Minnis has suggested that perhaps Aquinas has in mind an antiphon for the feast of All Saints, or perhaps, quoting Susan Ashbrook Harvey, just "a wider tradition" associating "sweet fragrance with the deaths, bodies, and relics of the saints and martyrs" (Minnis, *From Eden*, 205, quoting Harvey, *Scenting Salvation: Ancient Christianity and the Olfactory Imagination*, 227).
26 Bonaventure, *Commentaria in quatuor libros Sententiarum* IV, d. 49, p. 2, s. 1, a. 3, q. 1 c, 4:1018b–1019a.
27 Bonaventure, *In sent.* IV, d. 49, p. 2, s. 1, a. 3, q. 1 ad 1, 4:1019a.
28 Albert, *De res.*, tr. II, q. 8, a. 2, n. 58, 271a.
29 Albert, *De res.*, tr. II, q. 8, a. 2, n. 58, 272a.
30 Albert, *De res.*, tr. II, q. 8, a. 2, n. 59, 272a–b.
31 Albert, *De res.*, tr. II, q. 8, a. 2, n. 59, 272b.
32 Albert, *De res.*, tr. II, q. 8, a. 2, n. 58, 271a–b.
33 Albert, *De res.*, tr. II, q. 8, a. 2, n. 59, 272b.
34 Scotus, *Reportatio* IV, d. 49, q. 13; quoting Isaiah 40:31 (printed as *Ordinatio* IV, d. 49, q. 14, n. 5 [*Opera omnia*, ed. L. Wadding, 12 vols. (Lyon, 1639), 10:595]).
35 Scotus, *Reportatio* IV, d. 49, q. 13 (printed as *Ordinatio* IV, d. 49, q. 14, n. 7 [Wadding, 10:595]). I discuss these passages in my "Disability, Impairment, and Some Medieval Accounts of the Incarnation: Suggestions for a Theology of Personhood," *Modern Theology*, 27 (2011): 639–658, especially 652–653.
36 Aquinas, *Super sent.* IV, d. 44, q. 2, a. 3, qc. 1, co.
37 Aquinas, *Super sent.* IV, d. 44, q. 2, a. 3, qc. 1, ad 2.
38 Augustine, *De civitate dei*, XXII, c. 11, 2:586, ll. 23–26.
39 Durand, *Scriptum super I V libros sententiarum* IV, d. 45, q. 7, 4.4: 140–142.
40 Durand, *Super sent.* IV, d. 45, q. 7, 144.
41 Augustine, *Enchiridion*, c. 23, § 91, 98, ll. 93–99; see, Augustine, *Confessions and Enchiridion*, 392.
42 Augustine, *Enchiridion*, c. 23, § 92, 99, ll. 115–123; see, Augustine, *Confessions and Enchiridion*, 393.

43 Aquinas, *Super sent.* IV, d. 44, q. 3, a. 1, qc. 1, co., referring to Bonaventure, *In sent.* IV, d. 44, p. 1, a. 3, q. 2.
44 Albert, *De res.*, tr. III, q. 1, 305a.
45 Aquinas, *Super sent.* IV, d. 44, q. 3, a. 1, qc. 1, co.
46 Fiona Kumari Campbell, *Contours of Ableism: The Production of Disability and Abledness*, 73–74.
47 Campbell, *Contours of Ableism*, 75.
48 Brenz, *Recognitio*, 58.
49 I have recently attempted to develop an account of disability along these lines, understanding disability in terms of a mismatch between body, environment, and interests or desires: see my "Impairment, Normalcy, and a Social Theory of Disability," 705.

References

Primary Sources

Albert the Great. *Opera omnia*. Edited by Bernhard Geyer and others. Münster: Aschendorff, 1951–.

Alexander of Hales. *Glossa in quattuor libros sententiarum*. 4 vols., Bibliotheca Franciscana scholastica medii aevi, 12–15. Quaracchi: Collegium S. Bonaventurae, 1951–1957.

Alexander of Hales. *Quaestiones disputatae 'antequam esset frater'*. 3 vols., Bibliotheca Franciscana scholastica medii aevi, 19–21. Quaracchi: Collegium S. Bonaventurae, 1960.

Aquinas, Thomas. *Opera omnia*. Edited by R. Busa. <http://www.corpusthomisticum.org/iopera.html>.

Augustine. *Confessions and Enchiridion*. Translated by Albert C. Outler. Library of Christian Classics. Philadelphia: Westminster Press, 1955.

Augustine. *De civitate dei*. Edited by B. Dombart and A. Kolb, 5th ed., 2 vols. Bibliotheca scriptorum Graecorum et Romanorum Teubneriana. Stuttgart: Teubner, 1981.

Augustine. *De fide rerum invisibilium, Enchiridion* [etc.]. Corpus Christianorum series Latina, 46. Turnhout: Breopols, 1969.

Augustine. *De trinitate*. Edited by W. J. Mountain. Corpus Christianorum series Latina, 50. Turnhout: Brepols, 1968.

Bonaventure. *Opera omnia*, 10 vols. Quaracchi: Collegium Sancti Bonaventurae, 1882–1902.

Brenz, Johannes. *Recognitio propheticae et apostolicae doctrinae de vera maiestate Domini nostri Jesu Christi, de dextera Dei Patri omnipotentis*. Tübingen, 1564.

Duns Scotus, John. *Opera omnia*. Edited by L. Wadding, 12 vols. Lyon, 1639.

Duns Scotus, John. *Opera omnia*. Edited by C. Balić and others, 21 vols. Vatican City: Vatican Press, 1950–2013.

Durand of St. Pourçain. *Scriptum super IV libros sententiarum*. Edited by Fiorella Retucci and others. Leuven, Paris, Walpole, MA: Peeters, 2012–.

Praepositinus of Cremona. *De sacramentis et novissimis*. Edited by Daniel E. Pilarczyk. Rome: Editiones Urbaniana, 1964.

Secondary Sources

Bieniak, Magdalena. "Hugh of St. Cher (†1263) on the *dotes* of the Soul: A Question from Douai, BM, MS 464," *Bulletin de philosophie médiévale* 49 (2007): 67–90.

Campbell, Fiona Kumari. *Contours of Ableism: The Production of Disability and Abledness*. London: Palgrave Macmillan, 2009.

Cross, Richard. "Impairment, Normalcy, and a Social Theory of Disability." *Res philosophica* 93 (2016): 693–714.

Goering, Joseph. "The *De dotibus* of Robert Grosseteste." *Mediaeval Studies* 44 (1982): 83–109.

Harvey, Susan Ashbrook. *Scenting Salvation: Ancient Christianity and the Olfactory Imagination*. Berkeley: University of California Press, 2006.

Minnis, Alastair. *From Eden to Eternity: Creations of Paradise in the Later Middle Ages*. The Middle Ages Series. Philadelphia: University of Pennsylvania Press, 2016.

Pasnau, Robert. *Theories of Cognition in the Later Middle Ages*. Cambridge: Cambridge University Press, 1997.

Wicki, Nikolaus. *Die Lehre von der himmlischen Seligkeit in der mittelalterlichen Scholastik von Petrus Lombardus bis Thomas von Aquin*, Studia Friburgensia, NF, 9. Freiburg: Universitätsverlag, 1954.

10 Relative Disability and Transhuman Happiness
St. Thomas Aquinas on the Beatific Vision

Thomas M. Ward

Introduction

Many medieval Christian theologians taught that the highest human good is a certain kind of relationship to God, a relationship of *enjoyment*, often referred to as *beatific vision*, in which the intellect has immediate access to the divine essence such that the desires of the will are fully satisfied. It was a commonplace among these theologians that a human being does not have the ability to enjoy the divine essence exclusively by his or her own efforts. This disability is not just due to the fact that human beings were understood to be damaged by original sin. Even supposing there had been no sin, we still would not be able to reach the beatific vision by our own abilities. No other person or any created thing is equipped to help us; therefore, only God can raise us to that naturally unobtainable natural end of the beatific vision. On Thomas Aquinas's account of beatific vision – probably the most well-known medieval account – we need both an extrinsic power added to our nature and a divine actualization of that power; that is, God both adds an ability to our human nature that we do not by nature possess and also activates that power. Fancifully, to reach God's heaven, God himself must strap the rocket pack onto your back and then turn it on. This view warrants the following claims, which I want to develop and defend in this chapter: for Aquinas, human well-being does not consist in the full actualization of the powers intrinsic to human nature. In this respect, Aquinas's understanding of human being and well-being constitutes a radical departure from the eudaimonistic essentialism of Aristotle. Relative to the ones blessed with beatific vision, every merely human being, however excellent by Aristotle's standards, is disabled.

Relative Disability

Disability is a relative concept. A blind person and a rock are similar in that neither can see. But the rock is not disabled in virtue of being unable to see, whereas a blind person, just insofar as she is blind, is disabled. These judgments are warranted, if at all, because the abilities of some particular rock are not assessed relative to standards such as human nature, or human societies, or human subjective preferences, whereas the abilities of some particular human being are assessed relative to these sorts of human standards.[1] There is a legitimate question here about what warrants the ability-assessment of some particular human being relative to any of these standards, and in our own time, perhaps especially to the standard of human nature. This standard, for better or for worse, is the one most relevant to thinking through Aquinas's reflections on human well-being. Aquinas assumes that human nature gives us one kind of standard for making judgments about human well-being. Whatever the merits of this assumption on its own terms, it is worth thinking about, if for no other reason, because it is an assumption in play in our own ordinary-language practice of referring to persons who lack certain abilities as disabled. This practice invokes some, albeit hazy, notion of what it is to be human and what it is for a human to be well: we assume some norm about the abilities a human, qua human, ought to have and apply the label "disabled" to those who lack one or more of these abilities.

This is neither a consistent nor morally neutral practice. Judging by the grammar of disabled and cognate words in ordinary English, we all give ourselves a pass when it comes to *moral* defect, such that a person who lacks moral or intellectual virtues, but otherwise has "normal" physical and cognitive powers, is not described as a disabled person, despite the fact that moral defect is arguably more a hindrance to living a good human life than cognitive or physical disability. We judge by the wrong standards, to be sure, and a properly impartial practice of using the term "disabled" would leave us all disabled, and many of the able-bodied among us far more disabled than our physically disabled brothers and sisters.

Yet, inconsistent, unfair, and liable to abuse as our practice is, it is usually intelligible. And the practice is only intelligible with some idea in mind of what a human body or mind (and character!) *ought* to be. Moreover, we assume that a human being's having the abilities a human qua human ought to have is part of what it is for a human being to have well-being. Complete well-being for a human, by this standard, just is the life in which all abilities intrinsic to human nature are present and fully actualized. To the extent that a human being is disabled relative to this standard, that human lacks one or more goods that are part of what human well-being consists in. The practical impossibility of *perfect* well-being, by this standard, is no knock against the standard: as we (asymptotically, to be sure) approach the standard, we are happier; the farther away from it we are, the less happy we are.

Various lines of criticism can be pursued against this essentialist account of disability: metaphysical, epistemological, and ethical. Metaphysically, we might wonder whether there is such a thing as human nature, which can legitimate judgments about disability relative to it. Epistemologically, we might wonder whether, even if there were such a thing as human nature, we have or can have a sufficient grasp of it to legitimate disability judgments relative to it.

Ethically, we might interrogate the assumption implicit in disability judgments that the disabled person lacks some value that a "normally" abled person has. At one extreme, explicitly or implicitly a disabled person might be considered less valuable, objectively or third-personally, than a non-disabled person. Few would embrace such a position explicitly, though it seems to linger implicitly in some of our cultural practices, such as high relative rates of abortion of fetuses diagnosed with abnormalities such as Down's Syndrome. Even where we balk at deeming a disabled life less objectively valuable, we might wonder whether disability as such detracts from the disabled person's ability to live a life that is subjectively fulfilling for him or her, and how seriously to take first person reports, where they are possible.

It is probably impossible to say how seriously Aquinas would take first person reports of subjective well-being, but we can be certain he thought each mere mortal, in this life, however abled, not only cannot be perfectly fulfilled or happy but desires to be happier than he or she currently is. Aquinas's essentialism is metaphysically realist and epistemologically optimistic about human nature: there is such a thing, and we can know a lot about it. His essentialism also holds that there is a sort of happiness-lite which is available to some of us in this life and which has nothing to do with God, a natural fulfillment of human powers and desires which are accurately sketched in Aristotle's *Nicomachean Ethics*. No human life can perfectly live up to this standard as Aristotle himself was the first to admit, but the closer we get to this standard, the happier – relative to that standard – we are. But Aquinas's assessment of the imperfectability of human nature is far more dramatic than Aristotle's. Aquinas not only agreed with Aristotle that by merely human standards no human being can be perfectly happy; he also held that every human being by nature desires something – the infinite good – which it cannot by its natural powers achieve. Our natural desiring aims at a condition of life which our natural powers – all of them working together in concert, maxing out human nature – cannot attain.

If the abilities intrinsic to human nature are not sufficient to make it the case that, were those abilities fully present and fully actualized in some particular person, the person would not thereby enjoy complete well-being, then maxing out human nature is at best instrumental to or merely a part of complete well-being. That is to say, maxing out human nature is, at best, necessary but not sufficient for complete well-being. And this view is implicit in Aquinas's view that the highest human good involves an activity – enjoyment of God – which our nature does not equip us to perform. Yet it is, according to Aquinas, the one and only activity which can give a human life complete well-being. It is immensely attractive; it is longed for, explicitly by Christians and implicitly by everyone else. Human living is incomplete, unfulfilled, restless, without it. So, simultaneously, beatific vision is beyond human ability and is that in which complete well-being consists. Relative to those who have been given the ability to have beatific vision, *the saints*, as I will call them, we mere mortals, *wayfarers*, as I will call us, are disabled.

Transhumanization and the Preparation for Paradise

As a nice picture of what I have in mind by saying that relative to the saints, we are all disabled, I want to mention one aspect of Dante Alighieri's attempt to put the experience of heavenly transformation into words. In *Paradiso* I, Dante has just arrived in Paradise, guided by his beloved Beatrice. Blinded at first by the brilliance of Paradise, he turns his eyes to Beatrice and in that gaze undergoes a great change:

> 'Twas even thus a change came over me;
> As Glaucus, eating of the weed, changed race
> And grew a god among the gods of sea.
>
> Transhumanized—the fact mocks human phrase;
> So let the example serve, till proof requite
> Him who is called to experience this by grace.[2]

Transhumanization is a startling description of this change from wayfarer to saint. But Dante was not being licentious when he coined the term *trasumanar*. Similar thoughts, expressed rather differently, can be found in Aquinas's discussion of beatific vision. I'll discuss this in what follows, but first I want to spend some time setting up Aquinas's view by discussing his reasons for thinking that complete human well-being consists in something transcendent of human nature.

Aquinas on the Natural End of Human Nature

In Questions 1–5 of the First Part of the Second Part of *Summa theologiae*, Aquinas argues that there is one ultimate end of human life,[3] that this ultimate end is beatitude (*beatitudo*),[4] that beatitude cannot be found in any created thing,[5] that it in fact is found only in the beatific vision,[6] and that God alone makes us both able to have beatific vision and actually have it.[7] Human beings will everything they will for the sake of the ultimate end. This is evident because whatever they will, they will under the aspect of the good. Whatever is willed under the aspect of the good is willed either for the sake of some other good or for its own sake.[8] But there must be some good which we will for its own sake, since the goods that are willed move the will to its willing, and in essentially ordered series of movers there cannot be an infinite regress of movers.[9] So there must be some good on account of which we will all other goods and which we will for its own sake. Aquinas calls this good the complete good (*bonum perfectum*). All things act for the sake of their complete good, but humans do so with reason and will, and this warrants calling the human end beatitude.[10]

The complete good for a human being cannot be found in any created thing. This is because the complete good is a good which "totally satisfies a human being's appetite." The object of the will is the universal good, and this is found only in God. So only God can satisfy the appetite, and therefore only God can be the complete good for a human being, its ultimate end.[11] Aquinas's point here is that the will, by nature, desires goodness as such, not just this or that particular good. Whatever degree and kinds of created goods the will enjoys, it will always desire more goodness. Aquinas of course believes that there is such a thing which is infinite goodness, the source of all finite goodness. So this feature of the human will, its dissatisfaction with finite goodness, is not ultimately tragic: the heart's deepest desires can be realized.

God totally satisfies the appetite in a very specific way. It is not enough simply to know that God exists or that God is infinitely good. Unless the intellect has a vision of God's essence, it will not be satisfied. This is because, until we have such a vision, the intellect's ignorance of the essence of the First Cause of all things makes the will restless. By nature, we human beings want to keep asking *why?* until we get the deepest possible understanding. In this state of epistemic restlessness, we are not perfectly happy. Only when the intellect achieves the union with God in which God's essence is known can the will's appetite be satisfied.[12]

But this union with God, in which we find ultimate happiness, is beyond the natural powers of human beings. As Aquinas puts it, "The ultimate happiness that has been prepared for the Saints outstrips human intellect and will."[13] We can't get God in our intellects in the way required for beatific vision, because our intellectual powers are oriented toward material reality. No other creature can equip us for beatific vision, either.[14] So only God can do it for us.

You might think, with judgment, punishment, and reward in mind, that there is one way in which we do bring ourselves to beatific vision. After all, this vision is reserved for the saints, and the saints are the ones who have followed God's laws and have approached perfection in the love of God and neighbor in this mortal life. Beatific vision, you might think, is the reward for such a life. Aquinas only sort of agrees. He thinks that it is "fitting" that we achieve happiness by doing good works and receiving beatitude as a reward for those good works.[15] But Aquinas concedes that our good works play no real *causal* role in getting us to our reward. Aquinas reasons this way: rectitude or rightness of will is required for happiness; it is impossible for God to make an evil will happy, the will remaining evil. So the will has got to have rectitude logically *prior* to receiving beatitude. But, Aquinas continues, God could simultaneously cause the will to have rectitude and to receive beatitude. God, in his wisdom, does what is "fitting" and lets us play a role in bringing ourselves to have rectitude of will, at which point God takes over and raises us to beatitude.[16] However wise or fitting this is, however, Aquinas's reflections show that no human's activity, however morally perfect, is enough to compel or cause God to give that human beatitude. So blessedness is something we cannot do for ourselves and something we can't get God, through our good behavior, to do for us. We are in every way dependent on God for beatitude.

Aquinas on the Unnatural Means of Achieving the Natural End

So what is it that God has to do to us to give us beatitude? To answer, we turn from the early questions of the First Part of the Second Part to Question 12 of the First Part of the *Summa*. Here we get the marvelous claim that in the beatific vision, God himself – not an intellectual likeness of God, or a concept, or anything mental like that, but God himself – becomes, in Aquinas's words, "the intelligible form of the intellect."[17] At least part of what this amounts to is that in beatific vision, we have immediate cognitive access to God. We don't think God *via* any likeness or concept. When it's the divine essence we're cognizing, God himself plays the role a likeness or concept would play in the cognition of anything else.

This elevation to such sublimity (as Aquinas describes it) demands some special preparation of our cognitive faculties. We need a "supernatural disposition" added to our intellect, which Aquinas calls a "created light." Aquinas goes on:

> since the natural power of a created intellect does not suffice for seeing the essence of God ... it is necessary that this power of understanding be added onto it by divine grace. We call this augmentation of intellectual power the illumination of the intellect, just as the intelligible thing itself is called light or illumination .... Through this light [the saints] are made deiform, that is, similar to God.[18]

Here we have God first prepping the intellect to have beatific vision by adding to or augmenting the intellect with this supernatural disposition. So disposed, the intellect is then prepared to enjoy immediate cognitive access to God. Aquinas's talk of deiformity here should put us in mind of Dante's Glaucus image: just as Glaucus was transformed from man to god when he ate the magic seaweed, the saint changes from human to God-like in the beatific vision.

But this immediate cognitive access to God is not the whole story of beatific vision. Beatitude, as we've seen, involves the will's achieving its desire to enjoy the universal good. So it's not enough just to think the divine essence. The supernatural disposition of the intellect prepares the soul to cognize God in such a way that God is known to be a completely satisfying good with no possible drawback. The will responds to this clear intellectual vision of God with complete and unwavering love. As Aquinas says, "The vision of the divine essence fills the soul with every good."[19] According to Aquinas's understanding of the will, it necessarily wills (enjoys) God when the intellect has the power to present God to the will as unqualifiedly desirable. From this it follows that, having achieved beatific vision, it is impossible for the will ever to turn itself away from God. Thus, enjoying the goodness of God and secure in its ability to go on enjoying this goodness, the desire of the will is fulfilled. So the full story of beatific vision, for Aquinas, involves, primarily, the intellect's union with God as the immediate object of its activity and, secondarily, the will's necessary perpetual adherence to God thus cognized.

Aquinas Against the Idol of Human Nature

Let's take stock. From the preceding discussion of Aquinas on the beatific vision, it should be clear that the beatific vision is not *contrary* to our human nature in any way. The will, by nature, wills the universal good, which is God. The restlessness itself of the will is not due to a supernatural disposition whereby God suits the will to be happy only with God; that restlessness rather is just built into the nature of will. Thus, given our human nature as partially constituted by our faculty of will, it makes sense that God would provide a way to satisfy the will's transcendent longing. In this sense, beatific vision, while outside our natural powers, is the natural completion of the will's willing. While God must augment our nature in order to get us to beatific vision, this augmentation is to be expected given what the will is and given God's care for his human creatures. But the naturalness or expectedness of this augmentation still leaves it the case that beatific vision requires gaining a power that is beyond our nature. In beatific vision we remain human, but we are made more than human. We are, to return to Dante's word, transhumanized. (See Richard Cross's discussion of transhumanism in chapter 9.)

I said earlier that relative to the saints, we wayfarers are disabled. I hope now that we're in a position for this claim to make more sense. If the saints were non-human, not simply beyond the human, then success-in-the-category of sainthood would be as alien and irrelevant to us wayfarers as success-in-the-category of being a rock. It would make no sense for us to assess our own abilities as wayfarers against the standard set by the saints. But the saints are not non-human. We are supposed to be able to recognize in the saints the achievement of what we all long for: union with the supreme good, perfect beatitude, complete well-being. And, according to Aquinas, the saints have this achievement because they have an ability we wayfarers lack. Relative to the saints, we are not just differently abled, we are disabled, because that extra ability they possess is precisely what enables them to have the complete well-being we all want.

What this shows, I suggest, is that in Aquinas we see how human nature and human well-being come apart. A person in possession of all the powers intrinsic to human nature, full of virtue, blessed with all the goods of fortune, Aristotle tells us, the *eudaimon* must have – health, wealth, good looks, a good upbringing – is still radically deficient with respect to the one thing that can make his or her life completely blessed. Moreover, possessing all these goods is not even *instrumentally ordered* to complete well-being. For a Christian like Aquinas, believing that the good life according to Aristotle is the final word about human flourishing is idolatrous, because it implies that we have no need of God for our well-being. And believing that the good life according to Aristotle is instrumentally ordered to our supernatural end of union with God is heretical, because it is Pelagian: it assumes that by our own efforts, we can activate a beatifying response from God. So Aquinas opposes the whole Aristotelian tradition of identifying human flourishing with realizing the full potential of human nature. He is undoubtedly an essentialist, but he is a *transessentialist*.

Human Aspiration and Tragedy

Let me close by suggesting what an atheist or agnostic might be able to value in Aquinas's reflections on the beatific vision, as these pertain to the relationship between disability and human well-being. Suppose there is no God; then there is no beatific vision. But Aquinas's teaching about the will's restlessness, its natural tendency to go on desiring goodness no matter what degree or kinds of finite goodness it enjoys, is plausible. If it's right, then no finite good, *including complete success in the category of being human*, can be that in which human well-being consists. So an Aristotelian conception of human nature should not dictate the conditions under which a human being has well-being. Being *disabled*, in current ordinary linguistic practice, involves lacking some ability belonging to human nature, an ability which is taken to make one who has it better off, *ceteris paribus*, than another who lacks it. But if we have no good reason to suppose that success in the category of being human is the key to a happy life, then we should resist current practice. Human desiring does not max out when human nature maxes out, and maxing out human nature is not even instrumentally ordered to maxing out human desiring.

What to do then with this desiring, this infinite longing? Aquinas's answer is to affirm the longing but to reject as mere fantasy a trust that human medicine or politics or commerce will satisfy this longing. A different sort of answer is to reject the longing. It makes us restless; unhappiness is a necessary corollary of it. We might then acknowledge the wisdom in the Four Noble Truths, that human desire is the cause of suffering and the only way to alleviate suffering, and so achieve whatever degree of not-horribleness we humans are capable of achieving, is to quell desire through asceticism. A third way, more reflective of current practice in the so-called postmodern societies, is to go all in for desire but reject the transcendent and (by merely human powers) unreachable conditions for its full satiation. For all we know about the human condition in a godless world, we should let our restless wills seek out their own paths to their own versions of the best life. Of course, in such a world, it also turns out that human well-being is impossible. With a restless will and no God, human life is fundamentally tragic. Hopefully those inclined to this tragic vision can make the best of it. But making the best of it will not entail, or even make it likely, that only those lives possessing all the goods intrinsic to human nature are candidates for the best sort of happiness we human beings can have. In this respect, a modern hedonist consumerist and the medieval Dominican friar are allies.

Notes

1 In the language of some contemporary disability studies, we roughly can correlate the standards set by human nature, societies, and subjective preferences, respectively, with the medical, social, and cultural "models" of disability. Ronald Berger, *Introducing Disability Studies*, 26–30. Human nature considered as a standard relative to which we can assess disability is, depending on your metaphysical view about what a human person is, potentially more expansive than the medical model of disability. The relevant similarity is that the human nature model and the medical model each take it to be the case that there are objective facts about what it is for any human, qua human, to be and to be well.
2 Dante Alighieri, *Paradiso* I.67–72.
3 Quotations from *Summa theologiae* [=ST] are taken from the Dominican Fathers translation, easily found on the Internet at <http://www.newadvent.org/summa/>. Thomas Aquinas, *ST* I-II q.1, a.4–7.
4 Thomas Aquinas, *ST* I-II q.1, a.8; q.5, a.8.
5 Ibid., *ST* I-II q.2, a.8.
6 Ibid., *ST* I-II q.3, a.8.
7 Ibid., *ST* I-II q.5, a.6, 8.
8 Ibid., *ST* I-II q.1, a.6, co.
9 Ibid., *ST* I-II q.1, a.4, co.
10 Ibid., *ST* I-II q.1, a.8.
11 Ibid., *ST* I-II q.2, a.8.
12 Ibid., *ST* I-II q.3, a.8.
13 Ibid., *ST* I-II q.5, a.5, s.c.
14 Ibid., *ST* I-II q.5, a.6.
15 Ibid., *ST* I-II q.5, a.7, co.
16 Ibid.

17 Ibid., *ST* Ia q.12, a.5, co.
18 Ibid., *ST* Ia q.12, a.5, co.
19 Ibid., *ST* I–II q.5, a.4, co.

References

Primary Sources

Aquinas, Thomas. *Summa Theologiae*. Translated by English Dominican Fathers. <www.newadvent.org/summa/>

Dante Alighieri. *Paradiso*. Translated by Sayers and Reynolds. London: Penguin, 1962.

Secondary Source

Berger, Ronald. *Introducing Disability Studies*. Boulder: Lynne Rienner, 2013.

Contributors

Richard Cross is John A. O'Brien Professor of philosophy at the University of Notre Dame. He has published extensively on issues in medieval philosophy and theology with a particular focus on Duns Scotus. His most recent book is *Communicatio Idiomatum: Reformation Christological Debates*. https://orcid.org/0000-0003-1932-2993

Gloria Frost is Associate Professor of philosophy at the University of St. Thomas (Minn.). She has published articles on a variety of medieval thinkers and is currently completing a book on Aquinas's views about causal powers and efficient causation.

Jenni Kuuliala works as Senior Research Fellow at the Centre of Excellence in the History of Experiences at Tampere University, Finland. Her research focuses on late medieval and early modern hagiography, miraculous healing, disability, and lived religion. Her publications include *Childhood Disability and Social Integration in the Middle Ages: Constructions of Impairments in Thirteenth- and Fourteenth-Century Canonization Processes* (2016) and *Saints, Infirmities, and Communities in the Late Middle Ages* (2020). https://orcid.org/0000-0002-2770-2219

Miguel J. Romero is Assistant Professor of religious and theological studies at Salve Regina University. His published work includes "Aquinas on Happiness and Those Who Lack the Use of Reason" (*The Thomist*, 2016) and "The Goodness and Beauty of Our Fragile Flesh: Moral Theologians and Our Engagement with Disability" (*The Journal of Moral Theology*, 2017). https://orcid.org/0000-0002-5574-3157

John T. Slotemaker is Associate Professor of religious studies at Fairfield University. He has written *Anselm of Canterbury and the Search for God* (2018), with Jeffrey C. Witt, has co-authored *Robert Holcot* (2016), and co-edited *A Companion to the Theology of John Mair* (2015) and *Augustine in Late Medieval Philosophy and Theology* (2017). He is currently completing two books on medieval trinitarian theology.

Mark K. Spencer is Associate Professor of philosophy at the University of St. Thomas in St. Paul, Minnesota. He earned his PhD in philosophy at the University at Buffalo. He specializes in scholastic metaphysics and natural theology, phenomenology, and personalism, with a particular interest in issues having to do with the nature of the human person. He is the author of more than 30 articles on topics in these and other related areas. https://orcid.org/0000-0002-8829-9697

Kevin Timpe holds the William H. Jellema Chair in Christian Philosophy at Calvin University. His recent books include *The Lost Sheep in Philosophy of Religion: New Perspectives on Disability, Gender, Race, and Animals* (2019); *Disability and Inclusive Communities* (2018); the *Routledge Companion to Free Will* (2017); and *Free Will and Theism* (2016). His scholarly work focuses on philosophy of disability, philosophy of religion, metaphysics, and virtue ethics. https://orcid.org/0000-0002-3661-8166

Reima Välimäki is a postdoctoral research fellow at the Department of Cultural History, University of Turku, Finland. He obtained his PhD in 2016, and the book *Heresy in Late Medieval Germany: The Inquisitor Petrus Zwicker and the Waldensians*, based on Välimäki's dissertation, came out from York Medieval Press in 2019. Välimäki has been actively engaging in public history. Since 2015 he has worked as the historical expert of the Medieval Market event in Turku. Recently he has been taking part in two public history projects: 'Vihan pitkät jäljet' on the long history of hate speech (2017–2018) and 'Vammaisuuden vaiettu historia' on disability history (2017–2019). https://orcid.org/0000-0002-8301-6563

Christina Van Dyke is Professor of philosophy at Calvin University, specializing in medieval philosophy and the philosophy of gender. Much of her recent research combines those two areas and challenges the idea that women didn't do philosophy in the Middle Ages. She is currently completing a book, *A Hidden Wisdom: Medieval Contemplatives on Self-Knowledge, Reason, Will, Persons, and Immortality*, that focuses on what medieval contemplatives (such as Marguerite Porete, Hadewijch, Catherine of Siena, Angela of Foligno, and Mechtild of Magdeburg) have to say about self-knowledge, reason and its limits, love and the will, persons, immorality and the afterlife.

Thomas M. Ward is Assistant Professor of philosophy at Baylor University in Waco, Texas. He specializes in the history of philosophy, focusing on the Middle Ages. A 2009 Harvey Fellow, Ward is the author of *John Duns Scotus on Parts, Wholes, and Hylomorphism* (2014), as well as many research articles in the history of philosophy, including "A Most Mitigated Friar: Scotus on Natural Law and Divine Freedom," *American Catholic Philosophical Quarterly* 93:5

(2019), winner of that journal's Rising Scholar Essay Contest in 2018. https://orcid.org/0000-0002-5794-418X

Scott M. Williams (DPhil, University of Oxford) is Assistant Professor of philosophy at the University of North Carolina Asheville. He publishes in the areas of medieval theology and philosophy, philosophy of religion, and philosophy of disability. He has published several articles in philosophical theology on the Trinity and recently published a response article, in *Faith and Philosophy*, called "In Defense of a Latin Social Trinity: A Response to William Hasker." He is currently writing a book, *Henry of Ghent on the Trinity*, and is co-editing a special issue of the journal *TheoLogica* on conciliar trinitarianism. https://orcid.org/0000-0002-8401-0059

Index

Note: Page numbers in **bold** refers to tables and page numbers followed by "n" denote notes.

ableism 15, 39, 82, 85, 179, 206, 266, 270–272
accidents 29, 88, 95, 97, 247; as *propria* 36–37, 67–68, 76n73
Adams, Marilyn McCord x, 16, 19
agility 212, 259, 266–270
Albert the Great: and ableism 271; on agility of those in heaven 266–268; on disability and separated souls 236, 240, 247; on sensation for those in hell and in heaven 260–262; on slaves by nature and their dignity 151–152; and taxonomy of congenital disabilities 54, 56–65, 71
amentia (mindlessness) 14, 45, 135, 151–153, 158, 161, 163–164, 172–173
Amerindian peoples 17, 135–140, 158–161, 163–168
amniotic sac 62
Aquinas, Thomas: and ableism 271–272; and Albert the Great on taxonomy of congenital disabilities 56, 65, 69; and *amentia* 161–165, 172n55; on analogy 35, 44n63; and anthropology and disability 134–138; on beatific vision 282–283; on Christ and defects 210–213; on cognitive impairment and disability of separated human souls 236–242; and concept of disability 34–40; on concepts 26–32; on dignity 77n80, 85, 134–137, 140–141, 152–153; on human corporeal vulnerability 42n40; on *imago Dei/Trinitatis* 111–114; and intellectual disability 4; on knowledge of what it's like to be a separated soul 251n25; on lack of the use of reason, cause of 67, 155–156, 165; on perfectibility of human nature 279–284; and persons 83; and practical theology and disability 120; on procreation 73n26; and punishment model of disability for original sin 6; on ontology of rational powers 95–96, 116–117; on separated souls and infused intelligible species 244–247; on sensation for those in heaven and in hell 259–264; on slaves by nature 149, 151–158
Aristotle: on human happiness 279, 284; on hybrid species 72n8; and hylomorphism 55–56; on monsters, generation of 53, 75n63; on paradigm human beings 16, 205; on procreation 73n26; on sensation as passive 259, 262; and sexism 16, 229n48; on slaves by nature 142–151, 154, 158–159, 217
audism 179–180
Augustine: and ableism 271; on agility of resurrected human beings 269; on deafness and communication 181–183; on *imago Dei/Trinitatis* as *memoria, intelligentia, and voluntas* 109–111, 113, 118; on monsters 53, 157; and personhood 84; on resurrected women 217; on scars of resurrected saints 213; on sensation and resurrected human beings 260
Avicenna 74n36, 75n59, 251n19, 252n40, 268

barbarism 138, 142, 144, 151, 159, 161, 166
Barnes, Elizabeth 5, 7, 26–27, 34, 38–39, 45n74, 104n65, 226n13
Bartolomé de las Casas 136–140, 158, 160, 166–168
Basil of Caesarea 4, 90
beatific vision 30, 41n28, 247–249, 277, 280–284
Berkman, John 30–32, 34, 41n28, 42n40, 43n45, 120, 129n62
Bernard of Clairvaux 220, 228n43–44
Bernard of Trilia 239
blindness 6, 31, 52, 181, 187, 189, 205–206, 211, 213, 227n30, 248, 251n19, 277
body parts 57, 60, 62; as atypically small 57–59; and disproportionate quality of 61; as excessive in size 60; and extra members and conjoined twins 60; and missing bodily members 58
Boethius 81, 85–89, 92–99, 101, 104n52
Bonaventure: and ableism 271; on cognitive impairments of separated human souls 236, 244–245; on *imago Dei/Trinitatis* 114; on knowledge of separated human beings 250n16, 253n68; and *Meditations on the Life of Christ* 218; on sensation of resurrected human beings 265–266; on well-being of separated human souls 248
Bynum, Caroline Walker 226n18, 227n34, 229n49

Catherine of Siena 209, 223, 229n58
causation (or cause) 33, 52–54, 64–65, 96, 141, 156–157, 217, 253n68, 254n70, 265–266, 271, 281–282, 285; as the four causes (material, formal, efficient, final) 30, 36, 55–56, 58, 60–63, 68, 165, 186; as *sine qua non* cause 249
change 52–53, 261–264, 273n16, 280; as spiritual (intentional) 59, 262–263, 273n16; as substantial 55
climate: as cause of impairment or disability 139, 149, 151, 155–157, 159

cognition: and Aristotelian view of women 217; and death, before and after 260–261; and impairment 162; and infused species 240–244; and passive power 259, 261, 264; and personhood 97; and separated human souls 240–247, 253n67
concepts 2, 25–29, 35, 38–39, 41n15, 44n56, 52–53, 71, 82, 84, 86, 99, 115–116, 203, 238–240; and a mental word 27; and universals 27–28, 35, 99, 238, 241, 244, 260–261
confession 129n62, 183–185, 188–190, 192
congenital disability 51–71; and maternal imagination 53–54, 72n17, 72n20; and physical causes of 54; and sexual sin 51, 53, 64
consciousness 82–86, 101
consent 186–188, 193
Cross, Richard 2–4, 6, 25, 30, 33–34, 36–37, 243, 250n11, 252n48

Dante Alighieri 254n73, 280, 282–283
deafness 2, 26, 170–186, 188, 192–193, 194n9, 205
defects 6, 31, 74, 236
Derrida, Jacques 180, 194n3
differentia 27, 29–32, 34–36, 38, 42n40, 61, 87, 91
disability-positive 8–9, 11, 13–14, 16–17, 80–81, 86, 96–98, 100–101, 179
disability-rights 1–2
disability: being ignored 3, 25, 137, 182; and cultural model 13, 236, 240, 242, 247, 285n1; and definition of 1–2, 4, 17, 34, 225n2, 226n13; and health 3, 162, 180, 224, 284; and impairment 2, 33–34, 52, 235–236, 239, 241, 243; and intersection with medieval Christian philosophy and theology 1–6, 15, 179; and medical model 13, 51–52, 180, 236–237, 239, 285n1; and punishment model 6, 8, 30–31, 37, 65, 181, 236, 244, 248, 253n67, 261, 263, 271; and religio-moral account of 5–6; and social model 2, 46n81, 52, 236, 240–241, 243, 245; and well-being 1–2, 4–5, 7,

16, 38–39, 40n7, 97, 148, 235, 242, 247–249, 277–280, 284–285
disposition 141, 149, 156, 238, 247, 252n38, 262–263, 269, 271, 282–283
Dominican Order 140–141
Duns Scotus, John 6, 28, 33; on changes, natural and spiritual 254n70, 263–264; on disability, definition of 36–37; on disability and beauty 45n72; on female contribution to reproduction 56, 228n37; on motion of resurrected human beings 268–269; on *persona*, history of 94; on properties, communicable and incommunicable 86; on rational powers 96, 115, 245–246; on substance and *propria* 68, 76n73; on union of soul and body 249
Durand of St. Pourçain 252n37, 269–270

Eiesland, Nancy L. 5
embryo 51, 57–58, 60–62
Empedocles 56
essence 27–29, 36, 65–70, 76n73, 76n75, 86, 112, 171n35, 219, 237, 277, 281–283

Francis of Assisi 228n46
Franciscan 73, 186–187, 190–191, 197n62, 228n24, 238, 240, 242–245
Francisco Suárez 236; on community of separated souls 242; on motion of separated human souls 253n67; on separated human souls and intelligible species 240, 253n63; on union of human soul and body 249
Francisco de Vitoria: and remembering 'mindless' human beings 165; on slaves by nature and *amentia* 161–166

gender 216
genus 27, 29, 32, 34, 36, 41n22, 89, 91, 95
Giles of Rome 54, 254n70
God: as God the Father 86, 91, 111, 116, 215; as God the Son 87, 89–90, 94, 100, 111, 116; as God the Holy Spirit 91–93, 110–111, 116, 119, 253n62
goodness 143, 161, 166, 224, 281, 283–284
Gregory of Nyssa 81, 86, 89, 91–92, 109, 122n2

haecceities 36
happiness 31, 162–163, 213–214, 247–249, 279, 281–282
heavenly bodies 57, 62–63, 65, 266
Henry of Ghent: on human rationality 96; on *imago Dei/Trinitatis* 114, 118; on personhood and dignity 85, 87; on knowledge of separated human souls 252n35; on sensation of separated human souls 254n70
hermaphrodites 61
hierarchy 143, 153, 203
Hildegard of Bingen 53, 72n13, 223
hybrid species 53, 54, 72n8, 72n15
hylomorphism 37, 52, 54–55, 59, 70–71, 98, 101
human nature 16, 27, 30–31, 33–34, 36, 42n33, 42n40, 73n26, 85–87, 89–90, 94, 118, 134, 140, 143, 147, 152–153, 157, 160, 164–167, 206, 211–217, 223–224, 235, 248, 250, 277–280, 283–284, 285n1; and human body as ideal 7, 2–6, 211, 215–216, 222, 258–259, 266, 272; and states of 7, 8

imago Dei 17–18, 109–113, 115, 117–118, 120–121, 122n2, 151; and analogy 109–112, 115–118
imago Trinitatis 113–120; as *memoria, intelligentia, voluntas* 110–112, 114, 117–118
impairment *see* disability and impairment
incarnation 4, 30, 33, 42n33, 85, 87, 89, 93–94, 98–101
infirmities 42n31, 42n40, 43n45, 152, 172n55, 210–211, 218
intellectual acts 96, 152, 161–163; and modern personhood 81–86, 97
intellectual disability 4, 134, 138, 148, 152, 172n55
intellectualist 17–18, 109, 117–121, 122n2, 130n64
Islam 5, 19n14

Index

Jesus Christ 85–87, 89–90, 119, 207, 215, 218, 220–221, 229n49; and the Passion of 208, 210–211, 215, 223
Johannes Brenz 258, 272
John Mair 138–143, 145, 149, 151, 159–161, 164–168
John Maxentius 89–90, 92–93
Juan Ginés de Sepúlveda 139, 142, 165–168, 175n106
Juan de Quevedo 139, 160, 175n106
Judaism 5, 18n3, 19n14
Julian of Norwich 4, 220–221, 223–225

Kant, Immanuel 82–83
Kenny, Anthony 29
Kittay, Eva Feder 5, 102, 105n74
Kuuliala, Jenni 2, 196n36

Law: as Roman Law 93–94; as Canon Law 129n62, 180, 185–186, 188, 193
Leontius of Byzantium 89, 92
leprosy 64, 71n41
Locke, John 17, 51–52, 65–71, 76n73, 76n74, 82, 85–86, 101

Margaret Ebner 223–224
Marguerite d'Oingt 220, 223
marriage 75n60, 129n62, 184–188, 193–194
martyrs 16, 206, 213, 215, 220, 223, 226n14, 227n26, 227n290
Mary, the Virgin 215, 218
matter 55, 57–62, 65, 68, 70, 95, 98, 158, 217, 237–238, 240, 263
Matthew of Aquasparta 236, 244, 248, 252n35, 254n70
meaning *vs.* significance 2, 7; and understanding *vs.* overstanding 16, 81
Mechthild of Magdeburg 212, 223
memory *see imago Trinitatis*; power, as memory
menstrual blood 16, 55, 58–59, 68, 184, 228n40
methodology 3, 9, 38, 81; as evaluative 3; as historical 3; and medieval with a twist 9, 13, 18, 19n19
Metzler, Irina 37, 64, 71, 75n61, 182, 193, 194n9, 196n36, 253n67

miracles 190–192, 198n69, 198n70
mobility 34, 258–259, 266–270
monster 52–54, 57, 62, 64, 66, 71n7, 72n8, 72n10, 72n12, 73n26, 76n69, 203, 205, 226n9, 226n14
monstrous *see* monster
moral status 4, 9, 17, 51–52, 65, 69–71, 80–82, 84–87, 97–98, 100–102
mothers 16, 203, 206, 215, 218, 220–223, 225
mystics 16, 203, 206, 212, 223–224

Origen of Alexandria 109
original sin 4, 6–7, 17, 30–31, 37, 42n33, 45n69, 65, 181, 183, 211, 236; and fallen human race 8, 32, 43n46, 211, 213

passions 88, 139, 151, 205, 217, 220, 253n68, 262–263
person 17–18, 33, 41n28, 70, 77n78, 80–102, 110, 113–121, 130n65, 147–150, 153–167, 237–238, 242, 249, 250n1; as *hypostasis* 86–93, 99–100; and materialism 99–101; as *persona* 83–85, 87–90, 92–96, 98–101, 103n32
Peter Lombard 111–112, 114–115, 118–119, 121, 122n4, 186
phantasm 63, 238–241, 243–247
philosophy of disability, contemporary 2–5, 7, 15, 27, 38, 40, 81, 97, 101, 225n2
Porphyrian Tree 29, 41n22
power: as formative 56–65, 67–71, 73n26, 75n61, 75n63; as intellectual 67, 95–96, 98–101, 111–119, 243, 260, 281–282; as memory 111–119; as passive (*see* cognition and passive power); as volitional 95–96, 98–101, 111–119
Ptolemy 62, 141
properties: as communicable 86; as incommunicable 82, 85–86, 95–96
prosthesis 33, 240, 246
punishment model *see* disability and punishment model

race 72n8, 149, 155, 157; and being racialized 141, 148, 159, 161
ratio 35, 116–117, 187

rationality as use of reason 67, 134–140, 147–168
Raymond of Penyafort 184, 186, 189–190, 193
resurrected body 212, 254n73, 258–262, 267–272
Romero, Miguel 4, 40, 41n25, 42n40, 120, 129n62
Rusticus the Deacon 92–93

sacraments 129n62, 183–185, 193, 196n47
Salamancan Thomism 140, 158, 160–161, 167
sensation 63, 112, 120, 162, 258–262, 264–266; and spiritual reception of species 262
sex (sexual) 57, 60, 64, 217; and morality 75n60; as the sexes 61, 218, 223; and sexual sin 51, 53–54, 64, 72n13, 184–185
Shakespeare, Tom 5, 46n84
sight 52, 204, 260, 264–266, 271, 273n16
sign language 179–183, 188, 192–194
Silvers, Anita 5, 46n81
slave by nature 138–152, 157, 160, 163–164, 171n37, 217
Slotemaker, John T. 122n4
social history 7
Spanish colonialism 101, 138

sperm 55–57, 60–62, 64, 73n24, 75n63
spirits 63, 270
Stump, Eleonore 29, 41n22
substance 29, 33, 36, 41n22, 55, 59, 63, 66–68, 71, 86–89, 95–97, 101, 114–117, 237, 239, 247; and substantial form 55, 65–69, 76n73, 97–99, 104n70, 153
suppositum 86, 94–96
survival 143–144, 205, 273

teleology 204
Thomas of Chobham 185–186, 190
Timpe, Kevin 45n64
touch 212, 260, 262–266
transhumanism 259, 272–273, 280, 283
trinitarian theology 89, 110, 112, 116, 118, 125n30

universals 89, 241, 244; and *ousia* 86, 90–93, 99–100
univocal 26–28, 35–37, 39

Van Dyke, Christina 41n28, 227n25
volitional acts 96, 162; as power (*see* power, as volitional)

William Ockham 96, 109, 114–119, 121, 125n30, 128n46, 245, 247
Williams, Scott M. 102n17

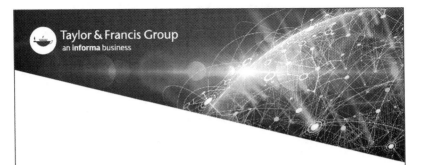

Printed in the United States
By Bookmasters